TRIUMPH OF THE LACK OF WILL

JAMES GOW

Triumph of
the Lack
of Will

International Diplomacy
and the Yugoslav War

Columbia University Press
New York

Columbia University Press
New York

© 1997 by James Gow

Printed in Hong Kong

Library of Congress Cataloging-in-Publication Data

Gow, James.
    Triumph of the lack of will : international diplomacy and the
Yugoslav War / James Gow.
       p.   cm.
    includes bibliographical references and index.
    ISBN 0-231-10916-4
    1. Yugoslav War, 1991 — Diplomatic history. 2. Yugoslavia —
Foreign relations.   I. Title.
DR1313.7.D58G69   1997
949.703—dc21   96-48545
                                        CIP

C   10 9 8 7 6 5 4 2 1

PREFACE AND ACKNOWLEDGEMENTS

The Yugoslav War of Dissolution was more discussed and analysed on almost all levels while it was still in train than any other conflict. The present volume began as part of that body of analysis, although I have had the advantage of concluding it immediately following the settlement of the conflict in Bosnia, with the signing of the Dayton Accords in Paris. The initial idea was to analyse the involvement of the international community in trying to end the war and the overall failure of those efforts. That objective had not altered by the time the final draft of the manuscript was completed. The ending of the war only served to strengthen and confirm the argument that was being made.

That argument was originally made at a conference in September 1993 and published in an article in a special edition of *The Political Quarterly* in 1994. It was at the suggestion of several colleagues that I undertook to expand that argument to book length, drawing on what was kindly judged to be a coherent set of analyses of the Yugoslav war from its outset. At several stages, the present volume represents an attempt to homogenise elements of that earlier work. In bringing together the various aspects of international diplomacy in the Yugoslav war in the current form, I am particularly indebted to the anonymous reviewer of the manuscript who in 1995 perceptively identified my original ambition: to use an argument which was new in 1993 for a volume to be finished in 1994. The demands of an agenda dictated by the continuing war meant that a project conceived at the beginning of 1994 was not finished before the year's end. The reviewer rightly suggested that by 1995, something new might need to be added. That suggestion forced a delay which serendipitously allowed for the end of the war to be incorporated in the analysis.

I have tried to meet two particular challenges in this book. One is to avoid the simplistic judgements made about international diplomacy during the course of the conflict. Instead, while identifying errors and weaknesses, I have tried always to place the analysis in the context of the complex interweaving of diverse international perspectives, concerns and commitments with the course of the fighting. As the central thesis in the book makes clear, however, this understanding is not blinkered to the critical political failings in the international community.

The second challenge I have tried to face is to provide, on the basis of available documents, accounts and discussions, a volume which will, as far as possible, stand the test of historians, thirty, or more years after the event, combing the archives to discover what really happened. At a minimum, I hope the book may be a benchmark against which to test their findings. There will certainly be scope for improvement on the basis of the new information which will inevitably emerge over the next thirty years.

The 'triumph of the lack of will' in the title is an obvious allusion to Leni Riefenstahl's cinematically remarkable celebration of Hitler's Nuremburg rallies. It is intended to convey the understanding that, scope and detail notwithstanding, the events in former Yugoslavia had strong parallels with events in Central Europe during the 1930s and 1940s. On one level, the title reads as a verdict on the establishment of an ethnically purified Serbian entity on Bosnian territory achieved in the face of collective international weakness. On another, it is a comment on the nature of the eventual success of international diplomacy in ending the war and deflecting the complete accomplishment of the Serbian project to create a set of independent or formally linked territories. That success underlined how relatively little was required to secure those achievements.

As ever in a project of this kind, there is a good deal of indebtedness and gratitude to be expressed. The financial support of the Harry Frank Guggenheim Foundation jointly to Christopher Dandeker and myself for work on peace support operations facilitated research which contributed to parts of this volume. Regarding content, I take any blame and credit for the book as is appropriate, but many people have had an influence on the evolution of my analysis and endured discussions and lectures with me. Whether adversely or positively critical, these have been to my profit. So many have helped that it almost seems invidious to name names — for fear of offence in missing out a particular individual. Acknowledging some individuals also seems unfair to the countless nameless officials working in government departments in several countries, especially in London and in Washington, as well as in international organisations, who were helpful and open in discussions, but who spoke on condition of anonymity. I wish, therefore, to acknowledge my indebtedness to them.

Finally, I wish to recognise the benefit I derived from discussion with or assistance from the following (and to apologise to anyone I have inadvertently forgotten): Marc Arnold, Jeremy Brade, Cathie Carmichael, Nebojša Čagorović, Abe and Toni Chayes, Mike Clarke, Ambassador Jose Cutilheiro, Chris Cviić, Christopher Dandeker, Andrei Edemskii, Espen B. Eide, Age Eknes, Greg Fox, Lawrie Freedman, Pete Gray, Catherine Guicherd, Sohail Hashmi, Jan Willem Honig, Miodrag Ivanović, Laza Kekić, Jen Kennedy, Aleksandar Korsik, John Lampe, Jenny Little, Suzanna van Moyland, Radojka Miljević, General Phillipe Morillon (retired), Andrew Muratore, Lord Owen, Minna Schrag, Jim Smith, Lt. General Sir Rupert Smith, Cornelia Sorabji, Shashi Tharoor, Mark Thompson, Mary Unwin, William Wallace, Graham Messervy-Whiting, Nick Wheeler, Simon Wilson, Susan Woodward, Charles Worth, Warren Zimmermann. I am also indebted to Angela Clark, Michael Dwyer and, especially, Christopher Hurst for tremendous and patient editorial work. Finally, it would be impossible not to be thankful to Peter and Dušica, to my parents and, above all, to marvellous Milena: their forebearance, support and faith makes me humble.

London, November 1996   JAMES GOW

CONTENTS

Part III

Part IV

MAPS

1. Republics of the SFRY with ethnic distributions

1

INTRODUCTION

The Yugoslav War of Dissolution finished two and a half years late. While it ought never to have occurred, it should certainly have been concluded in May 1993 when the Vance-Owen peace plan failed for want of the international political commitment, notably in the US, to oblige the Bosnian Serbs to accept it. When the war was brought to a close with the Dayton Accords and the signing of a peace agreement for Bosnia and Hercegovina in Paris, the most significant change at the international level was political commitment led by the US. The US position was not the only difference in the conditions affecting a settlement, but it was by far the most salient.

The US deserved credit for its role, eventually, in leading the way to a settlement. But, Washington could not avoid the judgement that it was responsible for the failure to stop the war in 1993 and to implement the Vance-Owen Plan. The agreement at Dayton, after two and a half years of drift and division, reflected the surrender of important principles for the international community: to resist ethnic purification and to oppose acquisition through force of contiguous territory for the Serbs in Bosnia. The American-made settlement abandoned these principles which had been part of Vance-Owen. Ironically, it was US criticism of Vance-Owen on the grounds that it did not do enough to uphold these principles which led to the plan's demise. The twinned failures of will and principle identified in the fate of the two plans lay at the heart of the international handling of the war. Although, ultimately, the most important aspect of the settlement in Bosnia was that it succeeded, that success could not erase the stain of failure imbued over four years. It deepened it.

Rarely, if ever, in history can so much time, energy, manpower, finance and diplomatic attention have been applied to a conflict with so little reward. The Yugoslav War of Dissolution came to concern all the major states and organisations with a stake in European security, as well as many outside that framework. Yet, only after four years of individual and collective effort had failed, was the war stopped. This volume aims to provide an interpretation of that collective international involvement and to identify the essential characteristics of diplomatic dereliction. As will be argued, these were bad timing, bad judgement, an absence of unity and, underpinning everything else, the lack of political will, particularly with regard to the use of force which was necessary if there were to be any chance of success. The critical difference between the failure of Vance-Owen in 1993 and the success of Dayton in 1995 was the absence and presence of these qualities.

The conflict in Yugoslavia presented the post-Cold War world,[1] and Europe in particular, with a critical challenge. The country which, because of its complex population structure and attempts at social, political and economic innovation, was so often characterised as the 'laboratory test case' for particular problems,[2] extended its reputation beyond its existence.[3] In its bitter dissolution, Yugoslavia, so long the guinea pig for students of internal factors, became the subject of international experimentation. It was the litmus test of a 'new world order' in which the old world would be made to work better through

---

[1] The term Yugoslavia is used throughout to refer generally to the territories of the Socialist Federative Republic of Yugoslavia (see below), both before and after the completion of that federation's dissolution. It is never used to connote the new 'Federal Republic of Yugoslavia', declared by Serbia and Montenegro in April 1992, and which continued, at the time of writing in the summer of 1995, not to be accorded *de jure* recognition through, *inter alia*, admission to the General Assembly of the United Nations and the Organisation on Security and Co-operation in Europe.

[2] On Tito's Yugoslavia as an ideal laboratory for political, social and economic theorists, see Bogdan D. Denitch, *The Legitimation of a Revolution: the Yugoslav Case*, Yale University Press, New Haven, 1976, p.17.

[3] The Yugoslav War of Dissolution generated a plethora of analyses, some well-judged, others not. It also spawned would-be PhD theses galore, most of which, to begin with, were more concerned with the same general questions, rather than the detail of particular aspects of the crisis. Indeed, there were so many aspects of the crisis that a healthy crop of doctoral theses two decades into the Twenty-First Century, could be anticipated, when the historians of the day get access to the official records on various aspects of the Yugoslav War.

international co-operation and in which new elements would be forged in the Yugoslav crucible.

The outbreak of war ran against the spirit of integration and co-operation which prevailed in the international community following the fall of the Berlin Wall in 1989.[4] The European Community (EC — later to become the European Union [EU] in November 1992), the North Atlantic Treaty Organisation (NATO), the Conference and Security and Co-operation in Europe (CSCE — later to become the Organisation on Security and Co-operation in Europe [OSCE] in January 1995), the Western European Union (WEU) and the United Nations (UN) had all been structured, explicitly or implicitly, by the Cold War. In its wake each was searching to re-orient itself and re-establish its identity, as were the various member states. In each case, however, the quest for change was predicated on the trend towards security through co-operation and increasing integration. The disintegrative crisis in Yugoslavia and the conflicts which followed undermined the philosophy of integration and confronted those engaged in integrative processes with a test of their abilities to deal with something which had come to be thought impossible in late twentieth-century Europe: the outbreak of armed conflict.

The performance of an array of institutions and the governments behind them, in particular of those most closely involved, the European Union (EU) and the United Nations (UN), was extensively criticised and condemned. There can be no doubt that the handling of the Yugoslav war was uneven and did not produce either immediate or complete success. From an early stage it was possible to judge that 'the "international community" has made a frightful mess of it.'[5] Outright condemnation of this failure was easy, although in the minds of many of those engaged officially at one level or another, this would be considered simplistic. The performance of the international community,

---

[4] The term 'international community', as Ken Booth, 'Military Intervention: Duty and Prudence', in Lawrence Freedman, ed., *Military Intervention in European Conflicts*, Blackwell for the *Political Quarterly*, Oxford, 1994, p.57 indicated, is somewhat nebulous. In the present volume it is used as a term of convenience to refer to the sum of states, international bodies and other international actors engaged with broadly common values and purpose within the framework of the collective regulation of international security questions.

[5] This editorial comment in *The Guardian*, 23 April 1992, was characteristic of judgements passed on the international involvement.

they would argue, had to be judged in the light of Yugoslavia's enormous complexity and contradictions, as well as the matrix of conflicting principles with which the crisis confronted the international community, adapting uncertainly to the post-Cold War: territorial integrity, the right to self-determination, the rights of minorities, the non-use of force and the right to self-defence, crimes against humanity and genocide. The intentions in this volume are to avoid the simplistic, to try to embrace the complexity inherent in the turmoil of international diplomacy and the Yugoslav War of Dissolution,[6] and, in place of glib and easy ridicule of international disarray, to understand the failings of international diplomacy and their consequences.

The terms 'international diplomacy' and 'Yugoslav War of Dissolution' require some explanation, as they constitute the core elements of this analysis. 'Diplomacy' is used in a straightforward way to refer generically to the management of international relations. It does not, therefore, refer to either the theory of diplomacy or the detailed art as practised by those charged with affairs of state. Nor, contrary to some interpretations, does it refer to an activity which excludes the use of armed force, or which may, indeed, be contrary to it.[7]

'International' could seem a rather tautological complement to diplomacy, but clearly is not. It is used, against the background of a trend towards co-operative and collective approaches to problems of European or global security, following the Cold War. This trend has been to distinguish a concern with the sum of efforts by individual states and, primarily, by collective action, from the efforts of any one state, group of states, or international organisation to manage their international relationships — in general, or in relation to the Yugoslav War of Dissolution.

Finally, the choice of term 'Yugoslav War of Dissolution' is important. It has three strands. First, it treats the armed conflicts in Slovenia, Croatia and Bosnia as part of one war. The factor which joins them is the dissolution of the Yugoslav state. 'Dissolution' is preferred

---

[6] For a comment on this phrase see next page.

[7] This use is not consistent with that of Keith Hamilton and Richard Langhorne, *The Practice of Diplomacy: Its Evolution, Theory and Administration*, Routledge, London, 1994, p.1, where diplomacy is defined as 'the peaceful conduct of relations among political entities, their principals and accredited agents'. For a forceful and comprehensive discussion of diplomacy, see Henry Kissinger, *Diplomacy*, Simon and Schuster, London and New York, 1995.

to terms such as 'secession', 'succession' or indeed 'civil war'. This reflects the accuracy of the term for both the actual processes which occurred and the way in which these were characterised formally by the agents of international diplomacy. It also reflects the weakness of the alternatives: 'secession' is clearly predicated on unilateral action, whereas the break-up of Yugoslavia was a process in which the federal bonds ceased effectively to operate; 'succession' implies that the focus of the war was control of the assets of the old Yugoslav state and the political order which followed it, whereas, as is shown below, the focus was statehood and borders; finally, in the transitional, hybrid (part internal, part external) nature of the armed conflicts, the primary, though not sole, element was the Serbian project to establish new borders with an ethnically pure population (see Chapter 2).

In fairness to those frustrated at the blunt end and in the backrooms of international policy, as well as in contrast to the plethora of facile and derisive commentaries made on international diplomatic efforts,[8] the present volume attempts to offer an account of international failure which, through a narrative built as comprehensively as possible on the detail available at this stage in history, reveals the complexity and the relative success achieved at certain times, in difficult circumstances,

---

[8] Amid the superficial and pedestrian attacks on international diplomatic floundering, as well as the impassioned and monodimensional assaults of, for example, David Rieff, *Slaughterhouse: Bosnia and the Failure of the West*, Vintage, London, 1995, which betray little understanding of international relations. Mark Almond's, *Europe's Backyard War: the War in the Balkans*, Heinemann, London, 1994, is a partial exception. Its mission is straightforwardly, vigorously and with rancour to damn international failure, like so many other pieces of writing on the topic. This is clear from the recognition that he was 'bound to offend foreign ministers and diplomats' by judging them to have 'laboured, postured and washed their hands of the problem in regular succession' (p.ix). From discussions with officials who dismissed the book because of its tone, this is what it did. Unlike many condemnations, however, it is vigorously written and, in essence, correct about the international failure. It does not, however, in those parts of the book dealing with international efforts, offer an understanding of the conditions which nurtured that failure, nor of the efforts actually made (indicated by a lack of references to official documents, or interviews with those involved). Consequently, there is no comprehension of the real points at which and for which the priests of international diplomacy could be held responsible for their failure. Nor, because of this, does he identify the characteristic cause of that failure — the absence of political will. My aspiration in the present volume is to provide an account which, among other things, reveals an understanding of the problems which will not offend foreign ministers and officials but may suggest those aspects of failure for which they could be expected to acknowledge responsibility.

within the context of a chastening failure. The international community's failure contained within it moments of achievement, as well as much that, given the circumstances, might well have been unachievable. Many aspects of the derided international involvement may well appear in a different light in the future — for example the role of UNPROFOR which may come to be regarded as more significant in enabling the Croatian and Bosnian armies opportunity to develop. It surely contained a little more of merit than its critics would allow. There were also significant, if small, ways in which the international community evolved, as a result of the Yugoslav farrago. None of this can disguise the reality, or diminish the magnitude, of an ignominious failure. Above all else, this was a failure of will.

To understand the failure of international efforts and the conditions for success, it is necessary to analyse in detail what the initiatives taken actually were. Although this may sound obvious, in four years of failed international attempts to stop the war in former Yugoslavia, it proved almost impossible for the great majority of both casual and serious observers to maintain a grasp on all that was happening at any given moment. For most people there were simply too many diplomatic undertakings, each couched in the complexity of the context in which they were made, as well as confronted by the complexity of the situation for which they were intended.

The result of this was less comprehension than there might have been of what was being attempted. This produced either heightened expectations, or underestimation, or simply erroneous interpretation. The greater part of this book offers as comprehensive account as possible of the political and military involvement of the international community in the Yugoslav War of Dissolution, interweaving description and interpretation. Without the detail it is not possible adequately to understand, let alone judge, the failure of international diplomacy.

This interpretation of international diplomacy towards the crisis, of necessity, includes analysis of the particular perspectives and roles played by the major states concerned with European security after the Cold War — Germany, France, the United Kingdom, the Russian Federation and the United States (all of which came to constitute the membership of the Contact Group which during 1994 led attempts to present a unified international policy towards the war). Comprehensive assessment of international activity provides the basis for identifying the four fundamental causes of international failure identified at the beginning. It is also the basis for arguing that international failure was a failure of will. Finally, it is the basis for demonstrating that these factors shaped the conditions in which agreement could be achieved at Dayton in 1995, two and half years after an agreement with more to offer in terms of principle was lost.

To understand the diplomatic developments with which the remainder of this analysis is concerned, it is necessary first to understand the context in which those developments occurred: the internal and external dynamics which precipitated the dissolution of Yugoslavia, as well as the war which surrounded that process. This is the concern of Chapter 2. The body of the analysis in the subsequent chapters is concerned with interpretation of international involvement in the war.The core of the book is organised in four sections, each with two chapters: early initiatives; military operations; major players; and peace plans.

The two chapters on the early initiatives cover the growing involvement of the EC and the UN, as well as the background role of other organisations, during the first year of the war. This was a critical period in which the overall international involvement was shaped, but in an essentially *ad hoc* way. Chapter 3 primarily traces the involvement of the EC from the declarations of independence by Slovenia and Croatia to the ending of armed hostilities in Croatia and the EC decision to recognise the independence of the republics. It argues that the initial, somewhat casual and limited engagement by the EC, defined the nature of future international involvement, notably the introduction of the UN, and most significantly determined a framework in which the independence of those Yugoslav republics seeking it could be acknowledged.

Chapter 4 argues that, although the EC had established a framework for recognition of Yugoslav republics, this was neither clearly understood, nor clearly implemented and supported. As a consequence, the focus shifted from Slovenia and Croatia, as well as the problematic but less painful case of Macedonia, to Bosnia. There, efforts to avert and manage impending crisis floundered, with the EC increasingly feeble in the diplomatic lead and the UN increasingly important, but at odds with its different selves and with the EC. The strong messages emanating from the UN Security Council, were not consistent with the views of the Secretariat, as one imposed sanctions regimes and the other began to manage a peacekeeping operation. More critically, there was increasing friction between the EC and the UN over Bosnia as violence was forced upon the country and UN peacekeepers were committed.

Chapters 5 and 6 consider the several military operations which were organised by the international community. The first of these chapters assesses the original UN peacekeeping operations in Croatia, Bosnia and Macedonia. The analysis reflects the degree to which the troops operating under the UN on the ground had come to be a substitute for successful diplomatic activity and the way in which the operations in former Yugoslavia were at the heart of innovations in peacekeeping in the 1990s. This involved the shift from traditional, strategically static peacekeeping, to operations in strategically dynamic situations and the evolution of concepts such as humanitarian intervention and preventive deployment.

The following chapter, focusing more on Bosnia, appraises the growing importance of using force and exercising coercion, as well as the problems that entailed. In particular, it focuses on evolving notions of using air power to provide support for protection of 'safe areas' and the problems of correlating this with forces on the ground, as well as diplomatically. It argues that creative use of coercive potential can be useful, but it requires an overall coherence of approach at all levels.

The overall lack of coherence in international approaches over four years of diplomacy, however much friction there was between organisations, was due to differences of perspective and opinion between the major players. Chapter 7 treats the three western European countries which played a central part in shaping international diplomacy over the Yugoslav War. Each brought its own framework of analysis of the conflict and each, as a consequence, had a different approach to the problem. Germany saw the war as a matter of self-determination and judged a strong approach to be necessary, under great domestic pressure. France was apparently contradictory in its approach to the war, but was in fact consistent with the French objectives of bringing the war to an early conclusion and promoting opportunities for France to have influence. London's position was one of pusillanimous realism, suffused initially with an interpretation of the conflict as ethnic and historical. As the conflict developed, the UK's position became central, its political nervousness and thorough analysis of what particular options would involve generally being the measure of the international position which emerged. These differing perspectives shaped EC involvement considerably and continued to be relevant after the stances of all three became more aligned.

Chapter 8 examines Moscow and Washington and the move in their relations from post-Cold War co-operation to largely polarised positions by 1993. Whereas the Russian Federation was strongly committed to all international and co-operative efforts, the US, while working in a co-operative framework, was reluctant to back a number of options. Central among these was the Vance-Owen Plan which Moscow strongly backed and opposed. For Moscow, particularly after an initiative for partial implementation of the plan, this was a clear sign that it had no choice but to take a more assertive position in its foreign policy. Washington's priority under both the Bush and Clinton administrations was to avoid placing troops on the ground in former Yugoslavia, although Clinton, especially, came under several influences to take a strong line. However, while the US analysis that the situation required a forceful approach was correct, it was never openly backed with an assessment of the implications for Washington of taking such a stand. Once this was reconciled, Dayton became possible.

In many, ways, although not exclusively, the US position was central to international policy. This can be seen clearly in the evaluation of the Vance-Owen and Dayton peace plans in Chapters 9 and 10. The former argues that the Vance-Owen plan was effectively killed off by Washington, which appeared not to understand key parts of it, with dismal impact on the Russian Federation. Central to the success of Dayton, in accomplishing a settlement, discussed in Chapter 10, was the role of the US and its commitment both to using force and to implementing the agreement.

Finally, the concluding chapter provides a comparative assessment of the content of the two peace plans and the conditions in which the two were under discussion. It does so on the basis of an assessment of the four fundamentals of failure identified; bad timing, poor judgement, a lack of cohesion and the absence of will to implement policies involving the use of armed force. With Dayton, the international community got less than it might have two years and half years before. The way in which Dayton succeeded also confirmed the way in which the international community had failed over four years. However, a settlement was achieved. As is argued at the end of the concluding chapter, for that settlement to become a genuine peace and for the international community to go some way towards removing the sense of failure, it was necessary for the international community to recognise the cardinal role of timing, judgement, cohesion and will. These were the qualities required of the international community to assure the peace agreed at Dayton and signed in Paris.

Given the intention in the present volume to provide a full account of international involvement in the Yugoslav War of Dissolution, it is necessary to cover the detail of international diplomatic activity thoroughly. At times this means presenting what might appear as one damned thing after another (a common impression, judging from many comments made to me by casual observers, of what the Yugoslav War of Dissolution was). This degree of detail is necessary for an accurate interpretation rather than the more usual approach to analysis of the difficulties of the Yugoslav conflict, which relies less on analysis of particulars and more on opinion, based on incomplete information and understanding. International involvement altered the conflict and catalysed developments in the wider world. The EC's initial, hubristic intervention, as armed conflict broke out at the end of June 1991, changed the assumptions of Belgrade's military leaders and placed a major international stake in the successful limitation and termination of the war — as is seen in the following chapter. That stake increased, the greater the involvement of, first, the EC (with support of the CSCE), then the UN, in conjunction with the EC (as the latter became the EU), followed by supplementary involvement by NATO and the WEU, and, in the beginning and end, the major states which lay behind the alpha-beta countenance of international bodies.

The increasing international stake in the Yugoslav war was in counterpoint to a reluctance and inability to use force. As emphasis grew on the role of diplomatic pressure, on peace support forces and on a set of coercive and quasi-coercive measures, which often proved hollow, there was no political commitment to follow through on initiatives. But, to be sure, there were things which could have been done. The most critical moment, in this respect, was the demise of the Vance-Owen Plan which presented the international community with a clear opportunity, in its own terms, but one which was dissolutely passed. In a conflict characterised by the craven use of force by limited military groups with limited resources, failure by those with superior armed potential to secure agreements or to preserve their own character and credibility could only result in an outcome which represented a triumph of that lack of will. Using that potential to secure agreement at

Dayton underscored this. Dayton was a triumph-settlement echoing with
the years of absent will. To shake of the ghost of failure, it was
necessary to ensure that the political commitment to build peace was
not lacking.

2

THE YUGOSLAV PROBLEM: CRISIS, COLLAPSE AND CONFLICT

International involvement in the Yugoslav War of Dissolution was inevitably riddled with complexity: Yugoslavia itself was complex, while multilateral diplomacy is rarely a straightforward matter. To understand the diplomatic developments with which we are concerned it is necessary, first, to understand the context in which those developments occurred. The body of the analysis in the subsequent chapters is concerned with interpretation of international involvement in the war. The purpose of the present chapter is to focus on the problem with which the agents of international diplomacy were confronted. In addition to analysis of the war itself, this means looking at the internal and external dynamics which precipitated the dissolution of Yugoslavia.

The war in Yugoslavia was a war for borders, statehood, identity and ideology. The conflict, while not inevitable, was inherent in the break-up of the erstwhile communist federation. As will be seen, the break-up of Yugoslavia was a product both of the historical peculiarities which turned the SFRY into an incubator for successor states and of the end of the Cold War. Not only did the end of the Cold War remove the restraint which East-West conflict had imposed on a fissiparous federation, it also created a particular environment. Yugoslavia's conventional strategic interest was lost, reducing international concern for its future. At the same time, the major powers were preoccupied with a variety of other questions, not least forging a new era of international co-operation, particularly over the Iraqi invasion of Kuwait. In these circumstances there was a strong sense that the

Yugoslav question was a collective concern. These were the sources of international involvement in the Yugoslav War of Dissolution.

Deconstructing Yugoslavia

Many Cassandras warned of Yugoslavia's demise.[1] Even before the man credited with keeping an impossible collection of communities and quarrelsome republics together — Josip Broz Tito — died in 1980,[2] there was speculation that Tito's federation would not survive his death.[3] That Yugoslav federation — the Socialist Federative Republic of Yugoslavia (SFRY) — comprised six republics and two autonomous provinces: Bosnia and Hercegovina (hereafter Bosnia), Croatia, Macedonia, Montenegro, Serbia and Slovenia — the republics; and Kosovo and Vojvodina — the provinces, both within Serbia.[4] The

---

[1] The following section is based largely on earlier research and a general understanding of Yugoslavia. For a full bibliography, see James Gow, *Legitimacy and the Military: the Yugoslav Crisis*, Pinter, London and St. Martin's, New York, 1992. In addition, a number of new books have emerged since then which appear in the bibliography to this volume.

[2] A number of good biographies of Tito have been written. Recent ones include: Richard West, *Tito and the Rise and Fall of Yugoslavia*, Sinclair-Stevenson, London, 1994; Jasper Ridley, *Tito: a Biography*, Constable, London, 1994; Stevan K. Pavlowitch, *Tito: A Reassessment*, Hurst, London, 1993 — which is more a fine essay on the essence of Tito's Yugoslavia, than a biography. In addition, there are some older, valuable contributions: Milovan Djilas, *Tito*, Weidenfeld and Nicholson, London, 1981; Phyllis Auty, *Tito: A Biography*, Penguin, Harmondsworth, 1974; and the original hagiography, Vladimir Dedijer, *Tito Speaks*, Simon and Schuster, New York, 1953.

[3] Tito himself noted and rejected this, looking to the army to carry forward his mantle and preserve the country: ' ...there are those who write that one day Yugoslavia will disintegrate. Nothing like that will happen because our army will ensure that we will continue to move in the direction we have chosen for the socialist construction of our country.' (Tito, quoted by A. Ross Johnson, 'The Role of the Military in Yugoslavia', in R. Kolkowicz and A. Korbonski, *Soldiers, Peasants and Bureaucrats: Civil-Military Relations in Communist and Modernizing Systems*, Allen and Unwin, London, 1982, p.189.

[4] 'Yugoslav' means South Slav. Each of the republics was constitutionally the sovereign state of one of the state-forming South Slav peoples (Serbs, Croats, Slovenes, Macedonians and, since the 1960s, Muslims), none of which had a 'home' state outside the Yugoslav framework (see Chapter 3). Of the Yugoslav communities, the majority spoke a variant of Serbo-Croat — the Serbs, Croats, Montenegrins and the Slav Muslims of Bosnia, Serbia and Montenegro; the Slovenes spoke Slovene and the Macedonians spoke Macedonian; in addition, there were a number of other small Slavic minorities, as well as a number of non-Slavic minorities of which the biggest group was the Albanians,

break-up of Yugoslavia, leading to superpower intervention, was the trigger for many a Third World War scenario.[5] Legend suggested that following Tito's death an Austrian newspaper ran the headline 'The People Are Not Out in the Streets'.[6] Yet it took ten years after the death of Tito for the Yugoslav federation to break up. To understand how and why the SFRY dissolved, when it did, means understanding what Yugoslavia was and what it had become, and that although the country was always uneasy it was not impossible: when it came, the Yugoslav break-up was the product of particular circumstances in the second part of the 1980s.

Yugoslavia was formed as the Kingdom of Serbs, Croats and Slovenes on 1 December 1918 (it was renamed Yugoslavia in 1929, after a troubled first decade). It was a product of circumstances at the end of the First World War and two ideas developed on either side of the historical divide between the traditions of the Western, Roman Catholic Church on one side and the traditions of the Eastern Orthodox and Ottoman Islamic churches on the other: Slovenes and Croats were Roman Catholic, Serbs, Montenegrins and Macedonians were eastern Orthodox, and in areas of Bosnia and Serbia, many Slavs converted to Islam — giving rise to the 'Muslim' population in those regions.[7] On the western side of the divide, in the Austro-Hungarian Habsburg Empire, the 'Yugoslav idea' emerged, in which a common state could provide the framework for the self-determination of all the South Slavs, who spoke either the same or closely related languages. On the other side Serbia gained increasing independence from the Turkish Ottoman Empire in the course of the nineteenth-century, 'narrow' Serbia (without

predominantly inhabiting the Kosovo province in southern Serbia. With the break-up of Tito's federation, only Serbia and Montenego continued a common existence as the 'home' states for Serbs and Montenegrins (to the unhappiness of some of the latter), while the other 'home' states became independent - although not without a violent challenge concerning whose 'home' it should be.

[5] For example, General Sir John Hackett, *The Third World War, August 1985: A Future History*, London, Sidgwick and Jackson, 1978.

[6] As this was related by the impeccable Dennison Rusinow, there can be little reason to suppose that this did not happen.

[7] On the evolution of the two national ideals, see Ivo Banac, *The National Question in Yugoslavia: Origins, History, Politics*, Cornell University Press, Ithica NY, 1984. On the history and evolution of each of the territories and peoples which formed Yugoslavia, including Bosnia and Hercegovina and Macedonia, see Stephen Clissold ed., *A Short History of Yugoslavia*, Cambridge University Press, Cambridge, 1966.

Kosovo and Vojvodina) becoming fully independent in 1878 and the idea was born of creating a 'Great Serbia' in which all Serbs would live — including those in Croatia-Dalmatia and in Bosnia[8] on the western side of the division between the Austro-Hungarian and the Turkish Empires. These ideas were not mutually exclusive, because Yugoslavia, in theory, could represent the achievement of both ideas.

In practice, the first Yugoslavia was characterised by nationalist problems. This was to a large extent because the Kingdom of Serbs, Croats and Slovenes was formed, essentially, as an extension of the existing Serbian monarchy. Although a 'State of Slovenes, Croats and Serbs' had been declared in October 1918, in Zagreb, as the Austro-Hungarian Empire was collapsing, the Habsburg South Slavs, with Italy about to annex lands promised to it by the Allies under the Treaty of London in 1915, were forced to join forces with Serbia, relying on the Serbian army and its position as one of the victorious allies to counter Italy. This union occurred within the framework of the Corfu Agreement of 1917, made between the Serbian government and the Yugoslav Committee in London, representing the Habsburg South Slavs.

The troubled history of the first Yugoslavia, in which the Croats in particular were discontented, ended in collapse as Germany and Italy invaded a weak and divided country on 6 April 1941. The Nazis were able to break the country up, making Serbia a German protectorate, annexing parts of Slovenia and Istria to Italy, and creating a so-called Independent State of Croatia on the territory of Croatia and Bosnia. There followed a many-sided war which was in part a civil war, in part a revolution and in part a war of liberation from the Axis occupiers. The main elements were the Germans and the Italians; Serbian Chetniks loyal to the Serbian monarch and to Royal Yugoslavia; the Ustasha, a fascist group, nurtured in Mussolini's Italy and installed to run the Independent State of Croatia — and which launched a campaign of terror and massacre against the Serbs within their domain; and the Partisans, a communist-led guerrilla movement under the command of Tito. The victors in that bitter war were the Partisans, who were able to recreate Yugoslavia as a federation in which, through the 'nation-state'

---

[8] It was the action of a Serb terrorist — the assassination of Austrian Archduke Franz Ferdinand, in the Bosnian capital, Sarajevo — seeking to promote this idea which triggered the First World War.

republics, each of the South Slav peoples would have both a framework for self-determination and a stake, theoretically, in the new state.

The communists never expected that these arrangements would have any meaning or real content in practice.[9] However, the history of Tito's Yugoslavia saw real authority and power pass from the federation to the republics. This trend emerged after Soviet leader Joseph Stalin expelled Yugoslavia from the communist bloc in 1948, forcing the Yugoslavs to develop their own 'road to socialism', so as to prove that, in the argument with Stalin, Yugoslavia was different from and better than the Soviet Union. The path chosen involved, on paper at least, limited decentralisation. As with the formation of republics, this was not intended to have genuine purpose. It was meant only for the sake of appearance. However, the history of the subsequent forty years was that of republican leaders increasingly wanting in practice what they had notionally on paper.

While Tito remained as President for Life, this system, codified in the 1974 Constitution, worked. After his death, with the captain and arbiter at the centre of republican quarrels gone, it became increasingly difficult to find a consensus on how to steer the Yugoslav ship. As the 1980s developed, Yugoslavia was enveloped by social, economic, political and constitutional crisis. It was impossible to agree on a way out of this compound crisis. In the end, the communist attempts to rectify the nationalist problems which undermined the first Yugoslavia satisfied no one. This created the conditions for Yugoslavia to fall apart again.

The arrangements of the 1974 Constitution in the end failed to satisfy everyone. It gave Belgrade, the federal and Serbian capital, too big a role for the comfort of others while leaving Serbia with a sense of injury — as was made clear in the 'Memorandum' drafted by the Serbian Academy of Arts and Sciences in 1986, which complained that the 'integrity of the Republic' had been "destroyed" and declared that 'the Serbian people cannot peacefully wait' in such a situation, and

---

[9] For an excellent account of the Yugoslav communists and the national question see Aleksa Djilas, *The Contested Country: Yugoslav Unity and Communist Revolution, 1919-1953*, Harvard University Press, Cambridge MA, 1991.

affirmed that Serbia would have 'define its national interests'.[10] This played an important role in the rise of Slobodan Milošević as leader of Serbia.[11] He came to power in 1987 promising to make Serbia 'whole' again by repairing the damage done by the 1974 Constitution and ending autonomy for the provinces. Milošević's campaign against the Albanians in Kosovo and for the restoration of the province to the republic, using 'street democracy', frightened other Yugoslavs. However, nobody was able to prevent a series of amendments to the Serbian and Kosovan constitutions forced through by the Milošević regime between the autumn of 1988 and March 1990, when Kosovo finally lost its autonomy completely. In the meantime, Belgrade curtailed Vojvodina's autonomy during 1989. It was significant that, particularly in the latter stages, there was no real attempt by federal bodies to impede the process.

Slovenia had initially made some attempts to defend the Albanians in Kosovo, in part because Slovenia itself felt threatened.[12] However, the Slovenes, in effect, abandoned the Albanians to nurture their own sovereignty. In September 1989, Slovenia adopted a series of controversial constitutional amendments, asserting republican sovereignty. As the one-party system gave way to multi-party elections in 1990, all the other republics made constitutional amendments.[13]

---

[10] *Naše Teme*, Vol.33, Nos 1-2, Zagreb, 1989, p.162. This draft document was not published, although its impact was considerable. A further draft was completed the following year, but was not published, either, at the time. Although it was circulated unofficially, it was not openly available until 1988.

[11] For an authoratative account (interweaving the words of the Serbian leader and other protagonists themselves) of Milošević's rise to power on the tide of discontent for which the 'Memorandum' was a catalyst, see *The Death of Yugoslavia*, Programme 1, Brian Lapping Associates/BBC, 1995. Milošević himself judged the removal of Kosovo's autonomy as a major achievement; see Milošević, *Godine Raspleta*, 5th ed., BIGZ, Belgrade, 1989, p.342.

[12] It was a major speech in defence of the Albanian position on Kosovo by Slovenian President Milan Kučan which was used by Dušan Mitević, Milošević's man at Radio Television Serbia, to stir Serbian opinion against the Slovenian leadership. See *Death of Yugoslavia*, Programme 1.

[13] For a more detailed account of this period see James Gow, 'Deconstructing Yugoslavia', *Survival*, Vol.XXXIII, No.4, Summer 1991, and *Yugoslav Endgames: Civil-Strife and Inter-state Conflict*, London Defence Studies No.5, Brassey's for the Centre for Defence Studies, London, 1991; see also Leonard Cohen, *Broken Bonds: The Disintegration of Yugoslavia*, Westview Press, Boulder CO, 1993.

The unbridgeable chasms between the positions of these new republican governments was reflected in constitutional debates at the Yugoslav level. The federation itself and its central institutions were increasingly irrelevant — as inter-republican constitutional arguments raged, the Federal Government of Ante Marković made valiant efforts to sidestep constitutional issues with a *de facto* economic reform programme which succumbed to republican power after six months.[14] Constitutional discussions revolved around two concepts for the future of Yugoslavia: federalism and confederalism. These reflected the old division of the Yugoslav idea. A new federation was proposed by Serbia, which wished to continue with a single state run from Belgrade. This was essentially a reworking of the federal constitution still officially operational it, and even seemed designed to optimise central control in clauses such as one overriding republican sovereignty to give federal documents and laws an 'obligatory' aspect everywhere in Yugoslavia.[15] Confederation was propounded by Slovenes and Croats who wished to reform Yugoslavia as a loose association of sovereign states, modelled on the European Community. The only firm feature of this proposal was the independence of sovereign states. From this basic point, anything else involving the transfer of measures of sovereignty to confederal bodies according to principles of international law was open to negotiation. Montenegro supported the Serbian plan; Bosnia and Macedonia were again caught in between, although they tended to favour a confederal alternative, with the former envisaging closer links and the latter weaker ones. These last two republics, the most vulnerable, subsequently made their own 'asymmetric' proposal.

A final phase of constitutional talks began in early 1991. As the divide between Slovenia and Croatia, on the one hand, and Serbia, on the other, was compounded by the ideological differences of the governments in those republics, the summits were destined to be deadlocked. The two camps were irreconcilable. As the leaders of what had come to be known, without question, as 'states' by all involved talked past each other, the changes under way became a source of tension and violence.

---

[14] See Gow, *Legitimacy*, pp.132-6.
[15] See the speech by Borisav Jović, Serbian member of the Federal Presidency, *Summary of World Broadcasts*, 19 October 1990.

After Croatia affirmed its sovereignty in 1990, ethnic Serbs living in parts of Croatia began to react, backed by Belgrade. They formed paramilitary units around police units staffed by Serbs and effectively cut off predominantly Serb-populated areas of Croatia from the rest of the republic. These areas, in which one of two adjacent villages could be Serb and the other Croat, possessed about half of the 600,000 Serbs living in Croatia (in total, 11 per cent of the republic's population). These moves were based on local fears, as long memories of atrocities committed against Serbs by Croat fascists during the Second World War were resurrected by the coming to power of a nationalist party in Croatia. However, they also appeared to be orchestrated from outside as Serbia gave its backing to the rebels. Milošević declared that the Serb nation was sovereign and that all Serbs therefore should live in one state — which meant that if there was not to be a Yugoslav federation, then attempts would be made to unite all Serbs.[16] Neither Croatia, nor Bosnia, where Serbs accounted for around 30 per cent of inhabitants, could be independent without trouble. As violence gripped Croatia and Bosnia in May 1991, both Milošević and opposition leaders made speeches containing the threat of war.[17]

However, Serbia stopped short of recognising a declaration of unification with Serbia made by rebel leaders. Serbia was clearly trying to intimidate other Yugoslav republics with the spectre of violence should they try to end the federation. Unless would-be independent republics wished to invite armed conflict and further destabilisation, they would have to accept Serbia's choice for the future of Yugoslavia, retention of the federation: but Serbia's behaviour only added to Croatian and Slovene beliefs that there could be no accommodation with the present Serbian leadership. The final signal of this came on 15 May 1991. Serbia and its satellites within the Collective Presidency of the SFRY decided to block what should have been the automatic rotation to the office of President of the Presidency that is, nominal head of the SFRY, to the Croatian representative, Stipe Mesić (that is,

---

[16] *Eastern Europe Newsletter*, 11 July 1990; on the questions of Serbian ethnic distribution and the "possible borders of a new Yugoslavia" which would be a common state for the Serbs, see the interview with Jovan Ilić, President of the Serbian Geographical Society, *NIN*, 8 October 1991; see also the discussion it evoked, *NIN*, 15 March 1991.

[17] See Gow, *Yugoslav Endgames*, p.59.

nominal head of the SFRY). The Serbian bloc did so to create conditions for a 'state of emergency' in which the army would declare martial law. Although Serbian representative to the Collective Presidency Borisav Jović had discussed this possibility with army chief General Veljko Kadijević, it did not emerge as Kadijević opted to act cautiously and, in his own terms, constitutionally.[18] From that point the SFRY, already crippled by the inter-republican wrangles which had littered the Yugoslav road to breakdown, ceased *de facto* to function. If it were needed, this was final confirmation for Slovenia and Croatia that the only solution for them was to leave a Yugoslav federation which no longer worked.

Yugoslavia and the End of the Cold War

For all the problems the Yugoslavs encountered in their relationships, which were the primary factors in the dissolution of the federal state, there was a crucial external dimension - the end of the Cold War. This event also represented the removal of a corset which had contained many of the straining bulges in the Yugoslav body politic.[19] Whereas during the Cold War the threat of Soviet annexation might always discipline fractious republican leaders, with the fall of the Berlin Wall that shadow no longer loomed. Moreover, the events elsewhere in Central and Eastern Europe in some senses accelerated developments in Yugoslavia: the Yugoslavs, and Slovenes and Croats, in particular, long used to being in the forefront of liberal modifications to the communist model, suddenly saw themselves being left behind.

Finally, the end of the Cold War was significant for Yugoslavia not only because it released the restraining corset, but also because it changed the country's international significance. It did so in two ways. First, it removed the strategic interest which the Cold War protagonists had shown in the country's fate: it was no longer important. Secondly, the fall of the Berlin Wall in 1989 heralded a new mood and era of co-operation in international security between the erstwhile adversaries of the Cold War. Taken together these aspects exhibit the significance of

---

[18] See *The Death of Yugoslavia*, Programme 2 for Jović's account and military intelligence film of the crucial meeting.

[19] The corset image is borrowed from Christopher Cviić, *Remaking the Balkans*, Chatham House Papers, Pinter for the RIIA, London, 1991, p.29.

the Cold War's conclusion for the Yugoslav War of Dissolution: it facilitated the disintegration of the federation by removing external strategic competition and permitted, even encouraged collective international attention.

For forty years Tito's Yugoslavia inhabited a world between East and West. In spite of the split with the Soviet Union in 1948, it retained a communist system, albeit a modified one. Indeed, that modified system emerged as a result of the rift with the Soviet Union in 1948. A number of factors fed into that split, although they coalesced essentially around the autonomous character of the Yugoslav revolution (which unlike the rest of Eastern Europe had not come under communist rule following Soviet victories in the Scond World War) and the related reluctance of the Yugoslav communists to follow Moscow's direction.

Differences between the two countries were evident in the military sphere where Yugoslavs who had won their own war resented Soviet military initiatives to turn what was ostensibly assistance into domination. Whereas Soviet military assistance had been initially welcome, it became clear that the Soviets were trying 'to encourage the transformation of the army into a conventional fighting force modelled on the Red Army and in the process subordinate it to Soviet control'.[20] Differences were also becoming clear in other areas, such as industrial policy with Stalin wanting to use Yugoslavia as a bread basket, whereas Tito wanted to industrialise the country in the same way as had happened in the Soviet Union. Soviet efforts to subordinate the Yugoslavs went against the grain of Yugoslav achievements. Backed by confidence from the war and popular support, Tito and the Yugoslavs even more strongly defied Stalin, after the decision to expel them from the Soviet sphere.

This was a manifestation of the Yugoslav communists' independent character, which had also shown itself in the period in which the split was generated. Yugoslavia had complicated Stalin's dealings with the West through ambitions to include Trieste in Yugoslavia and by support for the communists in the Greek Civil War.[21] In addition, Belgrade's military presence in Albania and its plans to annex its southern

---

[20] A. Ross Johnson, *The Transformation of Communist Ideology*, Press, Cambridge MA, 1972, pp.33-4.
[21] See, for example, Sir Duncan Wilson, *Tito's Yugoslavia*, Cambridge University Press, Cambridge, 1979, esp. pp.53-9.

neighbour caused concern in Moscow.[22] Similarly, it was an issue of independence which led directly to expulsion from the Cominform — the international organisation through which Moscow controlled other communist parties.

The issue was Tito's ignoring an instruction from Stalin to create a Balkan federation with Bulgaria. This was something which had been counter to earlier objections from Moscow about a project which, when the initiative to create a Balkan federation came from Yugoslavia, had been unacceptable. As with Tito's plans for Albania, the creation of a Balkan federation with Bulgaria appeared to Stalin as a bid to undermine Soviet control and to set Tito up as a competitor for leadership of the communist bloc. At a minimum, it showed that Tito had not grasped that the essence of Stalinism was obedience. However, by the time Stalin was instructing Bulgaria and Yugoslavia to form a federation, the perspective was very different for Tito. To have formed a federation with Bulgaria, in the circumstances, would have dissipated the Yugoslav leader's power base, as the Bulgarian party and the Bulgarian people would have had to be taken into account in making decisions. Because Yugoslavia did not comply, it was expelled.[23]

For a few years, Yugoslavia was given assistance by the West to help it survive Soviet pressure — something which was made easier for both sides by the links forged between the British and Tito's Partisans during the Second World War, at a time when Moscow was offering nothing but words. Yugoslavia became an important, albeit secondary factor in Western defence planning.[24] There was some discussion in Western chanceries about the possibility of trying to bring it fully into the West. That discussion continued into the mid-1950s as Yugoslavia and the Soviet Union flirted with full reconciliation after Stalin's death.[25] However, this was never a likely prospect as Tito never abandoned his commitment to communism or, more fundamentally, to the place where he had discovered it — the Soviet Union.

---

[22] As Richard West points out, the relationship between the Yugoslav and Albanian communist parties 'resembled that between the Soviet Union and Yugoslavia'. West, *Tito*, p.222.

[23] See Wilson, *Tito's Yugoslavia*, p.52-9.

[24] See Beatrice Heuser, *Western 'Containment' Policies in the Cold War: the Yugoslav Case*, Routledge, London, 1989.

[25] See Pierre Maurer, *La réconciliation soviéto-yougoslave, 1954-1958. Illusions et désillusions de Tito*, DelVal, Cousset, 1991, pp.402-34.

Even at the time of the break with Stalin, the Yugoslav leader 'could not imagine... that socialism could be built in any way that differed essentially from [his] understanding of the Soviet model' and the rupture seemed initially to be a misunderstanding which was not 'irremediable'.[26] Tito's ambivalence was most clearly demonstrated in the 1950s when, courted by Khrushchev, he was coming closer again to Moscow but had his hopes dashed by events in Hungary. He reluctantly supported the Soviet invasion on a temporary basis because Hungary had been undergoing a counter-revolution — that is, the communist regime was being overthrown. However, he insisted that once the aim of restoring socialist progress had been accomplished, Soviet troops should go. In this period Tito allowed the reformist communist Hungarian Prime Minister Imre Nagy Yugoslav sanctuary. While Tito could not countenance the end of a communist regime, because that would have implications for his own, he could not fail to back communists pursuing a separate road to socialism, because that too had implications for his position. When the Soviets reneged on promises about Nagy's future, made to get him handed over by the Yugoslavs, and had the Hungarian leader executed, Tito turned away again from Moscow.[27]

He was to follow the same pattern again in the 1960s, when a period of reconciliation was ended by the Soviet-led Warsaw Pact invasion of Czechoslovakia. Again Tito's longing for the respectful embrace of Moscow was disappointed. While Tito would never sacrifice his own brand of communism to the Soviets, it is hard to avoid the impression of an estranged lover who in his heart was always moved by the prospect of a reconciliation but, as soon as one seemed to be in the air, was swiftly reminded of the reasons for parting ways in the first place.[28]

Tito exploited Yugoslavia's position in the Cold War, playing one side off against the other with various benefits — in terms of trade and both financial and military assistance. Yugoslavia's independent character was also reinforced by Tito's role in promoting the Non-

---

[26] Dennison Rusinow, *The Yugoslav Experiment, 1948-1974*, Hurst for the RIIA, London, 1977, p.32.
[27] See Maurer, *La réconciliation*, p.161ff.
[28] See, for example, Maurer's account of the moves towards and then away from a Soviet-Yugoslav reconciliation in the mid-1950s (Maurer, *La réconciliation*).

Aligned Movement in which he and his Yugoslavia sought to be the leading force for socialist development in the developing world.[29] Although the Non-Aligned Movement had little of substance in it, it was important symbolically. In particular, it was important to Tito. Leadership of a movement embracing over fifty states gave him an international platform — allowing him diplomatic prominence and enhancing his reputation domestically. This last factor was notable in reinforcing the sense of an independent path, as well as the country's and its leader's importance in global politics.

His leadership of the Non-Aligned Movement was a vehicle for Tito to appear as leader of an international movement, as well as a an alternative socialist model — one not based on servitude to the Soviets — to the developing nations of the world. It was nonetheless conceived as a 'progressive' movement. In ideological terms it was united only by the collective purpose of the majority of its members, recently decolonised, to oppose anything western and imperial while not necessarily falling under Moscow's sway. The countries in the movement may be said to have been 'non-aligned against the West'.[30]

In spite of his orientation towards Moscow, because of the inherent problem in that relationship, Tito kept good relations with the West. This included personal friendships, such as that with Sir Fitzroy Maclean, the British Member of Parliament and soldier had been Churchill's special envoy to the Partisans during the war and who had become the only foreigner to be allowed to own property in Yugoslavia.[31] It also included positive diplomatic relations with prominent Western figures such as US Presidents Eisenhower and Nixon, as well as the British monarch who returned Tito's official visits.[32] Tito knew just how to maximise his own position by playing off East and West.

Independence from Moscow but adherence to communism left Yugoslavia with a pivotal position between East and West in the Cold War. Both sides at different times came closer to Yugoslavia, but for

---

[29] See Wilson, *Tito's Yugoslavia*, pp.132-4; see also Ridley, *Tito*, pp.345-63.

[30] Nora Beloff, *Tito's Flawed Legacy — Yugoslavia and the West. 1939-84*, Gollancz, London, 1985, p.159.

[31] Sir Fitzroy Maclean also prepared two biographies of Tito: *Disputed Barricades*, Jonathan Cape, London, 1957 and *Tito: A Pictorial Biography*, Macmillan, London, 1980.

[32] Phyllis Auty writes of the way in which Tito won the "admiration and liking" of numerous international personalities. (*Tito*, pp.340-1.)

both the main objective was to prevent it falling into the other's hands. This was clearly expressed by the newly appointed head of the British Embassy in Moscow in 1957:

With the diffidence appropriate to my lack of experience here, I venture the opinion that the tug-of-war in which we are engaged in Yugoslavia is one which we have no interests in winning so long as we can be sure of not losing it.[33]

For the West, certainly, strategic value in Yugoslavia lay in denying Soviet interests there and sustaining an icon of independence among communist parties.

During the Cold War, Yugoslavia had been of strategic importance in three ways. First, militarily, the 'Ljubljana Gap' — the valley in which the Slovenian capital lies — could have served for a rapid Soviet attack from Hungary into Italy (although this was never as much of a priority for NATO as the Central Front). At a minimum, therefore, to deny Yugoslavia to the Soviet Union was to make the defence of Italy and Austria easier. The second strategic factor was access to the Adriatic. Although the Soviet Navy could project into the Adriatic from the Black Sea, its position in the Mediterranean could have improved significantly had it been able to establish bases on the Yugoslav coast. In practice Soviet submarines were sometimes able to dock, with special permission, for servicing on the Yugoslav coast, but this was not a commitment of alliance and could not be guaranteed from the Soviet perspective. While from the Soviet point of view these strategic factors represented an interest in Yugoslavia, they were not so important that Moscow could not live without them.

Finally, and most significantly Yugoslavia was important to the West as a more Westernised alternative model of communism and to Moscow as the prodigal to be returned to the fold for fear of encouraging others: the existence of the Yugoslav variant of communism, in itself, undermined the Soviet claim to omniscience. As one, unusually subtle contributor to US Congressional debate argued in the mid-1950s, an independent but communist Yugoslavia was proof for communists that 'the Kremlin is not infallible' and that 'Soviet concessions on Yugoslavia' opened up 'the possibilities of ideological confusion and

---

[33] John Nicholls in a telegram to Foreign Secretary Selwyn Lloyd at the Foreign and Commonwealth Office, 15 January 1957, quoted in Maurer, *La réconciliation*, p.413.

division in the... monolithic Soviet bloc'.[34] Yugoslavia's development of its 'separate road to socialism' broke the cohesion of a single, Moscow-led communist world and, by offering an alternative which weakened the Soviet hold on Eastern Europe, subverted cohesion in the Soviet bloc: Yugoslavia established the principle that communist countries need not be subject to Soviet rule — and, if not Yugoslavia, then why not Hungary, or these strategic considerations were sufficient to make it important that Yugoslavia should become a part of the West. The strategic importance was to ensure that Yugoslavia did not return to the Moscow fold. What counted for the West was denying Yugoslavia to the Soviet Union. Indeed, the third ingredient meant that a partially reformed communist Yugoslavia was more important to the West as a virus which could infect the *corpus communisti* body than as a healthy member of the Western camp. However, once the Berlin Wall fell and the communist regimes in Central and Eastern Europe had collapsed, that purpose was gone. As communism dissolved and East-West co-operation developed, Yugoslavia ceased to be strategically significant.

When Yugoslavia broke up, it no longer fell into the 'have to do' category. Whatever importance it had, was no longer important enough to warrant serious attention — there was no critical reason for any external agent to ensure, or prevent, a particular situation in Yugoslavia. Despite this, it represented an important challenge, as a variety of interests remained. These stemmed from the new post-Cold War environment in Europe.

That post-Cold War environment had five key aspects: the shift from confrontation to co-operation between Moscow and the West; the Gulf Conflict of 1990-1; concerns for the problems inherent in the looming disintegration of the Soviet Union; the beginning of a partial withdrawal from Europe by the US; and the process of integration within the European Community before the transition to the European Union. In its own way, each of these seemed more important to those involved than the problems of Yugoslavia. Many have been tempted to suppose that preoccupation with these other issues meant that Yugoslavia's problems went unheeded. This was probably the case, much of the time, especially in most European countries, where discussions on the looming collapse of Yugoslavia were usually an afterthought, at most,

---

[34] Congresswoman Frances Bolton (Ohio), quoted in Maurer, *La réconciliation*, p.421.

on the agenda. However, they were not unnoticed and, according to one view from Washington, they were well noted and, then, expressly set aside as being too difficult:

There was no 'intelligence failure', no inattention due to preoccupation with the collapse of communism, or Iraq's invasion of Kuwait. Rather, despite considerable deliberation and diplomatic action, no good option emerged to arrest the accelerating, awful logic of breakup and war."[35]

In spite of Gompert's strong assertion, it is hard to believe that if there had not been such a co-incidence of major questions, there might have been more time for developing additional Yugoslav policy options.

After forty years of nuclear stand-off, the Soviet Union and the West, with the appointment of Mikhail Gorbachev as Soviet leader in 1985, began to wind down the Cold War. Gorbachev sought to bring 'new thinking' to bear on the world's, as well as his own country's, problems. All the bodies whose existence or nature were predicated on the Cold War — NATO, the EU, the WEU, the CSCE, the UN — had to adapt, or perish (as had the Warsaw Treaty Organisation and the Council for Mutual Economic Assistance, through both of which Moscow had exercised control on Central and Eastern Europe). The watershed in this process of de-escalation was the fall of the Berlin Wall in 1989 — both literally in October, but also metaphorically throughout Central and Eastern Europe in the second half of the year, as Moscow decided to release its grip on its Warsaw Pact satellites.[36] This, in particular, among a range of other positive developments, encouraged confidence between erstwhile antagonists. It also fostered co-operation.

The epitome of post-Cold War co-operation, in spite of the tensions which occurred between Moscow and Washington on occasion, was the international handling of the Iraqi invasion of Kuwait on 2 August 1990.[37] With a good working and personal relationship established

---

[35] David Gompert, 'How to Defeat Serbia', *Foreign Affairs*, Vol.7,3 No.4, July-August 1994, p.32. Gompert was Senior Director for Europe and Eurasia on the Bush Adminstration's National Security Council staff, charged with paying attention to Yugoslavia's disintegrative riddle.
[36] See Karen Dawisha, *Eastern Europe, Gorbachev and Reform: the Greatest Challenge*, Cambridge University Press, 1990.
[37] For a full account of the Gulf Conflict, see Lawrence Freedman and Efraim Karsh, *The Gulf Conflict, 1990-1991*, Faber and Faber, London, 1993.

between US Secretary of State James Baker and Soviet Foreign Minster Eduard Shevardnadze, added to a particular desire on the Soviet side, in line with 'new thinking', to see the UN activated for the kind of situation it was originally designed to deal with, a shared collective effort to respond to Iraq's invasion and annexation of its southern neighbour quickly emerged.

Under the auspices of resolutions passed by a UN Security Council working for the first time on the basis of co-operation between its Permanent Members, the United States led a military coalition against Iraq to restore Kuwait's territorial integrity. Amid the battlefield success and diplomatic rhetoric, the sense prevailed that the world had changed. That change was signified in US President George Bush's image of a 'new world order', although few noted that in other parts of the President's discourse it was made clear that this meant a better world, not a perfect one,[38] and even fewer understood that in reality this 'new world' would only be the old one working more in the way intended when the UN was established after the Second World War. Even though events in subsequent months were to tarnish the image of this 'new world', both directly in connection with the Gulf Conflict and generally in connection with the collapse of Yugoslavia, the impact of the civil war in Somalia and the conflicts brewing in the ruins of the Soviet Union, the idea that there were new standards remained, as did the emphasis, in spite of difficulties, on collective regulation of security issues.

If Gorbachev's 'new thinking' on the international stage transformed European security, the internal concomitant of this was restructuring and ever greater openness to discussion internally, all of which fuelled, or facilitated, the dismantling of the Soviet Union. The prospect that this giant multinational empire would break up caused grave concern in Western capitals, as much as it did in Moscow. Aside from a general preference for stability in international relations, there were major concerns for the impact of conflicts within the disintegrating Soviet Union upon the wider world and, most of all, for the fate of the vast

---

[38] See James Gow, 'Introduction', in Gow, ed., *Iraq, the Gulf Conflict and the World Community*, Brassey's for the Centre for Defence Studies, London, 1993, p.4.

Soviet nuclear arsenal.[39] In both Moscow and the West there was, essentially, paralysis as the hope that a Soviet break-up would not actually happen, the need to pretend that it would not happen (so as not to encourage it) and the impossible task of preparing for it all ran side by side.[40]

At the same time as co-operation was catalysing the end of Soviet hegemony, it was also easing the way for a partial American withdrawal from commitments to European security. The 'familiar patterns of trans-Atlantic relations' were being changed and challenged.[41] The US, traditionally torn between its universalist ideals and its isolationist instincts, quickly saw the end of the Cold War as an opportunity to downsize its military commitments in Europe. While this did not mean a full withdrawal from the European scene, it did mean that the US would not be prepared to take responsibility for leadership on European security issues, as it had during the Cold War, unless it had a particularly acute interest at stake. This reality was soon to be demonstrated when, in spite of policy statements about the continuing primacy of NATO in the management of European security questions, the US, reluctant to take responsibility, ceded the Yugoslav stage to the EC.[42]

The final element in the post-Cold War European security environment which set the context for international involvement in the Yugoslav War of Dissolution was the confidence and growing ambition of the EC as it prepared to become the EU. Working for a long time in the spirit of European Political Co-operation, in which, as far as possible, the Member States of the EC co-ordinated their foreign policies, by the beginning of the 1990s those Member States were looking to form a Union, one aspect of which would be the

---

[39] One of the earliest studies on this question was Kurt M. Campbell, Ashton B. Carter, Steven E. Miller and Charles A. Zraket, *Soviet Nucler Fission: Control of the Nuclear Arsenal in a Disintegrating Soviet Union*, CSIA Studies in International Security, No.1, CSIA, Cambridge MA, November 1991.

[40] See Dimitri Simes, 'Gorbachev's Time of Troubles', *Foreign Policy*, No.82, Spring 1991, esp. pp.115-17.

[41] Jenonne Walker, 'Keeping America in Europe', *Foreign Policy*, No.83, Summer 1991, p.128.

[42] Gompert, 'How to Defeat Serbia', p.36.

establishment of a Common Foreign and Security Policy (CFSP).[43] Spurred by the inability to make an adequate European response to the Gulf Conflict, impulses increased for the creation of CFSP. As much as the Americans were reluctant to take too much responsibility in Europe, the Europeans demonstrated a 'certain cockiness, even arrogance' in their continent's 'new vitality' at the end of the Cold War.[44] Obsessed with proving themselves, on the one hand, and preparing the difficult arrangements for their union, on the other, and with only half an eye on the problem itself, the EC was nonetheless in the vanguard of international efforts to deal with the dissolution of Yugoslavia.

The EC and the US were feeling their way towards a new relationship at the end of the Cold War, at the same time as they were each preoccupied with their identity and role in European security. Alongside this, there was considerable concern for the fate of the Soviet Union as it approached its demise. Finally, much of the diplomatic agenda in the crucial period before the dissolution of Yugoslavia was taken up with Iraq and the Gulf Conflict — which was both a manifestation of and a catalyst to co-operative approaches to international security, as well as the spur to heightened expectations of what this newly co-operative international community would achieve in the future. In this context Yugoslavia, previously the object of Cold War competition, became in its demise the subject of international experimentation.

Thus the end of the Cold War had three critical reverberations for Yugoslavia. First, it removed the external pressure created by East-West rivalry, in particular the threat of Soviet occupation which disciplined the vexatious Yugoslavs to avoid creating opportunities for a Moscow invasion. Secondly, external pressure evaporated because Yugoslavia lost strategic importance. This meant that outsiders were not sufficiently interested in the fate of the argumentative Yugoslav republics to act resolutely in response to trouble there. This in turn was because, with the end of the Cold War, although there was awareness of the imminent separation of the South Slavs' ways, there was a host of other issues which absorbed the time of international diplomats. The product of those agendas was a co-operative approach to dealing with problems of

---

[43] See Trevor Salmon, 'Testing Times for European Political Co-operation: the Gulf and Yugoslavia, 1990-1992', *International Affairs*, Vol 68, No.2, April 1992.
[44] Walker, 'Keeping America', p.128.

international security: at the end of the Cold War, the dissolution of Yugoslavia became a laboratory rat in experiments of collective international diplomacy.

The Yugoslav War of Dissolution

The dissolution of the SFRY was a product of the internal evolution of the federation created under Tito and a set of external factors associated with the end of the Cold War. By the end of 1990, at the latest, this combination of inner and outer influences had blended to make break-up inevitable. However, disintegration of the state did not necessarily mean war, even if, as in the Yugoslav case, it entailed evident characteristics of violent social unrest. There was a clear distinction between unrest and war. The essential part of that distinction was the role played by organised armed forces in the service of political aims. In the case of Yugoslav dissociation, it was the Yugoslav People's Army (JNA — *Jugoslovenska Narodna Armija*[45]) which made the difference between a chaotic divorce, peppered with violence and war.[46] It was the presence of the JNA or its direct offspring — the Croatian Serb and Bosnian Serb armies, in pursuit of Belgrade's project to create new borders — which meant that, rather than three separate 'wars of independence', there were three theatres and campaigns within one Yugoslav War of Dissolution.

In order to understand the failings of international diplomacy and to judge the critical failure of political will, it is necessary to grasp the character of that war. It was evidently a complex conflict, embracing a number of issues and parties — although for much of the time fewer than there seemed to be. It was a conflict which took most observers by surprise, not in its appearance but in some of its detail and intensity. It was certainly a conflict which, because of a certain amount of complexity and an even greater amount of apparent complexity, took some time to be understood. As will be seen below, there were five main features of the war: international involvement; the Serbian project

---

[45] Although this has often been translated as 'Yugoslav National Army', this is incorrect; 'People's' was the correct translation, in line with communist practice which created 'People's republics' throughout Central and Eastern Europe.

[46] James Gow, 'The Military in the Yugoslav War of Dissolution', *Storia delle relazioni internazionali*, Anno IX, No.1, June 1993.

for new borders; an imbalance of forces; coercion; and ethnic cleansing. Of these the defining property was coercion.

International involvement made a difference to the Yugoslav War of Dissolution. It altered the strategic environment in three ways. First, the initial EC intervention at the end of June 1991 appears to have been a principal element in prompting the JNA to make a reassessment and join with Serbian political leaders on a project to secure the borders of a new entity, inhabited almost exclusively by Serbs. The JNA leadership appears to have undertaken operations in Slovenia on the basis of two miscalculations. The first of these was that, in spite of evidence that Slovenia's Territorial Defence Force had been prepared to resist any JNA moves after the declaration of independence, the army assumed that a show of force would be enough to prevent Slovenian independence; when it began operations in Slovenia, the JNA was not going to war but was attempting to carry out a limited instruction from the federal government in Belgrade to take control of border posts in conjunction with units of the federal police. The second miscalculation was that, should the first assumption prove wrong, then the JNA would have the possibility of escalation — something which would, essentially, be backed by the outside world.[47]

However, Slovenia engaged the JNA in a series of armed clashes, and from the outset of armed hostilities the international community, in the shape of the EC's presidential troika, took an active interest and offered to mediate. As a result, although the JNA hesitantly began to escalate, including fifteen bombing or strafing missions in Slovenia, primarily against civilian targets, it was confused and constrained. Humiliated, unsure about using its firepower in an attempt to crush weaker Slovenian forces and concerned about the situation in Croatia, the JNA seems to have written off Slovenia to concentrate on Croatia.

At the same time it began a period of reassessment.[48] Having been surprised by EC involvement, the Belgrade military reconsidered its position, making assessments of the prospect of a Western military

---

[47] Miroslav Lazanski, 'Kuvajt na Alpima', *Intervju*, 23 November 1990; Janez Janša, *Premiki*, Cankarjeva Založba, Ljubljana, 1992, p.98; diaries of former Yugoslav Prime Minister Ante Marković, published in *Slobodna Dalmacija*, throughout September 1992.

[48] See generally, for example, *Vojno Delo*, God. XVIII, Nos 4-5, July-October, 1991; see also James Gow, *Yugoslavia and Lessons from the Gulf War*, Centre for National Security Studies, Los Alamos National Laboratory, Order No. 5-LE3-WO261-1, November 1992.

intervention. From the JNA leadership's point of view, the conclusions of this reassessment were extremely important. The JNA judged that a purely European military intervention in the Yugoslav conflict was improbable, but that there remained a need to be cautious about Western military action. It also judged that there was no prospect of preserving the SFRY and therefore that the JNA, according to Federal Defence Secretary General Veljko Kadijević, would have to fight for the borders of a 'new Yugoslavia composed of those peoples who wanted to live together in it and who would not allow the disintegration of such a Yugoslavia'. It became a priority to 'mount a counter-offensive which would confront the destroyers of the old Yugoslavia with a new Yugoslavia composed of those peoples who wanted to live together in it and who would not allow the disintegration of such a Yugoslavia'.[49] In effect, this meant a state exclusively for Serbs, as by this stage the majority of non-Serbs able to do so had demonstrated their preference not to continue as part of a Yugoslavia they judged to be Serbian dominated, while in many areas Serbian political activists were making it clear that, in spite of rhetoric to the contrary, they were not prepared to accept a continued equal co-existence.[50]

At the same time as the war in Croatia was being intensified, the JNA began a series of manoeuvres and movements across Bosnia and Hercegovina. These enabled the JNA to mobilise Serbs from Bosnia, at the same time as it was co-ordinating the mobilisation of the territorial defence forces in Serb-dominated areas with Serb political leaders. This

---

[49] General Veljko Kadijević, *Moje Vidjenje Raspada: Vojska Bez Države*, Politika, Belgrade, 1993, p.131. Kadijević's account seems to confirm the analysis made in James Gow in 'One Year of War in Bosnia and Hercegovina', *RFE/RL Research Report*, Vol.2, No.23, 4 June 1993. It might also be enough to persuade those, such as the asinine doubting Thomas, J.F. Brown (*Hopes and Shadows: Eastern Europe After Communism*, Longman, London, 1994, note 61, p.351) who, reluctantly accepting that there was evidence of preparations, persisted in supposing that this did not mean that there was intention and that those who had actually followed these events closely, such as myself, to whom he was making direct reference of the 'One Year of War in Bosnia and Herzegovina' article, were 'one-dimensional and unconvincing' to 'construe this capability as being proof that the JNA intended hostilities there'.

[50] See the reports of Bosnian Serbs political discussions in *Bosanski Pogledi*, 18 April 1991, still three months before Slovenia and Croatia declared independence and a full year before war came to Bosnia. Alongside these reports appeared a hauntingly premonitary cartoon depicting Muslims wearing crescent and star arm bands; this was an allusion to the Star of David arm bands Jews in the Third Reich were obliged to wear.

process of manoeuvre and mobilisation was judged by General Kadijević to be of 'vital significance' for the JNA, as much as to the 'Serb people in Bosnia and Hercegovina' which was 'by its geographical position and size, one of the keystones for the formation of a common state for all Serb people'.[51]

General Kadijević seems to have attempted to convey the impression that this project began in October 1991. However, he indicated that it had already been one of two options for JNA action in March, before the Slovenian and Croatian declarations of independence. There was good reason to suppose that it was begun in mid-August 1991. Co-incidental with the Moscow coup attempt of 18-19 August against Soviet leader Mikhail Gorbachev, the JNA intensified the war in Croatia and began the manoeuvres in Bosnia. It would seem that the war for new borders, which were also be carved from Bosnia, was launched at this stage. Although there were many voices attributing the war in Bosnia to the decision by the European Community member states and the United States to grant recognition of full independent international personality to the republic on 7 April, the war seems to have been conceived, planned and prepared, and implementation begun, some months before by the JNA and the Serbian Security Service.

The process of military preparation was accompanied by important political activity. This was the declaration by leaders of the SDS (Serbian Democratic Party — Srpska Demokratska Stranka) of the 'Serbian Autonomous Regions' (SAOs) of 'Hercegovina' (12 September), '[Bosnian] Krajina (16 September), 'Romanija' (17 September) and 'North-Eastern Bosnia' (19 September). These regions were the elements which would be used as the building blocks for the future Serbian entity in Bosnia.[52] Preparations were made for future adminstration and statehood, with 'shadow' governments being prepared and secret 'Crisis Headquarters' being organised for the moment when the 'Autonomous Regions' would form a 'Republic' and declare independence from the Bosnian state. This activity was based around the security service centres in the major town under Serbian control in

---

[51] Kadijević, *Moja Vidjenje*, p.144.

[52] These repeated the pattern which had occurred in Croatia. There, the declaration of two autonomous regions 'Krajina' and 'Eastern Slavonia, Baranja and Western Srem', was succeeded by the proclamation of a 'republic' 'Republika Srpska Krajina'.

each of the Autonomous regions.[53] The plan was given a military underpinning by the JNA. Bosnian Serb leader Radovan Karadžić and the local military commander at Banja Luka, General Nikola Uzelac, were clearly in collusion and conspiracy with the President of Serbia, Slobodan Milošević, as tapes produced by the last federal Prime Minister Ante Marković revealed.[54] In the following months, the JNA ensured that it was outside its barracks and began to establish itself, through constant manoeuvres, in the Bosnian countryside, taking troops and equipment out of barracks in towns, leaving behind only symbolic representation, visibly intensifying the process of preparation. Questions were asked in the Bosnian parliament on 12 and 21 September and by the Bosnian government. The JNA claimed to be 'defending Yugoslavia', as well as giving some indication of an alleged 'peace-keeping' role (this had also been the designation for the JNA's role in Croatia, before the declarations of independence and, even, during the sieges of Vukovar and Dubrovnik).[55]

The result of these preparations was that the Serbian camp had its forces pre-positioned in Bosnia to secure the infrastructure to be part of a mini-Yugoslavia, carved out of the republic, to be attached in the east to Serbia, in the south to Montenegro and in the west to Serb-populated and occupied regions in Croatia. In the period following the apparent decision of the JNA to forge the borders of a new Yugoslavia and the declarations of four SAOs in Bosnia and Hercegovina, in October, the Bosnian parliament faced with the challenges presented by the Serbian declarations of autonomous regions which clearly threatened the territorial integrity of the republic, the activities of the JNA, as well as rising tension and the emerging international framework for the dissolution of Yugoslavia, formally discussed and reasserted sovereignty. By this time, however, Bosnia was already heading for war.

Whereas there had clearly been plans to secure the borders of a new state at earlier stages, it appears only to have been as a reaction to the EC's intervention that the JNA finally took this option. It is conceivable

---

[53] See the 'Law on Government' of the 'Serbian Republic of Bosnia and Hercegovina' (later Republika Sprska); *Službeni glasnik srpskog naroda BiH*, 23 March 1992.
[54] See *Monitor*, 11 October 1991, taken from *Vreme*; see also Mark Mazower, *The War in Bosnia: An Analysis*, Action for Bosnia, London, 1992, p.4.
[55] See Gow, 'One Year of War'.

that political pressures from Belgrade might well have forced this option on the JNA anyway, as Serbian political leaders seemed to be working towards this outcome throughout. If only by influencing timing, the EC altered the strategic shape of the war.

The second way in which the strategic situation altered was the decision of the EC and its Member States later followed by other states to recognise the independence of Slovenia, Croatia and, eventually, Bosnia. This turned the conflict from one which, in terms of traditional international relations and of international law, was internal into one which involved four different states. This had major implications. For example, the borders of Bosnia and Croatia which were to be changed according to Serbian war aims, gained added significance as international borders and became a cardinal interest of the international community, as a whole. It also meant that Belgrade's sponsorship of and involvement in the war in Bosnia could be treated by the UN Security Council and mandatory sanctions applied against Serbia and Montenegro. In addition, this had implications for limiting the imbalance of forces in the conflict.

The third way in which international involvement altered the strategic picture was harder to assess. It would be difficult to make a definitive judgement on the real effect of some parts of the international intervention, particularly the insertion of a UN force in a strategically dynamic milieu in Bosnia. This involved arguments which might never be adequately resolved over whether UNPROFOR prolonged the war by feeding the combatants and by encouraging those in Bosnia — primarily Muslims — who benefited from humanitarian assistance not to capitulate when otherwise they would have done so in face of an inevitable Serbian victory.[56]

Such analysis seems to ignore the tendency in war for people to defend themselves and to fight to recover what is lost. In this sense it was always more likely that, rather than surrender, it would be a question of when and how the Bosnian Government, or the Muslims, would fight back. At the same time it was possible to speculate that the

---

[56] For an example of the opinion that international involvement prolonged the war in Bosnia, see Susan Woodward, *Balkan Tragedy: Chaos and Dissolution After the Cold War*, Brookings Institution, Washington DC, 1995, p.359; this judgement was one question mark against a book strong on detail, but confused as to whether it is a socio-economic analysis of dissolution, or an account of international policy.

insertion of UNPROFOR, by blunting the Serbian campaign through its presence, had created the time and space in which the Bosnian Government could organise a defence force and, by 1994, be able to mount increasingly successful operations. Without the presence of UNPROFOR, the Bosnian Government might not have been able to organise an armed force of that size at such an early stage.

Counter to this, some would argue (although on this there can be no reliable clear-cut judgement), was the impact of another result of international intervention. The sealing of a great imbalance in weaponry between the superabundant arsenal of Serbian forces on one side and their opponents' relative lack of arms on the other was a major factor in the war. This was a result both of the Serbs' inheriting most of the inventory of the JNA, while territorial defence forces in Slovenia, Croatia, Bosnia and Macedonia were stripped of their equipment, and of the imposition on 25 September 1991 of an arms embargo against the Yugoslav territories.[57]

The block on arms transfers was imposed on a war zone in which an overwhelming weapons imbalance existed. Those with the preponderance of matériel, within that imbalance, were attempting to create the borders of a new state and genocide. This left those without weapons unable to defend themselves and likely victims. At the heart of arguments around this were moral and practical questions. The moral aspect concerned whether or not the Muslim population in Bosnia (or indeed the authorities in Croatia and Slovenia) had the humanitarian right either to be protected by those with the wherewithal to do so or to try to defend themselves. While various European countries, under the auspices of the UN, tried to limit the extent of the horror in Bosnia through operations to provide humanitarian relief, the Bosnian Presidency and Government persistently called for the arms embargo to be lifted in their favour, arguing that the state and its threatened people should have the right to defend themselves.

All of this raised questions about the extent to which attempts to control arms supplies should take into account local specificities before action was taken. In the Yugoslav case imposition of the embargo was a well-meant gesture, but one which appeared not to have been thought through to its full implications which emerged as the situation deteriorated. The effect of the embargo was minimal on the side which

---

[57] UN Security Council Resolution 713, 25 September 1991.

had a preponderance of weapons and quite extensive on those without. As a matter of principle, it seemed questionable to impose heavy restrictions, no matter how well-intentioned those doing so might be, on all sides in a situation where the sides were grossly unequal. There could be little point in placing a blanket proscription on those who already had arms aplenty and it was hard effectively to defend decisions to subject those without the means of self-defence to a similar regime — unless action was taken on behalf of the victims — even though it coul be argued that the imposition of an embargo might limit the intensity of the conflict.

On the practical side, once the decision to apply an arms embargo had been made and once the only opportunity to relieve it had been passed over at the time of recognising the independence of the Yugoslav republics emerging from the dissolution, it was hard to get agreement to lift it. And in the case of Bosnia especially, it was hard to find out how certain categories of arms — especially tanks and big guns — would reach their destinations. In terms of decisions, the Bosnian Government often opined that the arms embargo was an illegal breach of its right to self-defence under Article 51 of the UN Chapter.

Legally and politically this was a non-issue. In terms of the UN Charter, Article 51 specified that it applied only until the Security Council had taken 'measures necessary to the maintenance of international peace and security' under Chapter VII of the Charter. The arms embargo was a Chapter VII measure taken by the Security Council regarding the territories of the SFRY — this was confirmed as the republics became independent. As per Article 25 of the Charter, in which all states agreed to be bound by Chapter VII resolutions, as well as the ruling in the International Court of Justice on Libya's appeal that the Security Council had acted unlawfully in applying sanctions against it[58] — the Security Council was supreme in these matters. That meant that the Security Council would have to vote to remove the embargo — always politically unlikely, given the positions of three of the Permanent Five Members — France, the UK and the Russian Federation (see Chapters 7 and 8).

---

[58] Paul Fifoot,'Functions and powers, and inventions: UN action in respect of human rights and humanitarian intervention' in Nigel Rodley, ed., *To Loose the Bands of Wickedness: International Intervention in Defence of Human Rights*, Brassey's for the David Davies Memorial Institute, London, 1992, p.155.

On purely operational grounds, getting heavy weapons to the Bosnian authorities relied on Croatian good will (not always there), to allow passage over land or transfer by air, which would have meant the US using C-5A Galaxy heavy lift aircraft — the only ones capable of doing this — to fly the weapons into Tuzla airport. To do that, the US would have had to secure the airport so as not to be subject to attack. To secure the airport would have meant the US going to war using personnel on the ground — something consistently ruled out (see Chapter 8). Therefore, although the arms embargo cemented an imbalance in weaponry which led to many calls for a change, it remained a fixture in the war, even as the Bosnian army, by obtaining substantial supplies of man-portable equipment and capturing some heavier weaponry, began to create more of an equilibrium on the battlefield.

The balance of forces was one factor determining coercion as the primary characteristic of the war, as was clear throughout much of the conflict in Bosnia. Coercion involves the exertion of strength upon a subject to induce a particular response. Whatever form it takes, coercive diplomacy is based on the capacity to hurt. In any form of coercion, influencing another party's behaviour is the essential characteristic. The coercer issues a threat that if a certain party does not modify its behaviour according to the coercer's will, then there will be a punitive consequence that it would be better to avoid. However, the pain which will be inflicted on the subject must satisfy us as coercers more than it causes us discomfort.[59] In the Yugoslav war, military weakness gave rise to coercive approaches. Limited forces and capability, added to a general lack of preparedness to engage in casualty-intensive conflict, created a conflict of coercive strategies. Coercion meant the avoidance of direct combat by all parties whenever possible — leading many military observers to suppose that it was hardly a war at all, as there was little evidence of tactical manoeuvre with armed forces. For all concerned, the essence of the conflict was to secure strategic, tactical and political objectives through the use of coercion, rather than through direct combat.

---

[59] See James Gow 'The Use of Coercion in the Yugoslav Conflict', *The World Today*, Vol.48, No.11, 1992. The understanding of coercion presented here draws on Thomas C. Schelling, 'The Diplomacy of Violence', here taken from John Garnett, ed., *Theories of Peace and Security: a Contemporary Reader*, Macmillan, London 1970.

This operated in three different ways. First, the weaker of the Yugoslav parties — that is the opponents of the JNA and Serbian forces — used their limited capabilities in attempts to coerce the Serbs, through indirect threat, into desisting from their attacks. The most successful was Slovenia which seized the initiative by launching a series of armed clashes with the JNA aimed at provoking international pressure — either political or military — which would achieve the twin aims of deterring JNA attacks and of securing international recognition of independence. This strategy worked, in large part, because Slovenia had learned much from the Gulf Conflict about media management and had established a major international press centre,[60] in advance of the declaration of independence and the conflict, from which the its authorities were able to present images of determined defence in face of the clumsy attacks by the JNA.

The second manifestation of coercion came from the occasional initiatives of the international community. The international response to the Serbian project incorporated a number of coercive instruments — political and economic sanctions, the insertion of an enhanced peace support force and the availability of air power to enforce agreements. The last of these was the most penetrating and forceful means of coercion embraced by the international community. However, in the course of 1994 the Bosnian Serb military commander General Ratko Mladić was able to conclude that by taking UN personnel hostage he could deter aerial attack, thereby providing his force with a seemingly effective counter-coercion measure. The apparent ineffectualness of international efforts following this, added to increasing humiliation of UNPROFOR by the Bosnian Serbs, provoked moves at the end of May 1995 to restore credibility to international efforts by the insertion of a combat-capable reaction force which would neutralise the hostage-taking tactic.

The essential ingredient in Serbian strategy was also coercion. Although strong in heavy weapons, Serbian forces lacked sufficient manpower to press the full advantage of their arsenal. Rather than commit troops, who were anyway reluctant and often untrained for close combat and street fighting, to casualty-intensive operations, the Serbian side adopted two coercive tactics. Both were aimed at the Bosnian population, particularly the Muslims, and at the Bosnian Government.

---

[60] See Gow, *Yugoslavia and Lessons*.

The first of these involved the besieging and stand-off bombardment of areas occupied by Muslims, or under the control of the Bosnian Government, using heavy artillery. Rather than move directly to defeat their opponents and occupy the areas, Serbian forces attempted to persuade them that the costs of resisting Serbian demands were too painful. The second tactic involved the use of 'shock troops' — paramilitary forces operating, until its formal demise, with the JNA — to enter smaller, more vulnerable towns and carry out a series of demonstrative atrocities: mutilation, murder and rape. The intention again was not to capture the area through direct combat but to induce capitulation and flight.

These tactics were commensurate with the Serbian strategy of ethnic cleansing. This relied not on direct combat with opponents but on the demonstrative capacity of the violence and the partial elimination of a population to induce mass migration.[61] The intended result of this was a contiguous set of ethnically pure territories — the mini-Yugoslavia as a common state of all the Serbs envisaged by General Kadijević or, a rotten rose by another name, the Greater Serbia, or Union of Serbian States, promoted by Serbian nationalists. Whereas ethnic antagonism may have been the primary motivation of Serbian nationalists, for the military ethnic cleansing had a practical strategic purpose. If there were no hostile or potentially hostile populations in the areas to be embraced within the new borders, then there could be neither political nor, crucially, armed opposition: in guerrilla war or terrorism, in Mao's famous dictum, the fighter is a fish in water, relying on a supportive community; thus to remove the community through ethnic cleansing was to leave the fish out of water.

The Serbian strategy was not clearly understood in the outside world, where many, including officials and their governments, saw only the incomprehensible mayhem of ethnic furies released from the grasp of history. The record showed that at least from the conflicts of the 1870s, through the first and second Balkan wars between 1911 and 1913, the First World War, the Second World War and indeed the Greek Civil

---

[61] Although introduced in the Yugoslav War of Dissolution as an integral part of the Serbian new state project, when Croat forces also engaged in an armed campaign to annex parts of Bosnia and Hercegovina and create what was called 'Herceg Bosna' during 1993, a similar pattern could be observed, as it could in some actions by Muslims fighting for the Army of Bosnia and Hercegovina.

War there had been a common pattern to conflicts. War in the region had been characterised by a loose-leaf structure of irregular forces which, as a contingency of war, carried out atrocious acts — mass rape, mass murder, gross mutilation, the razing of villages. They were often connected only by a dotted line to their political authorities who could then claim that the forces in question were not under their control.[62] This pattern was a contingent factor in the Balkan wars — it was the way things were sometimes done, not the point of doing them. The practice of the Croatian Ustasha regime during the Second World War moved towards something more purposeful with its creation of the notorious camp at Jasenovac and a tri-partite programme as, expressed by Deputy Leader and Education Minister Mile Budak in June 1941:[63] 'one-third of the Serbs we shall kill, another we shall deport and the last we shall force to embrace the Roman Catholic religion and thus meld them into Croats.'

The Serbian campaign of the 1990s for new borders inhabited by an ethnically pure population and free from potential unrest was clearly more than a happenstance of war. It had necessary strategic purpose. The systematic conduct of Serbian political and military forces — from the creation of Crisis Headquarters as shadow military-political commands some months before the war in Bosnia, the elaboration of bureaucratic arrangements, a consistent pattern of attacks and, especially in Bosnia, a network of concentration camps, some of which were also death camps — indicated a degree of organisation inconsistent with spontaneous contingencies of war. Whereas there was clearly an unpleasant tradition in the way war was waged in the region, the Serbian campaign of ethnic cleansing was qualitatively different in its systematic nature.

The Serbian project systematically to create, through violence that included ethnic cleansing, the borders of a new, ethnically homogeneous set of contiguous territories lay at the core of the Yugoslav War of

---

[62] This pattern and the links of the forces involved to relevant political authorities and state security services was noted in a report made under the auspices of the Carnegie Endowment following the Balkan Wars of 1911-13 (see, for example, pp.10 and 82-3). These were re-published as *The Other Balkan Wars: A 1913 Carnegie Endowment Inquiry in Retrospect*, with a New Introduction and Reflections on the Present Conflict by George F. Kennan, Carnegie Endowment, Washington DC, 1993.

[63] Quoted in A. Bell-Fialkoff, 'A Short History of Ethnic Cleansing', *Foreign Affairs*, Vol.72, No.3, 1992.

Dissolution. This project, underpinned by the Belgrade military, turned potentially violent unrest into war — albeit a war characterised by coercive tactics, including terrorisation, rather than direct combat. The complexity of the war both genuine and illusory, meant that for some time, it was hard for the international community clearly to see wood of the Serbian campaign from the individual trees of atrocity and ethnic combustion. It also meant that, for much of the time, international diplomats, as well as being concerned with a variety of other matters, could not be sure what the essence of the question was, let alone accept that the answer required clear, firm political will and preparedness to use force if necessary.

In the end the Serbian project was denied, although not completely defeated in Bosnia. In Croatia, the Croatian Army secured control of almost all areas of Croatia which had been held by the Serbs and gained diplomatic agreement on the return to its control of the one region, Eastern Slavonia, which the military did not take. In the course of these military actions, the Krajina region in the Dalmatian hinterland which for centuries had been home to Serb rural communities, were 'cleansed'. Although some tens of thousands of Serbs looked to return, many tens of thousands more would not. In the charmless analysis of Croatian President Franjo Tudjman, his country had been rid of a centuries-old problem.[64]

In Bosnia, the situation was less clear cut. By the end, Bosnian Serb forces were overstretched. Croatian forces, playing a substantial part in the war in western Bosnia, assisted the ever strengthening Bosnian Army to improve its position. By the end of 1995, Bosnia and Croatian forces, operating in alliance, had reduced the territory held by the Bosnian Serbs from 70 per cent to under 50 per cent.

Significantly, as the war turned in the summer of 1995, Bosnian and Croatian military efforts were complemented (whether or not by intention) by a substantial use of air power and artillery by NATO against the Bosnian Serbs following an attack on Sarajevo. With this, the Bosnian Serbs had little option but to turn to Serbia's President Milošević to negotiate and end to the war to avoid further losses. The result was to be agreement after three weeks of talks in Dayton, Ohio, sponsored by the United States, to an internal partition of Bosnia

---

[64] Speech at Split, 26 August 1995, broadcast live by Croatian television HRT (all channels).

between two entities — one Croat-Muslim, the other Serb. The Serbian project to change borders had been suffocated, but the Bosnian Serbs had emerged with a territory within Bosnia to call their own. In the end, they had not lost utterly. But, the Yugoslav War of Dissolution had concluded in favour of Slovenia, Croatia, Bosnia and Macedonia, as well as the international community.

The Yugoslav War of Dissolution, was a clash between state projects: those of Slovenia, Croatia and Bosnia and Hercegovina to be secured with independent international personality within their designated borders; and those of Serbia, throughout and Croatia, for a period in 1993, to create a set of ethnically pure contiguous territories cut from Bosnia and Hercegovina, in the Croatian case, and from Croatia, as well as Bosnia and Hercegovina, in the case of Serbia. In the end, the war was brought to an end in November 1995 as a result of the using force. The Serbian project was frustrated, in the end, by armed force and by diplomacy.

International Diplomacy and the Yugoslav War of Dissolution

The Yugoslav War of Dissolution and the international diplomacy which surrounded it were largely products of the ending of the Cold War. Although the decomposition of Yugoslavia stemmed from the internal logic of the dissonant relations between its decadent republics, which by the late 1980s had become embryonic states within a state preparing to emerge in their own right, the termination of East-West competition provided the context in which a parting of the Yugoslav ways became possible.

It removed the Cold War compress, and with it the lingering prospect of a Soviet intervention — something which had previously concentrated otherwise dissipatory Yugoslav minds. It had removed an immediate external strategic interest in the future of Yugoslavia — and, with it, the need for a rigorous approach to its problems.

Finally, it ushered in an period in which there was a confused confluence of several important streams of development in European and international security which meant that, apart from the devilish detail of Yugoslav dissolution, minds were often elsewhere and not sufficiently committed to dealing with the South Slav conflict.

Moreover, that new era was one in which there were new ambitions concerning issues of international security — those of the EC in particular, but also the general commitment of the international community, especially through the UN, to co-operative and collective responses to crises and conflicts. This was the source of international diplomacy in the Yugoslav War of Dissolution.

3

THE EARLY INITIATIVES:
FROM DECLARATION TO RECOGNITION

On 27 June 1991 a European butterfly fluttered its wings and the chaotic course of the Yugoslav crisis was irrevocably changed. The moment the Yugoslav storm broke violently on that day — with the JNA moving into Slovenia to assert federal authority and being met by armed resistance — the European Community (EC) embarked on a mission of crisis management. If that initial EC move did not necessarily change the course of history, it played an important role in determining the character of that history. From that initial EC intervention stemmed the two defining aspects of the Yugoslav War of Dissolution. The first was the decision of the Belgrade military to opt for a plan of war in which the borders of a new 'mini-Yugoslavia' for the Serbs would be established — an objective which dictated the strategy of 'ethnic cleansing'.

The second was the nature of the international stake in Yugoslavia's war and dissolution. All the subsequent international embarassments, as well as the occasional successes, were parts of a chain of events in which international credibility was increasingly at stake — a particular chain which began with the spontaneous decision of the European Council of the EC at its Luxembourg Summit in June 1991 to dispatch its troika to mediate.[1] From this ill-prepared initiative, a pattern of international diplomatic chaos was catalysed. Had the EC Summit not co-incided with the outbreak of armed hostilities in Slovenia and Croatia, EC action might well have been different.

---

1 The troika is explained below.

A summit after one week of fighting might still have decided to become involved, but it would not have done so without preparation, nor on the spur of the moment. Whatever action it took, it would have been with forethought and with a possibly more lucid sense of purpose (although, of course, this might have had a simliar outcome). As it was, the blending of a vague sense of responsibilties and the ill-conceived opportunism of those seeking to fashion a common European security policy condemned the EC and the international community as a whole to years of diplomatic tribulation and escalating responsibility in the conflict. In accordance with the image used in Chaos Theory,[2] as the EC butterfly fluttered its wings in Brussels, it turned a local storm pattern in the eastern Adriatic into an international diplomatic deluge.

Many of the difficulties in subsequent international involvement in the dissolution of the SFRY were determined in the first six months of the war. Although other international institutions were involved during those first six months of the Yugoslav War of Dissolution — such as the CSCE, the WEU and the UN — it was clearly the EC which took the lead in the international handling of the Yugoslav conflict, even after the burden of arranging ceasefires and discussing peace-keeping troops had been passed on from the Community to the UN. In particular, the EC was responsible for the troika which attempted to mediate and for the EC Conference on Yugoslavia. It was also the EC which, when other efforts]] failed, established the framework in which those Yugoslav republics seeking independence could gain recognition as independent international actors.

The Mainsprings of EC Intervention

The EC's crisis management enterprise changed the shape of the crisis and of the fighting. The Yugoslav army appeared to have made two assumptions: first, that a simple show of force — a few tanks on the streets and at the border posts — would be enough because the Slovenes would not fight, even though they had prepared armed forces; and secondly, that even if they were to fight, the army would be able to escalate with the backing of a world it believed had been urging it

---

2 On the 'butterfly effect' in chaos theory, see James Gleick, *Chaos: Making a New Science*, Cardinal-Sphere Books, London, 1988, Ch.1.

to maintain a single Yugoslavia at all costs.[3] The EC intervention meant that both assumptions proved to be wrongly founded. This in turn led the JNA generals into hesitant action caused by self-doubt and internal arguments about the way forward, as well as about what the EC would and could do.[4]

The JNA leadership was surprised by the EC's diplomatic intervention. One reason behind the EC's zeal in taking an unexpected crisis initiative was a quickly evolving sense its attitude towards Yugoslavia, before the declarations of independence, had inadvertently contributed to the situation in which there was a resort to force: another policy approach might have made it possible to avert violence (in this sense it was understandable that the generals were taken by surprise).

The EC's sense of responsibility was outweighed by another factor, probably the real mainspring of EC involvement — the nascent Common Foreign and Security Policy (CFSP) of the EC Member States, as they prepared for the Maastricht Summit in December 1991 (where the then-extant mode of European Political Co-operation in the EC would become, formally, a single policy area for a single European Union). In this context the EC was keen to exorcise the ghost of indecision and inaction during the Gulf Conflict the previous year.[5] It was, in the much derided announcement of Luxembourg Foreign Minster Jacques Poos, speaking as chair of the EC Foreign Affairs Council of Foreign Ministers, 'the Hour of Europe'.[6] To this extent Italian Foreign Minister Gianni de Michelis declared that Washington and Moscow had been 'informed', not consulted, about the mission of the EC troika of Foreign Ministers.[7] De Michelis even suggested that

---

3 For more detail on this, see James Gow, *Yugoslavia and Lessons From the Gulf War*, Centre for National Security Studies, Los Alamos National Laboratory, 5-LE3-WO261-1, November 1992.

4 Ibid.

5 See Lawrence Freedman and Efraim Karsh, *The Gulf Conflict, 1990-1991*, Faber and Faber, London, 1993, esp. pp.261-4 and 423; see also Trevor Salmon, 'Europeans, the EC and the Gulf', in James Gow, ed., *Iraq, the World Community and the Gulf War*, Brassey's for the Centre for Defence Studies, London, 1993.

6 See Catherine Guicherd's excellent, 'The Hour of Europe: Lessons from the Yugoslav Conflict', *The Fletcher Forum of World Affairs*, Vol.17, No.2, Summer 1993.

7 *The Guardian*, 1 July 1991. The US had, however, made it clear to the Europeans already during the Berlin Summit of the CSCE that a European desire to 'go it alone' would not be blocked.

the rapid dispatch of the troika constituted an EC diplomatic rapid reaction force.[8]

There was also diplomatic interest in Yugoslavia. In addition to the somewhat vain hope that claims to the right of self-determination might be exercised in a way which would not excite nationalist and territorial disputes elsewhere, there was concern to avert total economic collapse in the region and to avoid refugee problems. These were practical reasons for EC interest, in addition to which there was a question of trade. Yugoslavia was the main trade route between Greece and the other parts of the EC. There was, therefore, good reason to want peace on the territories of the SFRY. Moreover, the EC had economic influence. It was better placed than the US, for example, because of the amount of its aid and financial involvement in Yugoslavia. Whereas American aid was US$5m, the EC had large-scale aid and trade involvement: in addition to the EC's own links (£800m aid over five years and a 40 per cent share of Yugoslavia's exports), it was also co-ordinating the Group of 24 industrial nations' aid programme of 3.6 bn ecu ($4.1 bn).[9] It therefore had an instrument with which it could try to prevail upon the Yugoslavs.

Finally, the EC wanted to offer itself and its embrace for the various parties in the future, as part of the new, integrated Europe. This reflected not only the more concrete question of CFSP but values on a more philosophical or emotional plane. At this more abstract level one catalyst for European intervention was the European idea itself. This was shown in sometimes emotional reactions:

If Europe means anything as a concept, the civil war in Yugoslavia must be stopped. It is intolerable that, 18 months after the collapse of communism in Eastern Europe, two republics with democratically elected governments should be crushed by a communist-led army that appears to have brushed aside the politicians in Belgrade to whom it owes loyalty.[10]

In addition, in Germany the politicians and people, having invoked the principle of self-determination at the end of the Cold War, were emotional supporters of others making a claim on the basis of this 'fundamental' right (although they did not perceive that Croatia's independence would mean for the Serbs the kind of split into two states

8 *International Herald Tribune*, 1 July 1991.
9 *The Wall Street Journal*, 1 July 1991.
10 *The Independent*, 4 July 1991.

that the Germans had been happy to repair for themselves after forty four years although the position of the Serbs was more clearly analagous to that of the Germans in the inter-war period, with ethnic Germans living in mixed communities outside Hiter's Germany). However, it was not only in Germany that a swell of popular opinion, mobilised by television images, placed pressure on EC governments to act in Yugoslavia.

The majority of these considerations had been evident before the declarations of independence by Slovenia and Croatia had been made, and thus before armed hostilities began. As indicated, what made the difference and sparked the EC-led intervention was the co-incidence that the EC Prime Minsters and Foreign Ministers were all meeting together for the Luxembourg summit of the Twelve (the Members of the EC) as the fighting began. This made possible a rapid response, including a decision to act and the formulation of a plan for dealing with Yugoslavia. Because of this, the EC was quick of the mark in advancing its proposal within the CSCE framework because there was clearly a feeling that this was a European, not a transatlantic question. As much as the US had little inclination to get closely and immediately involved in Yugoslavia, there was reluctance in the EC to let the Americans be involved.[11]

The EC Troika

The European Community dispatched a mediation mission of three foreign ministers. The 'Troika' comprised the past, present and coming foreign ministers of the Presidency of the European Council of Ministers. In June its members were Gianni de Michelis (Italy), Jacques Poos (Luxembourg) and Hans van den Broek (the Netherlands) respectively. They took a three-point plan to Yugoslavia. This called for: a resolution of the presidential crisis which had precipitated the end of the SFRY through the appointment, as should have occurred automatically, in May, of Croatian representative Stipe Mesić; suspension of implementation of the declarations of independence for

11 Jacques Poos, speaking for the Luxembourg Presidency of the EC, declared: 'if one problem can be solved by the Europeans, it's the Yugoslav problem. This is a European country and it's not up to the Americans and not up to anybody else', (ITN News, 28 June 1991).

a period of three months; and the army's return to its barracks. This plan was borrowed from Ante Marković, the last Prime Minister of the SFRY, who had obtained agreement among the republican leaders to some of the details the previous Friday. The EC's 'success' was in reinforcing this.

The immediate and excessively triumphant return to Luxembourg following the first visit by the troika left the disputants to sort out the details. The prestige of a common foreign policy was put on the line without any guarantees that the brokered deal would be implemented. The session of the federal presidency to appoint Mesić did not materialise and the federal army, instead of returning to barracks as the government had agreed, continued to act on its own in Slovenia — 'out of control'. The Mesić appointment failed to happen because Slovenia refused to attend the 29 June meeting, declaring that it was no longer part of Yugoslavia and, so, its representative, Janez Drnovšek, had resigned. The meeting was therefore none of Slovenia's business.

Two days after claiming to have cobbled together a deal, the troika was back again. More bargaining led to another, more cautious expression of optimism. This package, in essence, was one which, had it been pursued some weeks earlier, might have facilitated a new, confederal Yugoslav community. But the fighting had transformed the situation. The JNA's action confirmed Slovenia in its determination to free itself from the rest of Yugoslavia. At the same time, the Slovenes' successful resistance had embarrassed the army and raised the stakes for it, while encouraging Croatia.

With the contending forces dispersed and with uncertain lines of political control, added to a blend of communist and Balkan duplicity, a ceasefire agreed at the centre proved difficult to implement. The terms of the ceasefire were critical, as they would determine the balance of power during the three months of bargaining envisaged in the EC proposal. If, as the Slovenes demanded, the JNA had to abandon its equipment and give up its mission to control Slovenia's borders, then it would effectively concede any influence in the breakaway republic.

The troika was, essentially, trying to bully the Yugoslavs into ceasing fire. De Michelis appeared to be cast in this role, arriving in Yugoslavia for the troika's second visit saying he was not interested in words, just in signatures. The EC and its member states backed up the troika's efforts to cajole the Yugoslavs into peace. An embargo on armaments and military equipment to the whole of Yugoslavia was imposed and there was an appeal to other countries to follow their lead. The EC also decided to suspend its second and third financial protocols with Yugoslavia — that is, to block aid worth £7-800m (although suspension was not put into effect because agreement was reached before this could happen).

That intervention succeeded in getting the Mesić appointment confirmed. However, the ceasefire agreement did not hold, in part because Slovene forces impeded the return of tanks to their garrisons, where it was feared that they could be repaired and refuelled for further attack. The JNA compounded this by launching its heaviest attacks to date, including aerial assaults, on the Slovenian capital Ljubljana.

Finally, on 7 July (with the backing of the CSCE) the troika succeeded in establishing peace in Slovenia. On the island of Brioni, once Tito's retreat, the EC mission got all the parties in the dispute to accept its plan. The EC had created the conditions for peaceful negotiations. Significantly, all parties agreed that a 'new situation' had arisen in Yugoslavia, requiring close monitoring and negotiation between the parties. Negotiations were to begin no later than 1 August and were to include all aspects of Yugoslavia's future, without preconditions. Although allegations persisted that both sides had breached the ceasefire agreement, on the whole it held because the JNA, in the absence of Serbian backing, had effectively conceded Slovenia. A function of its implementation was the 18 July decision of the federal authorities, including the Defence Ministry, to withdraw all JNA units from Slovenia within a three-month period.[12]

After Brioni the phenomenon of the troika was less prominent, as the Dutch Presidency of the Council of Ministers, which had begun on 1 July, became a leading element in galvanising EC efforts. It was the 'strong Dutch Presidency that made things happen'.[13] This included the organisation of a semi-military yet open and flexible monitoring operation. For the troika's final achievement at Brioni had been to gain agreement of all parties to the introduction of the European Community

12 Until the beginning of November, there were still 2,000 JNA troops with their equipment. This was because they had been unable to obtain permission for transit through Italy or Hungary and would otherwise have had to go through the war zone in Croatia to reach their destination in Serbia.
13 A British member of the European Community Monitoring Mission, interviewed by the author.

Monitoring Mission (ECMM).[14] This happened within the framework of the CSCE, although the EC was the driving force and leading element of CSCE activity. However, in the coming months, the main thrust of EC engagement was to be a peace conference in The Hague.

The EC Conference: Carrington's Mission

On 2 September, a ceasefire accord included agreement to begin talks on the future of Yugoslavia, to be held in The Hague. Only a day later, it was announced that the European Community Conference on Yugoslavia would be convened on 7 September in The Hague, under the chairmanship of Lord Carrington. Talks would be on the basis of three principles: no unilateral changes of borders, protection of the rights of all minorities, and full respect for all legitimate interests and aspirations.[15] The Conference proceeded alongside the ECMM's entry into Croatia and various efforts to obtain a durable ceasefire.

Carrington was widely perceived as a fine candidate for the difficult task ahead when he took up his role as the EC's representative and coordinator of the talks. As a former Secretary-General of NATO and, before that, the British Foreign Minister credited with the 1980 settlement on Zimbabwe, he had the diplomatic background to deal with the tortuous Yugoslav conflict, and was also widely regarded as having the personal qualities to be able to gain the trust of all parties.

The thankless nature of the task ahead was confirmed by the opening session of the conference. Although the Conference had been called on condition that the ceasefire was maintained, it began amid renewed fighting in Yugoslavia and with verbal offensives from both the Serbian and Croatian presidents. However, after the opening session the Conference became closed as Carrington began a series of private meetings with all the Yugoslav leaders and foreign ministers in an attempt to mediate.

Although Carrington initially insisted that an end to hostilities was a prerequisite for the Conference to proceed, he continued his work in

---

14 See James Gow and Lawrence Freedman, 'Intervention in a disintegrating state: the Yugoslav case'. in Nigel Rodley ed., *To Loose the Bands of Wickedness: International Intervention in Defence of Human Rights*, Brassey's for the David Davies Memorial Institute, London, 1992.

15 *Borba*, 5 September 1991.

spite of the seemingly unstoppable violence. On one occasion he appeared to have waved a magic wand as he conjured signatures to a ceasefire agreement not only from Croatia's President Franjo Tudjman and Milošević but from the Defence Secretary, General Veljko Kadijević, as well.[16] However, it was too much to expect that one afternoon with Carrington was enough to bring peace. As became the norm with Yugoslav ceasefires, signatures proved insufficient to halt combat.

The joint statement was flawed. It recognised that leaders could only pledge that 'everyone within our control and under our political and military influence should cease fire immediately'[17] — that is, they could not (or were not prepared to) guarantee that fighting would stop. In this the efforts of local mediation by ECMM members would continue to be more constructive than any kind of general agreement among the leaders. The Igalo agreement was also weak because it required that all forces should 'instantly and simultaneously withdraw from immediate contact and from actual or previous areas where hostilities have or are taking place'.[18] Of course, neither side was prepared in practice to do anything which would weaken its position without a guarantee that its opponent was reciprocating.[19] The lack of specificity involved virtually made the document null and void as it was signed.[20] Later efforts at arranging ceasefires increased specificity but did not diminish the growing perception that a lasting ceasefire was not a realistic possibility, as each agreement failed to be implemented or broke down with mounting ferocity.

In these circumstances Carrington had to forget his early statements that there could be no peace talks without a ceasefire and proceed with the Conference anyway. His evaluation was that:'by making progress — if we can make progress — we think it will be more likely that the ceasefire will hold and that we can get a solution that is acceptable to

---

16 At the signing in Igalo in Montenegro on 17 September, it was noteworthy that the hardline Chief of Staff of the JNA, General Blagoje Adžić accompanied Kadijević.
17 'Statement by Lord Carrington, the Presidents of the Republics of Croatia and Slovenia and the Minister of National Defence at Igalo on 17 September 1991'.
18 *Ibid.*
19 James Gow and James D.D. Smith, *Peacekeeping, Peacemaking: European Security and the Yugoslav Wars*, Brassey's for the Centre for Defence Studies, London, 1992.
20 See Smith, *Stopping Wars*, pp.164-72.

all the parties to the dispute.'[21] To this end the two expert groups that had been meeting intermittently on human rights issues and constitutional matters would be in session almost permanently.[22] A third group of experts later began work on economic affairs.

At the beginning of October the EC discussed the possibility of giving Yugoslavia 'diplomatic quarantine' — that is, removing recognition from the country and its official representatives. Although this did not necessarily imply recognition of the republics, it was a clear signal of the way the wind was preparing to blow. A day after this was discussed, and after the Serbian-JNA forces had received setbacks for the first time, Carrington was able to produce the most significant breakthrough to date — and perhaps of the whole dispute. On 4 October he secured Milošević's agreement to seek a political solution 'on the basis of the independence of those wishing it'.[23]

This solution would include a 'loose alliance of sovereign or independent republics' and 'adequate arrangements' for minorities and 'possibly special status for certain areas'. The key feature, however, was Milošević's acceptance that there could be no 'unilateral changes in borders'. Carrington, while recognising the amount of work and the difficulties which lay ahead, did not hesitate to recognise that this had been the major stumbling block and that it represented a major concession:

This is the first time that Serbia has recognised the right of other republics to self-determination — subject to respect for minority rights. By discussing issues such as the autonomy and special status for minorities we are going to the heart of the political problem. I hope this will speed up the political process for a ceasefire.[24]

In securing the Serbian President's recognition of the territorial integrity of Croatia, Carrington had achieved a major breakthrough. It would be hard for Milošević to backtrack on this public agreement. That

---

21 *The Financial Times*, 27 September 1991.
22 Delegations of experts were sent from each of the six Yugoslav republics. To these were added officials and legal experts of the EC and its member states.
23 *The Guardian*, 5 October 1991.
24 *Ibid.*

agreement provided the basis for the negotiators in The Hague and the EC officials to work towards a proposal for a political settlement.[25]

However, the path ahead remained rocky. Within two days the fighting intensified as the 90-day moratorium on the Slovenian and Croatian declarations approached its end which would be on 8 October. Croatia's President Tudjman, after a period of considerable pressure from his army of critics, ordered full mobilisation; the JNA responded with renewed vigour across Croatia, including bombardment of the historic port of Dubrovnik. The EC, on the basis of reports from the ECMM, identified the JNA as the chief offender and swiftly reacted. On 6 October, it set a deadline of midnight on 7 October for a truce, after which Yugoslavia's trade agreement would be suspended, ending all trade,[26] and sanctions would be imposed. A supplement to these measures was a threat that 'those responsible for the unprecedented violence in Yugoslavia, with its ever increasing loss of life, should be held accountable under international law'.[27]

The midnight deadline was met and a truce came into effect for several days, although not before the JNA air force had made an attack on the Presidential Palace in the Croatian capital of Zagreb. However, there were as ever pockets where the fighting persisted. With the assistance of EC monitors, both the JNA blockade of Croatia's ports and the Croatian National Guard's siege of federal barracks throughout Croatia (especially in the capital Zagreb) were lifted. The monitors were essential in enabling both sides to carry out their commitments, providing supervision and channels of mediation as the JNA began to leave its barracks in Zagreb (this process was halted half-way through as tension increased).

As clashes grew again, there was a strange interruption in the proceedings. Both Tudjman and Milošević were invited to talks with Soviet President Mikhail Gorbachev in Moscow on 15 October. Gorbachev got both men to agree to begin negotiations on peace within

25 It would also, as events turned out, provide the basis for EC arrangements for offering recognition of independent international personality to those Yugoslav republics seeking it (see Chapter 3).

26 However, UK Foreign Secretary Douglas Hurd noted that EC trade with Yugoslavia had become minimal and that any trade embargo would be ineffective without full UN backing. BBC Radio interview, cited in 'Weekly Record of Events', *Report on Eastern Europe*, 18 October 1991.

27 Quoted in *The Independent*, 7 October 1991.

a month.[28] This, while desirable, was odd: both sides were already involved in such talks in The Hague. Whatever was said went unrevealed, but after meeting Russia's President Boris Yeltsin and having a further session with Gorbachev the following day, Milošević and Tudjman emerged with different demeanours. It was obvious that the Serbian president was buoyant and satisfied, whereas his Croatian counterpart was unhappy.

Afterwards, while on the ground the Serb coalition pressed on, the Serbian stance at The Hague hardened. On the basis of the discussions with all parties in The Hague, Carrington and van den Broek offered the Yugoslav republics a plan for political redevelopment. That plan was to rearrange Yugoslavia along the lines of the EC itself .[29] Van den Broek stated categorically that border changes 'were not an option'.[30] This plan coincided with the various proposals advanced by Slovenia, Croatia, Bosnia-Hercegovina and Macedonia in the year leading up to the war. Significantly, a fifth republic, tiny Montenegro, also accepted the EC proposal.

Montenegro had been staunchly allied with Serbia throughout the years of crisis, although there had been attempts to show that it nonetheless had a separate identity and was not a vassal.[31] Now President Momir Bulatović told an emergency meeting of the country's parliament: 'We cannot adopt an in-between attitude. We can only accept or refuse.'[32] He added that refusal would mean international isolation and sanctions — something such a small republic could hardly afford. However, there was considerable discontent among the parliament's members.

With five out of six republican leaderships accepting the EC plan in principle, the only stumbling block was Milošević, who rejected it, although this rejection was not completely out of hand. His chief objection was the proposed position of the Serb communities outside Serbia. Having been classified as part of a 'nation' in the old Yugoslavia, these would now become 'national minorities'.[33] Serbia's

---

28 'Sovmestnoe Kommunike Presidentov SSSR, Serbii i Horvatii - Obobshchenie', *TASS*, 15 October 1991.
29 *Politika*, 19 October 1991; see also 'Draft Convention on...
30 *The Independent*, 18 October 1991.
31 See, for example, Wyjnaendts, *L'engrenage*, pp.107-10.
32 *Yuqofax*, No. 6, 31 October 1991.
33 See Chapter 3 for further discussion of this.

position was that these minorities should be 'sovereign'; this corresponded with the proposal of the Serbs in Croatia.[34] A further major stumbling block was the *quid pro quo* for Serb political autonomy in Croatia: restoration of autonomy for the Serbian provinces of Kosovo and Vojvodina, the removal of which had been Milošević's central political platform and only real achievement since coming to power in 1986. Suggesting this, he said, was interference in Serbia's internal affairs.

The Serbian President could not easily accept the proposal, given the pressure on him from powerful elements in the Belgrade parliament and the position of the Croatian Serbs. However, his scope for rejection was limited as the big guns of the United States and the Soviet Union were lined up behind the EC proposal, with threats of general international isolation and economic sanctions:[35] with five republics ready to head in one direction, it seemed there would be a shot-gun divorce if Serbia did not relent.

In addition to Serbia's leadership, its partner in the war, the JNA, repulsed the EC plan. Defence Secretary Kadijevic thought Carrington's plan would prove catastrophic and renewed charges were made that the plan was in effect 'Germany very openly... attacking Yugoslavia for the third time this century'.[36] He also bewailed the reality that the plan would mean the end of the JNA. The unsympathetic EC response to this sob-story was characterised by Carrington: 'The leadership of the federal army is acting in a totally unjustified fashion, bears a heavy responsibility and is accountable for what it is doing.'[37]

Milošević, along with the army leadership and Serb leaders from Bosnia and Croatia, publicly proposed an alternative plan for a 'mini-Yugoslavia' consistent with the military-political programme already being implemented, to include Serbia, Montenegro (which had been press-ganged by the Serbian President into withdrawing its agreement to the Hague plan), and whichever others wanted to remain part of a Yugoslav federation — the enclaves in Croatia and Bosnia would become 'autonomous federal units'. In this plan rearrangement of

34 *Yugofax*, No. 6, 31 October 1991.
35 *The Financial Times*, 19 October 1991.
36 *The Guardian*, 23 October 1991.
37 *The Independent*, 26 October 1991.

Yugoslavia would be according to referenda held on an ethnic, not a republican basis.'[38]

However, the Serb-coalition was doing little to encourage support for its position. The continuing bombardments in eastern Slavonia and especially the high-profile assault on the historic port of Dubrovnik raised international impatience with Serbia and the JNA. That impatience manifested itself in an ultimatum: Serbia was given one week, from 28 October, to accept the EC plan. Otherwise it would face comprehensive economic sanctions (although earlier statements that these would need to be backed by the UN were repeated). Moreover, if Serbia did accept, the Conference would continue with all six republics; however, if it did not, van den Broek warned, 'the Community will continue its patient negotiations with the five republics who are willing. This would be in the perspective of their right to independence.'[39]

This reflected decisions taken by the EC Foreign Affairs Council on 6 October,[40] two days after Milošević had accepted the principle of the republics' right to independence within borders. At that meeting it was agreed that Carrington would propose a Draft Convention envisaging the re-configuration of relations between the Yugoslav republics. In that agreement those republics seeking independence would gain it, subject to certain conditions including provision for minorities and the maintenance of a single economic space through a customs union. If the Draft Convention were not accepted, it was agreed, the EC would move to a position of working with those republics co-operating with the Conference in the light of their right to independence.[41]

Moreover, the EC Commission had by this time been given legal advice that it could act immediately to suspend its trade agreement with Yugoslavia and take punitive measures. The latter would include diplomatic quarantine of the federal Yugoslav state and of Serbia. The EC would then be in a position to 'take a series of positive measures to

38 *The Guardian*, 24, October 1991.
39 *The Guardian*, 29, October 1991.
40 'EC Declaration on the Situation in Yugoslavia', Informal Meeting of EC Foreign Ministers, Haarzuilens, 6 October 1991; Snežana Trifunovska *Yugoslavia Through Documents. From its Creation to its Dissolution*, Martinus Nijhoff, Dordrecht, 1994, pp.351.
41 'Recognition of the Yugoslav Successor States', Federal Foreign Office, Bonn, 10 March 1993, reproduced by the Embassy of the Federal Republic of Germany, London, 16 July 1993.

discriminate in favour of particular republics', said one official, even before formal diplomatic recognition.[42] Recognition itself would take a little longer but was now on the agenda. By the end of October, thirteen countries were accepting Slovene passports, though asserting that this did not constitute recognition. Italian Foreign Minister de Michelis said that the EC's aim was to wind up the peace conference by mid-December, by which time the 'treaty will be signed with the individual republics, and will represent official EC recognition of their independence'.[43]

At the beginning of November it appeared that EC efforts, backed by references to the CSCE and the UN, had produced the framework of, and encouraged evolution towards, a political settlement on Yugoslavia, albeit not a clean one. It was, however, one that after much deliberation was still rejected by Serbia. On several occasions the EC had made progress towards gaining ceasefire agreements or agreement in negotiations on the future of Yugoslavia, but only after exerting pressure on the less willing parties. In this the strong Netherlands Presidency of the EC Council of Ministers was extremely important. In the end, the conditions for truce were enmeshed with those for recognition.

Conditions for Truce and Recognition

Carrington had done extremely well in the circumstances, but not well enough. The dual role played by the EC of seeking to mediate both a ceasefire and a political settlement, more or less, ended with the so-close-yet-so-far failure at the end of October. At first, the Community appeared to be passing the baton to the UN, as the three of its members on the UN Security Council began to push for measures to be taken by that body, including its taking responsibility for dealing with ceasefire and peacekeeping discussions. This meant that by mid-November it was Vance, and not Carrington who was taking the lead in negotiations to

42 Abel Matutes, Vice-President of the European Commission, quoted in *The Guardian*, 29 October 1991.
43 Quoted in *The Guardian*, 1 November 1991. The Netherlands Presidency of the EC quickly supplemented de Michelis's statement with the clarification that 'the EC itself does not recognise anyone'. Recognition was a matter for the individual Member States, which of course operated with a high degree of co-ordination.

halt the fighting. Carrington and the Community, meanwhile, continued with the political groundwork.

The 'good cop/bad cop' teaming of the UN and the EC, which evolved more or less by accident, was both more acceptable to Serbia and more practical in terms of the quest to deal with the politics of the dispute. Serbia found the UN a more agreeable partner in talks because it did not appear to be driven by German ambition — as in Serbian eyes, the Community did — and forced the United States to take more obvious interest. The EC was freed from the responsibilities of neutrality involved in mediation and able therefore to assert its influence where this could be used to encourage political dialogue. In this sense the Serbian belief that it was a victim of German expansionism, expressed through the EC, did not impinge on ceasefire discussions in the same way as it had previously. As a result, the Community could take stronger positions without prejudging efforts to stop the fighting. Indeed, it was able to exert pressure over the political agenda in a way which created the conditions for the first really stable break in the seven months of fighting.

The UN envoy to Yugoslavia, Cyrus Vance, achieved a durable ceasefire agreement on 2 January 1992. With relative ease he had negotiated a ceasefire three weeks into November and gained agreement in principle for the deployment of a 10,000-strong UN peacekeeping force — if the peace were maintained.[44] This was the fourteenth ceasefire agreement of the war in Croatia and it fared no better than the previous baker's dozen. Eventually, on 3 January, a ceasefire came into effect which, though continually and increasingly broken by small skirmishes, essentially held in the succeeding months. As a result, the UN began to deploy a peacekeeping force in Croatia during the spring of 1992, although it appeared that the UN was really only being pressured into compensating for European shortcomings.[45] It was clear that such a peacekeeping force was going to be large, costly and faced with operational difficulties in what remained a tense, hostile and

---

44 *International Herald Tribune*, 25 November 1991.
45 The EC had no defence structures. The closest it had to any kind of defence capability was the Western European Union (WEU), composed of nine of its number. Although the French spoke of the WEU as the 'military arm' of the Community ready to move in when ordered and send whatever forces required to keep the peace in Yugoslavia, that was an aspiration, not a reality. The WEU lacked forces of its own and had no command structure. For more extensive discussion, see Gow and Freedman, 'Intervention'.

politically unresolved situation, as well as one in which the conditions for deployment had been hard to achieve.

There were three major reasons for the success of the January ceasefire. The war in Croatia had become stalemated in November, with neither side in a position to make significant progress.[46] At that time Vance had already been able to negotiate agreement for deployment of a UN peacekeeping force. This opened a way to a truce which avoided what could be interpreted on the Serbian side as open concession to German influence. Finally, the crucial difference between November, when both stalemate on the battlefield and Vance's embodiment of a neutral UN were present, and January, when a genuine ceasefire came, was recognition. Truce was only achieved as a result of the Community's decision in December to offer the possibility of separate diplomatic relations to those Yugoslav republics seeking independence.

Members of the Community had been getting ever more impatient, with Germany, in particular, pushing insistently for recognition of Slovenia and Croatia, and leaving no doubt that it would grant recognition before the year's end, even if this meant breaking ranks with Community colleagues. However, Yugoslavia was placed on the back-burner until after the dishes on the Maastricht menu had been cooked and consumed on 10 December. This was clearly a move to prevent the main meal at the EC's Maastricht Summit, the signing of treaties on greater European union, from being adulterated.

With Germany intending to recognise Slovenia and Croatia before Christmas, Vance apparently making no greater progress than his European predecessors and the negotiated political settlement which had seemed possible in October receding daily, the question of recognition came to the fore. Several EC members opposed this course for fear it would complicate the situation, not only in Croatia but in other Yugoslav lands, particularly Bosnia. The Germans, with backing from other members, countered that, on the contrary, recognition would be the decisive step which would break the circle of violence and induce a more compromising Serbian attitude. Whereas all the Member States had agreed, at the beginning of October, on the principle that the republics were entitled to independence, one or two states were, in truth,

46 See James Gow, 'Political-Military Affiliations in the Yugoslav Conflict', *RFE/RL Research Report*, Vol.1, No.20, 15 May 1992.

against recognising them as independent, while some others agreed on the principle but felt that the time for recognition was not yet ripe.[47]

Many hoped that there would be a peaceful outcome, including Bosnian President Alija Izetbegović who expressed the foreboding that the pace with which events progressed might condemn his country to war. He requested both German Foreign Minster Genscher and EC Conference chairman Lord Carrington not to precipitate him into a situation where the Bosnian authorities, unable to accept a Serbianised rump-Yugoslavia, would be forced to request recognition.[48] Bosnia was already infected with Serbian and Yugoslav military preparations for war and, while swift and decisive action was required to prevent a Serbian *fait accompli*, such action itself needed vision, clear preparation and commitment.

At the very least, EC recognition of Croatia would have implications for the other Yugoslav republics. Reservations about the impact of recognition on weaker elements of the Yugoslav structure, added to general reluctance to recognise precipitately, led the Community, supported by pleas from Lord Carrington, to persuade the Germans partly to delay recognition. This would permit it to happen in an ordered way, within a framework which gave Bosnia, Macedonia and, if it wished, Montenegro the opportunity to seek recognition.

After a long meeting on 16 December which continued into the early hours of 17 December, the European Council of EC Foreign Ministers discussed the question of recognition before emerging with a formula: the Badinter Advisory Commission to the EC Conference would be asked to counsel the EC on applications from the Yugoslav republics; applications would be invited from all the Yugoslav republics wishing to be recognised as independent; republics would be judged according to various guidelines, including conditions for individual and minority rights and the rejection of territorial claims; the Council of Foreign Ministers would then act in the light of the Commission's recommendations on 15 January. Thus in the space of half a year the EC had moved from a unified position on the maintenance of the

---

47 Among this latter group, the UK, in face of German intent, was widely rumoured to have struck a deal at Maastricht, in which the UK would go along with recognition, in the spirit of CFSP, in return for concesions on the Union Treaty.

48 Lord Carrington in 'A Soldier's Peace — with Major General Lewis MacKenzie (ret.)', Screenlife Inc., 1994..

Yugoslav state, through growing internal dispute and disarray on how to handle the war, to a common but harshly discordant policy on inviting those republics seeking independence to submit applications and undergo the procedure identified.

The imminence of EC recognition of Croatia's independence created a situation in which for the first time Serbia's interests would unquestionably be better served at the negotiating table. This was acknowledged by General Života Panić, then head of the Yugoslav army's 1st Military District and later to be Chief of Staff in the JNA's successor, the Army of Yugoslavia (*Vojska Jugoslavije* — VJ). In the army's journal *Vojno Delo*, he indicated that the army had been forced by the EC to stop short of its (still unspecified) goals in western Slavonia — what was to become, effectively, Sector West in the UN peacekeeping operation when it began.[49]

Before January the Serbian camp had evaded ceasefire accords because the Community had been unable to coerce more strongly for fear of increasing Serbian fears about Germany. For Serbia an EC-arranged ceasefire, backed by political coercion, could be interpreted as capitulation to Germany. A UN-brokered ceasefire on the other hand was, for Serbs thinking in those terms, an escape from the feared embrace of Germany: accepting arrangements made by Vance became an alternative to capitulation to the Germans.

Milošević and the army leadership also demonstrated a reawakened interest in the EC Peace Conference. Indeed, as Lord Carrington noted after the Conference re-convened on 9 January following a month-long gap, Serbian enthusiasm was far greater and its leadership 'more constructive', having 'obviously taken note' of the shift towards recognition of Croatia by EC members.[50] If Croatia was to be recognised, then Serbia's best chance now of benefiting from that situation was at the peace table.

Despite a remarkably brazen attack on two EC helicopters by JNA fighter aircraft, causing five deaths, the Community moved towards the 15 January deadline unruffled. That incident, representing perhaps a last

---

49 Col. Gen. Života Panić, 'Iskustva iz rata u Jugoslaviji moraju se analizirati na stranicima *Vojnog dela*', *Vojno Delo*, God. XIX, Nos1-2, January-April 1992, pp.222-3; this was also confirmed by General Veljko Kadijević, *Moja Vidjenje Raspada: Vojska Bez Države*, Politika, Belgrade, p.142.

50 'Weekly Record of Events', *RFE/RL Research Report*, Vol.1, No.3, 17 January 1992.

spiteful poke at the EC and a warning to those who would sign up for a UN peacekeeping force, was the only major infringement of the 3 January ceasefire. If the intention was to deter peacekeepers, the Security Council decision the next day to send 50 observers showed that it had not worked. Following the incident one of the main figures in the dispute, Federal Defence Secretary Kadijević, resigned. Ironically the replacement of this politically astute soldier with one far less so, erstwhile Chief of Staff General Adžić, made the political situation easier as Adžić's greater proximity to the Serbian leadership facilitated the army's 'withdrawal' from the old Yugoslavia which had had Kadijević's loyalty.

Milošević was clearly applying concerted pressure throughout the Serbian camp to allow deployment of the peacekeepers. In turn he arranged for pressure to be applied by most parts of the Serbian camp on the recalcitrant Babić to accept UN peacekeepers in Krajina. This included attempts to dislodge him, encouraging regional opponents against him and, according to the Krajina leader, being kidnapped by the JNA leadership, which tried to make him agree to the peacekeeping plans under duress.[51] Finally, the suggestion that Serbia, whether under that name or as Yugoslavia, would be recognised as the legal successor of the SFRY, as had Russia emerging from the Soviet Union, was an incentive for Milošević and his allies to be amenable in negotiations on peace, including a new-found, albeit temporary understanding for the situation of the Albanians in Kosovo. It was in these circumstances, and against the background of an EC failure to come up with an armed peacekeeping force, that the UN could begin the process of planning and deploying a peacekeeping force in Croatia.

Through its intervention the EC undoubtedly changed the course of the war, both in its intra-Yugoslav dimensions by undermining JNA assumptions, and in the international sphere by moving towards acceptance of the break-up of the SFRY. Even though, as is argued later, the German analysis was probably right concerning the situation in Croatia and anyway recognition was inevitable, the manner in which the EC arrived at and implemented the decision left whatever success might actually have been achieved in the shadow of a shambles. The

51 *Borba*, 3 February 1992.

idea of CFSP was tarnished, although it could be argued that there had been relative diplomatic successes in the course of the EC's involvement.

By the end of 1991 the EC had gone from brave optimism to dealing with the unpleasant and inevitable — and had already found the limitations of CFSP along the way. As will be seen at the end of Chapter 4, there were aspects of the problem the EC was not competent to deal with, notably the insertion of a peacekeeping force. This led the EC into an evolving and often awkward relationship with the UN. The EC, however, continued to take the international diplomatic initiative.

4

THE EARLY INITIATIVES:
FROM RECOGNITION TO RECKONING

Having shifted by the beginning of 1992 from pure mediation to bullying (albeit not without vicious disputes among some of the Twelve), the Council took one of the boldest moves in the course of the crisis — the decision to offer the possibility of granting recognition to those Yugoslav republics seeking it, in accordance with five conditions laid down as guidelines by the Council itself.[1] In January, the Council proceeded to grant recognition of independent international personality to Slovenia and Croatia. Applications for recognition by Bosnia and Macedonia were less straightforward.

Although EC involvement created a framework for the recognition of the independence of the Yugoslav republics which clarified certain legal and political questions in the international domain, this was neither clearly understood by many commentators, nor applied practically in a comprehensively successful way. In particular, the EC's attempts to manage the problematic case of Bosnia were to be a focus of attention and a source of friction with the UN.

Badinter: Sovereignty, Self-Determination and Nations

The Yugoslav War of Dissolution was about statehood, sovereignty, self-determination and, effectively, the meaning of 'nation', as well as

---

1 'Guidelines on the Recognition of New States in Eastern Europe and in the Soviet Union', adopted by the EC Council on 16 December 1991. See also Foreign Affairs Committee, *Central and Eastern Europe: Problems of the Post-Communist Era (First Report)*, Vol. I, HMSO, London, February 1992, p.xxi. For an excellent account of this process from a legal perspective see Marc Weller, 'The International Response....', esp. pp.586ff.

the identity and future of particular nations. These were the issues at the heart of the Yugoslav crisis and conflict, and it was the fall-out from them which provided the greatest repercussions for international security. It was therefore the understanding of these issues which defined the international perspective on the war.

In the two years leading up to the declarations of independence by Slovenia and Croatia, and in the wake of those declarations, different understandings on the question of right-holders with reference to the rights to sovereignty and self-determination were in conflict. These conflicting conceptions were addressed in the EC Conference on Yugoslavia, held first in The Hague and later in Brussels. In particular, they were considered by a legal advisory and arbitration commission established by the Conference under the President of the French Constitutional Council, Robert Badinter. It was their interpretation of constitutional and international legal matters which provided the framework for the Council of the European Community to act politically to settle these questions, at least in part.

The Advisory Commission based its opinions on the principles of public international law, with reference to the Yugoslav constitution and submissions from the various Yugoslav parties. The crux of this work was to try to advise the EC Conference on the place of the Yugoslav questions in the framework of international relations. Although, in the end, these questions were political, the legal circumstances were important. The break-up of Yugoslavia had to be placed in the context of the international system ordered on the principle of state sovereignty.

States are the necessary components of an international system, and the principle by which they are ordered is that of sovereignty.[2] Sovereignty is one of the concepts which falls into a category of ideas

2 On the central place of sovereignty in international relations, almost any introductory volume would offer illumination. Of particular specialist use are the following: F.H. Hinsley, *Sovereignty*, 2nd edn, Cambridge University Press, Cambridge, 1986; Alan James, *Sovereign Statehood: the Basis of International Society*, Allen and Unwin, London, 1986; James Mayall, *Nationalism and International Society*, Cambridge University Press, 1990. As well as the essentially political nature of the concept, sovereignty has obvious legal connotations which, as legal norms, are ultimately subject to the political action of law generation. For the perspective of international lawyers, see generally Ian Brownlie, *Principles of Public International Law*, 4th edn, Clarendon Press, Oxford, 1990.

where a great part of their value is to be 'essentially contested'.[3] In practical use, it has a number of purposes, as Alan James has pointed out.[4] Certainly, the meaning and content of sovereignty will often change, according to the need of a particular government at a particular time — it is a plastic term which means that governments can justify almost any action, whether assertive or contrite, in terms of exercising its sovereign rights. Essentially, this means the government has decided for itself what to do.

While often taken to be a fundamentally legal concept in international relations,[5] sovereignty is in reality both legal and political. Indeed it is ultimately a political concept because its basic meaning is the political supremacy to make law (even though, in modern practice, the makers of law are themselves likely to be subject to legal restraint). Sovereignty has taxed political and legal thinkers through the ages. Yet for all the thought applied to establishing what it could mean and who might possess it, in most cases the concept means only one thing: the sovereign, whoever or whatever it might be in particular circumstances, is the inalienable ultimate authority and thus has the right not to be overruled.[6] It is the 'power of action without being bounded unto others'.[7]

Self-determination is the right granted to 'all peoples' in, among other places, the UN Charter and the International Covenant on Civil and Political Rights (1966), in which 'the people' were given the right

3 Similar notions are liberty and justice — see W.B. Gallie, *Philosophy and the Historical Understanding*, Chatto and Windus, London, 1964, Ch.8.

4 Alan James, 'Sovereignty in Eastern Europe', *Millennium: Journal of International Studies*, Vol.20, No.1, 1991.

5 For this reason many international lawyers, in particular Americans, assume sovereignty to be not only a legal concept, but to refer to a 'constitution', because, in the United States, 'the Constitution' is held to be invested with sovereignty — although in reality domestic sovereignty is shared between the executive and legislative branches of government, the judiciary and the people. The case for purely legal conceptions of sovereignty is made, for example, by Gregory H. Fox, 'New Approaches to International Human Rights: The Sovereign State Revisited', paper for the SSRC-MacArthur Workshop on Sovereignty and Security in Contemporary International Affairs, Department of War Studies, King's College London, 3-4 December, 1993; Fox draws on Ian Brownlie, *Principles*.

6 See Michael Akehurst, *An Introduction to International Law*, Allen and Unwin, London, 1970.

7 Gordon Pocock, 'Nation, Community, Devolution and Sovereignty', *Political Quarterly*, Vol.61, No.3, 1990, p.323.

'freely' to 'determine their political status and freely pursue their economic, social and cultural development'. Although it is a general right which is usually assumed to include the right to statehood, in practice its application has been more limited.[8] The entities which have had claims to statehood granted have fallen into the following five cases: mandated, trust and other territories treated as non-self-governing under Chapter XI of the UN Charter; distinct political-geographical entities subject to *carence de souveraineté* (the only successful case here is Bangladesh); on the basis of a plebiscite held with the agreement of the parties involved in a particular territory; formerly independent entities reasserting their independence; and, following the demise of communist federation in Yugoslavia, the Soviet Union and Czechoslovakia, federating republics, constitutionally and legally defined as sovereign states, from a dissolved state. In spite of restriction in its application, however, self-determination had remained an evocative and affective symbol.

The Yugoslav constitutional-political dispute turned on the meaning given to 'nation'. Divergent interpretations of 'nation' produced radically different outcomes in terms of the compound concepts 'national self-determination' and 'national sovereignty'.[9] 'Nation' refers to people who are, with small exceptions, born together into a particular community. It may therefore refer to all the people born within the territorial boundaries of a political community in which they have citizenship rights — it is in this sense that US Presidents often address 'the Nation'. The word may also, however, allude to all the people born within a particular ethno-national group (which might be defined by, for example, genetic, linguistic, cultural and religious characteristics) irrespective of the territorially-defined political communities in which they find themselves.

8 In his important response to the UN Security Council's request for a report on the matter *Agenda for Peace: Preventive Diplomacy, Peacemaking and Peace-keeping*, the UN Secretary-General Boutros Boutros-Ghali rightly warns that unrestricted application of the principle could lead to unending fragmentation if every 'national' group claimed the right to form a state. UN Doc. S/24111 (1992).

9 It should be noted that although the term 'national self-determination' is in common use, only the term 'self-determination', without the 'national', appears in any of the fundamental documents, such as the UN Charter, which deal with the right to self-determination.

The two definitions of 'nation', — as all the people living within the territorial boundaries of a given political community and as all the members of a particular ethno-national group — can lead to terminological trouble where they do not coincide. (There are relatively few cases in which they even coincide approximately.) Thus, where ethno-national groups are found within different states, problems over sovereignty and self-determination may arise. These were sharply focused in the break-up of Yugoslavia, where the declarations of independence by Slovenia and Croatia, based in claims to sovereignty and the inalienable right to national self-determination of the republics as state-formations,[10] were directly opposed by a Serbian claim to the sovereignty of the Serbs as an ethno-national people, wherever they were to be found, with the fundamental and inalienable right to national self-determination. Both claims were made on the basis of the SFRY Constitution.

The right to self-determination, up to and including the right to secession, was granted in the preamble to the SFRY Constitution.[11] Each republic was a 'nation-state' formation endowed with sovereignty.[12] The republics were intended to be repositories of national self-determination for each of the Yugoslav peoples (*naroda*)

10 The Basic Constitutional Charter on the Independence and Sovereignty of the Republic of Slovenia and the Declaration of Independence adopted by the Slovenian Assembly on 25 June 1991 'proceeding from the will of the Slovenian people and the citizens of Slovenia as expressed at the plebiscite on the autonomy and independence of the Republic of Slovenia, held on 23 December 1990', noted that 'under the hitherto effective constitutional order, the Republic of Slovenia had the status of a sovereign state which exercised part of its sovereign rights in the Socialist Federal Republic of Yugoslavia' but continued that 'considering the SFRY does not function as a legally regulated state...the Republic of Slovenia is an autonomous and independent state [and] the Constitution of the SFRY is no longer in force in the Republic of Slovenia [and] the Republic of Slovenia takes over all the rights and obligations which under the Constitution of the Republic of Slovenia and the Constitution of the SFRY were transferred to the agencies of the SFRY' (translation of text reprinted in *War in Slovenia*, IN [Information from Slovenia Special Issue], Mednarodno Tiskovno Središče Ljubljana, Ljubljana, 1991, p.40; for documentation on Slovenian and Croatian declarations of independence, see Angelika Volle and Wolfgang Wagner, eds, *Der Krieg auf dem Balkan. Die Hilflosigkeit der Staatenwelt*, Europa-Archiv, Verlag für Internationale Poitik, Bonn, 1994, pp.136-42.
11 *Ustav Socijalističke Federativne Republike Jugoslavije*, Službeni List, Belgrade, 1991 (with amendments), p.9.
12 'The Socialist Republic is a state, founded on the sovereignty of the nation...'. *Ibid.*, Art.3, p.23.

— that is, state-forming nations.[13] These were contrasted with national minorities (*narodnosti*) which were taken to be members of an ethnic group which in general constituted a state-forming nation elsewhere — for example, the Albanians in Yugoslavia were a national minority because the place where they were a state-forming nation was Albania.

The SFRY Constitution, by referring to the sovereignty of the republics and the peoples, glossed over a complication which came to be important when the state broke up: within Yugoslavia each of the state-forming nations had its own sovereign state to look to, but logically this left, for example, Serbs outside Serbia as minorities within Croatia and Bosnia, but still members of a designated state-forming people. Thus the ethnic peoples in Yugoslavia had a constitutional role as 'founders of the member states of the Federation'.[14] So long as Yugoslavia remained a federation, it was possible to ignore the implicit technicality that if republic was a state founded on a particular ethnic people, then the logic which deemed Albanians, for example, to be a national minority in Yugoslavia, made Serbs outside Serbia and Croats outside Croatia national minorities too.

The general problem of defining the right-holder — that is, which 'nation' is the repository of these inalienable rights — is compounded in the Yugoslav case. '*Narodno samoopredeljenje*' ('national self-determination') intensifies the terminological tension. In Serbo-Croat, '*narod*' means both 'people' and 'nation'. In both senses it can refer to the ethno-national group or to the inhabitants of a state. This difficulty can be amplified by the possibility of translating 'United Nations' (that is, the global organisation of states) as '*Ujedinjeni Naroda*', or '*Ujedinjene Nacije*'.[15] The implication here is that, in Serbian minds, the term '*narodno samoopredeljenje*' was taken (both really and, where

13 Terminology in the Yugoslav context can be confusing 'at first sight', as noted in his discussion of the 1946 Yugoslav Constitution by Frits W. Hondius, *The Yugoslav Community of Nations*, Martinus Nijhoff, The Hague, 1968, p.138. Hondius provides the conventional interpretation of the evolution of these terms in Yugoslav constitutions.
14 *Ibid.*, p.247.
15 This should not be taken as a clear-cut distinction. Both *narod* and *nacija* could be used in both senses all Serbo-Croat variants. However, this example is offered to highlight the confusions and ambiguities involved. Hondius, *Yugoslav Community*, remarks on the appearance of *nacija* to refer to the ethno-nation in the drafting of the 1963 Constitution (p.249).

appropriate, disingenuously) to refer to the Serbian people wherever they were.

The ambiguity over self-determination in the Yugoslav context had peculiar features, but these were details which did no more than create emphases — they did not make the Yugoslav case unique. However, outside that context the issue was a little more clearly defined, if not more clearly understood generally. Indeed it was the general understanding of specialists received from previous periods, however different in which self-determination and sovereignty were key questions that guided the Badinter Commission in its attention to these questions regarding the break-up of Yugoslavia.

In this context Susan Woodward's judgements are mistaken.[16] She states that there was a 'lack of international definition of the practical meaning of self-determination';[17] that there was a 'blind spot about the relationship between nations and states and the meaning of national self-determination'; and that 'the EC decisions were not made on the basis of abstract principles or historical rights, but on the basis of rights embodied in the consititution' may need some qualification.[18] There was a practical meaning of self-determination; although there was indeed a blind spot among many commentators, this did not mean that there were no knowledgable and sighted people involved; and EC decisions were indeed based in rights obtaining from the SFRY and republican constitutions, but this was not exclusively the case, as the key principles, sovereignty and self-determination, were abstractions given practical character in limited circumstances.

First, it should be noted that all the Yugoslavs and Serbia preeminently, made their cases on the basis of the Constitution. It was not the EC which either imposed this framework or even simply accepted it from the Slovenes. Secondly, EC political action and the Badinter Commission's judicial opinions were not based solely on interpretations of the constitution but, crucially, on an understanding of the theory and practice regarding self-determination in international law, in particular the application of the abstract principle of *uti posseditis*

---

16 *Balkan Tragedy: Chaos and Dissolution After the Cold War*, Brookings Institution, Washington DC, 1995.
17 Ibid., p.165.
18 Ibid., p.205.

juris (see below).[19] For those — relatively few — familiar with the issue and its application in practice, the issues were far less problematic than many lay observers supposed when they tormented themselves in 'op. eds.' about conflicting claims. The reality that there were claims to self-determination being made, whether by the Serbs in Croatia and Bosnia, or by the Albanians in Kosovo, which could generate conflict was precisely because those particular claims could not be reconciled with conventional interpretation of the principle and practice of self-determination.

The opinions of the Commission effectively rejected the Serbian claim to sovereignty for the ethno-nation, deeming that sovereignty rested with the republics.[20] However, in response to a Serbian request for clarification on the right of the Serbs in Croatia and in Bosnia to self-determination, the Arbitration Commission was less categoric. It refrained from ruling that the Serbs in Croatia and in Bosnia did not have the right to self-determination.[21] Rather, it implied that there could be a second level at which self-determination operated, one in which self-determination was a principle which protected individual human rights, involving the possibility of claiming membership of an ethnic, religious, linguistic or other group, which groups were entitled to respect from governments under the imperative norms of international law (*jus cogens*).[22]

These opinions were based largely on traditional international law and convention, although there was an element of innovation appropriate to the circumstances. Whereas in theory self-determination might be applied at the lowest level to individuals, in practice it had only been applied in specific circumstances — and only with regard to

19 See Weller, 'International Response'.
20 Serbian President Slobodan Milošević later acknowledged that sovereignty had always rested with the republics and that Serbian proposals in 1990 had sought to include the tehno-nation as sovereign in constitutional reforms. *The Milošević Interview*, Brian Lapping Associates/BBC, 1995. For an alternative approach to that adopted here, conventionally and by the international community over constitutional questions in the former Yugoslavia, see Robert M. Hayden, 'Constitutional Nationalism in the Formerly Yugoslav Republics', *Slavic Review*, Vol. 51, No., Winter 1992.
21 See Marc Weller, 'The International Response to the Dissolution of the Socialist Federal *sic*. Republic of Yugoslavia', *The American Journal of International Law*, Vol.86, No.3, July 1992, p.591.
22 I am grateful to Benedict Kingsbury for this point and several others on which his perspective as an international lawyer brought benefit.

pre-determined territorial units, normally as part of a process of decolonisation.[23] What Badinter made clear was that the principle of *uti posseditis*, originally established in the context of decolonisation, was applicable. This meant that in the absence of peaceful agreement to alter frontiers which were changing status 'the former boundaries acquire the character of boundaries protected by international law'.[24]

This finding extended to the emerging states the protection of their boundaries in international law. It was supported by references to a number of non-binding international documents, including the Helsinki Final Act. Most important, however, it was backed by reference to the UN Charter. In effect the Commission's finding was that the republics were entitled to the protection and provisions of Article 2 of the UN Charter concerning the territorial integrity and political independence of states.[25]

The dominant aspect to note in all this was the sovereignty formally accorded to the various communist republics within their federations. This was the basis for the dissolution of those federal states. At the same time, in line with the generally felt desirability of limiting state fragmentation, the process of break-up was limited to the sovereign and federating states. Other territorial entities within those federations — the autonomous republics and *oblasts* in the Soviet Union and the autonomous provinces, such as Kosovo, in Yugoslavia — could not achieve independence in the same process because they were not endowed with sovereignty.[26]

23 See James Mayall, *Nationalism*, pp.55-6 and Brownlie, *Principles*, pp.170 and 596-7.
24 Opinion No.3, 11 January, 1992.
25 See Nigel Rodley, 'Collective intervention to protect human rights and civilian populations: the legal framework' in Rodley, ed., *To Loose the Bands of Wickedness: International Intervention in Defence of Human Rights*, Brassey's for the David Davies Memorial Institute, London, 1992, pp.14 ff.
26 The Kosovo Albanian leadership sought equal status with the sovereign republics in the EC Conference, arguing that representation on the collective Federal Presidency made Kosovo a federating unit. As Kosovo was constitutionally in a discrete, non-sovereign, category from the federating sovereigns — under Article 4, not Article 3, of the 1974 Constitution — its argument for equality was ignored. In retrospect, it might have been better for the Kosovans to argue differently: as Badinter invoked traditional anti-colonial principles, in order to understand the situation of the federating elements (*uti posseditis*), and given the territorial definition of the province, its constitutional status and the nature of Serbian rule there, the Kosovars could have played on Badinter's reference to colonialism and argued that their case was not so much one of messy dissolution of a

It was important to understand, in this context, that the break-up of Yugoslavia was not a question of minorities with autonomy in a region with defined territory seceding. It did not, therefore, imply more generally for other situations that there was a right of secession for minorities living in a defined territorial space.[27] Indeed the EC approach to the break-up of Yugoslavia and the other communist federations placed an important (and, in some cases, it could be argued, potentially unrealistic) limit on the dissolution of federations; there would be no endless process of minorities within minorities being accepted as state actors, as many including the UN Secretary-General Boutros Boutros-Ghali feared.[28]

What was critical in the Yugoslav case was that the federation was constitutionally a union of sovereign states (the republics being founded in the peoples, as per the discussion above), not a state in which autonomy had been devolved to minorities, in territorially defined regions. The issue in Yugoslavia was not secession but dissolution. Although Serbia had charged that other republics had seceded or would do so, the opinion of the Badinter Commission, on the basis of the SFRY Constitution and the basic principles of international public law, noted that 'the composition and workings of the essential organs of the Federation....no longer meet the criteria of participation and representativeness inherent in a federal state.'[29] As a consequence, the Commission concluded that Yugoslavia was in 'the process of dissolution',[30] which process it later judged to have been completed.[31] In essence, the independence of the Yugoslav republics was not so much a matter of secession, akin to the case of Bangladesh, but one of

---

federal communist state as one of straightforward colonialism.

27 In this context, Martin Rady ('Minority Rights and Self-Determination in Eastern Europe', *Slavonic and East European Review*, Vol.71, No. 4, October 1993, pp.717-28) was mistaken to suggest that 'the right to secession of a minority living in a defined territory' has 'now acquired a measure of legal recognition'. This was in part because he viewed Yugslavia as a question of 'constitutional devolution' which might 'convey the basis of a right to secession'. While it was not impossible that the eventual settlement of the war in Bosnia might have implications in this regard, to conceive of the independence of the Yugoslav republics and the role of the Badinter commission in this way was grievously to misunderstand that question.

28 Boutros Boutros-Ghali, *An Agenda for Peace*.

29 Opinion No.1.

30 *Ibid.*

31 Opinion No.8, 4 July 1992.

dissolution, more akin to decolonisation, in which the quality of pre-existing borders is changed as the international personality of a political-territorial unit is established.

The result of the Arbitration Commission's findings could be summarised by the following understanding on questions of sovereignty and self-determination. Sovereignty applied to territorial units. Self-determination, up to and including statehood, applied to such units. Self-determination could apply to other 'national' (that is, self-defining ethnic, religious, genetic, cultural, linguistic etc.) groups, as an expression of their members' individual human rights, but this would not include the right to form a state; it could, however, entail the right to levels of autonomy - that is, to political and cultural prerogatives and powers, perhaps of self-governance, operable within the boundaries of a state.

The blending of elements of international law (*uti posseditis juris*) with the provisions of the SFRY Constitution offered clarification of the issues at stake. Sovereignty and statehood were both linked to territory; national self-determination was linked to them in cases where 'nation' referred to the people living within the boundaries of a defined territorial unit; sovereignty, statehood and national self-determination were not necessarily linked, and were not juridically to be combined where 'nation' alluded to the members of an ethno-national community which formed part of one or more states, or territorial units with the potential to become states. However, the intellectual clarity that it was possible to derive from the Badinter opinions was muddied by the real waters of Yugoslav dissolution and the practical aspects of EC involvement in that process, especially in the case of Bosnia.

Bosnia: the Cutilheiro Talks

On the basis of the Badinter analysis, the Milošević concession of principle in October and the deadlock on the Carrington proposals in November, the EC moved offered the possibility of recognition to those Yugoslav republics seeking it. The outcome was mixed when judgements were passed on 15 January. Slovenia was recognised without question, but the other three applications were more problematic. The Badinter Advisory Commission recommended to the EC that Croatia should be recognised, but expressed a reservation that Zaagreb had not incorporated into law agreements to which had committed itself in the Draft Convention. This led many commentators, as well as the Serbs, to claim that Croatia had not satisfied the EC's conditions for recognition — missing two points, that the EC had issued guidelines not conditions, and that Badinter had recommended recognition. Recognition of Croatia caused friction, but this was little compared with the difficulties of Macedonia and, especially, Bosnia. Macedonia was recommended for recognition, but was left in limbo without formal EC acceptance of its independent international legal personality following a Greek veto.[32] However, the real nightmare was

32 The European Council, because of Greece's veto on the issue, did not grant the same status to Macedonia, although by the spring of 1994 a number of EC members were beginning to establish individual diplomatic links with it and it had gained admission to the General Assembly of the UN under the temporary name of 'former Yugoslav Republic of Macedonia' — FYROM. EC states eventually began to establish links after Greece and 'the former Yugoslav Republic of Macedonia' made an interim agreement to begin normalising their relations in November 1995.

Macedonia was a strange case. Badinter had no problems with Macedonia in spite of a curious clause inserted by the Greeks at the 16 December foreign ministers' meeting, which explicitly required a commitment 'to adopt constitutional and political guarantees assuring that it [the republic] has no territorial claim towards a neighbouring member State of the Community, and that it will not undertake propaganda hostile to that state, including the use of a name which implies territorial claims'.

Greece, however, persuaded its fellow *communautaires* not to recognise Macedonia. Its ostensible reason was that, despite duly made constitutional provisions stating that Macedonia had no territorial claims, a continued use of the 'historically Greek' name would imply expansionist claims on Greece. The odd proposition that tiny Macedonia, with a population little more than two million, its economy exhausted and with no armed forces represented a threat to a country which not only had its own armed forces but also the added benefits of EC and NATO membership (with the latter including American bases) was not summarily rebuffed by Greece's Community partners. Instead it was entertained, initiating an unnecessary bout of Balkan tension and the first notes of an extremely perilous round of 'Balkan musical chairs'.

Greece in fact had two real, if limited, interests in opposing Macedonia's recognition, neither of which concerned the improbable prospect of Macedonian territorial claims. One, perhaps the more significant, was that Greece had an ethnic Macedonian minority which it did not recognise beyond occasional admissions that its members were 'Slavophone Greeks'. It also had Turkish and Albanian minorities which it labelled 'Muslim Greeks'. Greece's real fear was that the existence of a Macedonian state might encourage its 'Slavophone' community to seek collective rights — and that this would have consequences for the Albanian and especially the Turkish minorities, as well as for relations with the kin-states, Albania and Turkey.

In this sense, a real if somewhat distorted fear lay behind Greek popular and political truculence over Macedonia. Cyprus occupied a prominent place in Greek consciousness.

Bosnia, where Badinter decided the situation was uncertain and might be clarified by the holding of a referendum on independence.

With the EC Council's decision to recognise the independence of certain Yugoslav republics, the purpose and work of the Carrington Conference — to negotiate an overall settlement of intra-Yugoslav disputes and the framework for future relations between the republics following the dissolution of the old federation — was obviated. Although Lord Carrington was asked to continue with the work of the Conference (to resolve matters such as formal succession, division of assets and repayment of debts), there was little scope for progress as the main negotiating incentive at his disposal, on behalf of the EC, was the attitude to recognition. With this gone, his resources were limited. The one area in which the EC could still concentrate its efforts, however, was Bosnia.

The Turkish intervention in northern Cyprus in 1974, linked to the position of ethnic Turks on the island, added to historic rivalries between the two countries and a series of other disputes, had great resonance among the Greeks. The island was not part of Greece — indeed it appeared to have been abortive moves by the Greek generals to invade the island which prompted the Turkish invasion. However, it was clear that Cyprus formed part of the Greek mental landscape and that, following the Cyprus model, any acknowledgement of a minority, especially Turkish, would imply eventual moves towards annexation. Thus, although the overwhelmingly greater part of the Greek response was hysterical, there was a grain of rationality and justification behind the emotion.

Greece's second reason for opposing Macedonian independence was its fear that Macedonia would become prey to Bulgarian expansionism. In this Athens's move was highly counter-productive. Greek obduracy only added to Macedonia's need to turn to Bulgaria and beyond that to Bulgaria's new friend, Turkey. These were both regarded by Greece as adversaries. The Greeks in reality got their calculations wrong: blocking recognition only drew attention to the Macedonian minority in Greece; and the surest way to have prevented Bulgaria's absorbtion of Macedonia either *de facto* or *de jure* — something both Serbia and Greece might have been prepared to fight about — would have been to support its independence.

In the mean time Macedonia was left in an uncomfortable limbo as the Serbian-dominated rump-Yugoslavia withdrew its army rapidly, leaving the small, impoverished country squeezed between it and Greece. Economically, politically and militarily vulnerable, Macedonia was only offered any comfort by Bulgaria. However, independence was always likely to be recognised sooner rather than later by the EC countries, which were impatient with Greece. This process began in the spring of 1994, with a number of European Union (as the EC had by then become) Member States opening diplomatic relations with Skopje, albeit still using the code-name 'Former Yugoslav Republic of Macedonia', which had allowed the republic to join the UN and was used in diplomatic circles to avoid greater difficulties with Greece.

While visiting Sarajevo on 6 January 1992, Carrington proposed the opening of a separate set of talks on the future of Bosnia within the framework of the EC Conference. With the Presidency of the EC passing from the Netherlands to Portugal, Carrington asked the Portuguese diplomat Jose Cutilheiro to take charge of these negotiations. Not only did Cutilheiro, formerly Ambassador to the Conventional Forces in Europe arms control talks in Vienna (eventually subsumed under the CSCE), have the advantage of high-level negotiating experience, but as he had the complete confidence of Portuguese Foreign Minister João Pinheiro, a more or less premanent link would exist between the Conference and the Presidency of the EC.

Following a preliminary meeting in Sarajevo at the beginning of February with the leaders of the three political parties representing the major communities of Bosnia, Cutilheiro began the real work of his sub-negotiations in the Portuguese capital, Lisbon, on 21-22 February. There the Ambassador made clear to all parties that there could be no question of tampering with the borders of Bosnia and Hercegovina, nor would there be any viable solution which did not take into account the existence of the three communities in the central Yugoslav republic.[33] Within this framework and against the background of the impending referendum on Bosnian independence from the defunct Yugoslav federation (to be held at the end of the month), the sub-conference would seek ways in which a constitutional future could be worked out for Bosnia.

Cutilheiro and Carrington proposed the idea of three 'constituent units' within Bosnia — in doing so they were desperately hoping to find a constitutional model which would not result in the Serbs initiating war.[34] Discussions took place around the idea of what was popularly and conventionally known as 'cantonisation' — although the actual term was not used in the Conference. The key element was that Bosnia would be divided into units defined by the principle of ethnicity. To anyone familiar with the map of Bosnia, this could only seem ridiculous

---

33 Henry Wynaendts, *L'engrenage*, p.159.
34 By this stage, it was clear that the Serbs had been preparing for the destruction of Bosnia for some time; see Chapter 1 and also Noel Malcom, *Bosnia: A SHort History*, Macmillan, London, 1994, p.224ff. The EC negotiators were attempting to find a way to stop preparation from becoming practice, as Carrington confirmed; *A Soldier's Peace with Lt. Gen Lewis MacKenzie (ret.)*, Sreenlife Inc., 1994.

(see Map 1). But, without any alternatives in the search for a way to avoid war, especially when political direction and backing — that is, a real policy — from the EC and its member governments were lacking,[35] the mediators were propelled to entertain discussion on the basis of what was essentially a Serbian idea supported by some Croats.[36]

Throughout 1990 and 1991, almost all political parties in Serbia proper, as well as Karadžić's SDS in Bosnia, had been arguing for the 'cantonisation' of Bosnia, still within the Yugoslav federation.[37] The model of Switzerland was invoked. The SDS sought cantons in order to create a confederal republic of three national communities. In December 1991, with the SDS adding to its complement of 'Autonomous Regions', published a plan and map in which 'national cantonisation' would result in around 70 per cent of Bosnia being covered by Serb cantons.[38] Ts although there could be no apparent sense in trying to divide Bosnia, given the ethno-demographic distribution of its population, there was taken to be at least some sense in accepting the principle as a basis for negotiation if it meant that the Serbs would not unleash a new, more vicious bout of armed violence. This was in essence a form of voluntary blackmail, which was to rank among the greatest of errors made in international diplomacy: the Serbian camp may have been intent on a programme of population purification in Bosnia anyway, but admitting the principle of ethnically determined territorial units was a cardinal mistake, since it bestowed approval on Serbian ambition and was in effect a charter for 'ethnic cleansing'.

The 'cantonal' notion of 'constituent units' had little attraction in itself for Bosnia's President Alia Izetbegović, either as head of the emergent state, or as leader of the Party of Democratic Action (SDA),

---

35 This opinion was expressed in private discussion by a very senior official.

36 Croatia's Foreign Minster at the time had already indicated that he was ready to accept pieces of Hercegovina, saying in January that concessions (over Krajina) could not be 'one-sided'; quoted in *The Guardian* 17 January 1992. However, the leader of the Bosnian branch of Tudjman's HDZ] at this stage, Stjepan Kljuić, supported Bosnia's integrity; see Milan Andrejevich, 'The Future of Bosnia and Herzegovina: A Sovereign Republic or Cantonisation?', *RFE/RL Report on Eastern Europe*, 5 July 1991.

37 See Andrejecich, 'The Future'.

38 Robert M. Hayden, 'The Partition of Bosnia and Herzegovina, 1990-1993', *RFE/RL Research Report*, Vol.2, No.22, 28 May 1993, pp.4ff.

the main party supported by the Muslims in Bosnia. Representing both the whole of Bosnia and a large part of the Muslim population which made up around 40 per cent of Bosnia's total, he favoured the retention of a unitary Bosnian state. But he was prepared to enter into talks on the basis of the EC proposals in the interests of both co-operating with the EC, on whose support he was to some extent dependent, and doing anything that might dispel the dark clouds of war gathering over his land.

The Croatian Democratic Union (HDZ) was broadly aligned with the Muslims. The sibling party in Bosnia of President Tudjman's ruling party in Croatia, it had been led by Stjepan Kljuić, a firm adherent of Bosnian unity — whereas many of his colleagues favoured partitioning the country between Serbs and Croats at the expense of the Muslims. As a result of fierce disputes within the party on the issue of 'cantonising' Bosnia, Kljuić was forced to resign as leader, to be replaced by an extremist from the 'Hercegovina' lobby, Mate Boban, who was a firm supporter of cantonisation and a close ally of President Tudjman. However, these internal differences in the Bosnian HDZ were of secondary importance. For the time being, the Croats' sole priority was to separate Bosnia from Serbia.

On the other side of the Bosnian independence equation, the leader of the Serbian nationalists, Karadžić, welcomed the idea of 'constituent units', but pressed on the sub-conference that only an extremely loose federation, or confederation, in which the Serbian unit was permitted to keep special links with Belgrade would satisfy the Serbs. This automatically set the Serbs and Muslims poles apart. Whether or not Karadžić would have settled for such an arrangement had anything of this type realistically been achievable is impossible to say without doubt. It does, however, appear highly improbable. Having begun to declare autonomous regions the previous autumn, having armed the local militias, having seen the JNA take positions all over Bosnia in preparation for war and finally, through these steps, having pushed the Bosnian authorities and the non-Serbian populations into a corner where they were being asked to accept unacceptable demands, it is hard to envisage Karadžić or his backer Milošević relenting unless something forced them to do so.

In this there were striking parallels between Bosnia's situation and that of Czechoslovakia in the 1930s. As Hitler used Henlein,[39] so Milošević used Karadžić. Konrad Henlein, leader of the Sudeten German Party, first destabilised the Sudetenland by mobilising the local German population, which had genuine grievances in the Czechoslovak state, before making demands for autonomy on the Prague government. These demands were in truth unacceptable, but the government acceded to them rather than face war. These were then increased to include the cession of the Sudetenland to Germany — another unacceptable demand which was granted to Nazi Germany at the Four Power Conference in Munich in 1938, where France and Britain, rather than face war at that stage, appeased Hitler. The Czechoslovaks, given little choice, ceded the Sudetenland, which was occupied by German soldiers. Having tried to provoke Czechoslovakia into prompting a Nazi invasion, with all its unacceptable demands met, Hitler's Reich annexed the whole of Czechoslovakia in the spring of 1939.

In one very clear sense, the EC took on the role France and Britain had played fifty-five years earlier at the Four Power Conference on Bosnia. It could not be said to be a great reflection on the individuals concerned (who were often unhappy at what they were doing), but in effect the EC and its ambassadors were urging Izetbegović in what was essentially an exercise in appeasement. While various elements in the international community were accused of appeasing the Serbian camp at several stages, it was at this time in 1992 that the real appeasement took place. Reports of 'ethnic cleansing' from Croatia could have left no doubt about Serbian performance,[40] while essentially unrealistic and, worst of all, misguided negotiations were held at which the weaker party was urged to make concessions to the bully, instead of being helped to stand up to intimidation.

The various Bosnians agreed to hold further sessions in March. In the mean time, the referendum recommended by the EC and conducted with EC assistance on Bosnian independence was held on 29 February and

39 A.J.P. Taylor, *The Origins of the Second World War*, Penguin, Harmondsworth, 1963, pp.192, 202-3.
40 Of particular note here is the testimony of the Head of the ECMM, Ambassador Dirk Jan van Houten on 'The Yugoslav Republics: Prospects for Peace and Human Rights' in *Hearing before the Commission on Security and Cooperation in Europe*, 102nd Congress, Second Session, 5 February 1992, US Government Printing Office, Washington DC, 1992.

1 March. The referendum asked:'Are you in favour of a sovereign and independent Bosnia-Hercegovina, a state of equal citizens and nations of Muslims, Serbs, Croats and others who live in it?'[41] 64.4 per cent of the Bosnian population took part in the referendum, of which 99.7 per cent declared themselves in favour of independence.[42] However, these were predominantly Muslims and Croats. The overwhelming majority of the country's Serb population — 31 per cent of the total — did not participate. Karadžić's SDS had called a boycott of the referendum. To help ensure that the boycott was effective, the JNA air force dropped leaflets urging support for the boycott, while the SDS and its militias in the 'Serbian Autonomous Regions' erected barricades to prevent ballot boxes being taken into areas under its control.[43] Although there could be no accurate gauge of Serb opinion because of these machinations, it would be dangerous to assume that there was not substantial popular support among rural Serbs for the Karadžić position. Thus the polarisation of Serbs, on one side, with Muslims and Croats, on the other, foreshadowed in the Lisbon talks, was reinforced by the voices — and the silences — of the peoples.[44]

While the recommendation on holding a referendum appeared to be 'rather proper and sensible to the EC', as Mark Thompson suggested, 'the proper decision for a constitutional lawyer to reach was not a proper decision for the EC to enact.'[45] For the leaders of the EC, testing their collective prowess in the field of security issues while hiding behind the quite justifiable recommendations of a lawyer on what was essentially a political question, was negligent. The failure to take firm action through a political decision to recognise Bosnia in January left the initiative with the Serbian camp.

41 Mark Mazower, *The War in Bosnia: An Analysis*, Action for Bosnia, London, 1992, p.7.
42 Commission on Security and Co-operation in Europe, *The Referendum in Bosnia-Hercegovina, February 29-March 1, 1992*, Commission on Security and Co-operation in Europe, Washington, DC, 1992, p.23, cited by Leonard J. Cohen, *Broken Bonds: The Disintegration of Yugoslavia*, Westview Press, Boulder, CO, 1993, p.237.
43 Noel Malcom, *Bosnia: A Short History*, Macmillan, London, 1994, p.231.
44 It should not be assumed, however, that all the Serbs held to the Karadžić line — clearly tens, if not hundreds, of thousands of them rejected his vision.
45 Mark Thompson, *A Paper House: The Ending of Yugoslavia*, Vintage, London, 1992, p.318.

Immediately tension grew, with the Serbs in Sarajevo erecting barricades on 1 March, on which day a shooting incident at a wedding in the city left one Serb dead. Karadžić, attempting to influence the outside world as much as the other communities in Bosnia, as well as other Serb leaders, renewed visions Bosnia's rivers flowing with blood. As the Dutch diplomat Henry Wijnaendts, involved in the negotiations at the time, noted, what Karadžić said was 'simple prophecy', for he had 'all the means at his disposal to make it happen' and would do so when the time came.[46]

EC diplomacy recommenced in Lisbon on 7 March and lasted for the next two days. These talks were effectively in checkmate. There had been progress on the prerogatives of the 'constituent units' during thirty hours of discussions, but none on the question of the territorial definition of the units. Briefly a miraculous agreement had looked possible on 9 March; although the territorial questions remained, there seemed to be accord on a plan for a federal constitution in which each of the 'national' groups would have a right of veto on any political issue deemed to be of significance. But this came to nothing.

Between 16-18 March, Cutilheiro returned to Sarajevo and again tried to roll his Sisyphean boulder up the Bosnian mountain. The Portuguese Ambassador brought with him a 'Statement of Principles for New Constitutional Arrangements for Bosnia and Hercegovina', drafted by EC Conference aides after discussions with the Bosnians. On 18 March the Serbs, Croats and the government in Bosnia signed the document. The statement divided Bosnia into 'three constituent units, based on national principles and taking into account economic, geographic and other criteria'.[47]

The country was to remain one, with a parliament comprising two chambers, one elected directly and the other formed by an equal number of representatives from each community. While the central government would have responsibility in a number of areas (defence and foreign policy, economic and financial policy, basic utilities and infrastructure), each of the communities would be able to veto in the parliament anything it judged to be against its interests. The 'constitutent units' would be responsible for all other matters which concerned them, in

---

46 Wynaendts, *L'engrenage*, p.160.
47 'Statement of Principles for New Constitutional Arrangements for Bosnia and Hercegovina',...

whatever way they chose, so long as their actions did not disrupt the independence and territorial integrity of Bosnia. The whole structure would also be overseen by a constitutional court, which included foreign lawyers to provide non-partisan arbiters in any potential disputes.

To the EC mediators, these principles constituted an attractive basis on which to proceed, even if it was predictable that each of the Bosnian communities would interpret the document in its own way. The Serbs saw it as meaning the territorial apportionment of the country according to an ethnic precept. Boban and the Hercegovina Croats saw a simliar scenario, although their minds were focused on Hercegovina, with scant regard for the majority of Croats in Bosnia who, living in central and northern Bosnia, would be likely to fall into Serb, or Muslim, cantons. Finally, the government-cum-Muslim view was that the country was so intricate in its ethnic composition that making the Serb and Croat versions of the country with its cantons would be impossible. Izetbegović and his colleagues were unhappy with the document, but found it acceptable because it retained a single state and in its internal dimensions would be unfulfillable.

Cutilheiro had not been unaware of the nightmare to come when it came to drawing maps.[48] The provisions of the statement had included the institution of a working group to 'define the territory of the constituent units'. This suited Karadžić who regarded even the signed document as no more than the 'basis for further negotiation'.[49] It was clear that the Serbian camp would use the combined threat of imminent violence, should the EC accept Bosnian independence, and the prospect that, as long as the Bosnian Serbs continued to negotiate, it would be unthinkable that the Twelve would recognise Bosnia, if that meant precipitating war.[50]

---

48 The reality that there were discussions on drawing maps places a not inconsiderable question mark over Lord Carrington's defence of the 'cantonisation' plan in a statement to the London Conference on 26 August 1992 when he defended the plan against those who criticised it for paving the official way to 'ethnic cleansing'. Much of what had been written, he said, was 'inaccurate', continuing that 'there was a clear understanding that the three "constituent units" envisaged under the agreement would not be geographical entities.' (Lord Carrington. 'Statement to the London Conference on Yugoslavia', 26 August 1992).
49 Quoted by Wynaendts, *L'engrenage*, p.164.
50 *Ibid.*, pp.164-5.

The Serbs had placed themselves in a controlling position. Added to what was already happening in Serb-controlled areas in Croatia and the logic of ethnic distribution in Bosnia,[51] this boded ill. Given the foregoing, while understandable hopeful thinking, it would be hard to credit the otherwise redoubtable Henry Wynaendts' statement that, as 'ethnic cleansing' had not yet produced its evils in Bosnia, an agreement was 'not unthinkable'.[52] His own assessment of Serbian behaviour in Croatia, added to a commonsense analysis of the Bosnian situation, ought to have made it clear, even if the diplomats' political masters were not prepared to countenance anything braver than vain hope, that there could be no 'divisions which would not leave hundreds of thousands of Bosnian citizens unhappy'.[53] 'Unless', as Mark Thompson impeccably crystallised the blindingly obvious, coercion were 'used to purify the units'.[54] If no one could anticipate the scale and malevolence of coercive purification in Bosnia, there was little reason for anybody in Wijnaendts' position not to recognise what could be expected if there were attempts to make a territorially defined ethnic cantonment in Bosnia. Of course, in mitigation of the Dutch emissary, it would be understandable if he and his colleagues, along with the Bosnian government, Bosnians and all well-meaning people wanted 'desperately to believe' in a peaceful outcome.[55]

Within days, the Statement agreed on 18 March was repudiated, formally by the Bosnian government and the HDZ, and, in effect, by the SDS. First, on 24 March the HDZ pulled out of the agreement, then a day later Izetbegović withdrew. Whereas the Croat repudiation was arguably based on the likely outcome of the plan itself — an estimated 59 per cent of the Croats the HDZ relied on for support would probably have been stranded in non-Croat cantons, had the agreement been realised[56] - the Bosnian President's renunciation was of a different character.

---

51 Reneo Lukić, 'Greater Serbia: A New Reality in the Balkans', *Nationalities Papers*, Vol.22, No.1, 1994, pp.62-3, highlights a number of the ECMM reports in the autumn of 1993 and early 1994 which registered Serbian action in Croatia.
52 *Ibid.*, p. 163.
53 Noel Malcom, *A Short History*, 233.
54 Thompson, *A Paper House*, p.320.
55 *Ibid.*, p.324.
56 Hayden, *Partition*, p.7

He did not merely reject the 'Statement' because of the 'implications for the ethnic division of the republic'.[57] Indeed Izetbegović and his colleagues were implacably opposed to any division of the republic. For the sake of peace, the government had accepted discussion on bases with which, in truth, it did not agree. It had undertaken negotiations, as with the referendum, at the behest of the EC — there was a realistic admission of the frail position of the Bosnian authorities mixed with a seemingly naive faith in the capacity of the EC to render a just and peaceful outcome in the country. However, the Bosnian leadership was now able to place its faith in another outside element, the United States.

The US Ambassador to Belgrade, Warren Zimmerman, advised Izetbegović that if he really did not like the agreement, he should not have signed it.[58] This was one of the first signs of a partial American return to the scene. Having left the Yugoslav stage to the European audition-seekers, as well as having refrained from following their January lead in recognising Slovenia and Croatia, the US was now preparing to return. This was partly the result of criticism that it had not been providing leadership of the Western world, partly the result of intensive lobbying in Washington by Bosnian representatives, especially the Foreign Minister Haris Silajdžić and future Ambassador to the UN Mohammed Šaćerbey,[59] which appeared to have convinced many in the American political elite of the need to act decisively to assist Bosnia.

As a result, the US was preparing to recognise Bosnia, along with Slovenia and Croatia, on 7 April. It was quite probable that by the time the Croats and the Bosnian government disavowed the Cutilheiro plan, there had been informal signals that the US was preparing to offer its recognition on the agreed date and that it would be leading the Europeans into recognition of Bosnia. That largely obviated the Bosnian government's need to follow EC suggestions. It also brought to an end

---

57 Cohen, *Broken Bonds*, p.237.

58 Zimmerman in discussion with the author. The then American Ambassador was telling Izetbegović to stay in line with his conscience and his political support, not that US support would be forthcoming in the event of catastrophe.

59 Silajdžić was to become Bosnian Prime Minster in 1994 and Šaćerbey Foreign Minister in 1995. Both Silajdžić and Šaćerbey had studied in the US and retained excellent contacts there, as, to a lesser extent, did Bosnian Prime Minister Ejup Ganić and other members of the Bosnian government, such as Minister for Humanitarian Aid Zlatko Lagumdžija. This group were known as 'the American Mafia' in the Bosnian leadership.

any prospect that the EC would be able to avert war through its negotiations, unrealistic though this was anyway.

Whereas there was an unconvincing hope that recognition might just serve to deter war in Bosnia as it had ended hostilities in Croatia,[60] there was also a crying need for further, stronger engagement. The odds were clearly stacked for the Serbian camp militarily, in the spring of 1992. It was probably understandable that the EC was trying desperately to do anything to avoid another bout of war which everyone had forewarned would be worse than that in Croatia had been — although nobody guessed at the cataclysm to come. Yet it seems (at least in retrospect) to have been a mistake not to allow, even to encourage, the Bosnian government to strengthen its position. In the absence of international measures, this would have meant lifting the arms embargo on Bosnia at the time of recognition.[61]

Having missed the opportunity for decisive action in January by granting immediate recognition, the EC, goaded greatly by the US initiative, proceeded to grant it in April when the more judicious action at that stage would have been to delay while either an agreement was reached (a negligible possibility) or the Bosnian authorities were given the opportunity and, from those willing to do so, the assistance required to resist Serbian might. When as much as possible of an armed capability was in place, ready to be delivered and used, then recognition accompanied by waiving of the arms embargo might have given the Bosnian government a deterrent capability. To have sought a little time to allow preparation in this would have been well judged. However, even if recognition could wait no longer, an international community not prepared to act itself should have revoked the arms embargo as it affected Bosnia. At the very least it was hard to imagine how doing this could really have made the situation there any worse.[62]

---

60 Cohen, *Broken Bonds*, p.238.
61 One of the interesting questions for those delving in official archives around 2021 could the extent to which this question was addressed and the arguments, if any, that were raised.
62 Of course, it has to be noted again that nobody, other than those planning it, could know quite how devastating the war would be.

The EC, the UN and the War in Bosnia

It would have been better, having failed to act decisively and recognise in January, to allow the talks more time. Recognition in April, in one sense too late, was also precipitate — not because it caused a war which negotiations could have prevented but because deferred recognition would have bought a little time both for the Bosnian government to prepare for the inevitable armed hostility and for the international community to prepare a co-ordinated follow-through to the act of recognition. One minimum step would have been to lift the UN embargo on arms transfers to Yugoslav territories in respect of the besieged Bosnian state — if in fact there was no international willingness to engage in a potentially large and awkward military engagement to enforce peace and order in Bosnia, as the adoption of measures under Chapter VII of the UN Charter, such as the imposition of an arms embargo might have implied.

Chapter VII of the UN Charter granted all member states the 'inherent right' to individual and collective self-defence.[63] This right was not inalienable, as many critics of international policy frequently argued with reference to Bosnia.[64] It was a right subject to the greater authority of the UN Security Council: nothing could impair the right to self-defence 'until the Security Council has taken an appropriate decision'.[65] This meant that once the Security Council acted under Chapter VII of the Charter, imposing mandatory enforcement measures on a country, defence and security matters with respect to that country became the business of the Security Council. Since the latter had passed Resolution 713, imposing arms sanctions on all territories of the former Yugoslav state, Bosnia's security should have been the responsibilty of the UN as it became independent. The implication of a state losing its inherent right to self-defence should be that the UN Security Council, on behalf of the international community, takes responsibility (in classic theory through collective security) for that state. The UN did not take responsibility for this situation.

63 Article 51.
64 Noel Malcolm, for example, wrote of the Bosnian government being denied the chance to 'exercise the normal right of any government to obtain arms for the defence of its people' (*op. cit.*, p.244).
65 Under Article 51.

As the situation in Bosnia evolved, the Security Council was to take further action under Chapter VII against Serbia and Montenegro (the 'Federal Republic of Yugoslavia') because of their role in the war in Bosnia, and against the Bosnian Serbs. In addition, a further Chapter VII measure, the creation and enforcement of an air-exclusion zone over Bosnia was applied generally. Eventually. there would be deployments of armed forces (see Chapters 5 and 6). However, these measures were always of limited value and reactive. In one sense they were the actions of a Security Council taking responsibility for the situation in Bosnia, in another they were the actions of a UN reluctant or unable to take as much responsibilty as the situation demanded. As a consequence, each measure taken was only partial and would require some further step to be taken in the future.

However, it was clear from before the start of the war in Bosnia that the UN (either its Member States, or the Secretariat) was unlikely to make the kind of major commitment which could have been as effective and relatively cost-free for the international community as rescinding the arms embargo. The one real step which was discussed was the deployment of a preventive peacekeeping force in Bosnia. Izetbegović had called for this already in the autumn of 1991. However, there was no interest then or in early 1992 when the Bosnian President reiterated his appeal, as UN Secretary-General Boutros Boutros-Ghali made apparent. This meant that the question would persist: might the horrors of Bosnia have been avoided if the UN had become involved there sooner?[66]

After the horrors began, the UN, alongside the EC, became further embroiled in the Bosnian bad dream. With the deployment of UNPROFOR in Croatia, the headquarters for the operation had been somewhat optimistically located in the Bosnian capital, Sarajevo. This was partly so that the mission would be based in neither Serbia nor Croatia. It was also in the hope that a UN presence might just help to avoid war. As it was, the UN came quickly under pressure to expand its role there as Bosnia became immersed in violence during April. In response to various pressures, including those from the EC, Boutros-Ghali sent Marrack Goulding, Deputy Under Secretary with responsibility for peacekeeping, to Bosnia in May to assess the conditions for mandating and creating a UN operation there. His

66 Wynaendts, *L'engrenage*, p.167 and 172.

conclusion was that conditions were not appropriate for sending a peacekeeping force to Bosnia. More pertinently, his report indicated the levels of violence and noted the siege of Sarajevo and, crucially, that the Serbs were attempting to create ethnically pure areas in line with negotiations carried out by Cutilheiro.[67]

In this period the Security Council was taking action against Serbia and Montenegro, identified as responsible for the war in Bosnia, demanding the withdrawal of the Yugoslav army from Bosnia in Resolution 743. The Serbian camp responded by declaring a new Yugoslav federation between Serbia and Montenegro (open to any other part of the former Yugosavia which wished to join later), and by dividing the army in two, with half being attached to the new state and half remaining in Bosnia to become the Army of the Serbian Republic (VRS). Almost all those staying with the VRS were Bosnian Serbs, reflecting the disproportionate numbers of *prečani* in the Yugoslav army.[68] This complicated matters but was not taken as representing withdrawal of the JNA — in any case, the new Yugoslavia continued to provide general military assistance to the VRS. Therefore, on 30 May the Security Council imposed economic sanctions on Serbia and Montenegro (Resolution 757).

In the mean time, the Bosnian cauldron had erupted furiously. In the week beginning 11 May, both the EC and the UN took decisions to withdraw their forces from Bosnia, thus accepting that there was nothing that either the ECMM or UNPROFOR could do in the circumstances.[69] (UNPROFOR, in fact, did not withdraw completely but retained a presence in the besieged city of Sarajevo.) An attempt was made to exclude the newly proclaimed 'third Yugoslavia' from the CSCE at the Helsinki follow-up meeting scheduled for July, but this

---

67 Secretary General's Report, UN Doc. S/23900, 12 May 1992.
68 A large part of the 60 per cent of JNA officers who were Serbs came from Croatia and Bosnia. These were those either who in their youth had been with the Partisans or who came from Partisan families. Serbs from those areas formed the core of the Partisan movement and the subsequent Yugoslav army in response to the 'ethnic cleansing' campaigns of Nazi-puppet Ustaša regime which ruled Croatia and Bosnia follwing the Axis invasion of the country in 1941. The violence of the Ustaša programme as Serbs were slaughtered or expelled drove local Serbs to join the communist-led Partisans because Tito's movement was providing active resistance to both the Ustaša and their Nazi backers. The Partisans were nonetheless an all-Yugoslav force, including Croats who opposed the Ustasha.
69 Cohen, *Broken Bonds*, p.241.

move was opposed by Russia. In the end Belgrade did not attend the summit at which Moscow agreed to exclusion, initially for six months although this was to continue until after the war in Bosnia had finished.[70] At the same time there was growing international indignation at the atrocious aggressive actions of the Serb irregulars and the JNA in Bosnia — the strategic programme of systematic murder and terror known as 'ethnic cleansing' was in full swing.[71] EC member states decided collectively to withdraw their ambassadors from Belgrade.

Serbia (or the new 'Yugoslavia') was being diplomatically isolated in the hope that this coercive pressure would force the Belgrade regime to stop the fighting. By now two things had been understood about the situation: first, that Serbia was overwhelmingly responsible for the gross violence carried out by the federal army,[72] and secondly, that the Serbian leadership did not respond to reason, but only to coercion. However, despite growing calls for stronger, even military, intervention to halt the carnage in Bosnia, the international community found itself hamstrung. The groundswell of support for some use of armed force did not appear to have sufficient political weight — although European and American leaders were clearly in the mood to employ stronger measures than before. Aside from the political-military uncertainties involved, armed intervention would probably require UN authorisation, which could not be guaranteed and which would also undermine UNPROFOR in Croatia, which it was still hoped would succeed.

The pressure to increase involvement as the situation deteriorated led to the UN Secretary-General recommending the formal expansion of UNPROFOR into Bosnia on 6 June, although the new mandate would restrict the role of the UN force to Sarajevo airport. Their task would

---

70 *The Times*, 11 May 1992.

71 The strategic purpose of 'ethnic cleansing' was to create areas from which potentially hostile, 'unreliable' populations which might mount political or armed resistance, were eradicated. For a harrowing, detailed study of 'ethnic cleansing' at work in one part of north-eastern Bosnia, see Hans Tretter, Stephan Müller, Roswitha Schwanke, Paul Angeli, Andreas Richter, *'Ethnische Säuberungen' in der nordostbosnischen Stadt Zvornik von April bis Juni 1992*, Ludwig Boltzman Institut für Menschenrechte, Vienna, 1994. (My thanks go to Peter Michalski for assistance where my understanding of German proved too limited for parts of this report.)

72 This was confirmed in the sanctions imposed on Serbia and Montengro by the UN Security Council, as well as by the accounts of many involved, such as former commander of UN Forces in Bosnia French General Philippe Morillon.

be to ensure the security and operation of the airport to enable flights carrying humanitarian assistance into the city which was by then entering its third month under siege. However, it was not until late on 29 June that the Serbian forces holding the airport relinquished control to the UN. This came in the wake of a surprise visit to the Bosnian capital by the French President François Mitterrand a day earlier. In the three weeks between Boutros-Ghali's announcement and the UN flags being raised over the tarmac at Sarajevo, elements in the international community, led by France, had begun to threaten the Serbs with a use of force. At the same time there had been arguments within the international community about Bosnia — whether force should be used, and how much force was enough force?

Mitterrand's flying visit to Sarajevo took virtually everyone by surprise. It was a strike in favour of action amid doubts and caution over what could be achieved. Mitterrand's initiative was aimed at both fellow leaders in the international community who were tending to wring their hands, counselling caution and displaying inhibition. This meant his colleagues in the EC who had shown themselves to be wary and believe that it was too early and dangerous to open the Bosnian capital's airport — this occurred only at the Lisbon Summit of the European Council on 27-28 June, immediately before Mitterrand's Sarajevo sortie.

It was also directed at the UN Secretariat, in particular the Secretary-General. The broad opinion was that it was too difficult at that stage to get the airport opened in order to create a humanitarian air bridge. This was the dominant view both in the UN and outside it. However, whereas the UN Officer Commanding in Sarajevo, the Canadian Lieutenant-General Lewis MacKenzie (before the Sarajevo command was created, Chief of Staff at UNPROFOR headquarters) expressed military caution,[73] there was a growing feeling that the Secretary-General was simply opposed outright to UN involvement in Bosnia, which he regarded as a 'rich man's war'.

Mitterrand's visit was significant in a number of ways. As an act it demonstrated to the more cautious and faint-hearted that things could be made to happen with a little boldness. A corollary lesson from this was, as General Philippe Morillon later pointed out, that politicians

---

73 Général Philippe Morillon, *Croire et Oser. Chronique de Sarajevo*, Grasset, Paris, 1993, p.94.

should be prepared to lead and be bold enough on occasion to ignore the cautious advice of officials.[74] Of course Mitterrand's initiative on this occasion was the exception rather than the rule in the course of the international approach to the problems of the former Yugoslavia. In addition, because things worked for Mitterrand that time, there would be no guarantee that they would in another situation.

Mitterrand's initiative was decisive in getting the airport at Sarajevo open because by going there he was able to demonstrate commitment to the Bosnian authorities, which in turn agreed not to make use of the airport — even for crossing it to get from one area to another — if the Serbs vacated it. The Bosnian agreement was decisive in persuading the Serbs that there would be no serious hardship in giving up the airport. On the negative side for the Serbs, their siege of Sarajevo began to be broken almost immediately as the French military landed the first humanitarian aid flight into Bosnia on 29 June, even before the Serbs had fully handed over to the UN. With all land routes into Sarajevo blocked by the VRS, the aerial lifeline was important for the embattled city.

The French President was also successful in shaking the UN into a fuller engagement in Bosnia, which might have been expected to complement the diplomatic initiatives of the EC. However, there were unfavourable by-products from Mitterrand's achievement. First, it placed a burden on the UN's limited resources in Bosnia. General MacKenzie had only four small battalions allocated (from France, Canada, Ukraine and Egypt — the French presence had been constant, even following the UN pull-out in May). These were not fully in place, but their task was to secure the runways, carry out engineering work and secure routes into the town. Although France, following the Presidential initiative, promptly supplied a parachute battalion and sappers, the strain on UNPROFOR in Sector Sarajevo was great.

One crucial by-product of French political success was the rapid deterioration in relations between MacKenzie and the Bosnian political

74 Morillon was deputy commander of UNPROFOR at the time of Mitterrand's jaunt to Sarajevo; he was later appointed as commanding officer in Bosnia when a separate UNPROFOR command was created there in September 1992; on leaving Bosnia Command in 1993, he returned to Paris to take up a post in the French Defence Minister's private office. On the credit due to his President for taking the initiative, see Morillon, *Croire et Oser*, p.94.

and military leadership. To do his job of securing routes into the town, MacKenzie's had to negotiate local ceasefires. However, it was the Bosnian army which was sometimes responsible for breaking those ceasefires — in the hope of provoking a US intervention which the 'American club' in the Bosnian leadership was sure would come. It was evident that, with the world's attention focused on the Bosnian capital, an amelioration of its circumstances would reduce the pressure for such an intervention: the siege of Sarajevo was perhaps more important to the Bosnian government than it was to the Serbs because of its potential to focus and mobilise support.

MacKenzie was angry that the Bosnian army was behaving this way and that his job was being made harder by the side his mission was (implicitly, at least) most likely to help. The Sector Sarajevo commander — somewhat understandably, if undiplomatically and counter-productively — openly criticised the Bosnian army for impeding his efforts to carry out that mission. As a result his relationship with the Bosnian authorities was irrevocably soured. Quickly he came to be regarded as a pro-Serbian 'Chetnik' by the press and population in Sarajevo, as well as by others outside Bosnia.[75] MacKenzie, aware of the hostility to him as an individual and the harm it was doing to the UN operation, as well as the danger in which it placed the troops under his command, resigned from his position at the end of July.

MacKenzie's predicament was one facet of unease in the UN Secretariat at involvement in Bosnia. Mitterrand's *coup* had placed further strain on the Secretary-General's adverse relationship with the

---

75 See, for example, the Pulitzer Prize-winning work of Roy Gutman, *Witness to Genocide*, Element, Shaftesbury (Dorset), 1993, pp.168-73. After retiring from the Canadian Army in 1993, MacKenzie confirmed this opinion by making a series of public appearances in the US, speaking for a Serbian lobby group. All of this, quite reasonably, emphasised the impression of apparent favour for the Serbs. MacKenzie's inner workings are unknowable, of course, but his behaviour could also be understood as frustration and (maybe paternalistic) incomprehension that there were people who thought that there was something better than the help he was trying to provide. The Canadian General, by his own account (and confirmed by Carrington), wanted a 14,000-strong military force in Sarajevo, prior to the conflict to deter the Serbs (*Soldier of Peace*). This is borne out by Morillon's judgement (*Croire et Oser*, p.96) and by the fact that MacKenzie, on his return to Canada, appeared to be largely responsible for ensuring that his country was among the first to submit comprehensive evidence on war crimes in Bosnia to the War Crimes Tribunal established by the UN.

Security Council and the EC: Mitterrand was head of a state which was prominent as both a Permanent Member of the former and a key member of the latter. Given Boutros-Ghali's reluctance to deal with Bosnia, Mitterrand's exploit not only showed that something could be done, but also meant the UN was going to have to do some of it. Increasingly Boutros-Ghali argued that so much more could be achieved if the resources being devoted to the UN operation in former Yugoslavia, especially anything to do with Bosnia, would be reallocated to other parts of the globe. Bosnia was a European matter, in the view of the Secretary-General, and it was only because it was in Europe that it was receiving so much attention when there were numerous cases which he regarded as similar, some of which were arguably worse, such as Somalia. Moreover, underscoring his hostility, he warned that increased commitment in Bosnia could only lead to a 'kind of Vietnam for the United Nations'.[76]

The friction between the UN Secretary-General and both his political masters on the Security Council and the EC came to its nadir in early July. Carrington, Cutilheiro and company had been continuing to pursue the diplomatic chimera of settlement, or even ceasefire, in Bosnia. On 17 July the EC team, at a meeting of the sub-conference on Bosnia in London, gained agreement on a ceasefire around Sarajevo in which all Serbian heavy weaponry would be placed under UN control. Boutros-Ghali, rather than welcoming this progress, took umbrage: what right, he intoned piously, did the EC have to make agreements on behalf of the UN without speaking to the UN first?

This was ostensibly a reasonable comment, even if it did seem to place institutional pride and jealously ahead of progress on peace in Bosnia. However, in reality the EC negotiators had been trying keenly to discuss the matter with Boutros-Ghali by telephone. Although he was understood to be there, he did not take Carrington's calls. It is easy to conclude that Boutros-Ghali was sulking, feeling that if demands continued to be made on the UN, then this would only be if the UN were involved from the outset in making arrangements for engagement. A ceasefire in a country where he felt the UN had little place, certainly as a surrogate for the EC when the latter could not deal with a problem

---

76 Boutros Boutros-Ghali, quoted by Cohen, *Broken Bonds*, p.242.

itself, was of far less importance than the question of the UN's status.[77] The EC, its member states and the Permanent Members of the Security Council were exasperated with the UN Secretary-General, reacting against his petulance, as well as betraying displeasure that a potentially pivotal opportunity to obtain a decisive concession from the Serbs had been lost. So too had momentum and any sense of cohesion in the ever more despairing efforts of various elements in the international community to bring an end to the war in Bosnia.

The destructive complex of Yugoslav problems, notably Serbian cunning and contempt, left all who touched it confused and confounded. There had been some achievements for international diplomacy, with what had proved to be limited means, in circumstances which became more difficult as time passed by, but even recognition of these limited achievements could not remove the indelible stain of failure — a defeat compounded by disarray. The EC had begun with bright hopes, but ended its solo phase struggling to maintain a common policy and turning to the UN to supplement its inadequacy as a peacekeeper. Although the UN-Secretary General proved reluctant to see the global organisation dealing with the Yugoslav War of Dissolution, he did not seem averse to provoking disputes to promote his own position. This resulted in some tension between the UN, in the form of the Secretary-General and the EC. Nonetheless, co-operation between the EC and the UN had begun promisingly, with both seeing value in the division of labour between them, the EC leading the diplomatic quest and the UN bringing its peacemaking experience to bear.

---

77 Explaining why the UN could not take on responsibility for implementing the agreement made by Carrington, on grounds of both practicality and principle, Boutros Boutros-Ghali said that, according to the UN Charter, the UN could make use of regional organisations to help in its work, but that there was no suggestion in the Charter that the opposite could apply (Secretary General's Report, UN Doc. S/24333, 21 July 1992).

5

THE MILITARY OPERATIONS: PEACEKEEPING IN CROATIA, BOSNIA AND MACEDONIA

As the international community strove to solve the Yugoslav War of Dissolution through high-level diplomacy, creating new relationships and bodies in the process, there was also effort and innovation on the ground. New instruments of peacekeeping were being forged in the Yugoslav crucible. UN peacekeeping generally was crossing new frontiers and,[1] in the Yugoslav region, in particular, a number of precedents were being set with regard to UN activity. The forces committed in Yugoslavia constituted the first UN peacekeeping mission in continental Europe. By the summer of 1994, it had become the largest ever UN peacekeeping operation, with over 36,000 troops deployed under three commands in Croatia, Bosnia and Macedonia. This was short of the total of 44,870 authorised by the UN Security Council but seemingly set to increase if peace could be established in Bosnia.[2] Moreover, in Macedonia armed US troops had been placed under UN command for the first time in the UN's first ever preventive deployment.

As international involvement in the Yugoslav War grew and the diplomats struggled to achieve a settlement, the role of the troops on the ground became increasingly important. This was because they carried the burden of containing the conflict, of limiting its scope — as indicated by UK Foreign Secretary Douglas Hurd who commented that

---

1 See Mats Berdal, *Whither UN Peacekeeping?*, Adelphi Paper No.281, Brassey's for the International Institute for International Relations, London, 1993.
2 UNPROFOR, 'Facts Sheet', UNPROFOR Headquarters, Zagreb, 29 June 1994.

peacekeeping was a 'growth industry' as international organisations would increasingly have to look at the possibility of intervening in countries to prevent unacceptable crises developing.[3] This underscored the critical point that the United Nations Protection Force (UNPROFOR, the designation was changed in the spring of 1995 to United Nations Peace Forces, UNPF, with the label UNPROFOR reserved for the Bosnia operation) had been deployed in a dynamic situation to serve the interests of the international community as a whole, and of the west European countries in particular, in response to what was an active security policy question. This was not a UN peacekeeping force being deployed in the traditional static, conflict termination role of classic UN peacekeeping.[4] UNPROFOR's role was as an active instrument of security policy and diplomacy.

It was the direct link to a high-profile and active peace-making process which gave UNPROFOR not only its size but also its significance. The existence of UNPROFOR was related to questions of European security policy, especially with regard to Bosnia Command

---

3 Douglas Hurd, quoted in *The Guardian*, 14 October 1992.
4 The degree to which the traditional principles of peacekeeping were evolving was a subject of debate. Although it is not the purpose of the present volume to deal with anything more than the substantive aspects of UN military involvement in the former Yugoslavia, the conceptual issues should perhaps be noted. In traditional UN peacekeeping, the strategic initiative lies with the hostile parties to a conflict which have decided to ask a third party, the UN, to supervise a ceasefire. This type of operation is characterised by three features: truce supervision by unarmed or lightly armed personnel, impartiaty and consent. This is a strategically static situation. By contrast, many UN operations in the 1990s took place in strategically dynamic situations: hostilities were not terminated, but continuing and the international force was charged with tasks of conflict mitigation, deterrence and protection and generally assisting in creating the conditions for settlement. As a result, the forces had to be far larger and better armed, could not count on consent and had authorisation for the limited use of force, which meant that perceptions of impartiality were not always easily maintained. For discussion of changes in international peacekeeping, see the following: John MacKinlay and Jarat Chopra, '2nd Generation Multinational Operations', *The Washington Quarterly*, Vol.15 No.3, 1992; MacKinlay, 'Improving Multifunctional Forces', Charles Dobbie, 'A Concept for Post-Cold War Peacekeeping' and Adam Roberts, 'The Crisis in UN Peacekeeping', all in *Survival*, Vol.36 No.3, Autumn 1994; Mats Berdal, *Whither UN Peacekeeping?*, Adelphi Paper No.281, Brassey's for the International Institute for Strategic Studies, Lodon, 1993; Espen B. Eide ed., *Peacekeeping in Europe*, Peacekeeping and Multinational Operations No.5, The Norwegian Instiute of International Affairs, Oslo, 1995; James Gow and Christopher Dandeker, 'Peace-support operations: the problem of legitimation, *The World Today*, Vol.51 Nos.8-9, August-September 1995.

(BH Command): UN involvement, as was affirmed in earlier chapters, was directly linked to EC initiatives. UNPROFOR was not only not a traditional UN peacekeeping operation, even in Croatia, where its origins were closer to traditional peacekeeping than in the two other commands. It was also, evidently, not a full peace enforcement operation either, but something in between: more than pure peacekeeping, but far less than peace enforcement. It contained enforcement components but relied broadly on a consensual approach as far as possible.

UNPROFOR as a type of operation was sponsored primarily by the UN Security Council, with the objectives of resisting undesirable and unacceptable trends (without resorting to war), of maintaining international norms as far as possible, and of pursuing the creation of conditions for a settlement to the conflict through the interaction of high-level diplomacy and the initiative of the force on the ground. Therefore, while the UN's major involvements in Cambodia, Angola and Somalia during the early 1990s were also shaping the future of UN activity in the sphere of 'wider peacekeeping',[5] it was the expanding size and scope of the force in Yugoslavia which did most to shape the international agenda.

As the international handling of the crisis evolved, the role of leading UN military personnel on the ground grew. In spite of the initial insistence by the UN Secretariat on a civilian commander and, following the departure of the original commander General Satish Nambiar, the realisation of this aim,[6] the initiative increasingly appeared to be with those on the ground, who were in a position to work on developing local ceasefires and able to seize opportunities to make situations better where possible. If events on the ground gave real definition to high diplomacy, then the work of those supposedly only

---

5 This was the term adopted by UK Land Forces for operations beyond traditional peacekeeping, in support of UN attempts to make, or maintain, peace. This type of operation was also known as '2nd Generation Peacekeeping' — see John MacKinlay and Jarrat Chopra, '2nd Generation Multinational Operations', *Washington Quarterly*, Vol.15, No.3, 1992.

6 The UN Envoy to ICFY, Thorvald Stoltenberg, became the civilian head of UNPROFOR in May 1993, as the UN Secretary-General's Special Representative. While retaining the ICFY role, he passed on the Special Representative's role to Yasushi Akashi, a Japanese diplomat with considerable UN experience, who became overall chief of UNPROFOR at the end of 1993.

responsible for implementing agreements and decisions of their international political masters was what might actually create the conditions for a settlement. In a sense, amid the haze of Security Council Resolutions, UNPROFOR's *de facto* mandate was to create and maintain stalemate on the ground to allow international diplomacy to work. UNPROFOR's record was mixed: whereas it could claim success in Macedonia, and to a lesser extent in Croatia, its successes in Bosnia, such as they may have been, were fraught with pressure and paradox — as is seen more fully in Chapter 6 where the focus will be on the issue of using force.

Peacekeeping in Croatia

UNPROFOR came into being on 21 February 1992 for an initial period of twelve months (six months longer than the customary initial period for UN peacekeeping forces), having been created to underpin the ceasefire between Serbian and Croatian forces in Croatia. Although its primary aim was to strengthen the 2 January ceasefire agreement negotiated by the UN Secretary-General's Special Envoy, Cyrus Vance (the Vance Plan), it also had the secondary aim of providing a symbolic presence in neighbouring Bosnia and Hercegovina which it was hoped would be sufficient to prevent the outbreak of armed hostility there.

The 15,000-strong force, with contributions initially from twenty-six countries, deployed in four sectors in Croatia — North, South, East and West with headquarters in the capital, Zagreb. The bulk of the force comprised military personnel, although there were also small police and civilian components, all under the command of the United Nations. UNPROFOR's mission was to provide United Nations Protected Areas (UNPAs), defined as areas in which Serbs constituted the majority or a substantial minority of the population, and in which 'inter-communal tensions' had 'led to armed conflict in the recent past'.[7]

The original UNPROFOR mandate was set out in four reports by the UN Secretary-General.[8] It was consistently emphasised that all arrangements would be interim ones, pending successful negotiation of a political settlement. Members of UNPROFOR were placed under the

7 UN Doc. S/23280, 11 December 1991.
8 Annex III, UN Doc. S/23280, 11 December 1991; UN Doc. S/23592, 15 February 1992; UN Doc. S/23777, 2 April 1992; and UN Doc. S/23844, 24 April 1992.

command of the Secretary-General and, theoretically, according to UN wishes, not permitted to receive operational orders from the national authorities. They were to remain impartial and 'normally' to use only minimum force when required in self-defence.

There was to be full demilitarisation of the UNPAs, envisaged in the Vance Plan, with full withdrawal of Yugoslav army forces from Croatia and local irregular units and other military personnel in UNPAs being disbanded and demobilised. Demobilisation meant ceasing to wear any uniform or carry any weapons. The weapons were to be handed over to the UN force for safekeeping.[9] After discussions with the parties, it was decided that the most practicable way to do this was for the arms to be placed 'in secure storage under a two-lock system'. One lock would be controlled by UN forces and the other by the president of the council of the *opština* concerned.[10]

In addition, UNPROFOR was to identify existing arrangements for local administration and confirm that the composition of these arrangements (including police forces) reflected the 'national composition of the population which lived in the area concerned before the recent hostilities'. Where this was not the case, UN forces were to arrange the necessary changes, in conjunction with existing local authorities. Beyond these functions UN forces were to monitor the work of local police forces and use their good offices to ensure that 'any changes to the *status quo* as regards other aspects of local administration are consistent with the spirit of the plan and pose no threat to public order'.[11]

The role of UN forces was to ensure that the areas remained demilitarised, to protect the indigenous population from 'fear of armed attack', and to help return displaced persons to their homes.[12] The UN High Commissioner for Refugees was asked to assume responsibility for designing and implementing a practicable scheme for achieving this. Confirmed violations would be taken up with the offending party and if necessary be reported by the Secretary-General to the Security Council. The plan clearly indicated that under no circumstances would serious violations be tolerated: 'If serious tension were to develop

---

9 Annex III, UN Doc. S/23280, 11 December 1991.
10 '*Opština*' refers to a local administrative district.
11 UN Doc. S/23592, 15 February 1992.
12 UN Doc. S/23280, 11 December 1991.

between nationalities in a UNPA, the United Nations Force would interpose itself between the two sides in order to prevent hostilities.'[13]

Fulfilment of the mandate proved problematic in several ways. Although the peacekeeping force was deployed and thus able to give a reasonable degree of interim security to the ceasefire, it was not able fully and altogether successfully to ensure that the provisions of the mandate were carried through in practice. As a result, there was scope for fighting to begin again in Croatia.

In general, demilitarisation was not accomplished. Although much weaponry was placed in store under the dual key system, some was not. Certain matériel, including armour, was painted blue and 'transferred' to the local police force. Indeed many members of the JNA, as well as the irregulars who were supposed to be disbanded, were transferred to these police forces. As this process occurred, the withdrawal of the JNA also proved to be an obstacle, although the eventual supplanting of the army by the new military-style police force meant that local radicals were able to accept the army's formal withdrawal. However, full demilitarisation was not forthcoming — and would not be, according to the Serbian leaders, until tension was reduced.

Tension was linked to the non-implementation of other features of the UNPROFOR mandate, particularly over displaced persons — the 275,000 Croats and others who had lived in the UNPAs before the war. The UNHCR insisted that conditions would not be appropriate for the return of populations until demilitarisation had been completed. In the mean time, the practice of expelling populations known as 'ethnic cleansing' continued with UNPROFOR powerless to stop it. []Although UNPROFOR could report cases of intimidation and ethnic cleansing to the local authorities, the responsibility for dealing with them rested with those same authorities, who could often be presumed to condone happening. These local administrations, formed by representatives of the Serbian political-military machine which had undertaken the war in Croatia, were generally unsympathetic (although former JNA officers were sometimes reported to take up matters in a serious way, unlike their irregular and civilian colleagues[14]). That the local police force was composed of Serbs ran against the provision in the Vance Plan to ensure that the police force and other parts of the local administration

---

13 *Ibid.*
14 This was reported by EC Monitors in interviews with the author.

should reflect the region's ethnic composition before the war — for this to be possible the return of non-Serb populations, among other things, as necessary. There was thus a somewhat absurd circle: return of populations required demilitarisation, demilitarisation required reduced tension, reduced tension required an end to attacks on non-Serbs, action to stop these required de-Serbianisation of the local authorities and police force — which required the return of non-Serb populations. Yet the UN representatives had no mandate to enforce the terms of the agreement to their deployment.

The failure to accomplish these aspects of the truce agreement fuelled growing frustration in Croatia and added to the fear that, whatever the formal agreements being made in The Hague, Brussels, London and Geneva, events were developing in a way which would in reality mean that the 'occupied territories' would be lost to Zagreb for ever. In Croatia UNPROFOR, having initially been welcomed by popular opinion had passed through a phase in which its misunderstood role was explained (and quite probably still not understood or believed), and within months of deployment had become an object of hostility.[15]

Finally, Croatia made attempts peacefully to return populations in spite of warnings from the UNHCR not to do so. UNPROFOR was mobilised to prevent this happening, an action that added to Croatian perceptions of UNPROFOR as something not only ineffectually confirming territorial losses through default, but actually acting against Croatia's interest. This kindled questioning both at popular and elite levels about UNPROFOR's presence.

The Croats' reaction to this situation was to make their own contributions to continuing tension, for example with their regular night-time hit and run attacks carried out by small units in the UNPAs. Sweeps by their forces in the 'Pink Zones' containing significant Serb communities and bordering on UNPAs, but not part of them, which were supposed also to be demilitarised, had the same effect. This resulted in protests to the Zagreb government by the UN and threats that sanctions could be imposed against Croatia if it did not stop.

---

15 See Vlatko Cvrtila, 'The Peace Operation and UNPROFOR — Croatian Media Reactions and Public Opinion', in Marjan Malešić ed., *The Role of Mass Media in the Serbian-Croatian Conflict*, Psykologiskt Försvar Rapport Nr.164, Streylsen för Psykologiskt Försvar, Stockholm, 1993.

Therefore, talk spread in Croatia about a military move to end Serb control. The Croatian army, apart from action in the 'Pink Zones', also quickly moved into parts of the Prevlaka Peninsula[16] after the ECMM, since EC and UN Special Envoys Lord Owen and Cyrus Vance, had negotiated the withdrawal of the Yugoslav People's Army and demilitarisation. While the 300-strong ECMM no doubt helped to limit the scope of the conflict in some parts of Croatia, as well as ensuring some local ceasefire agreements which resulted in implementation, and successfully accomplished their mission in Slovenia, perhaps its most significant achievement was to negotiate the withdrawal of the JNA from the Prevlaka Peninsula in September 1992.

When the JNA withdrew from the rest of Croatia, its units remained in Prevlaka. Eventually, in September 1992, the ECMM at the local level, and the representatives of the ICFY at the higher level, negotiated an agreement on Yugoslav military withdrawal from and subsequent de-militarisation of Prevlaka, at which the army was most unhappy. However, the Army of Yugoslavia (*Vojska Jugoslavije* — VJ) reluctantly withdrew, although it continued to claim ownership of Prevlaka. There remained the possibility, therefore, that the VJ might at some stage move to re-take the Peninsula.

The Croatian incursion into the area and its strategic importance at the entrance to the Bay of Kotor meant that, in spite of the ECMM's presence and efforts, Prevlaka would remain a vital issue. Croatia could claim that its move there was necessary in order to respond to Serbian bombardments of southern Croatia from Trebinje in eastern Hercegovina

---

16 The Prevlaka Peninsula is at the southern tip of the Republic of Croatia, on the north coast of the Bay of Kotor (Boka Kotorska). This small strip of land, 2,600 metres long by 150 metres wide — total area 99.9 hectares — dominates the entrance to the Bay of Kotor (*Vojska*, 1 October 1992). It was a key factor in the war in southern Croatia. Although part of the Republic of Croatia, the peninsula was owned by the Yugoslav People's Army (JNA). The operations in southern Dalmatia, the narrow hinterland to Dubrovnik known as Konavli, begun at the end of September were the only ones in Croatia carried out by the JNA alone — those in eastern Slavonia also involved irregular units organised in Serbia, those in central Croatia and Krajina involved local Serb populations. The region was strategically vital to the Yugoslav military. Without control of the southern tip of this region, the Prevlaka Peninsula itself, use of the naval base a Kotor in Montenegro would be difficult, given that entry to the bay would be controlled on the northern side by Croatia. The Bay of Kotor would be the only port left to the Yugoslav military if the whole of Croatia were to become independent and access to it would not be secure. Control of the northern side of the Bay was judged to be vital.

(perhaps using weaponry 'withdrawn' by the Yugoslav army). However, the action was nonetheless a clear violation of the agreement — as the President of the Federal Republic of Yugoslavia, Dobrica Ćosić, was keen to remind the UN Secretary-General and the two Special Envoys, complicating their dealings with the Yugoslav leadership.

In January 1993, the Croatian army carried out operations to secure the area of the Maslenica bridge in order to re-open it and restore north-south communications in Croatia, as well as the Zemunik airport near Zadar and, further south, the Peruča dam close to the border with Bosnia-Hercegovina. These operations achieved their aims. However, there were two adverse consequences. First, the Armed Forces of the Republic of Serbian Krajina (OS RSK) seized heavy weapons from the depots jointly controlled by OS RSK and UNPROFOR under the terms of the January 1992 ceasefire, and continued to use them daily for several months to fire on Croatian targets. Secondly, the military operations accentuated tensions with the UN. The operations were in breach of the ceasefire agreement, with Croatian forces entering supposedly demilitarised areas, albeit ones assigned to Zagreb authority and in which Serb forces had been slow to leave. The Security Council threatened to impose sanctions against Croatia, adding to uncertainty over the renewal of the UNPROFOR mandate at the end of its first year. The mandate was renewed for three months and then in July 1993 for a further three months, although this extension provided for a review after one month as a concession to Croatian wishes that the mandate should be renewed for one month only. This kind of uncertainty would characterise the UN's presence in Croatia throughout the war, although the mandate was always renewed.

As the UNPROFOR mandate approached renewal in September 1993, the Croatian army carried out another limited operation, *'Divoselo'*, similar to 'Operation Maslenica' in January. This time, the Croats took three villages in the northern part of Krajina, doing some 'cleansing' in the process.[17] Following the principle successfully established by the Serbs in Croatia and Bosnia, the Croatian army consolidated its success by withdrawing and allowing UNPROFOR to take over control of the area — thereby putting further strains on the peacekeepers, as well as freeing the troops engaged in the operation to prepare for another venture of the same kind. However, the Krajina Serbs responded with

---

17 *Večernji List*, 11 September 1993; *Nedjeljni Vjesnik*, 12 September 1993.

ferocity, launching rocket attacks on the outskirts of Zagreb, causing a sense of shock there.[18] This confirmed the limits of Croatian military potential at that stage and therefore the value of the UN operation to the Croatian authorities.

UNPROFOR's general unpopularity meant that the Croatian leadership would rely increasingly on channelling public dissatisfaction through civil protest against the UN force. In the summer of 1994 Croatian civilians began to blockade UNPROFOR posts - thus Zagreb had an alternative to armed action to appease its people and goad the UN. This only served to confirm that in more than one sense the Croatian government needed UNPROFOR: to save it from solving its problems with the Serbs in Krajina and to use as a scapegoat for those problems.

It remained quite likely, however, that Croatia would intermittently launch limited military operations to appease popular opinion, put pressure on the UN, and gradually to take control of territory in the UNPAs. In the spring of 1995, Croatia effectively removed Sector West from the map, as the Serbian forces within the sector were defeated. At the same time, a large part of the small Serb community remaining in the area went to Serb-held northern Bosnia as refugees. The UN force renamed UNCRO (the UN Conflict Resolution Operation in Croatia) in March was left standing as the Croatian army carried out a limited operation. Similar limited operations were to follow in August as authorities sought to control the whole of the country. They were also to be expected given that, although the UN force had stabilised the 1992 ceasefire in Croatia, it had never been able to play a role in implementing the Vance Plan, which went unfulfilled; it had also been unable to help Serb civilians in face of Croatia's steps to assert its authority. The flight of those Serbs into Bosnia was one small sign of the way in which the situations in Croatia and Bosnia were linked by the Serbian question — and by the UN presence.

Peace Support in Bosnia

The initial UNPROFOR mandate was restricted to Croatia, but the mission's headquarters were placed in the Bosnian capital, Sarajevo. Even when the Serbian assault on the city forced the UN to remove the headquarters to Croatia, an UNPROFOR presence was maintained in

18 *Slovenske Novice*, 14 September 1993; *Globus*, 17 September 1993.

Sarajevo with the mission's Chief of Staff, Canadian Brigadier (later Major-General) Lewis MacKenzie, attempting to act as a mediator.[19] However, as events unfolded in Bosnia, the UN role grew.

From November 1991 onwards, with the first official statement at the 9 December Plenary of the EC Conference in The Hague, there had been increasing and intensifying calls from the the Bosnian President Alija Izetbegović for the deployment of a preventive peacekeeping force to avert the outbreak of violence in his republic.[20] Similar calls for preventive deployment were made by military and civilian personnel engaged in the international effort, such as Lord Carrington. It is possible to imagine that if the UN had been prepared to take this unprecedented step, the Bosnian catastrophe might have been avoided (although there is much to suggest that this would not have happened).[21]

Instead, UNPROFOR's role in Bosnia began more three months into the conflict. Following the opening of Sarajevo airport in the wake of French President François Mitterrand's surprise visit at the end of June 1992 (see Chapter 4), an airlift to relieve humanitarian suffering in Sarajevo had begun. The flights, however, proved to be intermittent and in any case not sufficient to meet the humanitarian needs of the Bosnian capital. In addition, whereas airlifts could offer something to Sarajevo, they were not available in other parts of the country.[22] Representatives

---

19 MacKenzie was to describe the decision to base UNPROFOR in Sarajevo as a militarily 'dumb' decision. (*A Soldier's Peace — with Major General (Ret.) Lewis MacKenzie*, Screenlife Inc., 1994, BBC2 TV, 7 January 1995.)

20 Henry Wynaendts, *L'engrenage. Chroniques yougoslaves, juillet 1991-août 1992*, Denoël, Paris, 1993, pp.149 and 154.

21 This possibility was held out by Wynaendts, *L'engrenage*, p.172, who cited the opinion of Carrington and Izetbegović; this was reiterated by Carrington and General MacKenzie in *A Soldier's Peace*. There can be no doubt that a strong preventive deployment would have forced the Serbs and the JNA to reassess the project they had been preparing for several months and might possibly have shocked them into abandoning it. An early deployment would certainly, at a minimum, have placed greater obstacles in the way of 'ethnic cleansing'.

22 Many critics of UNPROFOR could not understand why Tuzla airport in north-eastern Bosnia was not used for airlifts into that region, which otherwise presented problems for those trying to approach by land as it could only be reached with great difficulty by road. Although UNPROFOR sought the opportunity to open the airport, this was a challenging prospect: the airport was generally vulnerable to Serbian artillery assault and the Serbs would only agree to the opening of the airport if the local Bosnian Army Command agreed, as with Sarajevo, not to exploit UN use of the airport; the Tuzla Corps command

of the UN High Commissioner for Refugees had made several efforts to get convoys of food and medicine to besieged communities in various parts of Bosnia, but had run into difficulties, even when the assistance of troops drawn (beyond their mandate) from the force of 1,500 based in Sarajevo was available. It was there difficulties which became the focus of international efforts.

Those framing policy felt unable to undertake more decisive military action both for practical reasons and because of the limits imposed by both the UN Charter and the conventions of international relations.[23] But, they wished to do something which would both send signals to Belgrade and the Bosnian Serbs, and make a positive contribution to the welfare of those suffering around the country. The answer seemed to lie in some form of 'humanitarian intervention' supported by armed force.[24] These circumstances led to the creation of a second element of UNPROFOR to escort humanitarian aid missions in Bosnia and Hercegovina. The original mandate for UNPROFOR in Bosnia, while designed to demonstrate international interest, to temper the war and to assist in creating the conditions for a settlement, was primarily humanitarian. This is because the international community turned to the UNHCR, which it designated as 'lead agency' to define the international mission in Bosnia.[25] That mission reflected a policy of 'comprehensive response', backed by major western governments.[26] The aim of this

was not prepared to make such an agreement and UNPROFOR was not prepared to enforce the opening of the airport.

23 On these limitations and the ways in which various crises in the early 1990s were leading to 'inventions' and 'innovations', which while apparently meagre in terms of the problems they sought to address, were radical departures which could only be made after serious consideration, see Paul Fifoot, 'Functions and powers and inventions: UN action in respect of human rights and humanitarian intervention' in Nigel Rodley, ed., *To Loose the Bands of Wickedness: International Intervention in Defence of Human Rights*, Brassey's in association with the David Davies Memorial Institute, London, 1992, pp.133-64.

24 On the issue of humanitarian intervention, see generally Rodley, ed., *To Loose the Bands*.

25 I am grateful to Warren Zimmermann for sharpening my focus clearly on the centrality of the UNHCR and the way in which the governments providing troops to UNPROFOR, in the absence of any clear and strong alternative course of action, left the UNHCR to determine international policy.

26 On the background to thinking on the policy of 'comprehensive response' to refugee problems, see Sarah Chapman, *Beyond Borders: West European Migration Policy Towards the 21st Century*, RIIA and Wyndham Place Trust, 1993, p.74ff.

policy was to assist as many people as possible to remain where they were and to avoid becoming refugees. Thus, although they might be dependent on international assistance, they would stay in their homes.

This approach served two main purposes. First, it relieved the international community of the burden of accommodating refugees elsewhere and accepting them as asylum seekers. Secondly, it confirmed the local UNHCR and broad international desire to avoid complicity in 'ethnic cleansing' and to assist in resisting that pernicious process. The aim was to give humanitarian aid to people in isolated communities, particularly those which the Bosnian Serbs had under siege, thus enabling those communities to hold out against the forcible pressure on them to leave. The initial mission given to UNPROFOR in Bosnia was to give military assistance to the UNHCR, facilitating the passage of convoys through difficult conflict zones and into towns under siege.

Although the new force component bore the same name as the operation in Croatia and was considered an extension of the peacekeeping mission there, its character would be quite different. Rather than peacekeeping, the role in Bosnia would be one of 'peace support' — that is a UN multilateral military operation in support of international peacemaking efforts. The mission in Bosnia would be to deliver aid, thereby implicitly sustaining populations under siege and putting a brake on 'ethnic cleansing'. This was never going to be an easy task and would require a better armed force than were usually deployed in the UN operations.

On 13 August 1992 the UN Security Council (Resolution 770) empowered states, acting nationally or through regional arrangements, to use any measures necessary to deliver humanitarian relief, including military measures, although it was explained that this was not a mandatory prescription for the use of force.[27] Discussion of the use of force made UN Secretary-General Boutros Boutros-Ghali nervous. He expressed fears in a letter to the Security Council that the use-of-force resolution could endanger UN peacekeepers already operating in Bosnia — and even those in Croatia — and hinted that they might be withdrawn by demanding 'adequate' advance warning of military intervention so that the threat to UN peacekeepers could be minimised. Those discussing the sending of armed escorts for the food and

---

27 Sir David Hannay, UK Ambassador to the UN, quoted in *The Daily Telegraph*, 14 August 1992.

medicine convoys allayed some of his fears, however, by moving cautiously. Those fears were also allayed by the decision to incorporate the enforcement mandate within UNPROFOR's mandate, as a further Security Council Resolution (776) on 14 September authorised the enlargement of UNPROFOR in Bosnia to implement Resolution 770.[28]

UNPROFOR in Bosnia was not charged with 'blasting its way through' to its point of destination.[29] Instead it was to escort the convoys in 'benign' ways, only using its armaments in self-defence if fired upon first (the French force at Bihać was far more assertive, given the scope Paris allowed it, than the UK contingent at Vitez which had very restrictive rules of engagement imposed by London). This avoided the obvious difficulties that could be envisaged if convoys got into frequent firefights. However, it also meant that there was a continuing problem of ensuring the passage of aid where the way was blocked by combatants. Although in this, as in most other matters, the Serbian camp was easily the worst offender, the UN Civilian Affairs representative Cedric Thornberry made it clear that all parties had frustrated the work of those attempting to deliver aid.[30]

The nature of the problems involved in the mission in Bosnia, the difficulties already experienced and, not least, NATO's need to establish a new role for itself,[31] all contributed to NATO contributing substantially to planning and organising UNPROFOR in Bosnia. This was although most of the relevant contributions were initially offered through the Western European Union (WEU) at the end of the London

---

28 Operative paragraph 2 of Resolution 776 explicitly stated that the enlargement of UNPROFOR was to implement pargraph 2 of Resolution 770 which accorded the authorisation under Chapter VII of the UN Charter permitting 'use of all necessary measures' to secure the delivery of humanitarian assistance.

29 Foreign and Commonwealth Office, 'UN Relief Operation in Bosnia-Hercegovina', FCO Former Yugoslavia Briefing Note, October 1992.

30 *The Guardian*, 24 November 1992.

31 The North Atlantic Treaty Organisation had been predicated on the overt Soviet threat to Western Europe. With the end of the Cold War, NATO remained as the greatest multinational military capability in history and as a transatantic political forum, but had lost its defining *raison d'être*. As a result, it began to seek new roles, one of which came to be support for UN forces and international diplomacy in the former Yugoslavia. See, for example, Stanley R. Sloan, 'US perspectives on NATO's future', *International Affairs*, Vol 71 No.2, April 1992.

Conference on Yugoslavia at the end of August 1992.[32] Under a French commanding officer, General Philippe Morillon, assisted by a British Chief of Staff, Brigadier Roddy Cordy-Simpson, the UN headquarters for the at first 7,000-strong UNPROFOR force was provided essentially by NATO which lifted infrastructure from the Northern Army Group Forward Headquarters in Germany to form the UNPROFOR Command in Bosnia (BH Command). This was a factor which greatly helped in setting up the operation: those involved had experience of working together, established working procedures and a common working language, English. The existence of a ready-made theatre command structure, into which others who joined the staff then had to fit, was a great benefit.

BH Command was split initially in two, with the main part at Kiseljak and a light command post in Sarajevo, where General Morillon based himself.[33] Over two-fifths of the Staff were provided by NATO.[34] In addition to the French and Ukrainian presence in Sarajevo under UNPROFOR's original deployment, but attempting to carry out the new UNPROFOR command's work, eight other countries contributed troops to the mission in Bosnia — and the French, already the largest contributors to UNPROFOR in Croatia, made a further contribution. The BH Command division of labour was planned as follows: UK, with Belgian and Dutch transport units, at Vitez; Spain at

32 Western European Union, *Communiqué*, Extraordinary Council of Ministers, London, 28 August 1992.
33 Général Philippe Morillon, *Croire et Oser. Chronique de Sarajevo*, Grasset, Paris, 1993, pp.110-13.
34 In terms of the history of NATO, it was an interesting development that French troops were taking part. Although this was not technically a NATO operation, it was to a considerable extent NATO organised and reliant on NATO, because the operation was beyond the alliance's designated area of operation, German participation was not possible under Bonn's own interpretation of its constitutional position at that stage. The places of German staff officers in the Northern Army Group Headquarters were taken by the French. This both represented a small step in the already signalled moves towards re-integration into the military structures of NATO but was consistent with traditional French practice because this *de facto* involvement with NATO was *de jure* NATO by another name — the UN. The appointment of General Morillon was undoubtedly due not only to his experience in Yugoslavia as Deputy Commander of UNPROFOR, but also to the benefit of sweetening French the French rapprochement with NATO. (Cf. Philippe Guillot, 'France, Peacekeeping and Humanitarian Intervention', *International Peacekeeping*, Vol.1, No.1, Spring 1994, p.40.)

Mostar; France and Portugal at Bihać; Denmark and Norway at Kiseljak; Canada and the Netherlands at Banja Luka.

However, this last contingent was unable to get its 100- strong advance unit into Banja Luka. Whereas the British-Dutch-Belgian element of UNPROFOR, based at Vitez, was functioning towards the end of November and beginning to use means such as the diplomatic skills of its commanding officer Brigadier Bob Stewart[35] to negotiate the passage of convoys, the Canadian-Dutch element which was supposed to operate from Serb-controlled Banja Luka, had not reached first base. In the mean time there was powerful evidence that large-scale, systematic 'ethnic cleansing' was being executed in the region.[36] The Canadians were instructed by the UN Secretariat to pay the Serbian authorities in Banja Luka $49,000 of a demanded $250,000, ostensibly claimed to defray 'administrative costs'. It was, however, an exercise in extortion and humiliation. The UN order constituted an unexpected interpretation of the authority to use 'all necessary means' in Resolution 770. The Canadians reluctantly carried out the UN's wish to comply with Serbian extortion on 9 November. However, Canadian delegations going each day to the outskirts of Banja Luka were still not allowed to enter the town to prepare for the deployment of UNPROFOR in this area.[37]

A number of operational problems emerged from the experimental experience in Bosnia. Among these was a concern about the use of intelligence. Traditional UN practice avoided the use of intelligence or covert methods, preferring instead to rely on information and the use of open channels of communication. Restrictions on the gathering and distribution of intelligence, however, made the operation in Bosnia more

35 See Morillon, *Croire et Oser*, pp.156-8; see also Colonel Bob Stewart, *Broken Lives: A Personal View of the Bosnian Conflict*, HarperCollins, London, 1994, *passim*.

36 On 1 December 1992, the UN Human Rights Commission met for only the second time in its history to vote to condemn the 'crimes against humanity' in Bosnia. US Secretary of State Lawrence Eagleburger named senior figures in the Serbian camp who had cases to answer. The list included the Serbian President Slobodan Milošević, the leader of the Bosnian Serbs Radovan Karadžić and the commander of Serbian forces in Bosnia, General Ratko Mladić.

37 The Canadian battalion was later to become the first element of the UN forces in Bosnia-Hercegovina to deploy in the Srebrenica 'safe area' demanded by the UN Security Council under Resolution 819 (supplemented by Resolutions 824 and 836), following a brief deployment in Macedonia as UNPROFOR's third command was set up there at the beginning of 1993.

difficult. Sometimes information could be crucial — it would be 'hard to envisage how convoy escorting can be carried out efficiently without an up-to-date picture of the military situation in the areas through which a convoy is to pass.'[38] As UNPROFOR found itself increasingly likely to come under hostile directed fire, there would clearly be a greater demand for this kind of information. The experience in Bosnia made it clear that the existing UN conventions on intelligence gathering and dissemination would have to be re-assessed by all involved.

A further aspect of peace support operations which became an issue was command, control and communications. UNPROFOR BH Command headquarters at both Kiseljak and Sarajevo ran into difficulties talking to each other, let alone Zagreb, New York or London. This was a question in terms of both the chain of command and the co-ordination of operations, and of the means of communication. Whereas the arrangements over BH Command, through use of NATO infrastructure, were important in ensuring co-ordination of the military side of the humanitarian operation in Bosnia, these were not repeated higher up the chain. BH Command had some difficulties co-ordinating with UNPROFOR headquarters in Zagreb, as well as with other UN agencies there.[39] A decision would be taken in Zagreb by UNHCR that a certain quantity of aid should be delivered to a particular point in Bosnia-Hercegovina. That decision would be taken without consultation with the local command and often not even communicated to it until an aid convoy was under way and requiring protection.

While these defects should not be exaggerated, they did add to the problems involved in a difficult job. Even greater problems arose in relations between UNPROFOR headquarters and the UN in New York. On the one hand, the UN's traditional mode of operation leaves little scope for initiative with most actions requiring clearance from New York, yet on the other there were complaints that the telephone in New York often went unanswered.[40] Similarly, a Land Rover badly

---

38 House of Commons Defence Committee, Fourth Report, *United Kingdom Peacekeeping and Intervention Forces*, HMSO, London, June 1993, p.xxxv.
39 Much of the analysis presented here is based on discussions with British officers returning from duty with UNPROFOR.
40 This accusation, attributed to General Lewis MacKenzie when he was Sarajevo Sector Commander in UNPROFOR, was as much a reflection of the limitations of the small peacekeeping staff at UN Headquarters as an accurate statement about the time spent at work by those in New York — many of whom could be expected to work long hours.

damaged in Croatia could not be written off and replaced for several weeks while authorization was sought from New York. A corollary of this was the reluctance of individual countries to contribute to UN operations in general and Bosnia in particular. Where the lines of command and control were uncertain, there was understandably a lack of confidence and an aversion to relinquishing national control where the organisational arrangements were weak.[41]

Communications in Bosnia were dependent on expensive commercially produced civilian satellite telephone systems, the use of which was not only expensive but sometimes inadequate. A better communications system was essential for a complex operation of this kind. One report on UN operations pointed out that the additional funding required would be both merited and well spent.[42] An added question, reflecting also on the question of UN 'information' practice, was the place of encrypted communications. While these were permitted within national contingents, as well as between UN headquarters in New York and the UN theatre headquarters, the general insistence on open means of communication was increasingly brought into question by the hostile circumstances in which forces found themselves.[43]

MacKenzie had actually called New York in a crisis, had been connected with a UN official at home asleep, who, according to MacKenzie, did not know what UNPROFOR was, where UNPROFOR was, or who MacKenzie was — in spite of the constant newspaper and TV coverage of the situation in Sarajevo which had made MacKenzie a real media 'star', according to his superior, General Morillon. (Morillon, *Croire et Oser*, p.17; for MacKenzie's account see *Soldier of Peace* and his autobiographical account *Peacekeeper. The Road to Sarajevo*, Douglas and MacIntyre, Vancouver, 1993; an extended account of Morillon's exchange with New York was provided in Jocelyn Coulon, *Les Casques Bleus*, Fides, Montreal, 1994, pp.226-7; cf. Colonel Austin Thorp, 'Minutes of Evidence', 27 January 1993, in House of Commons Defence Committee, Fourth Report, *United Kingdom Peacekeeping and Intervention Forces*, HMSO, London, June 1993, pp.47-8.)

41 This was one of the principle US objections to joining UN operations in Bosnia and elsewhere. The US did, however, set a precedent when it decided to commit a small contingent to UNPROFOR in Macedonia. However, the retention of national control was also an issue for countries such as Sweden with a reputation for accepting UN roles — see Christopher Brady and Sam Daws, 'UN Operations: the Political Military Interface', *International Peacekeeping*, Vol.1, No.1, Spring 1994, p.68.

42 House of Commons Defence Committee, *United Kingdom Peacekeeping*, p.xxxvi.

43 It was reported that the UK contingent in Bosnia had come under direct fire on about seventy occasions between deployment in the autumn of 1992 and April 1993. (*Hansard*, HC Deb, 20 April 1993, col 53.)

The degree to which UNPROFOR found itself in hostile circumstances related to questions about Rules of Engagement (RoE), which, though essentially a national affair, were directly related to the mandate given to the UN force and conditioned by the UN's traditional mode of operation. This limited RoE to the firing of a single directed round only when subject to directed incoming fire and when the source of that firing could be clearly identified. In situations such as that found in Bosnia, limitations of this type were impractical — particularly on those occasions as the mission developed when it became necessary to use air power in support of the troops on the ground. This tension was to grow in salience in the second half of 1993 (see Chapter 6). In the mean time the UN RoE in Bosnia were amended *de facto*.[44]

In spite of all its problems, UNPROFOR was undoubtedly alleviating some of Bosnia's misery and probably acting, if not as a deterrent, then as a presence which made the level of violence less than it might have been otherwise.[45] However, neither it nor the UNHCR and the International Red Cross, with both of which it was working, could be expected to handle the scale of the problem presented by hundreds of thousands of deportees and refugees without food, shelter and medicines and with nowhere to go, given the growing reluctance of other countries to accept them. In 1994, the UNHCR gave assistance to 3.7 million people within the territories of the former Yugoslavia, while over 600,000 former Yugoslavs were refugees in Europe. As a result of UNPROFOR's relative impotence, the warring armies in Bosnia increasingly came to despise it and to humiliate it.

---

44 Other specific concerns were raised by the UK House of Commons Defence Committee. These related to the status of the forces in relation to the governments of Croatia and Bosnia, the timescale for troop deployments in relation to their objectives, and welfare matters. Included in this last category were accommodation — it took several months before the UK contingent was adequately housed — and pay, with those displaced from UK contingents in Germany receiving 60 per cent cuts in their Local Overseas Allowance, while counterparts in other national contingents were receiving significant increases in pay. As UN peace support operations developed, it was likely to prove easier to remedy these smaller problems at the national level than to resolve some of the more critical issues involved in their overall management. (House of Commons Defence Committee, Fourth Report, *United Kingdom Peacekeeping*.)

45 In June 1993 UNPROFOR had assisted over 650 convoys in the delivery of more than 37,000 tonnes of food, medicine and clothes, in addition to which the air bridge to Sarajevo had carried over 7,500 tonnes of aid. (House of Commons Defence Committee, Fourth Report, *United Kingdom Peacekeeping*, p.xliv.)

Responses to these difficulties were inevitably complicated. UNPROFOR's mandate was derived from a vast number of Security Council Resolutions,[46] some based in Chapter VI of the UN Charter on the pacific settlement of disputes, and many in Chapter VII on enforcement measures. The tensions between these elements under different Chapters constrained UNPROFOR's scope for responding to Serbian taunts. Even more than this, however, caution in the UN Secretariat and in certain governments prevented it from giving the only kind of reply that would make a difference: a forceful one. As will be seen in Chapter 6, there was increasing pressure to resort to force, but tension and caution persisted. That caution was predicated on the complexity of the UNPROFOR operation — not only in Bosnia, but over the original assignment in Croatia, which was fraught with its own difficulties, and with the creation of a further mission in Macedonia. Here the UN had set a precedent at the end of 1992 by establishing a third element of UNPROFOR as a preventive deployment.

Preventing in Macedonia

Fears about the Yugoslav war spreading to the Former Yugoslav Republic of Macedonia (FYROM) led the UN Security Council to authorise the extension of UNPROFOR in a radically new direction.[47] On 11 December 1992, with Resolution 795, it announced the deployment of a precedent-setting preventive peacekeeping force in Macedonia. In creating an UNPROFOR command in Macedonia, the UN hoped that it would be able to avoid a further flaring of hostilities in the region by taking action it had failed to take in Bosnia and for

46 As of December 1993, there had been 54 UN Security Council Resolutions on the former Yugoslavia, all of which created the context for UNPROFOR's operation and approximately half of which defined some element of its complex mandate. The sum of these resolutions was contained in the UN Secretary-General's analysis of the UNPROFOR mandate referred to above — Secretary-General's Report S/1994/300, 16 March 1994.

47 Macedonia was admitted to the UN General Assembly, following the recommendation of Security Council Resolution 817 on 7 April 1993 as 'The Former Yugoslav Republic of Macedonia'. This was a temporary name to facilitate membership of the UN, given the outstanding questions raised by Greece on the use of the name 'Macedonia' which were otherwise blocking membership in a variety of international bodies. The label 'FYROM' was that used in UN and other official documentation to refer to Macedonia until such a time as the country's problems with Greece over the name had been resolved.

which it had been criticised — acting before fighting erupted in order to prevent it, rather than reacting to adverse circumstances when it was already too late do more than provide a palliative. The deployment in Macedonia represented a welcome effort to learn the lessons of earlier international failures to take preventive measures. With this in mind and many analysts foreseeing war in the southern parts of the old Yugoslavia, the UN Secretary-General and Security Council undertook to broach the virgin territory of preventive peacekeeping.[48]

At the end of November, Boutros-Ghali sent twelve peacekeepers to Macedonia. Their mission was to assess the possibility of deploying a larger peacekeeping force there, particularly along the borders with Albania and southern Serbia. This reflected the high degree of international concern about the growing prospect that a war in the southern tier of the old Yugoslav state would not be limited to the Yugoslav space, but would have regional ramifications. The US, for instance, otherwise regarding the Yugoslav troubles as a matter of less than strategic importance, saw that war in the southern Balkans could easily result in Greece and Turkey engaging on different sides and thus damaging NATO (at least as much as the arguments between Germany and some of the other EC states had damaged the Twelve as they prepared to become a Union). This led the US to warn that it would make a military response beyond the preventive UN deployment, if Belgrade initiated war in the south.[49]

The original deployment in Macedonia, made on 6 January, involved 147 Canadian soldiers who handed over to a combined Nordic battalion of almost 700 troops from Norway, Finland, Sweden and Denmark on 2 March. In July 1993[50] the UN force in Macedonia was supplemented by 315 troops who were the first committed by the US to an operation run by the UN, another precedent established in the Macedonian

---

48 Until that point, UN deployments had always followed the outbreak of conflict and, with a few exceptions — one of them Bosnia — had usually only deployed after a truce had been agreed and begun to be implemented by the hostile parties. (See Alan James, *The Politics of Peacekeeping*, Chatto, London, 1991 and John MacKinlay, *The Peacekeepers*, Macmillan, London, 1989.)

49 Nicole Gnesotto, *Lessons of Yugoslavia*, Chaillot Papers No.14, Institute for Security Studies/Western European Union, Paris, 1994, p.27.

50 This was pursuant to a supplementary Security Council resolution — Resolution 842, 18 June 1993.

operation.[51] A further 180 US troops joined what was by then FYROM Command following the transfer of a similar number of Swedes to reinforce BH Command in April 1994.[52]

FYROM Command set a precedent — not only because it was the UN's first preventive deployment, but also because it was the first UN armed peacekeeping mission with American troops.[53] The presence of US troops was double-edged. On one side of the blade, the sharpness provided by American forces added to the credibility of the symbolic deterrent element implicit in the mandate for FYROM Command. The reverse cutting edge, however, was that the distinctive war-fighting capabilities of American soldiers made them a potential risk as part of a sensitive, unique UN peacekeeping operation. Trained purely for combat, the US personnel were being asked to play a key role in a historic, high-profile, largely passive exercise in international diplomacy.

Not only was American adjustment to the type of mission a potential difficulty for the mission — so too was the possibility that the distinctiveness of the US personnel as combat troops could both appear provocative and undermine the international character regarded by the UN as essential for the legitimation of its operations. US commanders were said to 'go ballistic' if any soldiers came close to stepping out of

51 Steven R. Bowman, 'Bosnia and Macedonia: US Military Operations', *Congressional Issue Brief*, IB93056, Congressional Research Service, June, 1993.
52 The total strength of UNPROFOR FYROM Command at the end of June 1994 was 1,107. These comprised 95 Norwegians, 222 Finns and 121 Swedes in the 438-strong Nordic battalion, as well as 5 Danes and 541 Americans in the US battalion. In addition, there were 13 Military Observers, 26 civilian police and 84 other civilian personnel. (UNPROFOR 'Facts Sheet', Press and Public Information Office, UNPROFOR headquarters, Zagreb, 29 June 1994.)
53 The presence of US troops in UNPROFOR should be distinguished from the use of substantial numbers of US military personnel for the UN-authorised operation in Kuwait to evict the occupying Iraqi armed forces. It should also be distinguished from the deployment of the US military in Somalia where they were not technically part of the main UN operation, UNOSOM. Instead the American troops were deployed as UNITAF — the Unified Task Force — not as part of the UN operation, but with the 'UN' at the beginning as a diplomatic sleight of hand to allow their use but avoid placing them under UN command, which was unacceptable to the US. Unarmed US personnel had been observers with UNTSO but, uniquely in Macedonia, US military personnel were placed under the command of UNPROFOR.

line and damaging the peacekeeping essence of the operation.[54] In addition to US self-restraint, the presence of the Nordic battalion was critical in overcoming the potential problems associated with the US deployment. This happened in two ways. First, the approximate balance between the Nordics and the US, at fifty-fifty, was felt by those in FYROM Command to enable the harmonisation of both the deterrent and the peacekeeping elements of the mission and to keep the US profile at once high enough to be noticed but not so high as to send the wrong message.[55] Secondly, the Americans were able to benefit enormously from being deployed alongside a contingent from countries traditionally regarded as experts in peacekeeping: the most important benefit from the mission, according to the Officer Commanding the US Battalion, was getting to know the Nordic soldiers and 'the way they work'.[56]

The UN force was deployed along the border between Macedonia and Serbia, particulary the section with Kosovo. This was in response to the prospect of war coming across the border from Serbia and its primary day to day role was to monitor that border. Here were two scenarios. The first involved a Serbian move across the border to annex Macedonia: any likelihood of this had already diminished by the time the Macedonian element of UNPROFOR was deployed. The second possibility was that fighting could break out in Kosovo and spill over the border, with refugees also being pushed over the border in a new Serbian campaign of 'ethnic cleansing'. If Serbo-Yugoslav forces were to make incursions into Macedonia, therefore, this would not be directly to annex territory, an attempt to incorporate the small Serb-populated area near Kumanovo in northern Macedonian could not be excluded, or indeed the whole of the country if the Slav Macedonians sought an alliance against ethnic Albanians; rather, the incursion would be aimed at suppressing support for ethnic Albanians in Kosovo in the event of a conflict there. The latter would inevitably have bases in Macedonia, as well as using the north-western part of the country for transit between Albania and Kosovo. This was of particular concern because

54 Comment by US peacekeeper in Macedonia quoted by Suzanna van Moyland, 'Monitoring Macedonia', unpublished research paper, Department of War Studies, King's College London, October 1994.
55 *Ibid.*
56 Lt.-Col. Carter Ham, quoted in Richard Calver, 'Blessed are the peacemakers — Regulars, by God!', *UNPROFOR News*, Zagreb, June 1994.

in a Serbo-Albanian conflict in Kosovo the most viable land route for Albanian reinforcement and supply would be through western Macedonia, thereby implicating Macedonia.

This scenario was the reason for the deployment of UNPROFOR. The force was deployed symbolically to deter Serbian attacks and — its real mandate — to seal the border in the event of fighting in Kosovo. It was clear that, were this to happen, much would depend on the effect of the symbolic presence of the US contingent in the Macedonian capital Skopje — backed by the prospect of Marine and air reinforcements from the US carrier group positioned in the Adriatic. Formally, FYROM Command's mandate was to 'monitor Macedonia's borders with Albania and ...Serbia... and report on all activities that might increase tension or threaten peace and stability', as well as to 'stand between forces that would otherwise clash'. In broader terms the purpose of UNPROFOR in Macedonia was related to the potential threats to the peace in the country and 'by its presence to deter such threats from any source'.[57]

FYROM Command was split into three sectors by June 1994, north-east, north-west and west. The US battalion was deployed in the first of these, the Nordic battalion in the second and a group of thirteen Military Observers in the west (organised under the auspices of the CSCE and the EC). The most active sector of FYROM Command on the north-eastern border of Macedonia was taken by the Americans. The US battalion, sometimes only 500 metres away from the border and 2 kilometres from Yugoslav army positions,[58] observed and reported on the border, especially warning of 'conditions that might threaten FYROM or undermine its security'.[59]

Apart from one incident where an UNPROFOR patrol had strayed to the Serbian side of an unclearly defined border and was detained for a short time by the VJ,[60] the first real test of FYROM Command came in June 1994. VJ troops advanced to a strategic viewing point on Mount Straža on the border between Serbia (the Federal Republic of Yugoslavia) and Macedonia. According to Macedonian officials,

---

57 Secretary-General's Report, UN Doc. S/24923, 9 December 1992.
58 The nearest Macedonian military positions were seven kilometres behind UNPROFOR Observation Posts.
59 Lt.-Col. Carter Ham, quoted in Calver, 'Blessed are the peacemakers', p.11.
60 See James Gow and James Pettifer 'Macedonia - Handle with Care' in *Jane's Intelligence Review*, Vol.5, No.9, September 1993.

documentation on the delimitation of borders between republics in the old SFRY clearly indicated that the VJ troops had made an incursion on to the Macedonian side of the border — although Belgrade maintained that the observation point was one of a small number of border points which were subject to dispute.

UNPROFOR, however, successfully negotiated a withdrawal of the VJ forces, following a visit to Belgrade by the Norwegian FYROM commanding officer, Brigadier-General Tryggve Tellefsen. The VJ agreed to withdraw 500m., and as part of the deal Macedonian troops would not be deployed within 500m. of the border point on the other side. UNPROFOR would patrol the area in between.[61] Thus, apart from its liaison office in Belgrade during the spring of 1992 when it was first deploying to Croatia, and the liaison office it had maintained subsequently, UNPROFOR had a formal albeit *de facto*, role on Serbian territory for the first time.[62]

In addition to its primary preventive peacekeeping mission, FYROM Command collaborated fully with the other international activities in the country. It was charged with giving assistance to the Sanctions Assistance Missions (SAMs) monitoring the implementation of sanctions against Serbia and Montenegro. These, with around fifty personnel, had no power to stop and search, only to monitor and advise Macedonian customs officials of potential breaches. It was the job of the Macedonian customs officials to take action. The nature of Macedonia's borders with both Serbia (the Federal Republic of Yugoslavia) and the relationship between the Albanian populations in both countries, pitched against the small number engaged in SAMs, meant that UNPROFOR, as part of its broader monitoring role, could increase the scale of sanctions monitoring by helping the SAMs.[63]

UNPROFOR was also able to work co-operatively with the mediation and monitoring activities of the CSCE-EC Monitoring Mission which had already been deployed to Macedonia following the report of CSCE officials between 10 and 14 September 1992.[64] Whereas UNPROFOR

61 Van Moyland, 'Monitoring Macedonia'.
62 It should be noted, however, that an UNPROFOR liaison office had been kept open in Belgrade since the force was first deployed.
63 Van Moyland, 'Monitoring Macedonia'.
64 *CSCE Spillover Mission Monitor Mission to Skopje*, CSCE Document IV,8, Prague, 1992.

was a high-profile operation, the CSCE-ECMM was able to engage in quieter mediation, particularly by assisting in negotiations between different elements of the Albanian political community and providing channels for contact between the Ministries of Defence and Foreign Affairs in Skopje and both Albanian and Serb political leaders. In general this mediation, sometimes conducted in conjunction with the Chair of the ICFY Macedonia Working Group (German Ambassador Geert Ahrens) could claim to be successful.[65] This mediatory activity was supplemented by the presence of Hugo Anson, a Briton who, as Co-ordinator for Civil Affairs in FYROM Command and Delegate of the Special Representative of the Secretary- General, was able to use the 'good offices' given to the Special Representative of the Secretary-General, Yasushi Akashi, by the Security Council.[66]

In the main UNPROFOR, along with other endeavours by the international community, could be judged as having a beneficial effect in Macedonia. However, it was also conceivable that its deployment could contribute to internal problems in Macedonia.[67] In spite of UNPROFOR's intentions, it was possible that its preventive mission might augment the possibilities of internal violence in the medium term, even if it were successfully to stabilise the external borders of the country. The UN had to deal with perceptions by the Albanian minority that UNPROFOR was bolstering a regime which it feared was becoming more authoritarian. At the same time, Macedonians believed that the international presence placed to great an emphasis on Albanian concerns. If the tensions between ethnic Albanians and Macedonians, while predicated on the desire of large elements in the Albanian community for unification with the Albanian state, were to develop into hostilities, they would most likely form a low-intensity civil conflict.

However, in this UNPROFOR had no formal role. While troops deployed could informally help to keep relations stable, there was no authority for this. Were hostilities of some kind to break out, UNPROFOR would undoubtedly have to deal with them, complicating a relatively straightforward mission. Thus the notion of deploying an experimental, precedent-setting pre-emptive peacekeeping force in

---

65 Stefan Troebst, 'Macedonia: Powder Keg Defused?', *RFE/RL Research Report*, Vol.3, No.4, 28 January 1994.
66 UN Security Council Resolution 908, 31 March 1994.
67 See Gow and Pettifer, 'Macedonia'.

Macedonia was not free of hazards. It was not always clear that there was awareness of the adverse, as well as the undoubtedly beneficial, impact UNPROFOR might have.

It was certainly important to be aware of the particular difficulties of the situation and to avoid making the mistake of thinking that circumstances were the same as they had been in Bosnia. Deployment of a pre-emptive peacekeeping force in Bosnia might have helped to avert war there — it would certainly have created a physical impediment to the wave of Serbian incursions across the River Drina (which forms the border between Serbia and Bosnia) in the first week of April 1992 which were the vanguard moves of what, despite strong civil elements, was essentially a war of annexation. UNPROFOR in Macedonia, in this sense, could provide a trip-wire if something similar were to happen. In the mean time FYROM Command could be content that peace and stability were being maintained and that there had been no need to shift from observation to a more robust approach — which would bring with it trials comparable to those of BH Command.

The UN was much criticised, even from an early stage in Croatia and certainly it performed its roles with mixed results. It clearly could regard itself as having implemented a unique preventive operation with US personnel in Blue Berets in FYROM Command — although that success could never be confirmed. In spite of the difficulty of proving its success, the precedents set by FYROM Command carried positive connotations. Nonetheless there was reason to doubt if the precedents would be quickly followed. This was because of the peculiar circumstances in which FYROM Command had been created — as the third element of a large operation, created for security policy purposes and intended to contain a conflict which had already shown its character in three earlier and increasingly horrific bouts of fighting. Although a similar situation might arise sometime in the future, it was unlikely to do so quickly.

UNPF could probably also regard itself as having done a relatively successful job in Croatia — in its own terms and in terms of its formal mandate. It had assisted in stabilising the January 1992 ceasefire there at the same time as it saved both sides in the conflict from returning to a scale of armed conflict which neither could sustain successfully. However, it had been un able to assist in ensuring the implementation of key aspects of the Vance Plan which had made the ceasefire possible, especially the return of displaced people. Instead the inability of displaced people to return to their homes, with the UN perceived as being responsible, brought the position of the force into question. This also left it involved in a hostile relationship with the Zagreb authorities who could blame it for their own limitations, and humiliate it by carrying out limited military operations to take control of territory in areas of UN responsibility. Despite this, it was clear that the occasional skirmishes initiated by the Croatian army did not seriously disrupt the relative stability of the situation — to which the UN force had clearly contributed.

However, it was Bosnia which most defined success and failure. There the innovations involved in seeking to deliver humanitarian assistance saw the delivery of a great deal of aid, as well as an ever greater use of force. The circumstances in Bosnia were such that UNPROFOR, confronted with a number of difficulties, was under pressure to extend the scope for using force. Constantly interacting with events in the diplomatic sphere, UNPROFOR was not just a peacekeeping force: it was an instrument of international diplomacy which, however, events on the ground shaped for much of the time. In Bosnia, even more than in Macedonia and Croatia, UNPROFOR was a tool for managing a European security question. It was an instrument of international diplomacy and, in a partial sense, of European security. It was this position which meant that in Bosnia UNPROFOR increasingly met further dilemmas which required the use of force to be reconciled with a peacekeeping mode of operation. International politics, the situation on the ground in Bosnia and UNPROFOR's complex mandate generated difficult circumstances requiring a use of force, as will be seen in the following chapter. It also created a variety of other military roles too in support of it. These were largely executed by NATO, and thus emphasised UNPROFOR's position in a security policy equation for the international community.

6

THE MILITARY OPERATIONS:
PEACE SUPPORT AND COERCION

Although each command in UNPROFOR found itself in a different military-political situation and with a different role, the mandate for each was related to that of the other elements in the force. Thus the overall mandate for UNPROFOR, built through numerous UN Security Council Resolutions, was complex and sometimes contradictory. This complexity was at its greatest in Bosnia where there was always tension between different aspects of the mission. For some tasks (local mediation) the use of force had to be avoided. Others (armed protection of humanitarian convoys) rested implicitly on the capability of using force. Yet others (the protection of UN-designated 'safe areas') required the explicit threat to use force. One of the successes of UNPROFOR in Bosnia was to reconcile the contradictory elements of this complex and militarily ill-defined mandate, in which carrying out one part of the mission might make another part of it much harder to execute. In reality, however, the complex mandate gave room for manoeuvre, scope for interpretation and the possibility of a flexible approach, by turns delicate and robust, as UNPROFOR practised what was essentially its true role — peace support.

Peacekeeping is one element of peace support which, to paraphrase Clausewitz's famous dictum, is a continuation of policy by other means. Peace support denotes a multilateral military operation which serves the peace-making initiatives of international diplomacy.[1] Thus, whether the mission is straightforward interposition along an agreed ceasefire line,

---

1 Peace-making is understood as international diplomatic activity aimed at bringing a conflict to an end. The conventional UN usage of this term and others such as peacekeeping and peace-building can be found in Boutros Boutros-Ghali, *An Agenda for Peace* —, UN Doc. A/48/403.

or the delivery of humanitarian aid, or the defence of safety zones, or enforcement — or a blending of different activities, it constitutes peace support. The main purpose of this support is to 'buy time' for those engaged in the peace-making process to pursue a diplomatic resolution of the conflict.[2] However, where directed, a peace support operation can carry out specific tasks intended to move the diplomatic process along — whether this means taking on a new peacekeeping role, becoming the guardian of heavy weaponry, or acting as part of a coercive initiative. In the last instance, there be a place for the use of force or the threat of its use in peace support and peace-making activity. As in Bosnia, the key question concerns the operational conditions for the use of force.

UNPROFOR, in all commands, was allowed to use force in self-defence. However, in Bosnia the armament of the force was considerably heavier than usual for UN operations. The mission was not to 'blast its way through', but it had the capability and the authority to do so. In reality, the greater capability of the force in Bosnia meant that on occasions where the presence of the armoured convoys in itself was not enough, fire could be returned on those attacking a convoy. This was not infrequent: the British battalion in Bosnia between November 1993 and May 1994 returned fire sixty-seven times.[3] The principal distinction between BH Command and traditional UN practice came in the weight of fire returned; in contrast to the traditional single directed round of fire from light arms, BH Command forces returned fire using bursts from heavy cannons — and this on occasions destroyed gun positions belonging to one of the warring parties.[4] However, the big

---

2 Lord Owen explained that the success of UNPROFOR's 'humanitarian intervention' in Bosnia would depend on "whether it bought time for a peace settlement at the expense of prologing the war." (Lord Owen, 'Yugoslavia: the Lessons for the European Union', 1994 Sir Winston Churchill Lecture, Fondation Pescatore, Luxembourg, 11 March 1994.) It is, however, sobering to note the low number of cases — around 4 per cent — in which international diplomatic mediation resolves a conlict. (See A.B. Fetherston, 'Putting the Peace Back into Peacekeeping: Theory Must Inform Practice', *International Peacekeeping*, Vol1 No.1, Spring 1994, p.15.)

3 This figure was cited in discussion with officers of the Coldstream Guards which served as the British Battalion in this period.

4 Different contingents in Bosnia had distinct operational styles. The more heavily armed the contingent, the more likely it was to take an assertive approach. Thus General Morillon was able to comment that the exploits of the Cheshire Regiment under its commander Colonel Bob Stewart were made possible because of the Warrior armoured

question of using force related far less to activities of this kind by troops on the ground than to the use of force, particularly air power, in pursuance of other aspects of international peace-making. The following is an account of the tensions found in combining the forceful use of air power with a ground operation largely predicated on a consensual environment; also of the way in which the positive and creative potential for combining the modes of operation, demonstrated at the beginning of 1994, was lost in the UN's strategic failure at Goražde the following April and compounded at Bihać as the year ended.

The UN and NATO: Peace Support and Enforcement Measures

In total, armed forces — land, sea and air — from over thirty countries, co-ordinated by the UN, NATO and the WEU, were carrying out six discrete missions established by UN Security Council Resolutions. In addition to the peace support roles of UNPROFOR on the ground, there were naval and air missions. These included patrolling and enforcement of sanctions in the Adriatic Sea and on the River Danube; humanitarian airdrops; patrolling and enforcement of the air exclusion zone over Bosnia; close air support for UNPROFOR; and aerial defence of UN designated 'safe areas'.

Naval forces were engaged in sanctions enforcement. Although sanctions were imposed on Serbia and Montenegro in May (Security Council 757), measures to enforce them did not begin until 10 July 1992 when the WEU and NATO began an operation in the Adriatic which was also supplemented by an aerial component, provided by

vehicles they were using, which could be classed as 'veritable light tanks, very well protected and armed' and that as a result they could intervene in the thick of things and gain the respect of the combatants (Morillon, *Croire et Oser*, p.156). One British comment on others serving with UNPROFOR, such as the Canadians, was that only difference between them and the British was the degree of armoured capbility. An even stronger approach was taken by the Swedish Battalion which arrived with Leopard II tanks after BH Command was expanded in June 1993. Colonel Ulf Hendrikson commanding the force based at Tuzla announced that when he had arrived a checkpoints where soldiers refused to remove mines blocking the way, 'I have told the soldiers if they don't move the mines we'll blow their heads of,' adding with satisfaction, he had 'always gotten through.' (Reuters, 4 November 1993.)

naval patrol aircraft.[5] However, this operation had no authority to stop and search vessels suspected of breaking the embargo until Security Coucil Resolution 787 on 16 November 1992 authorised a right to stop and search both in the Adriatic and on the Danube (where the WEU countries had been assisting in enforcement since the London Conference in August).[6]

Based around NATO's Standing Naval Force Mediterranean (STANAVFORMED), this joint operation with the WEU was codenamed 'Sharp Vigilance'. After the sanctions regime on Serbia and Montenegro was tightened in April 1993 (Resolution 820), the naval sanctions enforcement operation was altered. The new round of sanctions prohibited any commercial vessel from entering the territorial waters of the Federal Republic of Yugoslavia and granted states enforcing this ban the right to use 'necessary means commensurate with the circumstances' to carry out this mission. This led, first, to NATO authorising the use of inert charges in Operation Maritime Guard.[7] Whereas there had been five known violations of the embargo by large merchant vessels before Resolution 820, following the stronger sanctions regime and the changed NATO enforcement practice there were only three further confirmed attempts to bust sanctions in this way and one suspected attempt to violate the regime.[8]

The naval sanctions implementation force was restructured in a more efficient way in June 1993 when the NATO-WEU Combined Task

5 NATO AWACS aircraft were also supporting the naval sanctions imlplementation mission from July 1992 onwards, operating not only from the Adriatic and from Italian airspace, but also from Hungarian airspace by agreement with the Hungarian government. As a result, Hungary became the first former communist country to gain significant Western hardware. The ending of the Warsaw Pact and the removal of Soviet air defence capability had left Hungary without control of its airspace. The US supplied Hungary, on favourable terms, with four radar ground stations and 144 'identification-friend-or-foe' systems for Hungarian aircraft. These both facilitated AWACS ability to monitor and strengthened Hungary against further violations of its airspace (there had been several, including one incident where Yugoslav planes dropped bombs on a Hungarian village during the conflict in Croatia in the autumn of 1991). (Charles Hebbert, 'Hungary's Military Reforms', *Jane's Intelligence Review*, Vol.5, No.6, June 1993, p.262.)

6 Between July and September 1992, 2,089 ships were inspected in the Adriatic. Of these 29 were suspected of breaching sanctions.

7 Maritime Guard was a discrete operation and comprised five destroyers (from Italy, Germany, Greece, Turkey and the UK) and two frigates (from the US and the Netherlands).

8 Lawrence Freedman, 'External Intervention in the Yugoslav Wars', unpublished paper.

Force 440, renamed 'Sharp Guard', came under a joint commander, rather than one for the vessels sailing with the WEU and one for the vessels serving with NATO.[9] Initially NATO and WEU had joint responsibility for the Adriatic as a result of inter-institutional diplomacy. Both forces had the same officer commanding who simply switched hats as appropriate. The somewhat farcical prospect of the Adriatic Sea cluttered with naval vessels performing a dance of flags around each other under a schizophrenic master of ceremonies led to a division of labour in which the WEU decided to concentrate on the Danube while NATO took full responsibility for patrolling the Adriatic.

The remaining missions — delivery of humanitarian aid to cut-off populations inaccessible by land, patrolling and enforcement of the air-exclusion over Bosnia, close air support for UNPROFOR on the ground and defence of UN designated 'safe areas' — involved the use of aerial capability. The first of these had two dimensions. The more prominent of them was the air bridge established to besieged Sarajevo following the surprise visit of French President François Mitterrand at the end of June 1992.[10] From then onwards, the supply of aid to Sarajevo by air was considerable — although the bridge was far from being open constantly as either fighting or sniper fire would result in closure. In the first five months of 1993, for example, 16,235 tonnes of aid were delivered by air to Sarajevo.[11]

The less prominent use of aircraft involved the use of airdrops, carried out primarily by US and German aircraft, to help sustain enclaves in eastern Bosnia which could not be reached by land convoys. These operations were conceived of by the US in place of preparedness to make a stronger commitment involving the deployment of its own troops; they were prompted by a (seemingly perverse) decision by the Sarajevo authorities on 12 February 1993 to refuse any further deliveries of aid until the inaccessible, predominantly Muslim communities in eastern Bosnia, numbering 100,000 people, had been

9 Operation Sharp Guard included eight ships from NATO's Standing Naval Force Mediterranean, seven from its Standing Naval Force Atlantic and six vessels flying under the WEU flag, as well as naval patrol aircraft.

10 See Chapters 3 and 7.

11. UNHCR 'Information Notes on former Yugoslavia', no.6/93, UNHCR-Office of the Special Envoy for former Yugoslvia, Zagreb, 25 May 1993. In addition, 14,900 tonnes of aid was shipped by land convoy to Sarajevo, bringing the total for the period to 31,135 tonnes.

given assistance. On 17 February the UNHCR stopped all attempts to get shipments to eastern Bosnia, including Serb communities, because of the Serb blocking of the convoys.

President Clinton met UN Secretary-General Boutros Boutros-Ghali on 23 February and afterwards announced that the US would begin to use Hercules C-130J aircraft to drop aid from 10,000 feet, including foodstuffs and medicine.[12] In the initial period, between 28 February and 21 May, the airdrop programme delivered 3286.3 tonnes of food and 79.4 tonnes of medicines to the Muslim enclaves at Srebrenica, Žepa, Goražde, Konjevici and Cerska[13] - although this was not enough to prevent the last two from collapsing in face of hunger and a Bosnian Serb onslaught.[14] In leading this humanitarian initiative, however, the US made it clear that it would be acting under existing UN Security Council resolutions as it embarked on this mission, for which a primary objective was not only to deliver aid and possibly assuage criticism, but also to put pressure on the Bosnian Serbs to allow the free passage of convoys.[15] In spite of this hopeful political purpose, the airdrop scheme was to continue for purely humanitarian reasons, albeit without the glare of public attention, during the following winter.

The 'no-fly' zone over Bosnia was established by Security Council Resolution 781 on 9 October 1992 and prohibited all military flights in Bosnian air space other than those on UN missions. However, implementation of this Reslolution was initially left to UNPROFOR, which was tasked with monitoring observance of the ban.[16] Serbian aircraft continued to violate the air exclusion zone, carrying out aerial attacks on towns such as Brčko and Gradačac. Under growing threats, particularly from the US, that the Resolution would be enforced, Milan Panić, Federal Yugoslav Prime Minster at the time, offered to transfer all Bosnian Serb aircraft to Serbia for safekeeping until the war was over. The Bosnian Serb leader Radovan Karadžić agreed to this with

---

12 *The Financial Times*, 24 February 1994.

13 UNHCR 'Information Notes on former Yugoslavia', no.6/93, UNHCR-Office of the Special Envoy for former Yugoslvia, Zagreb, 25 May 1993.

14 Lee Bryant, 'UNPROFOR's Mandate to Protect', *Balkan War Report*, No.18 February-March 1993, p.1.

15 Fiona M. Watson, *Peace Proposals for Bosnia-Herzegovina*, House of Commons Library Research Paper No.93/35, House of Commons, London, 23 March 1993, p.25.

16 The Security Council authorised the deployment of 75 military observers for this purpose on 10 November 1992 (Resolution 786).

Lord Owen, but he was overruled by the head of the Bosnian Serb air force at Banja Luka, who refused to give up the aircraft. However, even though the agreement with Owen was not implemented, the Bosnian Serbs largely refrained from using fixed-wing aircraft thereafter. They did, however, continue to use them on occasion and made ample use of rotary-wing aircraft.[17]

Eventually the international community moved to enforce the air-exclusion zone. Tired of constantly being frustrated by the Serbs across the board and, in particular, of the constant breaches of the no-fly zone with helicopters and a flagrant breach with use of a small turbo-propelled plane to bomb villages in eastern Bosnia in March 1993, the Security Council authorised the use of force to implement the 'no-fly' ban in Resolution 816 on 31 March. On 2 April NATO, having previously indicated its preparedness to do so, agreed to mount the first real-world operation in its history, pursuant to this Resolution. Following discussions and internal disagreements on the exact circumstances in which it would be permissible to shoot down aircraft breaching the air-exclusion zone, Operation Deny Flight began on 12 April.[18]

Operation 'Deny Flight' originally included twelve US Air Force F-15 and twelve US Navy FA-18 Aircraft, as well as eighteen F-16s from the Netherlands, ten Mirage 2000 and four Mirage FICRs from France and twelve Tornado F3s from the UK.[19] This force strength was later increased by the inclusion of a further six Dutch F-16s, a further six British Tornados with two VC10 in-flight refuelling tankers, eighteen Turkish F-16s and five NATO supply airacraft. In addition to these aircraft specifically deployed for the mission to bases in Italy, where they were directed from a headquarters at Vicenza,[20] NATO AWACS planes, already deployed in connection with the sanctions monitoring

---

17 By mid-March, the number of reported violations of the 'No-Fly Zone' since its creation on 9 October 1992 was 495. (Fiona M. Watson and Richard Ware, *The Bosnian Conflict — a turning point?*, House of Commons Library Research Paper No.93/56, 28 April 1993, p.2.)

18 Fiona M. Watson and Richard Hare, *The Bosnian Conflict — a turning point?*, House of Commons Library Research Paper No. 93/56, House of Commons, London, 28 April 1993, p.3.

19 The information in this section is derived from Freedman, 'External Intervention'.

20 This was the Headquarters for 5 ATAF (Allied Tactical Aif Force) in NATO.

missions over Hungary and over international waters,[21] gave assistance in terms of airborne command and control.

It was practice in this operation, however, to act with caution. Several warrnings would have to be given before any action could be taken. Moreover, most of the violations were made by helicopters and there was sensitivity with regard to the possibility that any rotary aircraft shot down might be found to have been carrying injured civilians — a possiblity which would have had embarassing repurcussions in spite of the flagrant illegality of the flight. Often helicopters were painted white and bore the sign of the Red Cross (this appears to have been especially true of violations made over Bosnian government controlled territory.[22] In one short period, 15-18 July, Boutros Boutros-Ghali reported that there had been seventeen reported violations, bringing the total for the whole period since imposition of the no-fly regime to 695 — a somewhat discouraging increase of almost 200 in the period after NATO began patrol and enforcement of the ban on 12 April 1993.[23]

It was notable, however, that only one of these flights was made by a fixed-wing aircraft. Moreover, this was one of only two incidents in which flights by fixed-wing military aircraft were recorded following the decisions in the spring of 1993 by the Security Council and the North Atlantic Council to use NATO to implement the 'no-fly zone'. The other occurred on 28 February 1994 and involved NATO aircraft shooting down four out of six Serbian combat aircraft over Bosnia after they had attempted to destroy munitions facilities. This Serbian operation demonstrated the collaboration between the various elements in the Serbian camp: pilots were transferred six weeks before the mission from the Air Force of the Federal Republic of Yugoslavia at Podgorica in Montenegro to Udbina in the RSK, from where the raids were launched against targets in Bosnia on behalf of the VRS. The two planes which avoided being shot down landed at the Banja Luka airbase

21 Hebbert, 'Hungary's Military Reforms', p.262.
22 See the 'Information on Flights in the Airspace of Bosnia and Herzegovina Not Authorized by the United Nations Protection Force (15-18 July 1993), attached as an Annex to the 'Note Verbale dated 19 July 1993 from the Secretary General Addressed to the President of the Security Council', UN Doc. S/24900/Add.63,.
23 *Ibid.,.*

in VRS-controlled territory.[24] The success of this enforcement action, added to the dearth of flights by fixed-wing combat aircraft in general, allowed the UN Secretary-General to conclude that 'Operation Deny Flight' had been 'almost entirely successful'. However, he was obliged to point out that the agreed NATO-UN procedures had not prevented many violations of the 'no-fly zone' by what he termed 'non-Combat aircraft', as he reported a total of 1,005 violations by mid-March 1994.[25]

For much of the time the 'no-fly zone' had been declared, there had been great reluctance to enforce it for fear of the adverse implications for UNPROFOR on the ground — hostage-taking and reprisals could not be ruled out as a Serb tactical response to the use of air power to enforce the air exclusion zone — although following the shoot-downs in February 1994, the Serbian response was muted. The same was even more true the possible use of air power in two other roles — close air support for the troops on the ground and enforement of UN Security Council Resolutions on the defence of 'safe areas'.

These roles were related, and the distinction, as much as anything, only reflected the slow pace at which the UN and the states involved were prepared to take evolutionary new steps. France, the Netherlands, the UK and the US made fighter and ground attack aircraft available through NATO, initially for the provision of close air support only. As with 'Operation Deny Flight', these forces were deployed to Italy, or on vessels in the Adriatic Sea — they shared the same command structure with 'Operation Deny Flight', and at certain stages some of the aircraft were shared.[26] Both roles, however, were contained in the mandate provided by the UN Security Council in Resolution 836 (4 June 1994). This emerged in relation both to Resolutions 819 and 824 which had designated a total of six 'safe areas' in Bosnia, and to the Washington Declaration of a 'Joint Action Plan' on 22 May 1993, which had effectively killed off the Vance-Owen Plan for peace. (See Chapter 9.)

The kernel of Resolution 836 was the decision to utilise air power to strengthen UNPRFOR's role in deterring attacks on the 'safe areas'. Following paragraphs in which UNPROFOR's mandate was extended

---

24 See James Gow, 'MIlitary Forces in Bosnia: Origins and Prospects', *Woodrow Wilson Center of East European Studies Newsletter*, September-October 1994.
25 'Report of the Secretary General', UN Doc. S/1994/300, 16 March 1994.
26 Freedman, 'External Intervention'.

to include, *inter alia*, the imperative 'to deter attacks against the safe areas' (5) and 'acting in self-defence, to take the necessary measures, including the use of force, in reply to bombardments against the safe areas... or to armed incursion into them,' (9) paragraph 10 authorised 'member states, acting nationally or through regional organisations or arrangements,' to take 'all necessary measures, through the use of air power, in and around the safe areas in the Republic of Bosnia and Herzegovina, to support UNPROFOR in the performance of its mandate...' The initial response of most relevant member states was to be cautious since the North Atlantic Council (NAC) on 10 June, the political decision-making body in NATO, limited its offer of assistance to the use of protective air cover in case of attacks on UNPROFOR. Thus although the Security Council Reslution authorised a broader use of air power, those at NATO in a position to offer it limited the Alliance's role at this stage. This was consistent with the interpretation placed on Resolution 836 by the Security Council in the discussion leading to its being passed.[27]

Such self-limitation in NATO was a result of Alliance politics. Aside from countries not directly involved in any likely action, such as Greece, which maintained reservations, there were differences between the major contributors to the mission. For some time, certainly since the advent of the Clinton Administration in January 1993, the US had been pressing for the admission of the use of air power in Bosnia against the Bosnian Serbs in order to break the siege of Sarajevo and other Muslim communities and to prevent VRS movements. The UK, the French and the Dutch, all with ground forces in UNPROFOR, were understandably reluctant to embrace the possibility of a substantial and antagonistic use of air power lest it place their troops in jeopardy. On the other hand, all of them, especially the French, were increasingly aware that there were circumstances, including attacks on UNPROFOR and clear defiance of its mandate, in which the credibility of international diplomacy and the UN force could only be maintained at all by a firm response to certain kinds of abuse.

Unease within NATO, UNPROFOR and the UN did not ebb away as arrangements for putting the NATO offer into effect were developed. The US wanted the commander in chief of Allied Forces South in Naples (CinC SOUTH — at that stage US Admiral John Boorda) to

---

27 I am indebted to Shashi Tharoor for this point of clarification.

command the use of air strikes with full freedom. France and Canada, however, wanted the UNPROFOR commander to have a veto on any use of air power. The compromise of a 'dual key' in which either military commander could block a decision by the other on air strikes was introduced. If either one vetoed a decision by the other, the matter would be referred to the NAC and the UN.

However, there seemed far more likelihood that, given the political sensitivity of the question, air strikes were far less likely to be a matter of operational dispute between CinC SOUTH and Commander HQ UNPROFOR than at the political level. Whereas the Security Council had lent its authority broadly to the use of air power, the UN Secretariat, as well as some senior figures at UNPROFOR, were clearly afraid of their possible outcome. Boutros-Ghali was keen to preserve for himself, or at a minimum his Special Representative, the final decision on the first air strike. Similarly, the NAC was reluctant to admit the possibility of aircraft firing without its taking a special decision to authorise it first.[28]

Thus practical instruments were put in place, including the deployment of Forward Air Controllers (FACs) in Bosnia, working with an Air Operations Co-ordination Centre (AOCC) established with BH Command Headquarters at Kiseljak. FACs could be deployed up to 45 kilometres from a target and use laser guiding devices to lead aircraft on to it, although in most cases in Bosnia visual contact would be important to ensure absolutely accurate targetting — more significant, even, than usual in a high-profile, sensitive UN peace support operation in which mistaken targetting, or the notoriously euphemistic 'collateral damage', was likely to become a major diplomatic embarassment.[29] Initially the FACs attached to UNPROFOR would be unable to talk directly to aircraft as radios suitable for UN use were incompatible with the aircraft communications — but by the time aircraft were firing in anger at Goražde in April 1994 this had been remedied and UNMOs were able to act as FACs for air strikes. Therefore, most messages would be relayed via the AOCC to Vicenza.

The political and operational difficulties associated with the co-ordination and use of air power in support of UNPROFOR went

28 Freedman, 'External Intervention'.
29 Group Captain A.D. Sweetman, 'Close Air Support Over Bosnia-Hercegovina', *RUSI Journal*, August 1994.

through a series of refinements in the course of the second half of 1993. However, this was nearly always in response to events. The most critical of these was the VRS's major assault and capture of Mount Igman and particularly the Bjelašnica Ridge, dominating the south-west approach to the Bosnian capital Sarajevo and strategically vital. By capturing the ridge the VRS completed its grip (already firm) on Sarajevo: it had the city fully ringed and had interrupted the one route which the Bosnian government and its forces had been able to use to bring in supplies. Both NATO and the UN had already made threats to take action against the VRS over the siege of Sarajevo. In this case NATO issued a demand for the 'stranglehold' to be released and the positions on Igman and Bjelašnica relinquished.

However, the threat of action did not become real. As NATO and the UN went through a time-consuming process of preparing the guidelines for a strike, the VRS was able to maintain its grip while at the same time becoming co-operative, so removing the need to carry through threats once the hiccups in the international system had been cleared. The VRS commander General Ratko Mladić achieved his main aim — closure of the route across the mountains which allowed limited resupply of his Muslim enemies — at the same time as he appeared to be co-operating with the UN by getting UNPROFOR to take over what was becoming another de-militarised zone. With UNPROFOR taking responsibility for this area General Mladić was free to deploy his troops to another front (having rubbed the noses of NATO and the UN in the mud by flagrantly defying the 'no-fly zone' with the televised use of a helicopter to move around his formations),[30] while his political associates were reaping the benefits of temporary co-operation.

On a number of other occasions there was friction over the question of using air power. In particular, this turned on the growing frustration felt with the UN Secretariat in New York. Leading governments in the Security Council and especially the practitioners on the ground became frustrated as they sought stronger action, particularly the use of air strikes. For UNPROFOR commanders, however, the problem was not just the extreme caution and delay of Boutros Boutros-Ghali, which meant that, although Close Air Support was called for, the moment for execution had passed by the time a decision came back from New York — this was almost inevitable, given a mandate of self-defence. The

30 Shown on 'Newsnight', BBC2 TV.

force commanders also despaired of the contradictory messages emanating from the Security Council: 'I don't read the Security Council resolutions anymore,' said Belgian Lieutenant-General François Briquemont — because they did not help him.[31]

By the beginning of 1994, UNPROFOR was on the point of adding to the number of generals it had already lost, through a variety of frustrations, ahead of schedule — the Canadian Brigadier-General Lewis MacKenzie and French Lieutenant-General Phillipe Morillon had both been forced to beat an early retreat. In the early part of 1994, both the Officer Commanding Bosnia, Briquemont, and soon afterwards the overall force commander, the French General Jean Cot, were lost to UNPROFOR. The UN, to paraphrase Oscar Wilde, seemed not so much unfortunate as careless — and indeed not so much careless as criminally negligent. The friction between the UN and its commanders was increasingly over the use of force: the commanders made calls for close air support, which arrived, but whereas action could only be effective if taken within minutes, clearance from the UN Secretary- General took six hours. Even though new arrangements transferred the final decision to the Secretary-General's Special Representative, Yasushi Akashi (from Japan), the reaction time still appeared too slow to be meaningful.

The paradox was that UNPROFOR in Bosnia could use force and could call on NATO for aerial support, but that this would present risks for UNPROFOR in Bosnia as well as for other elements of UNPROFOR, for the UN in general and possibly for relations between Russia and its Western partners. There was a basic tension: the uses of force discussed were part coercion, part defence — the former concerned protection of the 'safe areas', the latter protection of the troops in the force. Whereas there was no question in the minds of commanders and their national political masters about defence of their troops, there was concern that emphasis on the 'safe areas' as a whole had to be well balanced. For much of the time UNPROFOR was working well on the ground in ways that went largely unnoticed — through the Mixed Military Working Groups in Sarajevo and elsewhere carrying out local mediation between uniformed representatives of the parties.[32] Of course, UNPROFOR was also able to do this between

31 Quoted by Jocelyn Coulon, *Les Casques Bleus*, Fides, Montreal, 1994, p.199.
32 See, for example, General Phillipe Morillon, *Croire et Oser. Chronique de Sarajevo*, Grasset, Paris, 1993, pp.119-24.

civilians.[33] There was clearly a place for the threat of force, especially air power, and for its sophisticated employment — sometimes the threat was needed to push diplomacy along, and delicate use could demonstrate the credibility of threats.

Yet the use of force carried with it the danger that UNPROFOR's impartiality would be 'compromised'. Impartiality was regarded by the UN Secretary-General as the key to the operation's effectiveness: it was generally regarded by those engaged in peacekeeping as the hallmark of their trade. Once the UN took measures which effectively impeded the military progress of one party or another (most commonly the VRS), it was thought to encounter 'increased incidents of obstruction and harassment'.[34] However, in spite of Boutros-Ghali's hesitant approach to the situation, there was ample evidence that whenever there had been enough of a threat to put doubt in the minds of the parties, especially the Bosnian Serbs, it had produced a positive outcome and made the conduct of diplomacy easier:[35] conversely, the conduct of diplomacy had been much harder whenever it was clear to the parties — especially the Bosnian Serbs, as General Morillon pointed out — that the prospect of a use of force was remote. The more remote it was, the 'more Mladić believed he was entitled to do anything'.[36]

Whenever there was resistance and harassment, it proved to be temporary as the parties, usually the Bosnian Serbs, saw merit in keeping useful links with UN open. In terms of the carefully husbanded use of force, the crucial problem was not compromised impartiality — the evidence suggested that, while it was necessary to avoid being partisan within the conflict, it was right and proper for those engaged in the UN peace support operation as instruments of international diplomacy to be partial and committed to their mission and to the implementation of their mandate. Failure to do so would undermine the effectiveness of the force far more than any question of compromised impartiality through the clear, considered and concerted execution of their mission.

---

33 Morillon, *Croire et Oser*, pp.156-8; Colonel Bob Stewart, *Broken Lives: A Personal View of the Bosnian Conflict*, HarperCollins, London, 1993, pp.219-25.
34 'Report of the Secretary General', UN Doc. S/1994/300, 16 March 1994.
35 See below for further discussion of this point.
36 Morillon, *Croire et Oser*, p.193.

The alternative, with emphasis on the maintenance of 'neutrality' was in fact to corrupt the purpose of international diplomacy. Far more telling for UNPROFOR and the international diplomatic initiatives it represented than any suggestion of compromised impartiality through action was the prospect of compromised credibility where there was a failure to act, or, the failure to exploit success — which resulted mostly, as Boutros-Ghali lamented with some justification, from the inadequate provision of personnel to UNPROFOR by the member states for the new tasks resulting from success in difficult circumstances.[37] This was particularly true of the 'safe areas' in Bosnia.

Srebrenica: the Origins of the 'Safe Area'

The tension between the complementary yet contradictory needs both to use force and to avoid its use, as well as the associated problems, became encapsulated in the evolution of the 'safe areas' at Srebrenica, Sarajevo, Goražde and Bihać (in addition, there were 'safe areas' at Žepa and Tuzla]. In each the intertwined problems arose of using force, both assisting and exploiting its use through personnel on the ground, preventing situations in which those personnel would become vulnerable, and finally ensuring that the action of those on the ground was backed by timely and coherent political commitment. In all of these situations, there was an overlap between initiatives on the ground and those at the diplomatic level. There was great reliance on the personal role of the officers commanding in Bosnia, and the developments in these cases involved the generals both leading the international effort on the ground and acting as instruments of high diplomacy.

The notion of 'safe areas' first arose specifically over Srebrenica, where the small predominantly Muslim town in eastern Bosnia had become the focal point of a Serbian campaign to drive Muslims out of the Drina valley and where around 40,000 refugees from other communities in the region had fled. Eastern Bosnia had been swept by 'ethnic cleansing' campaigns in the first months of the war in 1992 — at which time numerous villages in that part of the country appear to have been razed. In the winter conditions of January and February, Muslim guerrillas and Bosnian Army II Corps units had conducted a series of raids in the area, capturing territory from the Serbs and putting

37 'Report of the Secretary General', UN Doc. S/1994/300, 16 March 1994.

pressure on the Serbs at Bratunac on the border between Bosnia and Serbia. In these attacks there seem to have been reprisal atrocities — meaning, at a minimum, summary executions.[38] The Serb response to these operations and to the pressure on Bratunac and the Serbian border, and needing to secure territory to frustrate the Vance-Owen Plan, which they were coming under pressure to accept (see Chapter 9) was to begin a crushing campaign to eliminate remaining Muslim communities in eastern Bosnia.

Not only was the VRS commander, General Mladić, turning the screw on eastern Bosnia through heavy firepower, he was also denying passage to UN aid convoys. It was for these reasons that UNPROFOR and the broader international community it represented faced demands for action to prevent massacre and starvation in the region. It was impossible for UNPROFOR, completely cut off by Serbian forces, to do more than guess and try to persuade the Serbs to allow access. Its commanders were sensitive to demands being made for action, but they were also cautiously sceptical: on other occasions the Bosnian authorities, militarily disadvantaged by the circumstances in which the war began and with a vested interest in prompting greater external engagement, had exaggerated situations. At Žepa, for example, they had played strongly on reports of cannibalism in attempts to sway international opinion, yet when UNPROFOR and aid convoys eventually managed to reach the enclave in eastern Bosnia, they discovered live cattle indicating that reports of starvation and cannibalism were exaggeration.[39] It was understandable both that the Bosnian government should use its ingenuity to try and improve its position, and that these efforts would make external actors, however sympathetic, doubtful of some of the claims made.

With reports from Muslims in the region indicating an accelerated Serbian military campaign and further 'ethnic cleansing', and the UN in New York pushing those on the ground to respond, General Morillon decided to set out for eastern Bosnia to see for himself, accompanied by a unit from the British battalion. Morillon and his team were forced to take a long route to the north and east (the eastern Bosnian enclaves

---

38 Morillon points out that the Bosnian army acknowledged this (*Croire et Oser*, p.132). The Bosnian Serbs, especially those who had fled to Bratunac, claimed more, saying that there had been massacres.

39 Morillon, *Croire et Oser*, p.133.

lay to the east and south) and delayed substantially along the way by the VRS at Zvornik, but eventually reached the Muslim communities in the Drina valley. On his first trip to the region, Morillon had reached Cerska which had already fallen to the Serbs and witnessed the vicious attack on Konjević Polje. On his second trip, the General negotiated his was to Srebrenica amid indications that a humanitarian and political nightmare could be under way there.

In Srebrenica Morillon argued with the local leaders that if they agreed not to carry out provocative attacks, he would be able to negotiate a ceasefire and obtain the deployment of at least two observers, as well as bringing in supplies by both road and air. The local community judged that Morillon was their best hope, effectively took him hostage — even though the UNPROFOR detachment would have remained anyway: as long as he was kept in the town, they could not be abandoned by the international community. Morillon tried at first to escape alone, but the locals prevented him. He then decided to stay, raising the UN flag and declaring that he would make his headquarters at Sarajevo telling both the Muslims and, in particular, the Serbs to 'understand... I am and I will stay in Srebrenica'.[40]

The result of Morillon's initiative was that once UNPROFOR was able to reach him again, land and air corridors briefly became open for humanitarian assistance, with food and medicine being flown in and the wounded being flown out by helicopter. On 13 March Morillon left Srebrenica for talks in Belgrade and at the erstwhile (and *de facto*) Bosnia Command headquarters at Kiseljak. Once out of Srebrenica, he was criticised both in Paris and in New York.[41] UN Secretary- General Boutros-Ghali accused him exceeding his mandate. There were French intelligence reports that as a result of this pressure an attack was being prepared on Morillon. Then it was decided to replace the outgoing overall commander of UNPROFOR, the Swedish General Lars Wahlgren, with the French General Jean Cot. This meant that Morillon was withdrawn to France, where he became special adviser to the Minister of Defence François Léotard. His legacy was to place a clear international stake at Srebrenica.

After 19 March, the VRS increasingly impeded the passage of convoys, so that by 16 April the UN Security Council declared

40 *Ibid.*, p.175.
41 Morillon, *Croire et Oser*, p. 180.

Srebrenica a 'safe area'. With the Serbs again bearing down on the beleaguered community, it decided that a stand had to be taken. This was almost certainly a reflection of Morillon's point about the international commitment to the town and its overwhelming refugee population. However, the magic ring of safety announced by the Security Council did not give effective protection, although a demand that 147 Canadian UNPROFOR personnel be allowed to deploy there was acceded to by the Serbs. (Mladić presumably judged that refusal might provoke an unacceptable international response, while UN troops, in effect, could hold the position for him indefinitely, freeing his men for use elsewhere.) The pressure arising from the Srebrenica situation was compounded by growing calls for other parts of Bosnia to be declared 'safe areas'. This is what the Security Council did in Resolution 824 on 6 May, adding Bihać, Tuzla, Sarajevo, Žepa and Goražde.

Following the demise of the Vance-Owen Plan, though ostensibly to keep its now non-existent prospects alive, the Security Council took a further step on the six 'safe areas'. In Resolution 836 (4 June 1993), acting under Chapter VII of the UN Charter on enforcement measures, it added to the 'safe areas' by authorising their military protection, not only by personnel on the ground but through the use of air power. The UN Secretary-General Boutros Boutros-Ghali reported that a further 34,000 military personnel,[42] including Forward Air Controllers (FACs) for assistance with air support, would be needed for UNPROFOR to secure the designated 'safe areas'.[43] However, the Security Council only authorised 7,600 further troops — it was difficult to find countries prepared to volunteer even that number for such a mission.

This presented both UNPROFOR and international diplomats with a serious problem when it came to protecting the 'safe areas'. Although something could be done with the limited troop levels available, it would prove difficult to make these areas genuinely safe without the consent of the VRS. UNPROFOR lacked the manpower to operate the 'safe areas' effectively. However, the broadened mandate opened up the possibility of using force both for peace support and diplomatically. The

42 This figure did not take into account any military personnel who might be engaged through national or other international bodies in air roles in connection with defence of the 'safe areas'.

43 Secretary General's Report, UN Doc. S/25939, 14 June 1993.

concept of the 'safe areas' would be given limited credibility if air power could be called in. However, awareness of a lack of personnel on the ground to combine effectively with air operations, plus understandable sensitivity about what might happen to the pockets of UNPROFOR troops in these areas should the VRS retaliate, lessened that credibility. The possibilities presented by these developments and their limitations were demonstrated at Sarajevo and Goražde in the first half of 1994.

Sarajevo, Goražde and Bihać: the Uses and Limits of Force

The opportunities opened up by this situation for combining high-level diplomacy, ground-level negotiation and the threat of a limited use of air power in a 'muscular' approach were demonstrated in early 1994 at Sarajevo following the arrival of Lieutenant-General Sir Michael Rose as officer commanding Bosnia Command.[44] It was evident in those early months in 1994, when some of NATO's coercive aerial capability was formally available to support UNPROFOR and international diplomacy, a meaningful air role depended on ground support. This support was necessary to identify targets or occupy positions from which the Bosnian Serbs had withdrawn or been forced out. There was an unavoidable need for military personnel on the ground to underpin diplomatic initiatives, particularly those which emerged from limited use of coercion (or the threat of it), but which could not be upheld without adequate follow-through on the ground.

Rose appears to have taken with him to the Bosnia Command clear ideas about what could be achieved through a robust approach — also at the local level. He seems also to have included the idea that there were also possibilities where well-trained professional soldiers were involved (able to co-ordinate effectively with pilots flying Close Air Support, or aerial defence of a 'safe area'). Such carefully husbanded use of air power in conjunction with troops meant that where a robust approach might strain the purely impartial character of a peace support operation, it would ultimately strengthen the operation by adding to its credibility. Indeed, it was important to distinguish between pure impartiality and non-partisanship, as well as between what might be

44 For a profile of General Rose and his initial impact on the situation in Bosnia, see Anthony Loyd, 'Universal Soldier', *The Times Magazine*, 23 April 1994.

termed emotional and technical impartiality.[45] The major consideration, however, was to ensure that suitable troops were available to capitalise on the localised gains of coercive diplomacy. However, there was hesitation in making such troops available in sufficient numbers.

There was a substantial debate in this context between the US on one side and Canada and the major European contributors on the other. The Americans were criticised for reluctance to engage seriously in the international effort, while making rhetorical policy statements which frustrated the efforts of UNPROFOR, ICFY, the UN and the Europeans. The US was inverting the dictum 'speak softly, but carry a big stick': there was much noise, but little action. The consequence of this was usually to blunt key diplomatic initiatives.

While the Europeans saw the US as doing anything to avoid having taking real responsibility, the US suspected European projects of being entrapment exercises. President Clinton clearly expressed this American fear at the time of the NATO summit in January 1994. For their part, the French at the same time made clear their desire to secure wholehearted US engagemen.

In this context the events surrounding the Sarajevo market square massacre on 5 February 1994, reportedly killing 68 people,[46] require some elucidation at various levels. This took place against the background of the new, confident and robust approach brought to the work of UNPROFOR Command by General Rose. In the words of one senior British official involved with the Bosnia operation, Rose 'threw double sixes' at Sarajevo — meaning that everything went not only right for the General but better than he could have hoped for, and more was achieved faster than expected.[47] He had been conducting talks within the Sarajevo Mixed Military Working Group on the demilitarisation of Sarajevo, and on the day the mortar shell landed in

45 By this I mean that senior military figures could not be blind to the physical realities of their environment, but could function on a different level technically, keeping from the parties any expression of their real feelings for the sake of pursuing an end to hostilities. This relates also to the distinction between being non-partisan — that is, not taking sides within a conflict — and being impartial in the perverse sense that impartiality may mean partiality to the international peace-making mission in which the force is engaged.

46 It may have been the case that not all those evacuated and treated as alleged victims of the attack in fact were so. A number of those being flown out of Sarajevo for treatment, however, were judged by those dealing with them to have old wounds.

47 Private discussion with the author.

the market square, he was meeting the various local military commanders to discuss the detail of a ceasefire package for the city.

The international response to the market square incident was uncharacteristically swift and strong. France called for a threat to use air power against the besiegers of Sarajevo which the US could not ignore.[48] There was hectic activity both in the Bosnian theatre and in the international arena, and on 10 February, following a request from Boutros-Ghali three days earlier, NATO issued an ultimatum to the Bosnian Serbs: they were given a ten-day deadline to withdraw their heavy weaponry from what would become a 20-kilometre radius heavy weapons exclusion zone around Sarajevo, or place it under UNPROFOR control — otherwise they would be destroyed by air strikes. Formally, Bosnian government heavy weapons would be subject to the same conditions.

It is important to note that while all this was happening in the diplomatic and coercive ionosphere, on the ground Rose was urgently capitalising on the commotion in the international environment to forge an agreement on the demilitarisation of Sarajevo. Already by 6 February he had agreement in principle on a ceasefire from the Bosnian Serbs, although the Bosnian President Izetbegović was insisting on a withdrawal of VRS heavy weaponry. By 9 February, Rose was overseeing the signing of a ceasefire agreement at Sarajevo airport. The following day, the NATO ultimatum was added to the brew.

At first it clearly made the Bosnian Serbs defensive. The VRS Chief of Staff General Milovanović insisted that the agreement on heavy weapons withdrawal was only 'oral', while by 15 February the VRS Commander General Mladić defiantly proclaimed that his army's heavy weaponry would never be withdrawn. Mladić was undoubtedly emboldened in this by the outright refusal of the Russian battalion commander in UNPROFOR Sector East in Croatia to redeploy to Sarajevo, as ordered by the UNPROFOR commander General Cot, unless ordered to so by Moscow. In addition, Russian special envoy Vitaly Churkin made it clear that neither he nor the Russian Federation was content with the ultimatum, suggesting that it might disturb the

---

48 Mariano Aguirre and Pedro Saez, 'Bosnia: después del ultimátum', Centro de Investigación para la Paz, *Papeles: Cuestiones internacionales de paz, ecologia y desarrollo*, No.50, CIP, Madrid, 1994, p.64.

careful balance achieved in the international approach to the Bosnian conflict.

In the end the Russians were able to contribute in a highly successful way to the resolution of the Sarajevo entanglement. The 800- strong Russian battalion quickly redeployed to Sarajevo in the days after 17 February. Although this was promoted as a diplomatic coup by both Russia and the West,it was in reality little more than agreement to implement the deal made by UNPROFOR under the threat of NATO air strikes. What was taken by many in the West to confirm a new anti-Western assertiveness could just as easily have been interpreted as successful teamwork.[49] Whatever the interpretation, the outcome was undisputed: as a result of the interaction of all concerned — Rose on the ground, UN, ICFY and Russian diplomats at the political level and NATO in the air — the bombardment of Sarajevo had been brought to an end (even if the Serbian blockade of the city would not be lifted immediately).

This incident showed that the coercive potential of air strikes could not be easily dismissed: the VRS had engaged actively in talks about an end to the bombardment even before NATO issued its ultimatum. The local accord on ceasefire and demilitarization of the Sarajevo averted air strikes. UNPROFOR and the continuing threat of air strikes ensured that, unlike on so many other occasions, the agreement made was followed through to implementation: in the past, the rule had been that promises would be forgotten as soon as external pressure was eased. Crucially, it was vital to occupy territory from which VRS heavy weapons had been removed and, most of all, to take charge of weapons being placed under the jurisdiction of UNPROFOR. This activity was inevitably manpower-intensive, and there was soon a call for an additional 3,000 soldiers to be deployed with UNPROFOR to make it possible for the Sarajevo agreement to work.

The momentum of the February events at Sarajevo, supplemented by NATO's shooting down of four Serbian aircraft violating the air exclusion zone (see above), gave an optimistic and emboldened aspect to the work of both UNPROFOR and the international diplomats

---

49 Of course, the non-visual, but largely co-operative, work of the russian special envoy Vitaly Churkin could not have such an obvious impact on perceptions as the TV and newspaper images of Russian troops arriving showing the thumb and two-fingered salute of the Serbian nationalists.

(especially as US diplomatic engagement had proved successful in curtailing the Muslim-Croat conflict in Bosnia in this period[50]). As an intense Serbian attack began rapidly overruning the UN-designated 'safe area' at Goražde, international actors engaged with greater confidence and buoyancy than usual. However, the events at Goražde were to lead to further lessons in the Bosnian school of peace support activity.

To begin with, the importance of troops on the ground was clear. Whereas UNPROFOR had been seeking a further 7-8,000 troops, the US decided, almost as the Security Council was due to vote allocation for them (in what could be seen again as an act of sabotage of UN efforts in former Yugoslavia) not to approve this number and reluctantly agree soon after to new budget allocations for 3,000. Although it can only be a matter of speculation, it is hard to avoid the conclusion that if General Rose had had even some of these supplementary 3,000 troops available to deploy to Goražde in time, that entire episode would have been strikingly different.

As it was, NATO carried out in support of UNPROFOR carried out the first real-world air-to-surface strikes in its history. In their detail and their broad effect these were ineffectual. They could also be regarded by the VRS as acts of provocation. The crucial problem was co-ordination between different levels in UNPROFOR and the UN and between the UN and NATO. The key questions were not operational but political. General Rose had called in air strikes on two occasions with mixed results, and now a heavy onslaught led to his making urgent further requests for authorization of Close Air Support action.

Seemingly nervous about the UN's position, the Secretary-General's Special Representative Yasushi Akashi refused permission, giving priority to limiting the scope of UN involvement in a hazardous, vexing and under-resourced operation. After the first two rounds of micro-targeted air strikes had halted the Serbian advance, but also after seeing a British Harrier jet brought down by the VRS, Akashi appears to have got cold feet as attacks striking into the 'safe areas' were renewed. Rose called for air strikes as information arrived that his troops had taken casualties. Although abysmal conditions made the use of air support critically difficult, at least as great a restriction was presented by Akashi. At that time at the headquarters of the Bosnian Serb leader Radovan Karadžić, he was reported to have offered Rose a

---

50 Aguirre and Saez, 'Bosnia: después del ultimátum', pp.66-7.

feeble response: 'How about Dr. Karadžić ordering an immediate ceasefire, allowing immediate evacuation of our people?'[51] Rose reacted strongly to this abdication of responsibility:'By the time the message gets to the units on the ground they will all be either dead or captured.'[52] No authorisation was given, in addition to which the aircraft overhead faced extensive visibility problems identifying targets on the ground. The outcome was that out of thirteen UN Military Observers rapidly deployed to Goražde, one soldier from General Rose's own regiment in the British Army was killed by directly targeted VRS fire and another wounded.

Rose was unable to respond immediately and strongly due to UN diplomatic dissipation.[53] He had to reassess his approach — although a NATO ultimatum threatening air strikes unless there were a ceasefire and VRS withdrawal from the centre of Goražde had resulted in a ceasefire and agreement to withdraw 3 kilometres. Late in the day, the NATO ultimatum to the VRS, threatening extensive action if it did not desist, had brought the Serb assault to an end which later stabilised conditions in the area. This had resulted in the local ending of hostilities, a Serbian withdrawal (albeit partial and very limited) and considerably better circumstances for the inhabitants of Goražde. Rose himself, on leaving his post in January 1995, was able to claim that events at Goražde had not been as they seemed to many outside.[54] This was not, however, a success to compare with Sarajevo. A small last-minute tactical success, it was a major strategic failure: it undercut the role that air power might play in the future.

Following the political uncertainty which accompanied the Goražde crisis, Rose changed the tone of his public statements, saying that he did not believe UNPROFOR was 'in the business of going to war in order to bring about conditions of peace'.[55] While he had never believed otherwise, making a statement of this kind was principally a way of indicating that he would be less likely in the future to take the robust approach adopted at Sarajevo and initially at Goražde. Goražde was probably the first military defeat Rose had experienced in his

51 Quoted in Anthony Loyd, 'Universal Soldier'.
52 Quoted in Loyd, 'Universal Soldier'.
53 Loyd, 'Universal Soldier'.
54 'Panorama', BBC TV, 23 January 1995.
55 Quoted in Loyd, 'Universal Soldier'.

distinguished career and was essentially a result of circumstance, UN inadequacy and betrayal of the General, of UNPROFOR and of the approach adopted early in 1994.

Moreover, if Rose had not had the loyalty of the UN diplomatic cadre, and one of his troops had died as the result, he was not going to allow a similar betrayal again. Like any good military commander, his loyalty was with his troops: if the UN could not be relied on to back him and the force in critical moments, then for the sake of the soldiers' morale and credibility it was simply better not to move to a use of force if the outcome might be, as at Goražde, the sacrifice of a good individual for nothing as the UN representatives vacillated. Without unequivocal political support, it was too dangerous to embark on this path: it was now a matter of 'no support, no action'. As a result the hero of Sarajevo in February, known affectionately as 'General Guns'n'Roses' by the Sarajevans, was unfairly to become vilified as a traditional UN 'pacifier and appeaser' by critics of UNPROFOR, particularly among the Bosnian leadership and in Washington.

General Rose's decision to act cautiously did not imply a view that selective use of air power for coercive purposes in conjunction with forces on the ground had no value, only that approptiate conditions and strong political will were required to back those on the ground.[56] The prospects for deploying air power in roles which blended both defence of a ground contingent or a 'safe area' with coercive purpose had been demonstrated. So had the boundaries of such action.

These were further confirmed at the end of 1994, as was the extent of the strategic failure at Goražde, with regard to Bihać. Bihać was a Muslim-dominated pocket of territory, on the border with Croatia, surrounded by Croatian Serb-controlled land across the frontier and Bosnia Serb-controlled territory within Bosnia. At Bihać, the Bosnian Army V Corps had launched an attack from within the designated 'safe area' which met with a powerful counter-offensive from the Bosnian Serbs, strongly supported by the Croatian Serbs striking from across the border. The combined VRS-Croatian Serb counter-offensive was crushing and the 'safe area' at Bihać was heavily bombarded and penetrated by Serb forces. UNPROFOR and NATO were unable to prevent the Serbs overrunning large parts of the 'safe area'.When

56 See Lawrence Freedman, 'Why the West Failed', *Foreign Policy*, No.97, Winter 1994-95.

UNPROFOR, supplemented by NATO Close Air Support and by air strikes, tried to deal with this situation, it was unable to deal with the strong Serbian pressure on Bihać.

As at Goražde, hiccups in the UN system, political hesitancy and, even more than in previous cases, the Bosnian Serb tactical response of taking UN personnel hostage (proving that they had the capacity to hurt the UN more and more easily than it could hurt them) caused problems. In addition the use of the Krajina Serbs both to assist the Bosnian Serbs and to complicate the situation, caused problems.[57] A further complication, from the point of view of the UN and the UNPROFOR commander, was that the immediate bout of hostilities had been launched by the Bosnian Army 5th Corps from within the 'safe area'.

As the UN and NATO tried to respond effectively, they were hampered by two critical factors — both of which had played a lesser part at Goražde in the spring. The first of these was variable weather which, though good for the time of the year and therefore helpful to the VRS, still presented obstacles to NATO pilots trying to identify specific targets for action. More important, the Bosnian Serbs had learned from experience the deterrent effect of taking UN personnel hostage. By effectively taking hostage large numbers of vulnerable UN personnel, the VRS innoculated itself against aerial action: it could hurt the international community in this way more than it judged it could itself be harmed through air attacks.

There was, however, a further variable. This was the Bosnian Serb use of assistance from their Croatian kin and, to a lesser extent, from anti-government Muslims in the area under the leadership of Fikret Abdić (whose self-proclaimed 'Autonomous Province of Western Bosnia' had been defeated by the Bosnian Army 5th Corps in August and whose forces had fled into Serb-held territory in Croatia, where some of them were effectively trapped, denied entry onto Croatian-controlled territory). Thus the VRS was able to respond to strong threats from the international community by allowing its partners to prosecute

---

57 The possibilities for using Close Air Support and air strikes creatively remained, but the severe limitations on them, certainly in the Bosnian context, were made clear in a report on UNPROFOR's mandate by the UN Secretary-General following the events at Bihać, which also reviewed the earlier events. ('Secretary-General's Report', UN Doc. S/1994/1389, 1 December 1994.

the campaign, even after it had concluded a cessation of hostilities agreement with the Bosnian army on the last day of 1994.

The involvement of the Krajina Serbs from Croatia was a particular problem for the UN and NATO as the Bihać area bordered on Serb-held territory in Croatia, but the 'safe areas' resolutions did not extend the scope for protective action to be taken outside Bosnia. In response the Security Council passed Resolution 958 on 19 November, in which the authorisation to use air power in and around the 'safe areas', originally given in Resolution 836, was extended to cover parts of the Republic of Croatia. Consequently, on 21 November the Udbina airbase, from which the Krajina Serbs had launched a number of air raids on the Bihać pocket, was subjected to a comprehensive NATO air strike. Although, following this action, the Krajina Serbs made an agreement, in Belgrade on 23 November not to engage further in Bosnia, in practice their involvement continued.[58]

The outcome of the Bihać incident was chastening. Whereas deterrents, strong ultimatums and limited action had helped to bring about a positive outcome at Sarajevo and played a mixed role at Goražde, in Bihać the threat and indeed the use of air power had prevented neither the VRS from entering the 'safe area' nor the Krajina Serbs from engaging in action against Bihać. This led to the conclusion that 'the extreme and unavoidable vulnerability of UNPROFOR troops to being taken hostage and to other forms of harassment, coupled with the political constraints on wider air action, greatly reduce the extent to which the threat of air power can deter a detrmined combatant.'[59] Thus the force configuration in UNPROFOR and an exponentially linked lack of political will for more extensive action which would effectively create pockets of enforcement action presented practical and political impediments to credible action.

Without a clear, efficient and rapid decision-taking chain, backed by political commitment to the operation and to the approach adopted, the force on the ground might easily find itself in difficulty. The credible threat of a use of force, on which a muscular peace support operation might sometimes depend, could be found wanting. An important feature here, absent in UNPROFOR but present in more normal military operations, would be preparedness to allow the theatre commander

---

58 See Secretary-General's Report, UN Doc. S/1994/1389, 1 December 1994.
59 Secretary-General's Report, UN Doc. S/1994/1389.

automatic authority to call in air power. To a limited extent there were efforts in UNPROFOR to make an arrangement of this kind, but nothing which would give a commanding officer confidence to embark on a course of action involving air strikes. Without clear support for and confidence in the theatre commander, a peace support operation such as UNPROFOR in Bosnia would be unable unlikely to function as successfully as it might.

The problems of Yugoslavia, particularly Bosnia, expanded the demands being made on the UN both practically and conceptually. The mixture of political, humanitarian and operational problems in Bosnia gradually led to a more coercive disposition there. While UNPF could probably regard itself as having done a relatively successful job in Croatia — in its own terms and in terms of its formal mandate — and implemented a unique preventive operation with US personnel in Blue Berets in FYROM Command, it was Bosnia which caught the attention both for its success and for its failure.

While the failings of BH Command could generally be ascribed to weak political support and stretched resources, its limited successes were achieved by credible threats to use force and by establishing support with all the parties — particularly through the work of liaison officers and to a considerable extent through the activity of individuals. UNPROFOR's most famous successes, such as those of Generals Morillon and Rose in Bosnia, came when the challenges were met promptly with confident improvisation and innovation, as well as preparedness to use force. Those occasions however, were always hampered by both political hesitation and a lack of follow-through, as well as other difficulties.

Often the initiative appeared to be with those on the ground and in a position to work on developing local ceasefires and to seize opportunities to make situations better where possible, but also relying on credible coercive back-up. However, there was little prospect of decision-taking authority being vested in the force commander. Events on the ground shaped international diplomatic activity much of the time. Supposedly only instruments of their international political masters, UNPROFOR's troops were carrying the initiative in attempting to create conditions for a settlement.

UNPROFOR represented an innovative and interesting attempt to square the circle of using armed forces without resorting generally to the use of armed force in combat to tackle the real problem in Bosnia: the Serbian military machine. The use of armed forces as an instrument of international policy to settle a dispute, with the restricted introduction of enforcement or coercive measures, had potential — as was shown in Bosnia. But that potential was predicated not only on the (undoubted) sophistication and competence of the military personnel involved, but also on the political commitment and resolve of those conducting, guiding or underpinning policy. There was certainly place for a peace support operation like UNPROFOR as an instrument of diplomatic policy involving aspects of coercion. But, as the strategic failure at Goražde revealed, the orchestration of that activity — particularly at the strategic level — had to be coherent, confident and communicated. Crucially, the same conditions for the successful operation of UNPROFOR — political commitment and coherence, particulary with regard to the use of force, were also the prerequisites for successful diplomatic initiatives. As will be seen in Chapters 9 and 10, this was critical in the success or failure of peace plans. As has been suggested throughout, however, these qualities were lacking as key governments at different times brought contrasting perspectives and policy positions to bear on the dissolution of Yugoslavia and its war, as will be shown in the following chapters.

7

THE MAJOR PLAYERS:
PARIS, BONN, LONDON

The international response to the Yugoslav War of Dissolution was manifest largely through multilateral organisations, such as the EU, the CSCE, the UN, the WEU and NATO. However, each of these bodies, while having some independent character, was essentially subject to the will of its member states, or at least of the most powerful and influential ones. All the major countries involved in the diplomatic handling of the crisis broadly adhered to a common approach for much of the time. Essentially that common approach combined reluctance to engage ground troops in combat roles, desire to contain and alleviate the impact of the conflict, and the aspiration to work multilaterally.[1]

However, within that broad shared framework there were strikingly different attitudes and views on certain crucial issues. These occasioned bitter disputes at certain points. The two major differences which emerged were between Germany and other Member States of the EC in late 1991 and, most divisively and persistently, between the US on the one hand and the Europeans and the Russians on the other, more or less from the beginning of 1993 onwards. The importance of these countries in the international diplomacy of the Yugoslav war, their differing perspectives and the need to harmonise policy between them resulted in the creation of a 'Contact Group' in early 1994.

1 The following chapter is based not only on the sources indicated, but also on numerous discussions with officials and others from the various countries and international bodies involved in the international diplomacy over the Yugoslav war. The text is suffused with an understanding derived from those discussions and benefits greatly, although unfortunately attributable credit cannot be given.

The Contact Group's original composition was seemingly accidental. Whereas the US and the Russian Federation (as a result of 'joint' initiatives at the beginning of 1994) were the core of the Contact Group, the UK, France and Germany came to be members in representative functions for ICFY, the UN and the EU. However, once Germany ceased to hold the Presidency of the EU, it continued to be a part of the Contact Group, remaining the EU representative. This confirmed that the countries themselves were the substantive members. The Contact Group was established because of the differences which had been revealed in the international community and which the parties to the conflict in the former Yugoslavia had attempted to exploit.[2] However, even within the Contact Group, there were to be divisions, as will be seen.

It is essential to any understanding of the international commitment in the former Yugoslavia to take account of the particular perspectives of the major actors. The purpose of the following two chapters is to make a comparative analysis of perspectives and politics in the five major capitals of the countries which formed the Contact Group — both because they were members of the Contact Group, but also because they were the most prominent and influential states behind the activity of the various international bodies. In each case, the emphasis will be less on comprehensively detailed accounts and more on capturing the important aspects of each country's approach. This chapter treats the policies and perspectives adopted by the former superpowers in the Cold War. For a variety of reasons, these two great powers only took more active parts once the Yugoslav War of Dissolution had become embedded as a critical test of international diplomacy — with Europeans having taken the initial challenge. In the present chapter attention focuses on the three EU members of the Contact Group — all of which, for all their sometimes obvious differences of opinion which deepened as the crisis lengthened, were generally united against the Americans. It considers first each country's perspective on the conflict, and then the way in which partly discrepant analysis begot radically divergent approaches to policy, especially at key moments and on major

2 The ICFY Steering Group Co-Chairmen, Lord Owen and Thorvald Stoltenberg, had been urging the formation of a group which could both co-ordinate policy between the major players and give them a more direct role in dealing with the various Yugoslav leaderships.

issues — such as recognition of the independence of those Yugoslav republics seeking it, the Vance-Owen Plan and particular aspects of the use of force.

All the three major international players studied here were undergoing a transformation of their relationships with each other and especially with the US. All of them also differed on aspects of policy. Perhaps the most critical difference, however, was the analysis of the conflict. As a multi-dimensional complex of problems, the Yugoslav War of Dissolution had, first of all to be interpreted. While no country had an absolute characterisation of the conflict and each was inevitably aware of the intricacies of the crisis, there were clear distinctions in the way they interpreted the crisis.

Paris and the Diplomacy of Difference: Cartesian Flexibility

Among the Europeans France probably had the most erratic approach to the problems of the Yugoslav war of dissolution, at least viewed superficially. In the course of the international involvement in the crisis, the French position moved from an étatiste-cum-Bonapartist attachment to the Yugoslav state and the Serbian cause at the outset, through various fluctuations, to being the principal advocate of air strikes against the Bosnian Serbs around Sarajevo in early 1994. In this sense the French understanding of the crisis moved considerably. However, as will be seen, the underlying trends remained constant. In true Cartesian style France had established principles and objectives and its interpretation of the events in Yugoslavia depended not so much on the events themselves as on whether they coincided with various French principles and objectives.

Foremost among these, apart from 'humanitarianism', was to promote France actively (as with the UK, as well) through various international bodies. For France the two most important ones were the UN and the WEU. Its initial enthusiasm for military intervention in support of the Belgrade authorities was motivated by a traditional French desire to give life to the WEU as opposed to NATO, thereby diminishing American influence. Thus the use of the WEU was what was important, not the purpose for which it might be used. Of course, the WEU had no military structures to be used, leading France increasingly to accept a compromise in which the WEU could be developed as the European pillar within NATO as US commitment was reduced. This comes as a result of the experience in Bosnia where France has recognised the great practical value of working with NATO structures and procedures.[3]

Among the various principles guiding French policy, the most significant was probably that 'difference'.[4] A priority continued to be asserting itself on the international stage. For a clearly medium-sized power which could no longer act unilaterally in most instances, the main opportunity to play a role on the international stage was through international bodies. From this point of view, membership of the EU, the WEU, NATO and the UN Security Council as a Permanent Member was vital to France. However, if this was necessary, it was also desirable to retain individual identity in order to maximise influence: being different meant that others in the same international bodies had to accommodate France, ensuring that French status and influence was not diminished.

France, particularly in its early analysis, understood the break-up of Yugoslavia in Bonapartist, state-centric terms. (Apart from anything else, acceptance of the dissolution of Yugoslavia was felt to have implications for France over Corsica.) The main issue was, therefore, the maintenance of the Yugoslav state — a perspective which led it, effectively, to support the Serbian side in the summer and autumn of 1991. This became an express attempt to counter what was seen increasingly as German support for Slovenia and Croatia, as well as to coerce Serbia. As it had done *vis à vis* Iraq for a period in the Gulf Conflict, Paris attempted to offer itself as Belgrade's old friend in the West in the hope that by keeping open a positive diplomatic channel there would be opportunity to influence the Serbs.[5] This approach was downgraded as the conflict continued and Belgrade's culpability in it

3 See Gow, 'The Policy Making Aspects of Peace-keeping, Intervention and Humanitarian Aid', Report of the Franco-British Council Meeting, London, 11 February 1994, the Franco-British Council, London, 1994; Jolyon Howorth, 'The Debate in France over Military Intervention in Europe' in Lawrence Freedman, ed., *Military Intervention in European Conflicts*, Blackwell for the *Political Quarterly*, Oxford, 1994, p.123.) The considerable French commitment in Bosnia was only one example of a general disposition to support UN activity around the globe. (See Phillipe Guillot, 'France, Peacekeeping and Humanitarian Intervention', *International Peacekeeping*, Vol.1, No.1, Spring 1994, p.30.
4 See, for example, Jean-François Deniau, 'Le Rang de la France', *Le Monde*, 7 September 1994.
5 Pia Christina Wood, 'France and the Post-Cold War Order: The Case of Yugoslavia', *European Security*, Vol.3, No.1, Spring 1994, p.132.

(whether the Serbian leadership, or the degenerate federal military) emerged more clearly.

By the end of 1991 France's understanding of the conflict had shifted and it could no longer sustain support for a unified Yugoslavia. Gradually, its position evolved into one which, on humanitarian, security and UN credibility grounds favoured the use of force against the Serbian camp — albeit in very restricted circumstances. France continued to regard the situation as enormously complex and to be treated only with great caution. However, its perception of the conflict gradually adjusted as events on the ground made clear where primary responsibility for the conflict lay. Nonetheless both for the sake of maintaining its international profile and in the cause of making diplomatic progress towards a settlement, France tried on a number of occasions to make a diplomatic opening to Serbia — for example, the joint initiative with Germany in the autumn of 1993 to offer the possibility (which many thought questionable) of a progressive easing of sanctions on Belgrade in return for co-operation in Belgrade to end the conflict.[6]

Initially, along with Spain, Greece and the UK, France had strenuously resisted an early move towards recognition of the independence of those Yugoslav republics seeking it. However, whereas the UK was initially against accepting their independence, it relatively quickly adjusted its stance to embrace the possibility of eventual recognition. France, by contrast, strongly resisted moves towards recognition as a matter of both principle and political propensity.

In typically Cartesian style, France was guided by the principle of preserving a centralised state. Thus in August 1991, at a time when various other members of the EC were moving at varying speeds towards accepting that Slovenia, Croatia and possibly other Yugoslav republics would become independent, in France there were arguments for an armed intervention by the WEU (of course a wholly unreal prospect) to help restore the Yugoslav state.[7] Although President François Mitterrand had signalled a theoretical preparedness to accept the possibility of independence for the Yugoslav republic, in very legalistic terms, it was stressed that this could only be acceptable within

6 See the article by French Foreign Minster Alain Juppé in *Libération*, Paris, 25 November 1993.
7 See Howorth, 'The Debate in France, p.116.

the framework of an international agreement where all issues had been settled in accordance with international law — as was intended to happen at the EC Conference on Yugoslavia chaired by Lord Carrington.[8]

There was, however, another important factor driving French policy to deny recognition and, after a common decision on eventual recognition was conceded in early October 1991, to slow down any recognition process. This was the desire, within the context of CFSP, to prevent German domination of the EC. Like the UK at the end of 1991, France was insisting that there were no differences on the principle of recognition, but only on the importance, for the sake of the coming CFSP conference, in ensuring that it was a common act, achieved in an orderly framework.

Another strand of French policy on CFSP was the elaboration of a European Defence Identity. For many years France had sought every possible opportunity to promote the Western European Union as the potential defence arm of the EC. In doing so it was attempting to create an alternative European structure for military co-operation to NATO — which it saw as primarily an instrument of an unreliable US policy.[9] In addition, it had taken an important role in creating a structure — the Eurocorps — which would begin to make possible the use of German troops outside a NATO context. The Eurocorps, originally formed only with German and French troops, was intended by the French as a further element in the construction of a European defence capability. Against this background, France advanced the notion of a WEU force being deployed in Croatia in the autumn of 1991. It was keen to form and send a force, but it was only prepared to do this in accord with other European countries, when a ceasefire was holding on the ground and the conditions for peace-keeping existed. France was eager to see such a force formed by the WEU as the seed for the creation and

---

8 Pia Christina Wood, 'France and the Post-Cold War Order: the Case of Yugoslavia', *European Security*, Vol.3, No.1, Spring 1994, p.134.
9 The French distrust of the US was due largely to the opposition of the US the joint French, UK and Israeli military operations against Egypt over the Suez Canal in 1956. The US effectively forced an end to the operation. The lack of American support was a catalyst for the French decision to possess an independent nuclear capability — the logic being that if the US could not be relied on to support its allies at Suez, there could hardly be confidence that it would really extend its nuclear umbrella to European countries if there were a Soviet attack on Europe.

elaboration of a 'European' defence force and hence a European defence policy. The British had been designated head of NATO's Rapid Reaction Force and it was suggested that this could be given authority by the WEU to act on its behalf. But at that stage this force, despite initial exercises, was still largely conceptual. The composition and logistics of any WEU force would either have to be worked out from scratch or borrowed informally from NATO.

Behind the scenes France had been drafting plans for an intervention in Croatia. This was how General Philippe Morillon had been engaged, as head of planning, until his appointment as deputy commander of UNPROFOR in the spring of 1992.[10] The intervention foreseen by the French at that stage would have been geared towards ending hostilities[11] within the framework of maintaining the integrity of the Yugoslav federation. As the conflict in Croatia developed, French insistence on restoring the federation and arguments for intervention faded in face of evident realities — although, when 'ethnic cleansing' emerged in Bosnia, there was again a strong desire in French popular and political opinion for intervention.[12] Planning for intervention, in the meantime, fed into support for a WEU peacekeeping force.[13]

By the end of 1991, France had accepted the break-up of Yugoslavia and gradually began to move away from an essentially pro-Serbian stance until eventually it was making what was probably the most genuine and clear-cut commitment to use force against the Serbian camp.[14] This shift can be attributed to four factors — here placed in

10 Général Philippe Morillon, *Croire et Oser — Chronique de Sarajevo*, Grasset, Paris, 1993, p.11.

11 This was confirmed by a very senior French officer in private discussion with the author.

12 Howorth, 'The Debate in France', p.111-12.

13 Wood, 'France', p.132.

14 This engagement may be judged more genuine and real on the grounds that France had already demonstrated its commitment through the deployment of 6,700 troops on the ground whose security could not be taken lightly, unlike US calls which appeared to contain considerable rhetoric and could certainly be made without responsibility for the safety of US military personnel. The genuineness of American clarion calls for aerial strikes was brought into question at the NATO summit on 10-11 January 1994 when the US appeared to have judged a French proposal for the co-ordinated use of air power around Sarajevo as a 'trap', preferring to concentrate on the Alliance's 'Partnership for Peace' proposal. (Wood, 'France', 148; *The Independent*, 27 January 1994. In fact, events were turned in the direction proposed by the French at the beginning of February when

reverse order of impact. First, the change of government in Paris and, in particular, the replacement of the 'pro-Serbian' Roland Dumas as foreign minister by the far more robust Alain Juppé,[15] made a big difference. Juppé and his colleagues had far fewer problems with the idea of moving closer to the formal military structures in NATO for practical reasons (while maintaining an emphasis on European and UN structures), as well as accepting military judgements that there were times and ways for the UN troops in Bosnia to use greater force.[16]

An important part in this shift was played by the French military, in particular by General Morillon, who had served with UNPROFOR as officer commanding Bosnia and Hercegovina. Although Morillon had been strongly opposed to any use of force in the early stages of his command, he had become convinced by the time he left of the need to use it in certain circumstances.[17] Morillon's assessment had a notable impact on the French government.

The third element in France's shift was ever greater familiarity with the situation on the ground and, in particular, with the limitations imposed by a lack of will to deal robustly with those responsible for the destruction in Bosnia — that is, France clearly recognised the Serbian camp's overwhelming responsibility for what was happening. Finally, the humanitarian nightmare in Bosnia was a major consideration. It was not possible to understand French activism in the international arena without being conscious of the enormous concern and pressure in France for 'humanitarian intervention'.[18] This characteristic of French thinking led Paris to propose, both in Bosnia and in other cases such as Rwanda, the creation of security zones to protect civilians faced with genocidal warfare. Taken together, these developments led to France favouring a stronger, more interventionary position.

French activism on the humanitarian aspects of the war in Bosnia, in particular, was a driving force for President Mitterrand's surprise visit to Sarajevo at the end of June 1992. As a result of his initiative, Sarajevo airport was opened to international aid, which effectively broke

a Serbian mortar shell landed in the Sarajevo market place.)

15 See Guillot, 'France, Peacekeeping'.

16 Alain Juppé, 'Address to the National Assembly, Paris, 12 April 1994', *Speeches and Statements*, SS/94/72, Embassy of France, London.

17 See Morillon, *Croire et Oser*.

18 Howorth, 'The Debate in France', pp.115-118.

the siege of the Bosnian capital for the first time. Mitterrand, leading the way on France's policy of difference, had been in the forefront of calls for a use of force to end the Serbian bombardment of Sarajevo, and taking the initiative to use France's posture of Serbian friendship to influence the Serbs and avoid a use of force.

These apparently contradictory positions can be explained by Paris's view of *le rang de la France* (France's international status) and the tactic for maintaining it — the policy of difference. This was supplemented by discrete approaches on forceful intervention, especially for humanitarian purposes, and on leaving channels open for pariahs. Thus, from the French point of view, the same policy could embrace the President of the Republic expressing his country's belief 'in the use of force, at least sufficient to guarantee the security of deliveries of humanitarian aid,' at the EC's Lisbon Summit,[19] and then using the Sarajevo visit to argue that his using the friendship card might offer greater possibilities of success than threatening the use of force.[20] It was probably true that the two had to go together to be effective.

Mitterrand's Sarajevo visit was a clear manifestation both of the policy of difference and of France's interventionist disposition in a further sense. While France had been urging armed intervention and had been prepared to take the initiative, the decision to go to the Bosnian capital was intended to show what was possible to the British, Germans and Americans, all of whom were refusing to consider action, arguing that the situation was too difficult. Mitterrand, travelling directly from the frustration of the Lisbon Summit, was determined on the basis of French military analysis, to demonstrate that enabling Sarajevo airport to be used by UNPROFOR, in line with UN Security Council Resolution 758 (8 June 1992), was feasible. Moreover, through his visit Mitterrand was able personally to obtain a commitment from Bosnian President Alija Izetbegović that Serb agreement to withdraw from around the airport would not be exploited by the Bosnian Army.[21]

By doing this, the French President could achieve a multi-layered success for the policy of difference. The less interventionist Europeans and the Americans had been shown what was possible; the airport was opened for aid and the siege breached — something which would

---

19 Quoted in Wood, 'France', p.138.
20 *Ibid.*, p.139.
21 Morillon, *Croire et Oser*, pp.93-4.

continue to be a source of French pride, as the 'French controlled airport' offered a lifeline through the 'dark days' of the winter of 1992-3;[22] and France had been able to avoid the need to use force — it had done this by offering, at one and the same time, its interventionist presence to the Bosnian authorities and its understanding and 'friendship' to the Serbs by making the Bosnian government agree not to exploit Serb withdrawal and the UN operation of the airport. However, a longer-term, more negative aspect would be that this initiative established a particular military involvement by the UN which, as it evolved, would inadvertently make stronger intervention of the kind advocated by Paris harder to accomplish (see Chapter 7).

The French interventionist disposition allowed it to be the axis of debates on the use of force. Where the Americans strongly favoured using air power against the Bosnian Serbs, and the British equally strongly opposed it, citing both the probable lack of utility and concern for their troops on the ground, the French, with a cautious but forceful approach and with troops on the ground, were decisive. This was a situation in which France promoted its self-interest through participation in a UN force, through its ability to influence discussion on the role of NATO, as well as the development of a European defence capability without the Americans, and finally through its role in determining whether or not force would be used in Bosnia.

Playing this role took France ever closer to full military re-integration into NATO.[23] In the course of UN military involvement in Bosnia, to which France was strongly committed, the UN established a working relationship with NATO (see Chapter 7). As this occurred, France — in order to maximise its influence, as well as for practical reasons — began to move back into the NATO military infrastructure, although some distance remained.[24] This also brought the French closer to the US than it had been since, at least, the 1960s.[25] In part this reflected the operational need for US support for the mission in Bosnia. It also represented an opportunity for unusual influence in Washington — which Paris used keenly to try to get the US to become more engaged

22 Tim Ripley, 'French Air Power in Bosnia', *Air Pictorial*, August 1994, p.353.
23 In 1966 France had partly withdrawn from NATO, refusing to participate in the integrated military command of the Alliance.
24 Gow, 'Policy Making Aspects'.
25 See Howorth, 'Debate in France', pp.121-22.

with its partners and allies in handling the conflict in the former Yugoslavia. This permitted France an important role in prompting co-ordination of international efforts through what became the 'Contact Group' in the spring of 1994, following UN diplomatic engagement.[26] Most of all, however, it meant recognition of the predominant role of the US in international security matters.

Therefore, although France and the UK had a considerable hold on the reins concerning the use of force, both were clearly subject to US pressure. When domestic pressures, particularly from Congress, began to place President Clinton in a position where he would have either to sacrifice his domestic reforms or succumb to demands for a use of air power and a lifting of the arms embargo, the Europeans, in spite of continuing grave concerns for their military personnel on the ground, acknowledged that there could be no interest in resisting an American President set on a particular course of action. Accordingly, in the late summer of 1994, they prepared to withdraw their troops from Bosnia.[27]

Although in the end this did not prove necessary because the US shifted course, it indicated that there were limits to France's ability to use its influence. The French approach to the dissolution of Yugoslavia had appeared contradictory, but had in fact been consistent, both in seeking an early end to hostilities and in improving France's position on the international stage. This latter aspect came through its diplomatic use of international bodies and, most of all, through the largest single commitment of military personnel to the international involvement in the former Yugoslavia. Above all else, the deployment of troops gave France credit with the US and the UK, for different reasons, and kept it a step ahead of Germany.

Bonn Backfiring: the Passion and Doubt of a Re-Emergent Giant

Germany had a radically different perspective from either France or the UK, particularly in the early stages of the crisis. It had been united in

---

26 Juppé, 'Address to the National Assembly'.
27 In the event, Clinton lost his health care reform bill for another year anyway, while the State Department and the NSC were judged, both at UNPROFOR HQ in Zagreb and in London, to have got 'cold feet' on their much vaunted proposals —·leaving French, UK and other troops with UNPROFOR in Bosnia through the winter of 1994-5.

1990, which revived the notion of self-determination in a European framework. As the Yugoslav state fell apart in 1991, Germany quickly changed from strong support for the Yugoslav state to support for those republics seeking independence — i.e. for what it regarded as self-determination.

The German Foreign Minister Hans-Dietrich Genscher argued strongly for the maintenance of the Yugoslav state throughout the developing months of crisis and in particular at the Berlin Summit of the CSCE only five days before fighting broke out in Slovenia and Croatia.[28] Popular opinion in Germany had already begun to swing heavily towards claims to independence by Slovenia and Croatia, with the Bavarian Christian Socialist Union (CSU), the ally of the ruling Christian Democratic Union of Chancellor Helmut Kohl, applying strong political pressure. CSU representatives accused Kohl of supporting 'the communists from Serbia' through the non-recognition of Slovenia and Croatia.[29] The growing political pressure in the country quickly pushed the Chancellor into assuring the 'troubled German public' on 2 July that he would press for the principle of self-determination which Germany itself had always sought.[30] Although Kohl was to balance this with a commitment to other CSCE principles such as territorial integrity, this was to be taken as the first 'direct support' for Slovenia and Croatia.[31]

For a country filled with the emotion of its own union at the end of the Cold War and celebrating the collapse of communism throughout eastern Europe, Slovenia and Croatia were understood as two more

28 On Bonn's early support for the Yugoslav state and, especially, Foreign Minster Genscher's support for Yugoslav Foreign Minster Budimir Lončar, see Nenad Ivanković, *Bonn: Druga Hrvatska Fronta*, Mladost, Zagreb, 1993, pp.13-24. For a surprisingly un-hysterical account of Bonn's shift from support for the Yugoslav state to promoting the cause of Slovenia and Croatia, see Milovan Radaković, 'Politički stavovi Savezne Republike Nemačke prema jugoslovenskoj krizi', *Vojno Delo*, Vol.XLIV, Nos 4-5, 1992. Radaković, writing in the leading Yugoslav military journal, recognised Germany's strong support of the Yugoslav federation before the conflict and the role played by domestic pressure in altering Bonn's course. The author then erroneously assessed that economic forces underpinning influential factors in German politics, such as the Bavarian CSU, had an interest, via the Alpe-Adria and (then) Hexagonale organisations, in the independence of Slovenia, Croatia and Bosnia.
29 Cited by Radaković, 'Politički stavovi', p.164.
30 Quoted, *ibid.*, p.165.
31 *Ibid.*

countries striving for self-determination and to throw off the communist yoke.[32] In this context the war was clearly seen neither as being to maintain the centralised state, which the French initially believed, nor as the ethnic struggle discerned by others. It was a war of aggression by communist-led Serbia and the JNA against the emerging democracies in Slovenia and Croatia. Thus for Germany the conflict was essentially a question of the right of Slovenia and Croatia to self-determination, spiced with outrage at the behaviour of the Yugoslav military and Serb forces in the conflict.

It was these strong domestic interpretations which guided German policy on the dissolution of Yugoslavia. Although the US had been keen to press Bonn into taking a more significant role on the international stage and to provide leadership in Europe as the US gradually withdrew from the leading role in matters of European security, this could not intself explain the German stance. Nor could the interpretation often offered by Germany's critics: hegemonistic ambitions in the region. Germany was fumbling its way towards a role in new circumstances, but because of its history was highly sensitive to the way in which other countries perceived it.[33] Far more persuasive explanations could be found in the emotional impact both of the idea of self-determination and

32 It is striking that the German embrace of Slovenia and Croatia under the umbrella of self-determination, fuelled as it was by a spirit of the rejection of communism, failed to notice that, as for the Germans, the idea of living all together in one state was important to the Serbs — and living together in one state is what the dissolution of Yugoslavia meant for the Serbs who were spread in large numbers in two republics outside Serbia — Croatia and Bosnia. This observation should not obscure the real nature of Serbian policy, as identified in Chapter 2. See James Gow, 'Serbian Nationalism and the Hissssing Ssssnake in the International Order: Whose Sovereignty? Which Nation?', *Slavonic and East European Review*, Vol.72, No.3, Summer 1994.

33 Marie-Janine Calic, 'The German Perspective on the War in the Former Yugoslavia', paper for international conference on the Yugoslav conflict, University of Keele, 19-20 September 1994; on German sensitivity to others' perceptions of them, of their country and of its historical character, see Security for Europe, *Final Report*, Center for Foreign Policy Development of the Thomas J. Watson Jr. Institute for International Studies, Brown University, Providence RI, December 1993; see also Harald Müller, 'Military Intervention for European Security: the German Debate', in Lawrence Freedman, ed., *Military Intervention in European Conflicts*, Blackwell for *The Political Quarterly*, Oxford, 1994, pp.139-40.

of images of violence;[34] strongly coloured press coverage, added to familiarity with the Croatian coastline where many Germans took their holidays;[35] the presence of a large Croatian émigré community among the 450,000 Yugoslavs in Germany (to which were added 324,000 refugees in the first months of the war); and the Bonn government's political problems in persuading its people that the country was not giving away more than it was gaining in the Maastricht Treaty on European Union — recognition of Croatia and Slovenia was thus important to limit criticism on Europe and was therefore a 'direct result of Kohl's surrender at Maastricht'.[36]

While the US opposed recognition of Slovenia and Croatia in the second half of 1991, it remained largely in the background on the issue. The foreground was held by the Europeans and above all by the Germans, who were making ever stronger moves in the direction of recognition within the EC collective framework and threatening to act unilaterally outside it. Following the 6 October European Council meeting, at which it was agreed that, if the Draft Convention in which Carrington would propose a re-arrangement of the Yugoslav republics giving independence to those seeking it, subject to conditions — were rejected by any of the republics, then it would be necessary for the EC to work towards a solution with those republics co-operating with Conference, in the light of their right to independence. This move was

---

34 The emotional content of the German response to events in Croatia and Bosnia was evident even in the language used by officials, as could be seen in written briefing material issued by the German Federal Foreign Office. While the content of the German analysis was not unreasonable, the tone in which it was sometimes expressed was not rounded in the usual manner of offical briefings. For example, although Belgrade's role could not be questioned, it was surprising to find a more journalistic than diplomatic characterisation of it: 'The Serbian leadership itself had done all that it could to undermine the state created by Tito by systematically unleashing Serbian nationalism since 1987' before its campaign of 'revenge and conquest'. ('Recognition of the Yugoslav Successor States', Federal Foreign Office, Bonn, 10 March 1993, reproduced by the Embassy of the Federal Republic of Germany, London, 16 July 1993.)

35 To some extent *Die Welt* columnist Carl Gustav Ströhm embodied both German journalistic and tourisic commitment to Croatia — having been there for the first time as a motor-cycling tourist to Tito's communist Yugoslavia in 1954, as he pointed out in a collection of his articles published in the Croatian daily *Večernji List*. See Carl Gustav Ströhm, *Što Sam Rekao Hrvatima*, Alfa, Zagreb, 1994, p.8.

36 Wolfgang Krieger, 'Toward a Gaullist Germany? Some Lessons from the Yugoslav Crisis', *World Policy Journal*, Spring 1994, quoted by Calic, 'German Perspective'.

re-inforced on 28 October, at which point the EC gave Serbia a one-week ultimatum on accepting the Hague document.[37]

Following Belgrade's rejection of the Carrington plan at the beginning of November, Germany, backed by a majority of EC Member States, began to move towards recognition of those republic's seeking independence — with the only question being that of timing: Germany, Denmark and Belgium favoured recognition before Christmas, as Chancellor Kohl informed a press conference in Bonn on 5 December, whereas other Member States were either undecided, or in favour of a slower approach.[38] These forceful initiatives by Germany stemmed from its interpretation of the conflict as an act of Serbian aggression against democratic, independence-seeking republics entitled to self-determination, as well as the analysis that only a strong move, such as recognition, would change the conditions of the conflict sufficiently to persuade the JNA to cease its operations in Croatia.[39]

Eventually the EC decided to invite applications for recognition from the Yugoslav republics for independence after the 16 December 1991 meeting of the European Council.[40] At that meeting, criteria for recognition were elaborated and it was stated that the EC would seek the advice of the Advisory Commission to its Conference on Yugoslavia, headed by the President of the French Constitutional Court Robert Badinter on the suitability for membership of those republics which made applications. This represented a common policy position among the EC Member States, following rough arguments behind the scenes in the previous months and reports of considerable trade-offs in the negotiations on the Maastricht treaty on European Union, which was signed on 10 December at the EC Summit.

However, this apparent harmony, encompassing a German diplomatic success, did not last. The Germans were under fierce domestic pressure

37 'Recognition of the Yugoslav Successor States'; see also, Ivanković, *Bonn*, pp.98-103.
38 See Henry Wyjnaendts, *L'Engrenage. Chroniques yougoslaves, juillet 1991-août 1992*, Denoël, Paris, 1993, p.129, and Ivanković, *Bonn*, pp.131-6 and 143-9.
39 An end to hostilities and agreement to withdraw had been achieved in Slovenia as early as 18 July 1991, while the war intensified in Croatia, lasting until the beginning of January 1992.
40 The European Council was the executive political body within the EU — the point at which the ministers in each policy area from the Twelve would come together to establish policy. In terms of CFSP, the relevant meetings were the monthly Foreign Affairs Councils and the half-yearly Summits of Heads of State and Government.

to act immediately on Slovenia and Croatia. The Bundestag had already voted unanimously to mandate the government to recognise the two independence-seeking republics before Christmas and popular opinion was running high. This pushed Chancellor Helmut Kohl to take further initiatives which could only cause additional hostility among the other EC members. Only one week after establishing a common EC policy, including the process of taking advice from the Badinter Commission and the priority of acting jointly Bonn announced on 23 December that it would recognise Slovenia and Croatia and establish diplomatic links on 15 January.[41] Although arguably this *de facto* recognition was arguably technically not breaking ranks with the other EC Member States because *de jure* recognition would not actually take place before the agreed date of 15 January,[42] it made a mockery of the mechanism of taking counsel from Badinter's Commission by taking its opinions and the reactions to them of other Member States for granted. Moreover, and more important, this move to temper domestic pressure destroyed any pretence of a common foreign policy.

All this came at a moment when Germany should have been able to claim acknowledgement for what had been accomplished. Events on the ground appeared to be proving the German analysis to be sound: recognition appeared to have ended the war in Croatia. Moreover, had it behaved otherwise, Bonn might have been able more easily to avoid blame for the war in Bosnia. Recognition of Slovenia and Croatia did not, as many have asserted, prompt the war in Bosnia — that had been coming since the previous August-September.[43]

However, the circumstances in which recognition came soured relations among the Western powers and cast the twin shadows of blame and shame on Bonn — even where this was not merited. Intra-European antagonism on the question of recognition became bitter when, seven days after agreing a common approach, Germany announced that it would recognise Slovenia and Croatia on 15 January — thus breaking ranks with the rest of the EC. Even though the Twelve

---

41 A German Foreign Ministry press statement had already indicated on 19 December that Bonn would enter into negotiations with the Yugoslav republics on diplomatic relations and that 'in the case of Slovenia and Croatia recognition will be formally declared as soon as the above [EC] conditions are met.' (Quoted in Ivanković, *Bonn*, p.150.)
42 *Ibid.*, p.148.
43 See Chapter 2.

had agreed after much argument on a common policy, CFSP was left critically damaged as Germany inflamed its fellow *communautaires* — it seemed that any prospect of CFSP being intensified for the 1996 Inter-Governmental Conference at which Maastricht would be reviewed was restricted by the friction over recognition. As a consequence of its panicked blunders, the Germans, clearly stung by the criticism engendered and by a sense of the fear they had generated in Europe, retreated into the background on security questions in general and on the Yugoslavia conflict in particular.

After the tension over recognition of Slovenia and Croatia, the main priority for Germany came to be re-harmonisation of its position in the EC and the strengthening of a common approach. The scope for Germany's policy initiatives was constrained by the reaction to its 'Croatia fever', as well as by the reality that, while it might judge a forceful approach to be the most appropriate, there were too many factors, including domestic inhibitions and external perceptions, which made this highly unlikely to become German policy.[44] German consolidation tallied with growing Franco-British co-operation on the former Yugoslavia.

As the conflict developed, Germany continued to play a strong role, but in a more demure fashion — even though throughout the conflict, it maintained the frame of analysis established in the first days of the conflict, namely support for the right to independence of the former Yugoslav republics and support for the republics themselves once independent (especially war-ravaged Bosnia).[45] Nonetheless, its views were adapted to circumstances and became more sensitive to some Serbian questions. Following Genscher's replacement as foreign minister by Klaus Kinkel in 1992, Bonn's perspective settled on a policy to contain the conflict in accord with other members of the international community.[46] Bonn committed itself fully to supporting international initiatives, whether with other countries, such as the US (on a proposal to lift the UN arms embargo in favour of the Bosnian government) and France (on the easing of sanctions against Serbia and Montenegro in return for co-operation from the Serbian President Slobodan Milošević in ending the war in Bosnia), or through

44 See Security for Europe, *Final Report*, pp.12-13 and 29-30.
45 See Calic, 'German Perspective'.
46 Calic, 'German Perspective'.

international bodies like the UN, the EU, ICFY and, significantly in terms of Germany's diplomatic evolution, the Contact Group. Membership of this body represented for Bonn a small step towards an equal and responsible role on the international security stage — one which would not count against the German Foreign Minsitry's long-term ambition to acquire a permanent seat on the UN Security Council.

Alongside this diplomatic growth, Germany was gradually shedding some of its constitutional, if not political and psychological, inhibitions over the deployment of its troops outside narrow NATO contexts.[47] Among other developments, this meant allowing its military personnel to fly with the NATO AWACS operations in support of UN Security Council resolutions on Bosnia, Croatia and sanctions. However, of the major Western states only Germany played no prominent part in the drama surrounding the use of force. This was due to Germany's domestic constraints on the one hand, and sensitivity to its external perceptions on the other. The domestic constraints included not only interpretations of the German Constitution, involving arguments that the deployment of German forces outside NATO was not permissible (a view eventually dismissed in the constitutional court), but also considerable inhibition over participation in any military activity, let alone armed intervention.[48]

Nonetheless, Germany made military contributions in four areas: to the NATO AWACS airborne monitoring and control flights in connection with 'Operation Deny-Flight' (patrolling and enforcement of the UN air exclusion zone over Bosnia), as indicated above; to the NATO-WEU joint sanctions monitoring fleet in the Adriatic; to the airborne delivery of humanitarian aid to Muslim enclaves, cut off and besieged in eastern Bosnia during 1993; and to the air element of the reaction force added to UNPROFOR in June 1995.[49] In addition, the

47 See Müller, 'Military Intervention', pp.128-37.
48 In late summer 1992, only 44 per cent of Germans supported the idea of Germans being used for *unarmed* peacekeeping and only 14 per cent supported the idea of German troops participating in a UN peace enforcement operation (Müller, 'Military Intervention', p.139).
49 This last contribution was the most radical. However, it was judged in both Bonn and Brussels that the value of specialist German Tornado aircraft equipped for air-defence suppression was such that there would be less sensitivity about deploying them for use in support of UNPROFOR and NATO than there would be in Germany and elsewhere if it emerged that lives were lost because these unique aircraft had not been allowed to

Bundeswehr staff conducted extensive planning for the deployment of troops in the former Yugoslavia — although it should be noted both that there was never any question of deploying German troops, and the German army's senior officers felt exactly the same doubts concerning military engagement in Bosnia as their counterparts in other Western countries.[50] There was never any question of German troops being deployed, not only because of popular disapproval but also because there was great sensitivity over the way in which Germany was perceived by its allies.

For Germany, despite the internal pressures and the policy perspective which had pushed the issue of recognition, the most important aspect of the Yugoslav war was its relationship with its partners and allies. Initially Yugoslavia had seemed like a great opportunity for the new Germany to lose some of its foreign policy inhibitions in the EU context, but in the end, after the discordant debate on recognition, the priority for Bonn became the need not to offend the sensibilities of others in the EU and NATO. This created conditions in which, unavoidably, it was forced to shed some of its military inhibitions.

London and Pusillanimous Realism

Britain played a central and major role in the international handling of the War of Dissolution in Yugoslavia.[51] That role was harshly criticised at different times and from different sources. Allegations were made that British policy was pro-Serbian,[52] that it was a policy of appeasement and indifference.[53] In the summer of 1993, the UK Prime Minister John Major was forced uncomfortably to depart from his

participate in missions.

50 Calic, 'German Perspective'.

51 For a more detailed and expanded version of the present analysis on UK policy, see James Gow, 'British Objectives, British Objections and the Yugoslav War of Dissolution', in Alex Danchev, ed., *International Perspectives on the Yugoslav Conflict*, Macmillan, London, 1996.

52 See *The Independent*, 8 September 1993.

53 See Jane M.O. Sharp, *Bankrupt in the Balkans: British Policy in Bosnia*, Institute for Public Policy Research, London, 1992, pp.19-20, where the recent record on Bosnia was judged to be 'comparable with Neville Chamberlain's appeasement of Hitler in the late 1930s'.

prepared text during an official visit to Malaysia after the Malaysian Prime Minister Mahathr had delivered an open and direct attack on British policy towards Bosnia.[54] In mid-October, US President Bill Clinton, while rounding on his European allies in an interview for the *Washington Post*, picked out the British especially for their resistance to his preferred option for Bosnia — a partial lifting of the UN-imposed arms embargo on the territories of the former Yugoslav state.[55] As early as December 1992, the Bosnian President Alija Izetbegović asserted that the British were 'the biggest brake on any progress' towards solving his country's war, an accusation which many observers echoed as they assessed the UK's policy as being 'bankrupt'.[56]

While UK policy was less than glorious and, in the end, a failure, it shared those qualities with the policies of other major actors in the international community. The UK may have stood accused because it played a more significant role in the diplomatic treatment of the crisis than most other states — including the supply of a small secretariat to the EC for the duration of the Hague Conference and for a long period at ICFY,[57] an active role at the UN and the sending of the second largest contingent of troops to operate with UNPROFOR. This reflected both its strong commitment to ending the war in former Yugoslavia and its engagement as a major actor on the international stage, as well as its analysis of the various aspects of the situation, both intra-Yugoslav and international.

The UK's initial analysis of the conflict was, like that of the French, conservative and restrained. However, whereas the dominant question for the French was the maintenance of an integral Yugoslav state, the UK originally saw the war in Yugoslavia primarily through ethnic and historical glasses. The Yugoslav conflict was understood less in terms of the modern dynamics of disintegration and more in terms of historic animosity. 'The dispute within Yugoslavia,' was, in the view of Minster of State Douglas Hogg, 'largely ethnic and historic'.[58] While, even at

---

54 Mirza Hajrić, 'Mejdžorova posljednja jesen?', *Oslobodjenje*, 1-8 October 1993.
55 *The Washington Post*, 6 April 1993.
56 Quoted in Sharp, *Bankrupt in the Balkans*, p.1.
57 Both, of course, obtained indirect and irregular support from other countries and organisations.
58 Evidence to the Foreign Affairs Committee, Foreign Affairs Committee, *Central and Eastern Europe: Problems of the Post-Communist Era*, First Report, Vol.II, HMSO, London, 1992, p.58.

early stages, the UK had no problems in clearly identifying the Serbian leadership as the source of war, or in advocating economic sanctions, particularly on oil,[59] the dominant tendency was to see the inter-communal element in the war, the aspect of villages and neighbours fighting with each other.[60]

This vision was reinforced by reflections on the situation in Northern Ireland. It was believed that there were strong parallels between Yugoslavia and Northern Ireland as irremediable inter-ethnic conflicts. This led to the understandable notion that it would be unwise to volunteer for a second experience like Northern Ireland. Whereas the deployment of UK troops on sovereign territory was considered a necessity, a similar deployment in Yugoslavia was very much a contingency to be avoided.

Although the primary characteristic of the early British analysis was a rather unfocused vision of an ethnic maelstrom in Yugoslavia, it altered as the conflict developed. In line with its partners in the EC, London came to see the issues at stake more clearly in terms of order among the sovereign republics which had formerly been part of Yugoslavia, two of which were subject to Belgrade-induced attempts at dismemberment. The very nature of that attempted dismemberment, however, only served to stress that the internal, ethnic dimension highlighted in the early phases could not be dismissed.

Beyond this there was recognition that, whatever happened, the UK would not be acting separately in terms of action. All British activity would be channelled through multilateral agencies — primarily the EC, but also the UN, NATO, the WEU and the CSCE. It was through membership of such international bodies that the UK put its security policy into effect.[61] The eventual commitment of troops to UNPROFOR in Bosnia, for example, cannot be understood without awareness of the importance for the UK of being seen to play an

---

59 *Ibid.*, p.59.

60 I have often argued elsewhere that this was only one of two roads to war in Yugoslavia — and the lesser of them. (For example, see Gow, 'One Year of War in Bosnia and Hercegovina', *RFE/RL Research Report*, Vol.2, No.23, 4 June 1993.) The other, the ambitions of political elites was by far the more significant, something which the UK Foreign and Commonwealth Office was later to acknowledge through its role in the imposition of comprehensive economic sanctions against the Serbian leadership.

61 This was partially stated in Foreign Affairs Committee, *Central and Eastern Europe: Problems of the Post-Communist Era*, First Report, Vol.I, HMSO, London, pp.xvi-xvii.

important role in both the EU and the UN.[62] In these international
bodies the UK saw not only forums in which to amplify British status
on the international scene, but also the framework preventing others
from making radical moves which it regarded as unsustainable, rash or
running ahead of their own analysis of what such moves might imply.
This was the case in the earlier stages of the war with recognition of the
independence of the republics seeking it and later with US advocacy of
lifting the UN arms embargo in favour of Bosnia and launching air
strikes on Serbian forces in the country. Although at a relatively early
stage, and certainly by the end of October 1991, the UK understood that
those republics would eventually be recognised, it placed great emphasis
on the circumstances and timing of recognition.

This represented a pre-disposition to orderly ways of carrying out
action, but also harked back to the original analysis of the crisis. It was
feared, as the then EC Envoy to Yugoslavia Lord Carrington had made
clear, that recognition without an overall settlement would be likely to
make matters in the former Yugoslavia worse.[63] In any conflict
characterised as ethnic, according to the British analysis an external act
in favour of one belligerent against the interest of the other could only
antagonise the latter and incite further bloodshed.[64] This interpretation
was primarily based on caution, rather than on any principle or political
preference, and had the objective not only of ending the war as soon as
possible, but also of achieving a settlement — within the framework of

---

62 There were limits to this UK commitment, however, such as the imperative not to do
anything which would call into question the 1994 Defence White Paper 'Options for
Change'. Under 'Options', cuts were being made in the UK armed forces. An unstated
imperative guiding action was the requirement not to do anything which might reverse the
decision to cut the armed forces. This was evident in the initial briefing given to Colonel
Bob Stewart, battalion commander of the first British troops to go to Bosnia with
UNPROFOR, after the UK Government had relented on its decision not deploy its armed
forces in the former Yugoslavia: involved in deciding on the appropriate force to send,
he was told that the absolute ceiling was 1,822 personnel. (Bob Stewart, *Broken Lives:
A Personal View of the Bosnian Conflict*, HarperCollins, London, 1993, p.15.) However,
this proved not to be an absolute as the decision was taken, in September 1992, to deploy
2,400 troops in Bosnia. In the summer of 1993, 'Options' itself was reviewed and ground
force cuts restored and cuts in the Navy introduced.
63 Lord Carrington, 'Intervention to the London Conference', 26 August 1992.
64 For an exposition of essentially British reservations on involvement in ethnic conflicts,
see Robert Cooper and Mats Berdal, 'Outside Intervention in Ethnic Conflicts', *Survival*,
Vol.35, No.1, Spring 1993 (although one of these, Berdal, was Norwegian).

CFSP. However, CFSP was also an essential mechanism for restraining partners and allies from action which, in London's view, might cause more harm than good.

London adopted this wise owl position over US initiatives on Bosnia also following the inauguration of President Bill Clinton. The Clinton Administration came into office advocating a policy of 'lift and strike'. Both elements of this policy, especially the arguments on the benefits of lifting the arms embargo, ran into analytical walls in London. Moreover, the UK attempted to counsel the US on the two questions it had experience. It had already examined lifting the arms embargo as an option and on military intervention could by this stage count on the support of those with which it had already discussed the uses of force. Britain had sought to restrain France in the early phases of the Yugoslav War of Dissolution in September 1991, over deployment of a WEU interposition force in Croatia, an idea eventually rejected.[65]

A partial lifting of the arms embargo was considered by London at the same time as plans were being made to contribute troops to UNPROFOR. This option was rejected for a variety of reasons, including among other things the expressed fear that more arms would only encourage reciprocal bloodshed, that there would anyway be considerable practical obstacles to supplies reaching the Bosnian army and that if it did prove possible to get the embargo partly removed, there was no guarantee that the Bosnian army would be victorious or that there would not be pressures at some later stage to send troops to its aid.

Moreover, it was regarded by the Europeans as unrealistic to think that the categories of weapons the Bosnian army required would reach it unless the US went to war on the Bosnian side, a possibility both the Bush and Clinton administrations had repeatedly excluded. Taken together, these points made the UK government reject the idea of lifting the arms embargo. Instead, other ways of offering assistance were considered. It was hard to gauge accurately where the weight lay in the balance between the reluctance to become embroiled militarily and the pressures to intervene. There was some debate about sending a large expeditionary force, but the UK mandate was restricted, in the end, by rules of engagement only permitting return of fire if the source of fire had been clearly identified.

65 *The Financial Times*, 1 October 1991.

The US reluctance to commit its ground forces in the Yugoslav theatre was decisive in determining Britain's attitude to the use of armed force — both its initial opposition to any military deployment and its insistence on the type of operation which eventually began in Bosnia. While the British had no interest in committing forces themselves, the apparent impossibility of deploying American troops in the former Yugoslavia was interpreted by London from the outset to mean that there could be no armed intervention. Without the US army, the Europeans alone would not have sufficient troops available to mount a serious expeditionary force — even if this were judged desirable or necessary.

UK resistance to an armed intervention arose not so much from concerns about the complexity of the battle on the ground (although, of course, such concerns existed), but because there was no political will either in the UK or elsewhere available to mount an expeditionary force, as the Foreign Secretary Douglas Hurd strongly counselled analysts to recall:

> The only thing which could have guaranteed peace with justice would have been an expeditionary force.... And no government, no government has at any time seriously proposed that. And that I think is a line which should run through any analysis because it cuts out so much of the rhetoric which has bedevilled this.[66]

With every government nervous of embarking on an adventure for which it had little stomach, the UK troop commitment made some sense. Deployed, at least partly, with the implicit hope that their presence and that of other NATO troops would be a symbolic deterrent, the UK troops with UNPROFOR in Bosnia were given a mission which could be carried out without serious risk of difficulties and heavy casualties.

However, there should be little doubt given Britain's greater general inclination than most countries to use a military option, as well as the implicit sub-text of its security policy — tuck under America's wing — that if there had been any possibility of US ground troops being deployed, it would have joined in international action. Without US ground troops, the UK (and France, the other major — and larger —

66 Interview, Channel 4 TV, 'Diplomacy and Deceit', 2 August 1993, *Bloody Bosnia*, Media Transcription Service, M2578, p.4.

Triumph of Lack of Will

contributor of troops in former Yugoslavia) could only envisage intervention as an act of folly, given the reality that, without US involvement, the European allies in NATO simply did not have enough troops to make sure that a fiasco would be avoided.

As it was, the US was only interested in using its air power. Air power was generally regarded as likely to require a follow-up with ground troops, and this raised two matters. One was the implication that the UK and other troops on the ground might have to take this role. The other was that the soldiers in Bosnia, as well as those in Croatia, might become targets and would certainly have to curtail their humanitarian operations. Advocates of air strikes suggested that UNPROFOR could withdraw and the Bosnian army provide the ground follow-up — but this led straight back to the debate on lifting the arms embargo, which was weighed against the lives being saved and the humanitarian work being done by the UN troops in the country.[67]

The UK did not rule out the use of selective air strikes. Indeed, on six occasions in 1994 it was prepared to use them. Its support of the US preference for using air power increased following the appointment of Lieutenant-General Sir Michael Rose as head of Bosnia Command in UNPROFOR. The UK authorities were obliged to back their own general and persuaded by his judgement that there were very limited objectives which could be achieved by the judicious use of air capability. These were either to give UNPROFOR credibility or to prod the diplomatic process — and were demonstrated on a small scale by the conduct of British troops on the ground throughout Bosnia,[68] and on a larger scale at Sarajevo in February 1994, when the twenty-two month bombardment of the city was brought to an end for several months through the threat of air strikes on Serbian positions around the city.[69] Of course, both Rose and his political masters in the UK remained acutely aware of the limitations of using air power, particularly in the context of a UN operation — as was demonstrated in the events at Goražde the following April. Thus the UK position

---

67 On the US-UK differences, see Fiona M. Watson and Richard Ware, *The Bosnian Conflict — a turning point?*, House of Commons Research Paper No.93/56, 28 April 1993.

68 The British battalion in Bosnia returned fire sixty-seven times between November 1993 and May 1994. (This figure was cited in discussion with officers from the Coldstream Guards which served as the British battalion in this period.)

69 For a more comprehensive treatment of these events, see Chapter 7.

shifted slightly after the appointment of General Rose to an admission of the practical need for it on occasion.

This was also, it appeared, a way of improving relations with the US, which generally welcomed signs of more forceful action. Moreover for the sake of its trans-Atlantic bridges, the UK did not rule out the possibility of withdrawal and lifting the arms embargo, although it was extremely difficult to imagine these happening in practice. However, its judgement continued to be that more could be done through UNPROFOR than through the uncertain and difficult course of withdrawal and lifting the arms embargo. The UK therefore continued to place the overwhelming emphasis on a consensual approach to dealing with the protagonists in the war.

Finally, UK objections over certain questions concerning the use of force mostly had to be divorced from UK objectives, which were to end the conflict, restore regional peace and stability and to resist the Serbian war campaign — albeit not through force of arms. In terms of UK security policy and global standing, the objectives were to ensure a prominent role and to prevent commitments being made by partners and allies that would be impractical or unacceptably costly.

However, the long-term cost of the UK's opposition to US policy could not be easily assessed. But, there had been damage to the so-called 'special relationship' between the two and where that left the UK's tuck-under-the-American-wing policy remained to be judged. While the UK's attitude was always negative, in practice, it did more than most other countries and its actions were usually commensurate with the international environment in which they arose. However, these were never commensurate with the circumstances of the Yugoslav War of Dissolution.

Most of the UK's 'objections' over the issues surrounding the use of force (including the arms embargo) were founded on sound analysis of the circumstances — although there remained points on areas in which questions might be asked, depending on views of the strength and competence of the various forces in Bosnia and Croatia. (The UK position seemed to exaggerate the strength of the Bosnian Serbs, especially). However, the UK analysis had one critical feature: the determined reluctance of political leaders in all the major countries, with the UK in the forefront, to commit ground forces in the former Yugoslavia. While Douglas Hurd was correct to emphasise the reluctance of various governments to become engaged in a major intervention, it would be wrong to suppose that in doing so he was implying that the UK wished to see action but was restrained by the lack of enthusiasm for such a project on the part of those governments. If anything, Hurd and the UK government were backward at going forwards: rather than attempting to lead the international community and persuade the US in particular to take action (as commentators frequently supposed would have been the case had Margaret Thatcher still been Prime Minister), Hurd reacted swiftly to subdue discussion of using force whenever the issue arose.

In spite of sometimes receiving advice from officials to the contrary, UK politicians, like their counterparts elsewhere, shrank from more decisive action — and where their counterparts were more enthusiastic, sought to place any possible use of force in a soundly reasoned context. The UK political leaders could nonetheless be criticised for their outright nervousness, for their failure to take a leading role in drumming up support for more forceful international action and for their acceptance of apparent half-measures and symbolic gestures in the hope that these would be enough. The major fault with British policy, therefore, was its pusillanimous realism.

Involvement in the Yugoslav war shaped and catalysed the transformation of West European security after the Cold War. It both revealed differences and consolidated new arrangements. The biggest policy conflicts among the Europeans emerged, unsurprisingly, around the big policy issues for the international community: recognition of those Yugoslav republics seeking to establish independence and aspects of the use of armed force. The divergent approaches to these issues taken by the major EU countries was informed both by differing perceptions of the conflict and by a disparity in objectives at various times.

However, for all there differences the Europeans had more in common with each other for the most part of the war, than with their allies in the US. The major European countries shared a policy approach based on two main activities — UNPROFOR and the UN-EC sponsored International Conference on Former Yugoslavia (ICFY). Moreover, in spite of the difficulty of the recognition question and its impact on the evolution of CFSP, Yugoslavia was an opportunity for Germany to begin its transformation from humbled penitent to responsible giant in the framework of European policy. But most of all

France and the UK, traditionally distrustful of each other even as allies (especially from the British side), began to form an axis for military-political policy and activity in the European context. This emerged after both countries made sizeable deployments of armed forces to operate with UNPROFOR in Bosnia and with the WEU and NATO in support of UN Security Council Resolutions.

The two were thus able to dominate the debate on the use of force because of these troop; the verbal gambits of others would always run up against feet on the ground. When France with the largest contingent in the former Yugoslavia decided that there was a need for force and that it could be used purposefully, others were obliged to take the matter seriously and act accordingly. Increasing Franco-British co-operation on security policy was a positive by-product of the international involvement in the war — one likely to have major ramifications for the future development of the EU, the WEU and NATO as organisations and European and Mediterranean security in general. In particular, it meant a stronger independent European capability. This would have deep longer-term implications for both Russia and the US.

8

THE MAJOR PLAYERS: WASHINGTON AND MOSCOW

Washington and Moscow began the final decade of the twentieth century in an historically positive register. The end of the Cold War had given way to a relatively harmonious spirit of international security co-operation in which there was increased emphasis on normative values. Although there were moments of disharmony, the use of the UN Security Council as the authority for a co-operative approach to the regulation of international order was embodied in the handling of the Gulf Conflict at the beginning of the 1990s. This was a manifestation of the 'New World Order' characterised by the US President George Bush — a world 'freer from the threat of terror, stronger in the pursuit of justice, and more secure in the quest for peace'.[1] The relative terms used by Bush implied a better world — one which would be not so much new as the old one upheld and its values given sustenance. However, Bush's words were generally taken as superlatives implying a situation already in being, and created a swell of optimism.

By the beginning of 1995, the initial shine of the 'New World Order' had been rubbed off by Somalia and Rwanda, among others, and, above all by Bosnia. For differing reasons, neither Moscow, nor Washington, was to the fore in the first months of conflict in the dissolving Yugoslavia. Indeed, it was not until the beginning of 1994 that Moscow and Washington began directly co-operating over the Yugoslav war. That co-operative effort was to give birth to a further manifestation of

1 US President George Bush, 'Toward a New World Order', Address to joint session of Congress, Washington D.C., 11 September 1990, *USIS Wireless Service*.

international co-operation: the Contact Group (see Chapter 10), the forum for a co-operative international policy effort to achieve settlement of the problems arising from the violent dissolution of Yugoslavia. However, the underlying truth was that both the Contact Group and the bi-lateral Russian-American initiatives which made it necessary, were reflections of the need to hold inconsistent policy strands together.

The Contact Group was at once both a mechanism for providing a co-ordinated international policy and a device in which the rifts between disparate capitals and bodies might be submerged. Similarly, US-Russian joint initiatives were an attempt to reconcile divergent views of the conflict and how to address it. Although both capitals of the Cold War superpowers, in the spirit of post-Cold War co-operation, had shown deference to the EC in the early phases of the conflict (and both were acutely aware of parallels for the collapsing Soviet Union at the time), both later became more engaged.

However, during 1993 the positions of both Washington and Moscow evolved in contrary directions, as will be shown. Up till 1993, the two capitals had broadly lent their support to the work of international agencies, Washington with more commitment than Moscow. However, for both, these were years of domestic reorientation, international readjustment and redefining identity. During 1993 the US, under the Clinton adminstration, in effect broke with the co-operative approach to international security. In taking an independent line, the US was attempting to satisfy the traditional and contradictory impulses of its foreign policy: principled idealism and isolationism. Eventually Washington returned to a policy based on support for multilateral initiatives as a way of spreading US responsibility in the international system, though it did not do so without oscillating policy preferences.

While the US under Clinton was moving back towards support for collective initiatives, Moscow, ironically, was evolving towards a more differentiated policy in which co-operation with the West was downgraded and subject to considerations of Russia's influence and status. This irony was compounded by the reality that Moscow's drift from co-operation was due largely to the failure of international mechanisms in this critical period — a failure resulting from Washington's uncertain support for and effective opposition to the Vance-Owen Plan. Consequently, the fruits of post-Cold War co-operation would begin to turn sour.

In the Mirror: Moscow's Perspective on Stability and Status

As the Yugoslav War of Dissolution progressed, Moscow was transformed from the capital of the Soviet Union into the capital of the Russian Federation — a transformation of historic proportions, requiring a period of adjustment and consolidation. This and indeed the transformation of Europe were the result of 'new thinking', the co-operative approach to international security which emerged in the last years of the Soviet Union.[2] That approach was carried forward into the early post-Soviet period, when Moscow's foreign policy was more unambiguously committed to co-operation with the West than before — including on Yugoslavia. In later phases co-operation would continue, but with a shift from unhindered internationalism towards re-nationalisation of foreign policy. Moscow's perspective on the war and dissolution in Yugoslavia was therefore set very firmly in its own ontology and Moscow was able to guide itself in a period of existential adjustment by reference to events in Yugoslavia.

In a sense the dissolution of Yugoslavia meant more to Moscow than to any other major capital — the war and destruction among the Yugoslavs provided a 'horror mirror' for Moscow[3] which it could not fail to interpret as an anti-model for the dissolution of the Soviet Union. Both were multi-national communist federations, based on the formal sovereignty of the federating republics. A key element in Moscow's understanding was, therefore, that the events in disintegrating Yugoslavia reflected on, and had implications for, the situation in the dissolving Soviet Union; so too would the way in which the rest of the world reacted to the break-up of Yugoslavia.

At the time of the declarations of independence by Slovenia and Croatia, the 'mirror' factor made Moscow view the Yugoslav question as one of keeping the fissiparous republics in one federation. Straightforwardly, this was because the prospect of independent Yugoslav republics would seriously undermine efforts to retain equally

2 On Gorbachev's 'new thinking', particularly the desire to see a greater role for institutions such as the UN, see Michael McGwire, *Perestroika and Soviet National Security*, Brookings Institution, Washington DC, 1991, esp. pp. 229-9.
3 Nadia Alexandrova Arbatova, 'Horror Mirror: Russian Perception of the Yugoslav Conflict', paper presented at the Consensus Building Institute Conference on 'Russian and American Perspectives: Ethnic Conflicts in the Former Soviet Union', Harvard University, 25-26 October 1994.

centrifugal Soviet republics in the Union — in the same period there had been considerable problems with the evolving independence movements in the Baltic Republics, Moldova and, most critically, Ukraine:[4] after the failed Moscow coup attempt of 18-19 August 1991 only three Union republics had not formally declared their independence by the end of that month (the Russian Federation, Kazakhstan and Turkmenistan) and Moscow recognised the independence of the three Baltic States, which were subsequently admitted to the CSCE and the UN in September. The tension between pressures for independence and efforts to retain a stabilising framework was to remain throughout the six months following the declarations of independence — in which the EC was leading international efforts to resolve the crisis in Yugoslavia, by seeking to establish a new common framework for its republics.

Conscious of avoiding a repetition of this in the Soviet Union, the last Soviet leader, Mikhail Gorbachev, while passively supporting EC initiatives, proposed a new arrangement for his decaying federation — a Union of sovereign republics.[5] This in many ways mirrored the EC proposals for the Yugoslav republics in The Hague (discussed in Chapter 3). However, Gorbachev's efforts to get agreement to his plan for new relations between the Soviet republics failed. In the Yugoslav context, it was becoming clear by the end of 1991 that restoring a common Yugoslav framework would be impossible. At the same time the Gorbachev plan was lost in face of overwhelming support for independence in a referendum in Ukraine, followed by the Russian Federation, Ukraine and Belarus (the three founding members from 1922) declaring the end of the Soviet Union and its replacement, as of the last day of 1991, by a Commonwealth of Independent States. From that point on, Moscow's perspective was that of the Russian Federation — which had already indentified common ground with Slovenia as early as 1990 when both were challenging federal order.

For the newly independent Russian Federation, the troubles in Yugoslavia could be interpreted in two ways. First, in face of pressures for the break-up of the Russian Federation into its component non-sovereign republics and regions, there was a need to consolidate and to

---

4 See Hélène Carrère d'Encausse, *La gloire des nations — ou la fin de l'Empire soviétique*, Fayard, Paris, 1990.
5 See Geoffrey Hosking, *A History of the Soviet Union, 1917-1991*, Fontana, London, 1992, pp. 492-3.

assure the integrity of the Russian Federation. As with Yugoslavia, there had been a formal dissolution of the communist federation into its constitutionally sovereign republics — and, as in Yugoslavia, there had been challenges from within the newly independent states, sometimes involving war. Moscow's priority was to adjust to the new situation and to secure the Russian Federation. With Yugoslavia this meant upholding the integrity of Croatia and Bosnia as states — as a mirror for proper relations between the former Soviet republics.

At the same time, easy parallels could be — and were — drawn between the position of the Serbs and the Russians, and Serbia and Russia in their respective former federations:[6] in both the capital of the republic was the capital of the federation, both had historical geo-strategic weaknesses (being landlocked and with vulnerable borders) and fears of Turkey, and, most crucially, both had been the largest single population group in the former federation and had large a diaspora in the other republics.[7] The parallels between the two situations, irrespective of the detail on the ground, enhanced the sympathy for the Serbs in certain political spheres in Moscow.[8] This was based not so much on the often-cited historic alliance between fellow Slavs (a notion undermined by various realities in history, such as the 1948 Moscow-Belgrade split and Serbia's support for the attempted coup in Moscow in 1991), as on a fusion of perceived memories in the Second World War in which the Croats had sided with the Germans and events in Belgrade and Yugoslavia distracted the Nazis sufficiently to delay the

6 Andrei Edemskii, 'Russian Policy Towards the War in Ex-Yugoslavia, 1991-94', unpublished paper, Slavonic and Balkan Studies Institute, Academy of Sciences, Moscow.
7 It should be remembered that, while ethnic Russians were in an overall majority in the Soviet Union, the Serbs in Yugoslavia were only around 35 per cent of the population, but formed the single largest ethno-national community. (Foreign and Commonwealth Office, 'Some Aspects of Ethnic Minority Problems in Yugoslavia', Annex F, Foreign Affairs Committee, *Central and Eastern Europe: Problems of the Post-Communist Era*, First Report, Vol. II: 21-II, House of Commons Session 1991-92, HMSO, London, 1992. p.41.)
8 See, for example, the letter signed by a number of significant 'conservative' figures in *Sovetskaia Rossiia*, 21 January 1993, reprinted as 'Verim — Prizyv Budet Uslyshan' in *Iugoslavskii Krizis i Rossiia: Dokumenty, Fakty, Kommentarii (1990-1993)*, Sovremennaia Istoriia Iugoslavii v Dokumentah, Vol.2, Fond Iugoslavianskih Issledovanii i Sotrudnichestva 'Slavianskaia Letopis', Moscow, 1993, pp.401-3.

onslaught on the Soviet Union and thus allow winter to assist Moscow in defending the homeland.[9]

In addition to this, for many tied to Cold War ideas, the West remained the enemy — therefore, sympathy and support for Belgrade flowed strongly, as it had for Saddam Hussein's Iraq.[10] The Serbs were seen as being persecuted by the West in preparation for action against 'the Slavs' similar to that against Iraq in 1991.[11] Indeed, there was more emphasis on Russia's need to oppose the West than to 'stand up for fellow Slavs'.[12] The combination of parallel situations and sympathy gave rise to the Russian leadership's need to conduct a 'balanced and objective policy'. That policy was 'balanced' in the sense that it regarded all Yugoslav political and military leaders as bearing responsibility for the war,[13] and balanced Russia's interests on both sides of the borders-versus-diaspora issue, as well as accommodating internal criticism with co-operation in international diplomacy.

Moscow's balancing act, given the parallels between the positions of the Serb populations in the break-up of Yugoslavia and of the Russians in the Soviet dissolution, also revealed a fundamental contrast. Whereas the political leaders in Belgrade had used the issue of kin-populations and their security to stir the ingredients of war and foster campaigns for border changes, their Russian counterparts had striven to stabilise situations through legal and political provision for ethnic Russians in the newly independent states, as well as, crucially, to consolidate borders — thereby proving their credentials as responsible actors in international society.[14]

The Yugoslav case in itself was of little direct interest to Moscow, either before or after the end of the Soviet Union. It was, however, of

9 This point was impressed on me in discussion with Aleksandar Korsik, First Secretary at the Russian Embassy in London — who stressed that this was an emotional response rather than one based on objective analysis; see also Arbatova, 'Horror Mirror'.

10 See James Gow, 'The Soviet Union', in Gow, ed., *Iraq, the Gulf Conflict and the World Community*, Brassey's for the Centre for Defence Studies, London, 1993.

11 'Obrashchenie k Slavianskomu Kongressu', in *Iugoslavskii Krizis*, pp. 359-60; see also, Arbatova, 'Horror Mirror'.

12 J.B.K. Lough, *Constraints on Russian Responses to the Yugoslav Crisis*, Occasional Brief 22, Conflict Studies Research Centre, RMA Sandhurst, June 1993.

13 Summaries of the principles of Russian policy appeared in *Kommersant*, 2 April 1993 and *Nezavisimaia Gazeta*, 29 April 1993.

14 See Carole Birch, ed., *Russia: A State of Emergency?*, Centre for Defence Studies, University of London, 1993, pp.36-7.

some interest as a point of reflection for the experience of Soviet dissolution, as a vehicle for co-operative foreign policy with the West, and as a cause for debate in Moscow, where the official line on all these questions was by no means the only one. Indeed, the strength of dissident voices was to grow with time until there was a significant impact on the tone of Moscow's policy — although the substance of that policy remained broadly the same.

The debate in Moscow on events in Yugoslavia reflected debates on 'the Russia question'.[15] It was conducted between 'romantic nationalists' or the 'ideological and imperial', on the one side, and 'pragmatists' or those committed to 'new thinking', on the other.[16] The former group contained the small but vocal group of 'pan-Slavists' who identified with the Serbs as 'brothers'. It also included those who, in terms of debates about Russia's own predicament, thought of it as more than the Russian Federation — but also as embracing either the whole of the former Soviet Union, or those parts of it inhabited by Russians and Russian-speakers.[17] The pragmatists were those who saw Moscow's priorities as preserving the integrity of the Russian Federation, establishing as orderly an environment as possible in the former Soviet space, based on international norms, and renewing and improving relations with the West in the spirit of liberal international co-operation — as begun in the last years of the Soviet Union.[18]

For both groups international involvement in the war in the remains of Yugoslavia presented an opportunity to demonstrate Russia's

---

15 *Ibid.*

16 Andrei Edemskii, 'Russia and the Former Yugoslavia: the Meaning of the Balkans', Paper at the Conference 'Semantics and Security: the Meaning of the Balkans', School of Slavonic and East European Studies-Centre for Defence Studies, University of London, 21-23 September 1994; Hannes Adomeit, 'Russia as a "great power" in world affairs: images and reality', *International Affairs*, Vol.71, No.1, January 1995.

17 Edemskii's label 'romantic nationalists' in this context is useful shorthand, but may also be slightly misleading because some of those interested in the restoration of the old Union, or in 'protecting' Russians in the 'near abroad', were either Soviet and communist (rather than 'romantic' and 'nationalist'), or pragmatists who saw safeguarding the interests of Russians as a matter of practical necessity if the Russian Federation particularly, and the post-Soviet space in general, were to be stabilised.

18 The most prominent and committed member of this grouping was Foreign Minister Andrei Kozyrev — who summarised the essential features of both the Yugoslav disintegration as an anti-model for Moscow and the policy of international co-operation in his article 'The Lagging Partnership', *Foreign Affairs*, Vol.73, No.3, May-June 1994.

continuing greatness as a world power. For the ideological-imperial 'nationalists' events in Yugoslavia were understood as an opportunity to assert Russia's greatness through competition. For the new-thinking reformist-internationalists (or Atlanticists) it was an opportunity to show that Russia could wield 'soft power', i.e. 'exert influence... through "persuasion", without the use of force'.[19] As international involvement in the war in Bosnia, in particular, evolved, Moscow came to adopt a more assertive approach towards Western and particularly US policies. In part this shift was in response to a series of internal factors: the activism of more 'conservative' elements in political debate and in seeking power; the growth in popular support for those more conservative forces and the parallel popular disillusionment with the reform process; the acute pain of economic dislocation, accompanied by a lack of Western direct investment (which bolstered the growing support of the conservatives); and finally the disillusionment of the internationalists with the reform process and, most of all, the demoralisation of being unable to demonstrate backing and respect abroad for Russia and Russian initiatives.[20]

Although all these pressures had been building for some time, it was the private realisation that its opinion did not carry the appropriate weight which seems to have persuaded Moscow that its previously unfailing support for international efforts counted for little. Moreover, in spite of attempts at positive presentation, the critical opportunity to demonstrate Russian 'soft power' influence to offset growing domestic criticism was disregarded by Washington: this was the initiative for 'progressive implementation' of the Vance-Owen Plan. While trends had been developing before the effective Washington 'snub' in May 1993, that experience in particular appears to have moved the Atlanticists in Moscow towards a more assertive (and sometimes antagonistic) role which would both appease internal critics and reveal Russia's continuing strength to the doubting world.

19 Institut Evropa, Rossiskaia Akademia Nauka. *Novaia geopoliticheskaia situatsia v Evrope, pozitsia Zapada i intersy bezopasnoti Rossii*, Institute of Europe, Moscow, 1994, p.67, quoted in Adomeit, 'Russia', p.67.
20 This interpretation is adapted from Adomeit, 'Russia', pp.58 and 63.

Moscow Policy Approaches: Co-operation and Assertion

Moscow's policy on Yugoslavia was overshadowed throughout the crisis by its own political situation; indeed it was of some significance as a forum for the conduct of internal disputes. Entwined with domestic considerations and the complications of the new Russia establishing itself in the world, policy was multi-layered and came in many waves, some cross-cutting. This made it hard sometimes to discern either shifts in policy or, more often than not, continuity in policy. Many superficial policy changes were temporary feints by the Russian Foreign Minister, Andrei Kozyrev, to shake off the conservative sharks seeking to oust him.[21]

The multiple waves of policy may be marked by three tide-changes. The first phase was that in which Moscow policy broadly shadowed and supported other international efforts; the second covered a transitional period in which expansive support for Western approaches was in question, but co-operation continued with Russia increasingly seeking to play a more prominent role and moving towards an independent, assertive line; and the third was characterised by Russian assertiveness, clearly based on the importance of promoting Russia as a 'great power'. Throughout, Moscow was offering support for international initiatives, although it was increasingly clear from the assertive approach that this could not be guaranteed — and moreover that whatever its commitment to multilateral initiatives, it was prepared to act unilaterally.[22] The central difference between the three streams was that in earlier periods Moscow made assumptions about its equal status, but later took it upon itself to ensure that it had an identifiable, separate role and was not taken for granted by its Western partners. The tide turned on Russian policy in the wake of the demise of the Vance-Owen Plan.

The pronounced shift in the character of Moscow's co-operation with Western countries from the spring of 1993 was both in response to growing domestic criticism of what was perceived as a pro-Western sell-out, and to the realisation that, as time went on, the behaviour of elements in the West gave grounds for some of the criticism, as well as for re-appraisal. Although opinion was swelling in support of a Russia-

21 See Stephen Sestanovich, 'Andrei the Giant', *The New Republic*, 11 April 1994, p.27.
22 See Pavel Baev, 'Russia's Experiments and Experience in Conflict Management and Peacekeeping', *International Peacekeeping*, Vol.1, No.3, Autumn 1994, pp.251-2.

first policy before May 1993 it was Washington's rejection of its proposals on implementation of the Vance-Owen Plan which confirmed for Russia that it would have to reconsider its approach and ensure its equal status on the international diplomatic cast-list. The end of the Vance-Owen Plan was thus also the end of Moscow's unadulterated co-operation with the West.

Moscow's broadly supportive policy came in two phases. The first covered the final months of the Soviet Union — either side of the August coup attempt. Throughout this phase, Moscow took a back seat. It offered its support, before the putsch, to EC efforts to maintain some form of Yugoslavia. After August, with undercurrents of change leading the Soviet Union towards its end, it continued to back EC initiatives, even as these initiatives were themselves turning towards acceptance of the inevitability of Yugoslavia's dissolution.[23]

Only on one occasion did the failing Soviet Union officially (although there were unofficial exchanges between the Soviet and Yugoslav generals) take specific action over the crisis in Yugoslavia. This was in October, when President Mikhail Gorbachev invited the Serbian President Slobodan Milošević and Croatian President Franjo Tudjman to Moscow, offering to mediate. That meeting resulted in a statement,[24] but no progress towards resolution of the conflict — suggesting that the event was designed more for Gorbachev's own purposes in a hopeful attempt to persuade the Soviet republics to form a new union and avoid the fate of Yugoslavia.[25] Thereafter the events in the Soviet Union superseded Soviet foreign policy, paving the way for Russian foreign policy — the second phase of passive support for Western approaches.

---

23 Moscow's support became more clear-cut after the events of August. Before this, there had been no objections and implicit indications of support from the Ministry of Foreign Affairs, both singling out Europe in international co-operation (29 June 1991 — see *Iugoslavskii Krizis*, p.58) and in CSCE approval of EC activity. Explicit support was offered to the 'initiative of the Twelve' on 19 September 1991 — see *Ibid.*, p.63.

24 'Kommiunike o Vstrepche v Moskve Prezidentov M.S. Gorbacheva, S. Miloshevicha i F. Tudzhmana' (15 October 1991) in *ibid.*, p.64; also reprinted in *Iugoslaviia v Ogne: Dokumenty, Fakty, Kommentarii (1990-1992)*, Sovremennaia Istoriia Iugoslavii v Dokumentah, Vol.I, Fond Iugoslavianskih Issledovanii i Sotrudnichestva 'Slavianskaia Letopis', Moscow, 1992, p.187.

25 See Edemskii, 'Russian Policy'.

Russian foreign policy started on a high note of co-operation. At the UN Security Council Summit in January 1992, President Boris Yeltsin, regarding Russia as much as the West as the beneficiary of the disappearance of the Soviet Union, announced that Moscow and its former adversaries were now 'allies'.[26] Throughout the following year, Moscow would lend its support to the initiatives of others — the deployment of UNPROFOR in Croatia, the imposition of sanctions against Belgrade, the extension of UNPROFOR to Bosnia — in what was regarded by (even sympathetic) critics at home as 'hyper Westernism'.[27] During this period there was growing criticism from the parliament, beginning in June 1992, following Russia's support for the imposition of sanctions against Serbia and Montenegro in May.[28] Prominent individuals, such as the chairman of the Parliamentary International Affairs Committee, Yevgenii Ambartsumov, charged that in applying sanctions and supporting the suspension of Belgrade from the CSCE, Moscow should pursue its own interests rather than allow its foreign policy to be dictated by American electoral politics.[29]

This kind of criticism inspired Kozyrev to play a prank on his counterparts at the CSCE Summit in Helsinki on 9-10 July 1992, when he briefly shocked the world by condemning Western policies and warning that Belgrade could count on Moscow's military backing against the West.[30] However, he quickly assured his Western counterparts that the speech had only been a ruse to warn them of what was likely to come if others, lurking in the background, gained power. However much Kozyrev may have been kidding, he soon began to follow a more determined line, generally continuing to support Western approaches, but strongly emphasising the need for political rather than military approaches to the settlement of the Yugoslav conflict.

---

26 Quoted in Adomeit, 'Russia', p.45.

27 Arbatova, 'Horror Mirror'.

28 'Postanovlenie Verhovnovo Soveta Rossiiskoi Federacii', 26 June 1992, in *Iugoslavskii Krizis*, p.111.

29 *Izvestiia*, 30 June 1992; for further examples of critics urging the need to follow Russian interests, see Adomeit, 'Russia', pp.52-3.

30 This performance was curiously mis-attributed as being in December by Renée de Nevers, *Russia's Strategic Renovation: Russian Security Strategies and Foreign Policy in the Post-Imperial Era*, Adelphi Paper 289, Brassey's for IISS, London, July 1994, p.38; it was further mis-attributed as being not only in December but also in Stockholm by Hannes Adomeit, 'Russia', p.45.

The London Conference at the end of August to heal wounds in the international community and renew diplomatic efforts provided the Russian Foreign Minster with a vehicle for his policy of active co-operation through political measures. So began the second, transitional wave of Moscow policy. This period again fell into phases; first, active diplomatic support for co-operative political approaches to the crisis; secondly, the attempt to identify a 'special role' with a positive and distinctively Russian character in support of international diplomacy, but at the same time counter to any moves by the US to pursue a more forceful approach; and lastly a more negative, distinctly Russian role, in conjunction with the UK and France, in blocking US impulses partly to lift the UN embargo on arms transfers to the territories of former Yugoslavia to assist the Bosnian authorities. Throughout this transitional phase Moscow appeared increasingly to take on the role of Belgrade's protector, although in reality it was more interested in shaping a particular position for itself while continuing its support for international diplomacy.

From the London Conference in August 1992 to the following February, Russian policy on Yugoslavia had four principles — virtually dictated by the vote in Parliament at the end of June.[31] First, there was a need to be even-handed and to place equal responsibility on all sides. Secondly, Russia should be actively concerned with the Yugoslav problem and make its voice known in international diplomacy, vigorously supporting the mechanisms of the London Conference but insisting that final decisions be made by the Security Council, thereby ensuring Moscow's involvement. Thirdly, it sought to prevent the introduction of new Security Council resolutions, in particular issues that included the possibility of using force against the Serbs. Finally, the Russians put their weight behind the potential of the new federal leaders in the rump 'Federal Republic of Yugoslavia' (Serbia and Montenegro), Prime Minister Milan Panić and President Dobrica Ćosić, as vehicles of

---

31 These characteristics are derived from Edemskii, 'Russian Policy'; Deputy Foreign Minister Anatolii Adamishin gave an official version of Russia's approach, in six points, to a session of Parliament on 17 December 1992 — see the excerpts 'Iz Stenogrammy Zasedaniia Verhovnovo Soveta RF' (17 December 1992) in *Iugoslavskii Krizis*, pp.130-43, esp. pp.133-5).

anti-war and anti-Milošević sentiment. A crucial element in all of this was support for non-violent means and for 'constructive forces'.[32]

Support for the apparent opponents of Milošević was central to this Russian approach, since it provided an instrument for ensuring a political approach. The message was elementary: the international community should not threaten force against the Serbs or Serbia since to do so would only damage the prospects of Milošević's opponents who if not hamstrung by international pressure against Serbia, would win the December 1992 presidential elections.[33] Following their victory, Serbia's support for the war in Bosnia would be curtailed and there would be a political solution. The outcome of the elections, however, undercut Russia's position. Milošević defeated Panić[34] — a prelude to his arranging a vote of no-confidence in him as Yugoslav Prime Minster and so ending his period of office.[35]

This approach worked well for Russia until the elections; it was able to be fully engaged, to a great extent setting the agenda. ICFY and the other major powers shared Russia's view that 'constructive forces' had to be given a chance — even if any understanding of the way Milošević ruled would counsel that this was a hopeful rather than serious prospect. Russia was playing a strong role, supporting the extension of UNPROFOR into Bosnia (despite some misgivings in Moscow conservative circles about the nature of the force and NATO's involvement) and complementing international activity — indeed, being possibly the most seriously engaged and positive diplomatic supporter of the ICFY Co-Chairmen Vance and Owen.[36]

The exhaustion of Moscow's approach, based on energetic support for a political solution resulting from constructive forces in Belgrade, left ICFY as the main pillar of its continuing and firm orientation

32 Oleg Rumianstev, *ibid.*, p.137.

33 Panić was thought likely to obtain 70 per cent of the vote in presidential elections in Serbia against Milošević — see *ibid.*

34 In reality, the man Moscow backed got nowhere near the 70 per cent of the vote foreseen in Moscow only three days before the election; Milošević took 55 per cent of the vote to Panić's nonetheless creditable 34 per cent (*Kommersant*, 25 December 1992).

35 See James Gow, 'Serbia and Montenegro: Small 'FRY' — Big Trouble', *RFE/RL Research Report*, Vol.3, No.1, January 1994.

36 Graham Messervy-Whiting, *Peace Conference on Former Yugoslavia: the Politico-Military Interface*, London Defence Studies No.21, Brassey's for the Centre for Defence Studies, London, 1994, pp.18-19.

towards co-operative diplomatic activity and the pursuit of political settlement. This co-incided with the advent of the Clinton Administration and the prospect of a radically different US policy which would seek to help the Bosnian government by lifting the arms embargo and taking a more coercive diplomatic stand against the Bosnian Serbs, including air strikes. This led to a new Russian position — partly in response to positions adopted in the opposition.

There was considerable pressure on Russian foreign policy to block any moves by the incoming US Administration to move away from the political sphere. The inherent antipathy to using force among those leading Russia's 'internationalist' policy was augmented by an overwhelming vote in Parliament — 162 to 4. This challenged Moscow's partnership with the West on former Yugoslavia, even though the total of those voting was only a fraction of the total parliamentary membership.[37] The opposition objected to the Foreign Ministry's lecturing 'Slav brothers'; favoured unconditional support for fellow Slavs against Islam and the Vatican; was for lifting sanctions against Serbia and imposing them on Croatia; was against the Vance-Owen Plan, which compromised Bosnian Serb interests; and opposed the (purportedly) sycophantic policy towards the US.[38] Kozyrev and the Foreign Ministry, therefore, had two reasons to adopt a new approach: to offset the Americans and to appease the growing opposition to co-operation with the West in Moscow, not only by more extreme groupings but also by many in the centre of Russian politics.[39]

The new policy was contained in an eight-point plan distributed to members of the UN Security Council in late February 1993 by the Permanent Representative of the Russian Federation, Ambassador Yulii Vorontsov.[40] The main elements of the plan included renewed and vigorous implementation of the UN arms embargo on Bosnia, an implicit threat to impose sanctions against Croatia if there were further

---

37 Allen Lynch and Reneo Lukić, 'Russland und der Krieg im ehemaligen Jugoslawien', in Angelika Volle and Wolfgang Wagner, *Der Krieg auf dem Balkan. Die Hilflosigkeit der Staatenwelt — Beiträge und Dokumente aus dem Europa-Archiv*, Verlag für Internationale Politik, Bonn, 1994, p.130.

38 *Kommersant*, 2 April 1994.

39 See Nevers, *Russia's Strategic Renovation*, pp.30-33.

40 See Lynch and Lukić, 'Russland', p.130. The eight points were published in *Rossiiskaia Gazeta*, 26 February 1993 — reprinted in *Iugoslavskii Krizis*, p.180.

hostilities there,[41] and strenuous commitment to the Vance-Owen Plan, in which the important possibility of Russia's contributing to a multinational implementation force was stressed. At the same time Moscow was striving to co-ordinate with Washington: following America's appointment of a Special Envoy to ICFY, Ambassador Reginald Bartholomew, it appointed Deputy Foreign Minster Vitalii Churkin as its own Special Envoy.[42]

This policy translated into pressure on all parties to sign the Plan. On 9 March Yeltsin warned that 'Russia would not protect those who set themselves against the international community'.[43] He further suggested that a second London Conference should be convened to dot the i's and cross the t's on the signed Plan.[44] However, as the Bosnian Serbs rejected Vance-Owen, Kozyrev struck out with a strong and positive approach, intended to counter any US-led moves to use force against the Bosnian Serbs and to keep international diplomatic efforts alive.

After the Serbian rejection, there was still at least one way forward for Kozyrev: to agree to deploy new forces in Bosnia to take a 'step by step' approach[45] — which meant 'progressive implementation' of the Vance-Owen Plan.[46] This could have meant using of armed forces to begin implementation of the Plan in areas under the control of Croatian and Bosnian forces, as well as the establishment of 'safety zones'. Kozyrev was prepared to offer Russian troops for this, even though there would likely have been difficulties supplying the large contingents

---

41 The Croatian Army had initiated a series of limited operations in the area of Maslenički Most in January 1993 — see Chapter 5.

42 Churkin was to become a particularly significant figure, whereas Bartholomew remained in the background, to be replaced later in the year by Ambassador Charles Redman. Churkin worked himself into the remarkable position of enjoying the confidence of all involved in the Yugoslav imbroglio — at least until April 1994, when he abandoned talks with Bosnian Serb leaders in exasperation. Although remaining notionally attached to ICFY, he was appointed Ambassador to Brussels and Liaison Official with NATO — a positive sign for the West.

43 Quoted in Edemskii, 'Russian Policy'.

44 *Ibid.*

45 Lough, *Constraints.*

46 *The Daily Telegraph*, 17 May 1993.

implied.[47] 'Progressive implementation', in Kozyrev's view, implied the gradual dampening of the flames in Bosnia.[48] The initiative was resoundingly rejected in Washington, although it had some support from other key states (see Chapter 9). In reality, if the war was to be stopped — and both lives and treasure saved for the future — there was little real alternative to this approach, which was 'risky, politically unpopular, but the only efficient measure'.[49] Partial implementation, at least creating 'safe provinces' with secure logistics lines — and possibly the means to end the fighting — offered the last chance to achieve a settlement which, at least in a limited way, upheld international norms. It was the most astute way forward for the international community.

As a result of the US rejection, not only was the last real opportunity for a principled international settlement of the conflict in Bosnia lost, but the foreign policy tide in Moscow turned. For the remainder of 1993, Moscow's transitional period evolved into its third phase — in which it moved to forceful assertion of a policy based on 'an understanding of its national interests',[50] rather than seeing its primary national interest in international co-operation. From this point on, foreign policy was increasingly geared towards Russia being taken seriously and respected by the West as a 'Great Power'. This was to be the chief characteristic of this wave of Russian policy.[51]

Throughout 1993, Russia continued its full support of international diplomatic efforts to find a new plan, such as the 'Union of Republics' notion (see Chapter 9). It also fully engaged in a multilateral effort with France and the UK to oppose US pressure for a move to make air strikes and lift the arms embargo. In part this was still evidence of Moscow's commitment to international co-operation. However, it also manifested a realisation that its faith in Washington had not been returned and that, in line with the criticisms in Russia of a 'policy of

---

47 See Elaine M. Holoboff, 'Russian Views on Military Intervention: Benevolent Peacekeeping, Monroe Doctrine, or Neo-Imperialism?', Lawrence Freedman ed., *Military Intervention in European Conflicts*, Political Quarterly Special Edition, Blackwell for the Political Quarterly, Oxford, 1994, p.167; see also Lough, *Constraints*, and Arbatova, 'Horror Mirror'.
48 This is discussed in further detail and in context in Chapter 9.
49 Arbatova, 'Horror Mirror'.
50 Nevers, *Russia's Strategic Renovation*, p.38.
51 See generally Adomeit, 'Russia', who points out that the underlying current was moving in this direction as a result of a number of factors.

national humiliation',[52] it would not only play an active and individual role in the international concert on Bosnia but no longer shy from playing an assertive and, if necessary, discordant role.

Following the December 1993 elections in Russia, which saw an anti-reformist majority elected in Parliament, an assertive 'neo-imperial' line was firmly established in Moscow foreign policy. The election results confirmed the 'retrenchment' in foreign policy[53] — which had been coming since Kozyrev's realisation in the spring that 'Russian foreign policy inevitably' had 'to be of an independent and assertive nature'. This emerged from the recognition that 'the only policy with any chance of success is one that recognizes the equal rights and mutual benefit of partnership for both Russia and the West, as well as the status and significance of Russia as a world power.'[54]

This did not mean the end of all co-operation and partnership — only that Russia could not be taken for granted and had to be treated with respect and as an equal. If it should be turned away, as on taking the Vance-Owen Plan forward, or ignored, as at Sarajevo in February 1994, it would steer its own course regardless of the West, especially Washington, and if appropriate cast the shadow of a return to 'the old benefactor-client relationship that played such a pernicious role in the regional conflicts of the Cold War era'.[55] It heralded the beginning of a period in which Moscow would feel able both to imply that it had a veto on expansion of NATO and to apply force against the rebel Chechen Republic by the end of the year.

In the course of the Yugoslav conflict, not only had Moscow evolved from the capital of the Soviet Union to the capital of an independent Russian Federation, but its foreign policy had changed from increasing partnership and co-operation with the West to limited co-operation in which the assertion of Russia as a 'Great Power' and the prospect of competition rather than partnership were once again present. From the onset of international involvement through to the collapse of the Vance-Owen plan, Moscow's broadly supportive policy went through three evolutionary phases: passive and more or less unadulterated acceptance of Western enterprise; highly active co-operation with Western

---

52 *Ibid.*
53 Nevers, *Russia's Strategic Renovation*, p.38.
54 Kozyrev, 'Lagging Partnership', p.61.
55 *Ibid.*, p.66.

initiatives, against the grain of growing criticism in Moscow; highly active co-operation in which Russian initiatives were present, both to demonstrate Moscow's independence to its critics and to divert the possibility of an American move to the use of force with the advent of the Clinton Administration in Washington. In spite of co-operative undertakings with the Clinton White House, it was the US approach which led to the abandonment of wholehearted international co-operation by Russia.

The retreat from internationalism in Moscow policy, both in general and over Yugoslavia, was a response to underlying political pressures from the parliamentary opposition and to growing disillusionment with the West among the reformist leadership. The latter focused on the 'paucity of Western support' for the reform process,[56] and what was felt to be a disappointing *de facto* rejection of Russian co-operation from the moment of high hopes in January 1992 when Yeltsin saw Russia and the West as allies. Demonstrable success would have been the best way of forestalling domestic criticism of this policy approach. To have embraced the Kozyrev proposal on partial implementation would not only have gone far to quell the war in Bosnia and facilitate a resolution of the conflict (thereby saving Bosnia and its people from the continuing privations of war), but it was the last chance for the Kozyrev school in Moscow to demonstrate that Russia was taken seriously as a partner by the West and that wholehearted co-operation, in general and on former Yugoslavia, was the best option. Instead the rejection of Kozyrev's initiative demonstrated even to the liberal-reformist Atlanticists running Russian foreign policy that two-way co-operation was not automatic. Moscow therefore had to alter its path.

Although this did not mean the end to Moscow's co-operation with the West, it signalled a firm application of the brakes — and the loss of an opportunity to establish a co-operative mechanism for dealing with European security problems, including those faced by Russia within the former Soviet Union. Whatever co-operation remained possible, Russian behaviour in Chechnia indicated that an important opportunity had been missed. That chance evaporated in Washington on 22 May 1993 when US policy laid to rest the Vance-Owen Plan.

56 Nevers, *Russia's Strategic Renovation*, p.28.

In Search of America: the Reluctant Superpower's Perspectives

Washington's interventions in the international treatment of the Yugoslav conflict increased as the war progressed. This was partly a result of the need to adjust to its place in the post-Cold War world. It was also due to a strengthening perspective on the crisis as one in which the principal characteristic was Serbian aggression, which emerged critically after Bill Clinton became President at the beginning of 1993. The US initially viewed the conflict as a blend of aggression, ethnic assertion, self-determination and state preservation, but as the conflict moved to Bosnia, it saw that particular former Yugoslav republic (unlike Slovenia and Croatia) as a wholly innocent victim of circumstance and Belgrade's military planning. With Clinton in the White House, the interpretation of the conflict as a war of aggression would dominate, with important consequences not only for US policy but for relations with Moscow and international policy as a whole.[57]

Even though international responsibility in the Yugoslav War of Dissolution can be attributed to the vanity of the EC's off-the-cuff diplomatic intervention in June 1991, the opportunity for that intervention was provided by the absence of US leadership. The collapse of Yugoslavia thus became the first major issue of Western security since the 1956 British-French-Israeli debacle at Suez in which the US had not led the way. Throughout the Cold War, US leadership had been exercised primarily through NATO in which Washington had 'formed up': that is, the US would make a proposal and the allies would form up around it or oppose it.[58] Most important, America's allies could assume that the US would take the lead and provide 'by far the greatest substantive expertise'.[59]

A modified version of this process had been transposed to the UN Security Council and the broad community of states forming the UN

---

57 I grateful to a number of Washington officials, especially at the State Department, who were extremely helpful in guiding my understanding of US debates on and approaches to the Yugoslav conflict. There thoughts and contributions are often insinuated in the present analysis. Unfortunately, I was not able to gain similar assistance at the political level — something which would undoubtedly have enhanced my understanding.

58 Jenonne Walker, 'Keeping America in Europe', *Foreign Policy*, No.83, Summer 1991, p.129, points out that forming up did not mean that Washington necessarily got its way — it was quite possible that European allies would offer opposition to an American initiative.

59 *Ibid.*

during the Gulf conflict. The US had taken the initiative and then set about persuading not only its long-time allies but other capitals, including Moscow, to lend their support to what was essentially a US-led venture with international authority. The disintegration of Yugoslavia represented a break in this pattern. There had been a brief backstage talk by US Secretary of State James Baker to the various Yugoslavs on the eve of the declarations of independence, but when the show began the Americans were absent. From that absence and the EC attempt to take the initiative the concatenation of delusions, fallacies and failures which has constituted international treatment of Yugoslavia's dissolution followed.

Washington's initial absence can be partly explained by its analysis of the crisis and coming conflict, partly by the attitudes of those in the Bush foreign policy team, but mostly by its hesitant attempt to reposition itself in the international system. Thus, while there may be some justification for believing that in 1991 the Gulf conflict and the difficulties of the then Soviet Union meant that the US had less time and resources to devote to the questions posed by the Yugoslav break-up, it would not be true to say that the Americans were caught completely off guard, with their attention elsewhere. However, the effort made in the Gulf Conflict, which momentarily appeared to be the herald of a new age, was more probably 'the last gasp of a morally and politically clearer age'.[60] The expectations raised by the success of the Gulf operation were to cast a shadow over subsequent US policy on Yugoslavia and elsewhere.

The US perspective on the crisis in Yugoslavia embraced elements of all three European views during the Bush Administration. The Bush team, according to one individual involved,[61] had taken a good look at the problems of Yugoslavia and judged from the outset that it was too difficult, that there was nothing which could usefully be done to avoid a violent break-up, and that there was no reason strong enough to justify an armed intervention in what was understood as a complex mixture of the three perspectives held by America's European allies.

---

60 Michael Mandelbaum, 'The Reluctance to Intervene', *Foreign Policy*, No.95, Summer 1994, p.3.
61 David Gompert, 'How to Defeat Serbia', *Foreign Affairs*, Vol.73, No.4, July-August 1994, pp.32-5. Gompert was Senior Adviser for Europe and Eurasia in the Bush Adminstration's National Security Council staff.

The CIA had given warning in 1990 that the Yugoslav federation would almost certainly break up in the following eighteen months and that violence was likely to accompany the process.[62] Thus, there had not been a failure of intelligence to understand what was happening in Yugoslavia. Moreover, already in 1990 the US had made some efforts to mitigate the coming disaster in Yugoslavia. For example, through NATO it had attempted to address the problems arising in the disintegrating federation, but a proposal for consultations was not adopted, with the French, according to David Gompert, 'accusing the United States of "overdramatizing" the problem'.[63] Despite this attempt the US mostly went against both its traditional practice and its stated policy on the primacy of NATO in European security after the Cold War until well into the conflict in Bosnia. Instead it encouraged the Europeans to take the initiative and offered to provide support.

The US had offered encouragement to the Europeans for three reasons — because its initiatives had been rebuffed, because EC countries were keen to be treated as a single diplomatic entity which would fly the flag of common foreign and security policy, and most of all, because there was a belief that no good policy options existed and, whatever these options might be, more influence lay with the EC. This made it easier for Washington to hand the baton to Brussels. Had there been a clear policy objective, urgent leadership would probably have been furnished.

As it was, the US judged that break-up was inevitable and that it could not be peaceful (although there could be no prediction of the actual scale of violence[64]). In the US view, Serbia was 'usurping power', Slovenia was resolutely set on escaping Serbian power, Croatia was determined to be independent and would follow Slovenia, and the Serbs both in Croatia and in Belgrade would not allow an independent Croatia without a fight (which would also implicate the JNA). Beyond this lay the uncertainties of what might happen in Bosnia, Macedonia and Kosovo. The US therefore began with a primary interest in avoiding a war in the Balkans — which it saw as highly likely, anyway, and a certainty if the Yugoslav federation were to break up.

62 Roy Gutman, *A Witness to Genocide*, Element, Shaftesbury (Dorset) 1993, p.xxiv.
63 Gompert, 'Serbia', p.35.
64 See *Ibid.*, pp.33-4.

This general sense among Bush Adminstration experts of being confronted with an insoluble problem was possibly compounded by the attitudes of the individuals involved. While there could be little doubt that the Serbian President Slobodan Milošević was the chief villain of the piece, there was a tendency to place almost equal blame on the independence-seeking republics for which there was 'scant sympathy'.[65] Some alleged that this was due to the presence of a 'Belgrade Mafia' in the Bush team.[66] In particular, it was argued, the Belgrade experience of Deputy Secretary of State Lawrence Eagleburger and National Security Adviser Brent Scowcroft, as well as their later interests, enhanced their support for the State Department analysis that unity was the best option and that Slovenia and Croatia were the problem.[67] This may have been particularly telling in internal debates between the Departments of State and Defense, in which the latter was reported to have argued for a managed dissolution of both Yugoslavia and the Soviet Union.[68]

Probably the most decisive element for the US was its attempt to establish its own position in the post-Cold War world. Although Washington had successfully led the UN-authorised coalition in the Gulf conflict, that example of activism was against the grain of an American withdrawal from always playing the most prominent role on every issue in either the Western Alliance or the international system. This did not mean complete withdrawal, but greater selectivity over the areas in which the US would engage and whatever the issue, a greater need to work on a basis of partnership rather than leadership.[69] In facing the

---

65 *Ibid.*, p.33.

66 Gutman, *Witness*, pp.xxiv-xxv.

67 Eagleburger had been US Ambassador to Belgrade in the late 1970s and was widely reported to have established a good social relationship with Milošević at that time while the latter was working at Beobanka, a major Belgrade-based bank. Eagleburger had what he described as a 'well-tested working relationship' with the Serbian President (quoted in Leonard J. Cohen, *Broken Bonds: the Disintegration of Yugoslavia*, Westview, Boulder, 1993, p.216). After leaving the US Foreign Service in the early 1980s, he became a director of Yugo America, the American branch of a Serbian-based car manufacturer, as well as President of Kissinger Associates (of which Brent Scowcroft, who had been air attaché to Belgrade in the 1960s, was Vice President), a representative firm which carried out business with Yugoslav state companies.

68 Gutman, *Witness*, p.xxiv.

69 Walker, 'Keeping America', pp.140-2.

questions posed by Yugoslavia as well as the EC's desire to be taken seriously, the US was quite prepared to abdicate leadership.

It was not merely content to do so over Yugoslavia; it was actually eager to do so — for two reasons. The first was a sensitivity of the way the US was perceived in the world. Washington had been subjected to accusations that it had manipulated the UN and other countries for its own purposes in a form of neo-imperialism. The US was concerned lest, in the wake of the Gulf conflict, 'a leading role in Yugoslavia would imply that it could and would act as international policeman, even in an area of more immediate importance to America's rich European partners.'[70]

A concern in Washington for the way in which it was perceived was tied to a second reason for refraining from leadership. This was the desire not to become burdened with practical responsibilities. Had the US sought to provide leadership through NATO, it would have been obliged to back its words with force — in terms not only of a specific threat, but of whatever it would have to do to prevail if the initial action proved insufficient: once it had made a commitment to use force, it could not avoid taking whatever action might prove necessary to avoid failure. Thus it could not rely on inducing a desired response with limited threats and action, and, because it had no desire to carry out extensive operations, the 'consequences of guessing wrong were prohibitive'.[71] Because the costs of involvement might prove greater than the Bush Administration was prepared to countenance, it was judged better not to enter the frame to begin with.

That judgement was predicated on an analysis at the outset similar to that of the UK about the historic and ethnic dimensions of any Yugoslav conflict — aspects which meant that the US were to become committed to a policy involving force, the conflict would have more in common with Vietnam than Kuwait. The need to commit large ground forces in a complicated conflict risked unending and unacceptable escalation. This was compounded by the critical judgement that the US

70 Gompert, 'Serbia', p.41; discussions with senior officials in the State Department indicate that the desire not to be seen as the sole superpower and hegemon was a serious consideration for the US.
71 *Ibid.*, p.40.

had no direct interests at stake in the region now that the Cold War had passed.[72]

Whereas the US initially shared both the UK's view of the complex ethnic character of the conflict and France's proclivity for opposing Slovenian and Croatian independence in its first phase, it also shared the German analysis that the war was one of Belgrade-led aggression, especially when conflict came to Bosnia. It was reinforced there by the appreciation that, whereas Slovenia and Croatia had brought suffering upon themselves through irresponsible behaviour (in US eyes), Bosnia was an innocent victim of circumstance and well-planned Serbian aggression.[73] This was the view of the Bush Adminstration, but remained tempered by other concerns. With the arrival of Bill Clinton in the White House, this element came to dominate the US perception of the conflict.

In the early days of the Clinton Adminstration, the American analysis of the war in Bosnia was as a 'conventional case of aggression by one state (Serbia) against another (Bosnia)'.[74] In the case of Bosnia, the perception of an act of aggression was compounded by the (generally accurate) judgement that the Serbian camp was wreaking violence on a largely undefended Bosnian population. This interpretation of the war in Bosnia had been prominent in the Clinton election campaign, when as a candidate Clinton had cited Bosnia as an example of the Bush Administration's supposedly ineffective post-Gulf Conflict foreign policy, marked by 'indifference' to human rights abuses: 'Once again the administration is turning its back on violations of basic human rights

72 Michael Brenner, 'Les Etats-Unis et la crise yougoslave', *Politique Étranger*, April 1992, p.330.

73 See for example Warren Zimmermann's interview with Liljana Smajlović, 'Moja uloga u Bosni', *Vreme*, 27 June 1994.

74 Robert W. Tucker and David C. Hendrickson, 'America and Bosnia', *The National Interest*, Fall 1993, p.15. The authors correctly point out that in the US there was generally a highly simplified understanding of the conflict, rightly pointing out that the conflict was not conventional in the sense understood. However, their analysis of what the issues and facts of the Bosnian case were — including the judgement that 'the recognition of Bosnia's independence itself constituted an illegal intervention in Yugoslavia's internal affairs' (p.17) — was fallacious. Cf. James Gow, 'Serbian Nationalism and the Hissssing Ssssnake in the International Order: Whose Sovereignty? Which Nation?', *Slavonic and East European Review*, Vol.72, No.3, Summer 1994.

and our own democratic values.'[75] The Clinton Adminstration, it was promised, would be more active.

No Action to Limited Action: US Policy from Bush to Bill

The Clinton criticisms of the Bush Administration's attitude to Bosnia focused on the notion that the Bush White House had missed the point and was failing to discharge its responsibilities to the world by cravenly allowing atrocities to pass without decisive action. The reality was that, along with other members of the international community, the Bush team had acted to the extent of its desired, or required, commitment — and had been careful to avoid suggesting action beyond what it was prepared to do, or what was consistent with its co-operation with other key elements involved in the international handling of the Yugoslav conflict.

With the Clinton Adminstration there was to be a radical difference. Instead of harmonising its policy preferences with both the degree to which it was prepared to make practical commitments and with its allies and partners in the international community, the new White House had a tendency to pronounce on principle, prevaricate in practice and pre-empt the policies and plans of others. While its stand on principle against 'ethnic cleansing' and the use of force in the attempt to create new borders could not be faulted as such, it was never commensurate either with circumstances or its own degree of commitment, given its absolute domestic priorities. Consequently, as will be seen, US policy approaches graduated from virtually no action to little action — the sum of which was to distract international diplomacy and divert any pressure for serious engagement by the US.

As Yugoslavia entered its final collapse, the Bush Adminstration, somewhat unrealistically, favoured the unity of Yugoslavia because it believed this held out the best prospect of avoiding a war. At the same time as formally backing unity, according to senior officials, the US favoured a confederal rearrangement of the Yugoslav republics.[76] However, the US did not make this preference known, perhaps because

---

75 Quoted in Elizabeth Drew, *On the Edge: the Clinton Presidency*, Simon and Schuster, New York, 1994, p.138.
76 *Ibid.*, p.34; this was also related to the author by Warren Zimmermann, US Ambassador to Belgrade at the time.

it could not,[77] although in reality the only possible way of avoiding violence was international admission of the possibility of a confederal arrangement, or an asymmetrical association — moves which would have evened the diplomatic and political odds.[78]

On the eve of the break-up of Yugoslavia and the outbreak of hostilities, the US introduced subtle modifications into its position. While Secretary of State James Baker and Ambassador Warren Zimmermann insisted strongly that they stood for the retention of the Yugoslav state, they also, quietly and largely unnoticed, added that, even though they were in favour of Yugoslavia, they could not stand against democracy.[79] In spite of this nuanced openness to the possibility of re-arranging the Yugoslav republics, the US was to maintain a hard line against recognition until after the EC had decided to grant recognition to Slovenia and Croatia in January 1992. The US made efforts towards the end of 1991 to dissuade the EC in general and Germany in particular from resorting to early recognition outside the framework of an overall agreement.

The Baker-Zimmermann meetings with the various Yugoslav leaders in June, whatever the role played by various Washington personalities and their supposed pro-Serbian sympathies in earlier debates, gave rise to one of the key reasons for an American abdication on Yugoslavia during the first six months of conflict and a lack of sympathy for Slovenia and Croatia. This was the personal response of key figures such as Zimmermann and Baker. At meetings with all the Yugoslav leaders on 21 June, Baker and Zimmermann believed that they had obtained assurances, as well as from Belgrade, from Slovenia and Croatia that they would not act unilaterally and precipitately. When both issued declarations of independence on 25 June, the Americans were

77 Dennison Rusinow, 'Yugoslavia: Balkan Breakup?', *Foreign Policy*, No.83, Summer 1991, p.158.
78 See *Ibid.*, as well as James Gow, *Yugoslav Endgames*, London Defence Studies No.5, Brassey's for the Centre for Defence Studies, London, 1991.
79 Secretary of State James Baker said this to Yugoslav generals and Serbian leaders on his visit to Belgrade on 21 June 1991, according to Warren Zimmermann, who was at Baker's side, in discussion with the author. (It should be noted, however, that the Yugoslav generals appeared to believe that they were 'only doing what Mr. Baker told them' when they began operations to keep Yugoslavia together. See Janez Janša, *Premiki*, Mladinska Kniga, Ljubljana, 1993, p.98.)

affronted at what they regarded as treachery.[80] In a sense, they sulked for six months and left the Yugoslav bill to be picked up entirely by the Europeans, who had already been pushed to the fore, and some of whom were only too keen to demonstrate what they could achieve without Washington.

Following the EC decisions on reconition, the US began to shift its policy. This was to bring Washington more into line with Europe, but was also driven by analysis of the situation recognition had created in Bosnia. It was the assessment that Bosnia was a victim of circumstance and likely also to become a victim of aggression that led the US to lead the otherwise cautious Europeans towards full recognition of Bosnian independence in April 1992 in the hope that, as in Croatia, internationalisation of the conflict might discourage Serbian attacks.[81] In this same period, after the Bosnian President Alija Izetbegović signed the 18 March agreement in Lisbon on the 'cantonisation' of the country, he divulged to Zimmermann that he did not actually agree with it. Zimmermann told the Bosnian President that he was under no obligation to sign documents with which he did not agree.[82] Subsequently Izetbegović withdrew his agreement to the Lisbon document.

In doing so, he was taking confidence from American sympathy — something which became characteristic of the US-Bosnian relationship. The US was more overtly sympathetic and committed to defending the principle of a multicultural Bosnia and to the protection of the Bosnian Muslims in the face of 'ethnic cleansing', above all by the Bosnian Serbs but also by the Bosnian Croats. As a result of America's more apparent support, it was hard to avoid the conclusion that the Bosnian leadership believed that more substantial assistance would be forthcoming.[83]

Further evidence of US commitment came in Washington's efforts to secure the imposition of two packages of sanctions on Serbia and Montenegro for their involvement in the war in Bosnia, the first in May 1992, the second in May 1993. Moreover, it was the US, through

80 This is based on discussions with Zimmermann. See also his remarkable personal account: Warren Zimmermann, 'The Last Ambassador: A Memoir of the Collapse of Yugoslavia', *Foreign Affairs*, Vol.74, No.2, March-April 1995.
81 *Ibid.*
82 *Ibid.*
83 See Tucker and Hendrickson, 'America and Bosnia', pp.18-19.

Acting Secretary of State Eagleburger, which pressed the question of war crimes, following revelations of widespread Serb atrocities, as well as detention camps in some of which Muslims were killed, for example that at Omarska.[84] Following President Bush's defeat in the November 1992 presidential elections, Eagleburger published a list of ten Serbian political and military officials suspected of involvement in organising and carrying out 'ethnic cleansing'. Finally, 1992 and, in effect, the Bush Administration finished with a curt Christmas Day warning to Belgrade that there would be a forceful US response if it initiated hostilities in Kosovo.[85]

However, however much the Bosnian leadership and others might perceive Washington to be the most openly supportive among the major capitals, it was not offering much. Indeed, the fact that many in the US felt that Washington had been found wanting in the summer of 1992 was exemplified by State Department Desk Officer George Kenney, as reports emerged of extensive 'ethnic cleansing' and Serbian detention and even death camps. He became the first of a succession of officials to resign, unable to countenance Adminstration policy.[86] This represented a principled and emotional position which characterised US policy far more than any other major country's — increasingly after the advent of the Clinton Administration.

Action and Distraction: the Clinton White House and US Policy

It was notable that one of the principal architects of President Clinton's Bosnia policy, National Security Adviser Anthony Lake, was a defender of State Department Yugoslav Desk Officer George Kenney's resignation, having resigned himself over US escalation of the Vietnam war into Cambodia over twenty years earlier.[87] Adherence to the principle of resisting 'ethnic cleansing' was an essential strand in US thinking, both at the State Department and in the Administration. However, this was countered by a continuing reluctance to engage

---

84 Gutman, *Witness*, p.90.

85 *New York Times*, 28 December 1992.

86 Kenney, in an explanation of why so many officials had resigned from the Department of State over policy on Bosnia, accused the US of effective complicity in genocide. (George Kenney, 'Complici di un genocido', *La Repubblica*, 28 August 1993, in association with *War Report*, London.)

87 See Drew, *On the Edge*, p.143.

militarily to prevent what was happening in Bosnia. Whereas the Bush Adminstration, in spite of an apparently stronger commitment to Bosnia, had broadly aligned itself with international efforts, given its inhibitions on using force, the Clinton Adminstration arrived with a policy position which it believed overcame the need to deploy US ground forces and which would only engage US air power for a limited period. This was the 'lift and strike' blueprint.

It had become clear that only a serious and forceful approach would persuade the Bosnian Serbs to desist. There was no political constituency in Washington for the engagement of US troops. Even the advocates of US intervention mostly believed that this should be restricted to aerial commitment only. In this context 'lift and strike' provided an appealing formula. The US would be taking a principled position to resist Serbian aggression and support the efforts of the Bosnian government by securing a restricted lifting of the UN arms embargo against the territories of the former Yugoslavia in favour of the Bosnian authorities, providing air deterrence to prevent Serbian forces taking advantage of a transitional period and avoiding a commitment of US forces on the ground.[88] The deceptively simple recipe was flawed — not least in the disruption it would cause in relations with allies and partners, especially the UK and France which had troops deployed with the UN force in Bosnia.[89]

Hence, the US under Clinton began to urge its European allies to take more decisive action against the Serbs (and in certain periods, such as the autumn of 1993, the Croats). This strong, clear interpretation of the conflict as a matter of inter-state aggression set the US apart from its European allies, even the Germans who were increasingly persuaded of the hybrid nature of the war. As a result of divergent perceptions of the conflict, there were substantial differences of opinion on questions of purpose and policy between America and the Europeans and between all four major Western countries.

---

88 Lawrence Freedman, 'Why the West Failed', *Foreign Policy*, No.97, Winter 1994-5, p.64.
89 Drew, *On the Edge*, p.155; see also Thomas J. Halverson, 'Explaining American Yugoslav Policy: Why Washington's Commitment is the Shape of Things to Come', paper for the International Conference on the Yugoslav War, Keele University, 19-20 September 1994.

The most critical difference came on the vexed question of the Vance-Owen Plan (which will be] discussed in Chapter 9). The new Administration strongly criticised the Plan, made a less than complete offer to support its implementation (in the event of the Bosnian government and the other parties agreeing to it), which was later effectively withdrawn, and adumbrated a policy which both ran counter to the efforts of all engaged in the international handling of the conflict, such as the UN and Washington's partners and allies, and revealed a determination to avoid deploying ground forces. Although there were unavoidable hiccups created by the transition from the Bush team to Clinton's which affected US policy towards the Plan, a more important determinant of the US approach to Vance-Owen was the attitude of the Administration. This can be understood in two ways — the general tenor of Adminstration policy and specific apprehensions.

The essential contradictions which characterised US policy throughout the Clinton regime were, therefore, thrown into sharp relief in the handling of the Vance-Owen Plan: the impulse of moral indignation to act was in conflict with an overriding desire to protect an all-important domestic agenda from the damaging intrusion of foreign policy entanglements. At the general level, from the outset, the chief foreign policy aim of the Clinton White House was as far as possible to keep clear of foreign policy. This meant avoiding new initiatives which could be demanding and ultimately distracting. Domestic reform was all.

The new Administration was guided by the need to avoid the fate of the last great domestic reform-oriented White House, under President Lyndon Baines Johnson. Johnson's domestic reforms had been sunk by entanglement in Vietnam. For the Clinton Adminstration it was essential that there should not be another Vietnam — which also meant no foreign policy commitments with the potential to backfire and so make the passage of difficult domestic legislation on health care reform, the economy and crime even harder than they would be anyway or even impossible.[90] Thus, there would be strong limits on any area of US foreign policy, especially one as complex and uncertain as the war in Bosnia.

---

90 This interpretation is based on observation of Administration behaviour, as well as discussion with officials in Washington which tended to confirm it. On Clinton's difficulties in getting essential legislation, see Drew, *On the Edge, passim.*

Nonetheless, there was a stated commitment to increased action on the war in Bosnia, as well as a genuine moral impulse for it. Even before his inauguration, the President-elect declared that 'the legitimacy of ethnic cleansing cannot stand'.[91] Clinton appears to have been affected personally by reports of the situation in former Yugoslavia and by the urgings to 'do something' of those such as Elie Wiesel (who deeply impressed the President in his lecture at the dedication of the Holocaust Museum in Washington on 21 April 1993).[92] Clinton was confused, in policy terms, between the emphasis on domestic affairs in his Administration and his personal reaction both to the events in Bosnia and to the charges of others.

The essential contradiction in his own position and that of his Administration was encapsulated in one sentence on 20 April: 'The US should always seek an opportunity to stand up against — at least speak out against — inhumanity.' As Elizabeth Drew, an informed and incisive observer of the Clinton White House, observed, there was 'quite a disparity within that one sentence'.[93] In reality, Bosnia policy in the Clinton Administration was 'a study in ambiguity' and its 'implementation an exercise in futility'.[94]

Against this background, the Vance-Owen Plan met with specific misgivings on the part of the new Administration at three levels. First, there was understandable ethical concern. Although there were divisions within the Administration on the degree to which this should be allowed to affect policy (with Defence Secretary Les Aspin most clearly against taking a strong interest in the Bosnian question), for the President, his Vice-President Al Gore and for the National Security Adviser Tony Lake there was a strong emotional and moral issue to be addressed. This involved the twin duties to reject aggression and to take a stand against 'ethnic cleansing'. The Plan, accompanied by the continuing implementation of the UN arms embargo against the former Yugoslav territories including Bosnia, appeared to be a device for forcing the

91 Quoted by Drew, *On the Edge*, p.139.
92 *Ibid.*, pp.135 and 153.
93 *Ibid.*, p.153.
94 Michael Brenner, 'The United States Perspective', paper for Winston Foundation Project (CeSPI), Spoleto, 2-3 December 1994.

Muslims to surrender and for rewarding the Serbian camp.[95] There was a clear view, shared by Clinton, Gore and Lake, that, in a similar position to the Bosnians', they would want the right to have weapons to defend themselves against aggression and 'ethnic cleansing' — Clinton rhetorically repeated the telling question: 'How would Americans react if others told them that they could not have arms to defend themselves?'[96]

Secondly, there were diverse political considerations. These embraced the need to accommodate political lobbies supporting the Bosnian cause — which were a growing force in Congress, where the Bosnian government had been using connections established by the American-educated members if its leadership and representative agencies to lobby strongly. In addition, there was considerable informed debate on the issue of intervention.[97] There was also pressure from both the media and public opinion. The liberal press, notably through the reporting of joint Pulitzer Prize-winners John Burns in the *New York Times*[98] and of Roy Gutman in the more populist *Newsday*,[99] as well as the opinion columns of, among others, Anthony Lewis in the *New York Times*, accompanied TV images from Bosnia — both the constant coverage of dedicated news stations such as CNN and the committed reporting of the ABC network, particularly Peter Jennings's 'Special', broadcast as the Vance-Owen Plan was being debated in the spring of 1993.

In addition to press pressure, public opinion polling had shown a considerable increase in support for American action. Although there were some reports identifying 60 per cent opposition to

95 This was a view for which there was much support in Congress. See, for example, the comments by Senator Joseph Biden in Sub-Committee on European Affairs of the Committee on Foreign Relations, 'Hearing. American Policy in Bosnia', 18 February 1993, US Government Printing Office, Washington DC, 1993, p.24.

96 See Drew, *On the Edge*, pp.150-1.

97 See, for example, 'To Die in Sarajevo: US Interests in Yugoslavia — A Symposium', *Policy Review*, Fall 1992, in which a selection of leading conservative foreign policy specialists in September 1991 offered opinions.

98 A contentious, negative critique of reporting, such as that by Burns, appeared in Peter Brock, 'The Partisan Press', *Foreign Policy*, No.93, Winter 1993-4.

99 For a collection of the reports on Bosnia for which he was awarded the Pulitzer Prize, see Roy Gutman, *Witness to Genocide*, Element, Shaftesbury, 1993.

intervention,[100] these tended to be based on partial information and limited knowledge. In-depth polling revealed opposition in the order of 60 per cent only to unilateral US intervention, whereas there was consistent support in polls where the possibility of multilateral action for intervention was posited — support was never below 50 per cent and in the most thorough polling averaged 60 per cent.[101] Even though the image and memory of Vietnam preyed heavily on the minds of political leaders dedicated to domestic issues,[102] pressure of this kind had to be taken into account. At the same time, the superficial uncertainty shown by some contradictory polls, added to a distrust of popular support, fuelled the judgement made by Stan Greenberg, one of Clinton's 'floating' consultants, that polling could not be a guide to reaction following any presidential announcement of involvement.[103] Thus the Administration had to balance political pressures and demands for action against its outright opposition to engaging ground forces in Bosnia.

The question of deploying ground forces was related to the third level of Adminstration opposition to the Vance-Owen Plan. This involved its practicability. The assessment of the US and of other countries and NATO was that the Plan could not be fully implemented. The number of internal borders that the ten-province plan would have created was regarded as unenforceable. This generated the dismal judgment that the

100 For example, it was reported in February 1993, that 60 per cent of US citizens were against intervention. (*Washington Post* and ABC Poll, reported in *Mladina*, 23 February 1993.

101 See Steve Kull and Clay Ramsay, *US Public Opinion on Intervention in Bosnia*, Program on International Policy Attitudes, CISSM, School of Public Affairs, University of Maryland, 15 May 1993, esp. pp. 1, 5 and 6. The same authors and Program carried out a follow-up study a year later which generally consolidated the earlier findings — *US Public Attitudes on Involvement in Bosnia*, Program on International Policy Attitudes, CISSM, School of Public Affairs, College Park MD, 4 May 1994. In the latter, deeper study — which also conducted a general analysis of all polls carried out on Bosnia in the previous year, it was found that the completeness of information in a question, among other things, such as mitigated loss of American lives, was an important factor in determining the degree to which support for involvement was greater than the baseline figure of 45 per cent (with baseline opposition to involvement at 10 per cent).

102 For one example of discussion on the continuing need to address the 'Vietnam syndrome', see Waltraud Queiser Morales, 'US intervention and the New World Order: lessons from Cold-War and post-Cold War cases', *Third World Quarterly*, Vol.15, No.1, 1994.

103 Drew, *On the Edge*, p.150.

'only thing worse than the failure of Vance-Owen would be the success of Vance-Owen.'[104] This, in addition to the principled objections that the Bosnian government should not be forced to accept a plan which rewarded 'ethnic cleansing', and the intelligence assessment that the Bosnian Serbs would not accept it, made Vance-Owen unattractive. The degree of opposition was based on an ideal of implementation in what were assumed to be far from ideal conditions — there was no sense that the doubts generated by this vision might be outweighed by limited implementation which would halt the war. As a result, rather than seek to use the plan to stabilise Bosnia, the US preferred to see the Vance-Owen Plan killed off in the Washington Declaration of May 1993 (see Chapter 9).

In putting an end to the Vance-Owen Plan, the US was acting in a way which could be seen as one of three mutually contradictory elements: placing principle before pragmatism in rejecting an ethically corrupt plan; placing pragmatic wisdom before principle in allowing the war to continue rather than deploying troops to blunt it; and ensuring that there would be no possibility of the US being obliged to honour a commitment to deploy troops on an implementation mission, thus in theory keeping the domestic policy agenda from being spoiled by any possible military fiasco abroad (although, ironically, this was to happen in Somalia, not Bosnia — and, like the failure in Vietnam, it was not properly understood[105]). Whichever of these was the genuine or most important explanation for US policy, the reality which followed confirmed the inherent tension within the Clinton Administration's policy on former Yugoslavia. It also set the US on a policy odyssey which would last another year.

By the end of that year, although the inherent contradictions would remain, the real thrust of policy was based on the realisation of the need to gauge policy in terms of real commitment and the need to work with others, rather than openly against the grain of what others were doing. This meant trying to repair the great strain and damage done to relationships with allies within NATO as well as to NATO itself. The same was true for the crucial and historic 'strategic partnership' with Russia, as well as trying to replace some of the opportunities lost — in

104 John Fenske, 'The West and the "Problem from Hell"', *Current History*, Vol.29, No.577, November 1993, p.355.
105 See Morales, 'US intervention', pp.88-91 and 94-6.

Bosnia and in relations with other major international actors — for which the Vance-Owen Plan had represented the best option.

Washington's policy odyssey began — and, in a sense, was already completed — as its lack of commitment to the Vance-Owen Plan and its promotion of the 'lift and strike' option (see Chapter 9) created an environment in which the Bosnian Serbs could safely fail to 'ratify' the signature of their leader Radovan Karadžić, free from the international pressure which had persuaded him to sign at the beginning of May. With cruelly ironic timing Clinton and Secretary of State Warren Christopher were both having a change of heart. In the first week of May Christopher, failing on his somewhat unconvincing and ill-thought-out mission to convert the Europeans to the 'lift and strike' option, began finally to focus 'on what a loser this policy was'.[106] This feeble effort was made in spite of the clearly stated objections of the British and French, as well as the disapproval of the Russians.

In Europe it had been realised that the only way to convince the British and French would be to threaten the future of NATO. But although that could realistically be expected to turn them round to supporting US policy, it would also necessarily mean both gambling heavily on the policy and making it an American responsibility, requiring US leadership. But from the outset the US had wanted to avoid leadership, looking to the Europeans to carry the burden and provide back-up where necessary. It was neither prepared to act unilaterally, having clearly committed itself to 'multilateralism', nor to provide leadership.[107] As there was absolutely no will to shift on this issue, the Adminstration's policy had run into a dead-end.

At the same time as Christopher was struggling unavailingly, the President began to waver on US Bosnian policy. Reportedly[108] he had become deeply impressed by reading one book — from the myths of history and ethnic furies school of quasi-analysis.[109] As a result of this and Christopher's rejection in Europe, 'lift and strike' was put on hold, but there was no firm policy decision to replace it. Consequently a year

---

106 Quotation attributed to a senior official close to Christopher by Drew, *On the Edge*, p.159.
107 F. Stephen Larrabee, *Politique Étrangère*, Année 59, No.4, Winter 1994-5, p.1044.
108 Drew, *On the Edge*, p.157.
109 Robert D. Kaplan's *Balkan Ghosts: A Journey Through History*, St. Martin's Press, New York, 1993; for a telling critique of 'dangerous nonsense', see Noel Malcolm's review 'Seeing Ghosts', in *The National Interest*, Summer 1993.

of 'rift and drift' followed, as relations with the Allies in NATO and with Moscow were tattered and the Adminstration could not decide conclusively what to do.

With 'lift and strike' on hold but not removed from the agenda — and indeed with 'strike' looking increasingly likely as circumstances demanded action and the British and French traded agreement on a little bit of strike to avoid lift — US policy, somewhat apart, shadowed the main trends in international activity. ICFY, following the demise of Vance-Owen, had continued to pursue a settlement through the 'Union of Republics' notion of July 1993 and the HMS *Invincible Acquis* from September the same year. In these negotiations the US was holding out for a better position for the Muslims in any three-way deal. The new US approach, after May, was nonetheless geared towards obtaining a settlement. There continued to be a threat of using air strikes either multilaterally or unilaterally, but these would now be clearly linked to diplomatic purpose, with emphasis in the first phase on lifting the siege of Sarajevo before a second phase anticipated the use of air power to push the parties towards an agreement.[110]

Although this policy could be regarded as having led eventually to progress at Sarajevo in February 1994, in conjunction with bilateral initiatives with the Russian Federation and multilateral ones within the Contact Group (in which the initiative of the US Ambassador in Zagreb, Peter Galbraith, was critical), the reality was that following initial US reluctance to be drawn into action, the French had played the critical role in bringing about air strikes, and various others had performed significant parts in making it work.[111] Subsequent initiatives through the Contact Group including the 'take-it-or-leave-it' approach which the Bosnian Serbs were to reject, left the Clinton Adminstration, in spite of its own (by this stage clear) assessments of its 'real', but 'limited' interests in Bosnia,[112] to return to its point of departure in August 1994: 'lift and strike'.

---

110 See Drew, *On the Edge*, p.275.
111 *International Herald Tribune*, 15 February 1994.
112 US Secretary for Defence William Perry, quoted in Thomas Halverson, 'Explaining American Yugoslav Policy: Why Washington's Commitment is the Shape of Things to Come', paper for International Conference on the Yugoslav War, University of Keele, 19-20 September 1994. See also Warren Zimmermann's piece 'The Balkan Imperative' in *The Washington Post*, 24 April 1994, where a complementary set of 'major' but not 'vital' interests was outlined.

However, no sooner had the UK and France implicitly acknowledged that US pressure would be irresistible and that 'lift and strike', along with withdrawal of UNPROFOR, would be inevitable,[113] than the US in September placed a six-month moratorium on its call to lift the arms embargo.[114] Ironically the Clinton Adminstration, having ebbed and flowed in arguments with its Allies on the arms embargo question, pulled back from the brink when finally forced to confront the real implications of withdrawal, lift and strike, and renewed its efforts to engineer an acceptable settlement.

This was perhaps the ultimate example of uncertainty and incoherence in policy which had characterised the Adminstration — torn between understandable emotional reaction, outrage and a stand on principle, on the one hand, and facing up to inescapable realities and responsibilities of action, as well as President Clinton's surpassing devotion to domestic policy, on the other.[115] The President 'provided no steady leadership on the subject within the government, to the American people, or internationally'.[116] The about-turn (suspended) on policy towards Bosnia was confirmation that the US, especially under a domestic-oriented Administration, was facing grave difficulties in adjusting to the post-Cold War world. This was damaging both to the US itself and to its relations with other countries. In Elizabeth Drew's assessment, whatever the right policy might have been — and the major debates on it showed the enormous potential for difference — it was clearly wrong to have such an inconsistent policy, or indeed no policy at all: 'The President talked too much about what he was going to do — and then didn't do it.'[117] This inconsistency lay at the heart of US

113 UK Foreign Secretary Douglas Hurd began to signal this, probably before it had been accepted as inevitable, in a speech in June recognising that there were pressures 'beyond the borders of Bosnia' which created a 'real risk' that the arms embargo would be lifted and UNPROFOR's position would become 'impossible', forcing it to withdraw. (Douglas Hurd, 'Annual Diplomatic Banquet Speech', *Arms Control and Disarmament Quarterly Review*, No.34, July 1994, pp.49-50.)
114 This call was supported by Bosnian President Alija Izetbegović.
115 David C. Hendrickson, 'The Recovery of Internationalism', *Foreign Affairs*, Vol.73, No.5, September-October 1994, gives a good account of the disconnection between Clinton's internationalist foreign policy commitments and his 'desire to focus on America's internal renewal...the main reason for his election', (p.27).
116 Drew, *On the Edge*, p.283.
117 Drew, *On the Edge*, p.284.

policy on former Yugoslavia under Clinton — and thus at the heart of international diplomatic efforts.

The truth was that, while President Clinton's heart was clearly in the right place, his domestic programme and political judgement countered any impulse to 'do the right thing' in Bosnia. This resulted in a half-way house policy which made diplomacy more difficult: it was never clear whether it was half-way up or already half-way down. Moreover, eighteen months into the Clinton Presidency there had come to be a clear understanding, somewhat late in the day, that maintaining the international 'concert' formed with Russia and the Europeans was more important than 'the precise disposition of the Bosnian civil war'.[118] In particular, having made 'strategic partnership' with Moscow an early priority,[119] the Clinton White House had missed chances to consolidate that partnership and thereby damaged its prospects. Nonetheless, much damage had already been done.

In defence of the US position under Clinton, there could be no doubting the importance of stressing matters of principle and of refusing on that basis to contemplate agreements which would place a seal of approval on reprehensible Serbian acts: there should be no more 'Munichs'.[120] Moreover, any assessment of the Adminstration's performance on former Yugoslavia, as well as on a number of other issues, had to take into account the unhappy inheritance from the Bush era.[121] However, there could be no escaping the conclusion that lack of preparation, internal confusion within the Administration, uncertain and fluctuating policy and the (at best) self-deception involved in making promises which were either untenable or which there was no intention of honouring, was damaging if not deceitful.[122] As a result,

118 Hendrickson, 'Internationalism', p.41.
119 See Michael Cox, 'The necessary partnership? The Clinton presidency and post-Soviet Russia', *International Affairs*, Vol.70, No.4, October 1994.
120 This point was put to the author with conviction be a senior State Department official.
121 See, for example, Anthony Hartley, 'The Clinton approach: idealism with prudence', *The World Today*, Vol.49, No.2, February 1993.
122 For example, following events at Goražde in April 1994, the Croatian newspaper *Nedjeljna Dalmacija* (20 April 1994), speculated as to whether this had been a 'Western catastrophe, or Clinton's deceit?' The idea of deceit and 'trickery' in US foreign policy was also found elsewhere — Jonathan Clarke, formerly a British official in the UK Embassy in Washington, warned that Americans would "turn away from war begun in trickery", in a piece published in the *Los Angeles Times* on 13 April. See also Clarke's 'Commentary', *Los Angeles Times*, 26 October 1993.

there was disillusionment and a lack of confidence both at home and in the world.[123]

In the course of the conflict in Yugoslavia, the attitudes of both Washington and Moscow were evolving, in relation both to the conflict itself and to the position of each in the world. Up till 1993, Washington under the Bush Adminstration and Moscow, in the spirit of international co-operation with which it had ended the Cold War, backed the efforts of international bodies. However, for both capitals these were years of domestic re-alignment and redefinition of their roles in international society. During 1993, ironically, they crossed in opposite directions. While the passage of both countries was part of a general re-orientation after the Cold War and a reaction of the Clinton Democratic Adminstration to being in office, it was the latter which bore the responsibility for the final dereliction of international policy.

Three important consequences stemmed from the Clinton approach. First, the stand on principle against 'ethnic cleansing' without being prepared to do what was necessary to stop it, i.e. intervene meant that the Vance-Owen Plan was condemned to failure and the people of Bosnia to almost two further years of war. Secondly, an irreversible shift in Transatlantic relations had been catalysed, with the Europeans chastened into preparing for a new world order in which the comforting (or discomforting) American leadership of the Cold War years would either be absent or if present, unreliable. Finally, the opportunity to embrace the Russian Federation in international mechanisms for dealing with conflicts such as Bosnia was badly damaged and possibly lost. Although there would be other proposals in the hope of ending the war and salvaging some international honour, with the Clinton Administration in particular able to claim credit, this was the point from which there could be no escaping the reality of international failure.

123 See Hendrickson, 'Internationalism', pp.27-8.

9

THE PEACE PLANS:
VANCE-OWEN AND ICFY

Throughout international involvement in the Yugoslav war, there were attempts to draw plans for peace and conclude agreements based on them. The first of these were drafted within the framework of the European Community Conference on Yugosalvia (see chapters 3 and 4). The most significant initiatives, however, were the Vance-Owen Plan and the Dayton Accords. The latter, which finally brought an end to armed hostilities in November 1995, will feature in Chapter 10. The Vance-Owen Plan will be the focus for the present chapter which charts its origins, its progress and its demise. The Vance-Owen Plan is significant because, more than any other undertaking to secure peace, it offered an opportunity to bring the war in Bosnia to an end on terms which would combine peace with principle. It also provided a focal point and a policy objective for cohesion in the international community. Its demise, however, was due to international division, as will be seen.

Ironically, its origins were in efforts to reduce friction among international actors. When Lord Carrington, chairman of the European Community Conference, seemed to have reached an agreement on a ceasefire and in particular on arrangements for the UN to take control of heavy weaponry, tension between the EC and the UN reached breaking-point. The UN Secretary-General expressed his pique at the EC negotiating team's affront in making agreements on behalf of the UN — to look after heavy weapons — without even discussing the matter with UN representatives (although efforts had been made to contact Boutros-Ghali who was unavailable). Consequently the tension was resolved by the establishment of a joint conference to give new life to wilting international diplomacy, as well as to soothe relations between the EC and the UN. This also followed suggestions by the Serbs that the UN should be involved in the talks and a call by the French Foreign Minister Roland Dumas at the Munich summit of the G-7 for enlargement of the EC Conference which, it was felt, had become exhausted.[1]

Proposed, finally, by the UK Presidency of the EC, the conference was to be held in London and would bring the UN to centre-stage, alongside the EC, in the international-Yugoslav arena. The essential division between the two in terms of tasks was to remain — the EC would pursue the diplomatic cause and the UN would primarily be responsible for operations on the ground. However, the two would be working more closely together, as the upshot of the London Conference was to be the creation of a jointly-run International Conference on Former Yugoslavia (ICFY) to replace the Carrington Conference. However, as will be seen, even though the UN and the EC had formally joined forces, this would not mean international consensus on handling the tribulations of Yugoslavia. A joint EC-UN initiative would result, as will be argued, not only in the creation of the international community's best opportunity to achieve its aim of stopping the war in Yugoslavia, resisting ethnic purification and preventing the Serbs from establishing a set of contiguous territories through the use of force — the Vance-Owen Plan. But it was also to result in a failure to make the most of that chance as it was killed amid international disagreement, to be succeeded by an ethnic partition plan emanating from the Serbs and Croats. For one moment in the spring of 1993, there was a clear opportunity to bring the Bosnian war to an end on terms which would, however imperfectly, secure the aims and principles which were at stake for the international community. These were prominently framed at the London Conference.

The London Conference

The London Conference was held on 26-7 August 1992, co-chaired by the UK Prime Minister John Major (who was formally responsible for calling the Conference) as the President of the European Council, and

---

1 Henry Wynaendts, *L'engrenage. Chroniques yougoslaves, juillet 1991-août 1992*, Denoël, Paris, 1993, p.178.

the UN Secretary-General Boutros Boutros-Ghali. It marked the end of the European Community Conference on Yugoslavia. In addition, the London Conference would give new impetus and clarity to the international quest for peace and principle amid the wreckage of the old Yugoslav state.[2] By the end of the Conference it looked to those engaged on the diplomatic search that this had happened: there was general agreement on principles and on a programme of action which would have immediate affect,[3] both on the ground and in Geneva where the International Conference on Yugoslavia spawned by the London Conference would go into permanent session. However, the initial optimism was soon to fade as the international community, pleased with what it had achieved at London, rested on its limited laurels. The coercive current underlying the Conference was relaxed, meaning that important momentum and accords, aside from the creation of the Geneva conference, were lost.

One immediate development at the Conference which symbolised the fresh approach promised by the Conference was a changing of the EC guard. Lord Carrington resigned and his place as EC Special Envoy was taken by David Owen like Carrington a former UK Foreign Secretary and prominent political figure who had recently been elevated to the status of 'Lord'.[4] Owen's choice, in itself, was a signal of strength and coercive intent: he had only several weeks before the Conference prominently called for the use of air power against the Serbs in Bosnia. Owen was to become co-chairman of an international conference on the former Yugoslav state which, unlike its EC predecessor, would go into full-time operation in Geneva. Owen's co-chairman was the UN Secretary-General's Special Envoy, Cyrus Vance (who was to be succeeded in May 1993 by the Norwegian Thorvald Stoltenberg).

The international atmosphere in the run-up to the Conference was heavy with both the prospects of strong coercive action and

2 The French Foreign Minister spoke of the need to 'reinvigorate the political process'. (Untitled text of speech by Roland Dumas, French Foreign Minister, London, 26 August 1992.)

3 Some, including Lord Owen (in comments to the author), doubted how 'general' the agreement on principles was, believing that the parties had clearly demonstrated that they would sign or agree to anything for one or two days.

4 Carrington agreed to remain involved as a member of the Steering Committee of the International Conference on Former Yugoslavia in Geneva which was created by the London Conference.

international capitulation to the realities of Serbian territorial acquisition in Bosnia: were the Serbs to be bombed or were they to be rewarded? In truth, there was never any intention in the international community to concede Serbian gains on the ground — only to reinforce the principle that borders should not be changed through the use of force. While there were real pressures for a use of coercive force against the Bosnian Serbs as the awful picture emerged of 'ethnic cleansing', including concentration camps, as well as systematic rape, killing and terrorisation, there remained great qualms about taking military action. These contradictory concerns had resulted in UN Security Council Resolution 770 on 13 August 1992. This authorised 'all necessary measures' to be taken in order to ensure the delivery of humanitarian aid.[5]

The sense of international impatience and willingness to coerce was carried into the Conference. The UK Prime Minister John Major, in his opening address as co-chairman, indicated that the need for a peace process 'should be coupled with the necessary international pressures to bring success'.[6] Others at the Conference were more specific than Major in identifying elements which could be included in a pressure package — the admission of observers in a number of places in the former Yugoslavia, especially Serbia and Montenegro, a tightening of the trade embargo, expulsion of Serbian representatives from international bodies, and the setting up of an international tribunal to try those guilty of, or responsible for, crimes against humanity.[7] The US

5 The language used was a direct echo of the phrase 'all necessary means' used in Security Council Resolution 678 (29 November 1990) which had authorised the international military campaign to evict Iraq from its occupation of Kuwait in the Gulf Conflict. It was intended to convey the impression that similar force would be used, even though its linkage to humanitarian assistance indicated that the Resolution carried no serious intent to engage in a major armed intervention — something almost all governments had ruled out from the very beginning of the war.

6 'Text of the Opening Speech made by the Prime Minster the Rt. Hon. John Major MP to the London Conference at the Queen Elizabeth II Conference Centre, London', 26 August 1992. It should be noted, however, that as Major went on to indicate some of the measures which might be taken to bring pressure to bear — such as tougher sanctions and isolation — he carefully avoided any hint of a resort to armed force.

7 'Text of Intervention by the Netherlands Minister for Foreign Affairs H. van den Broek at the London Conference on Yugoslavia 26/27 August 1992.' Others supporting further action in their interventions at the Conference included German Foreign Minister Klaus Kinkel, Canadian Foreign Minister Barbara MacDougall, Danish Foreign Minister Uffe

Acting Secretary of State Lawrence Eagleburger spoke of 'punishing and quarantining aggression', while squarely placing the blame on the Serbs:

> I represent a government, in fact, which historically had enjoyed a special relationship with the people of Serbia.... But it is Serbs, alas, who are most guilty today of crimes which mimic those of their former tormentors... And it is the Serbs who face a spectacularly bleak future unless they manage to change the reckless course their leaders chose...[8]

Finally, apart from the implicit threat of coercion in Security Council Resolution 770 and the various statements at the Conference, there was a specific military proposal: French Foreign Minister Roland Dumas called for the creation of an air-exclusion zone over Bosnia — this would ban all military flights, other than those authorised by the UN, and would thus ease humanitarian flights into Sarajevo and deny the Serbian camp its absolute military advantage in the air.[9]

However, for all the sense of purpose in the various interventions at the London Conference, there was also a sense that this vocal coercion could be unnecessary. This was because of a letter sent to the President of the UN Security Council by Yugoslav Prime Minister Milan Panić on 17 August.[10] In that letter, Panić outlined a number of important commitments of principle on behalf of the Federal Republic of Yugoslavia, some of which he reiterated in his address to the London

Elleman-Jensen and Austrian Foreign Minister Alois Mock.

8 'Intervention by Acting Secretary of State Lawrence S. Eagleburger at the London Conference, Queen Elizabeth II Conference Center, London, United Kingdom', Office of the Assistant Secretary/Spokesman (London, United Kingdom), US Department of State, 26 August 1992. Eagleburger, formerly US Ambassador to Belgrade, had a reputation for having close links with individuals and businesses in Serbia — this added to the force of his intervention. Eagleburger had been a prime actor in the 'Friends of Yugoslavia' group which in the 1980s had co-ordinated trade and assistance with Yugoslavia in the interests of stabilty following the death of President Josip Broz Tito in May 1980.

9 Dumas sought surveillance and reconnaissance flights over Bosnian territory and introduced the idea of controlling Bosnian air-space. (Untitled text of speech by Roland Dumas, French Foreign Minsiter, London, 26 August 1992.)

10 Panić was a Belgrade-born US citizen who owned a successful pharmaceutical business and had returned to become Prime Minister of the Federal Republic of Yugoslavia. This was generally regarded as a move by Serbian President Slobodan Milošević to improve his country's image in the US.

Conference.[11] These included a categoric opposition to the use of force to change borders between republics, acceptance of the international borders formed between the Federal Republic of Yugoslavia (Serbia and Montenegro) and other republics as a result of the dissolution of the old Yugoslavia (including an announcement that Belgrade had officially recognised Slovenia and was prepared to recognise the other republics), meaning that the new Yugoslavia had no territorial claims on any of its neighbours, and that it rejected the 'barbaric practice of ethnic cleansing in any form'.[12]

To emphasise this last point, Panić told the conference that he was prepared to 'bring to justice' any Yugoslav citizen against whom there was evidence of involvement in 'ethnic cleansing' and reported the arrest of five people, including the mayor of Hrtkovci in Vojvodina, the previous week.[13] He also announced that he had sacked Mihail Kertes, the Deputy Interior Minister, on the question of 'ethnic cleansing'.[14] The immediate reason for this dismissal, however, was the discovery by the British Security Service (MI5) that Kertes was bugging Panić in his discussions with UK Prime Minister John Major and other Western figures at the Conference. That discovery gave Panić the initiative at the London Conference in handling Milošević and others in the Serbian camp: at one stage in the Conference, Panić famously told Milošević to 'shut up' — the Federal Prime Minster held a higher position than that of a republican president and was therefore in charge.

Milošević was quiet throughout the Conference as the Serbian side made a number of agreements and, in some cases, even made offers, such as that by the Bosnian Serb leader Radovan Karadžić to withdraw from two-fifths of the land occupied by Bosnian Serb forces. By the end of the Conference it seemed that much progress had been made. This was reflected in the documents created by the Conference which

11 Letter from Prime Minister, Federal Government, Federal Republic of Yugoslavia to the Honorable Li Daoyu, President of the Security Council, the United Nations, New York, NY, Belgrade, 17 August 1992, signed Milan Panić; 'The Speech of Mr. Milan Panić, Prime Minister of Yugoslavia', 26 August 1992.

12 *Ibid.*

13 *Ibid.*

14 Kertes was Deputy Federal Interior Minster and head of the Yugoslav Security Services, and was widely understood to have been responsible for organising the distribution of weapons to Serbs as Yugoslavia broke up, as well as organising 'ethnic cleansing' campaigns.

were the basis for the peace and pressure process to be continued at the International Conference on Former Yugoslavia and elsewhere.

The London Conference issued a number of documents. The most important of these were the 'Programme of Action on Humanitarian Issues Agreed Between the Co-Chairmen to the Conference and the Parties to the Conflict', 'Statement of Principles', 'Work Programme of the Conference', 'Specific Decisions by the London Conference', and 'Statement on Bosnia'. The 'Programme of Action on Humanitarian Issues' was effectively an agreement signed by all three leaders in the Bosnian war to allow the delivery of humanitarian aid under the terms of Security Council Resolution 770 — using armed guards but without having to use armed force. The 'Statement of Principles' was important because it established the standard by which all the parties to the negotiations, most notably the Serbs, agreed to be judged. In total there were thirteen principles, of which the central ones were the non-recognition of all advantages gained by force, the respect of human rights and implementation of constitutional guarantees on human rights and fundamental freedoms of the members of ethnic and national communities, compliance with the Geneva Conventions and the fundamental respect for the independence, sovereignty and integrity of state borders.[15]

The 'Work of the Conference' document created the organisational framework and established the fundamental principles for the major International Conference which would go into permanent session in Geneva until the dissolution of Yugoslavia had been settled. The Conference in Geneva was to be understood as a continuation of the London Conference which represented the first Plenum of the International Conference on Former Yugoslavia. As in London, the full International Conference in Geneva would be under the Permanent Co-Chairmanship of the Presidency of the EC (later the EU) and the Secretary-General of the UN.

---

15 The others were: the imperative to respect ceasefires; the need to engage in negotiation on the basis of the principles outlined; commitment to seek and accept a final settlement on all questions of succession to the Former Yugoslavia; the obligation to comply with UN Security Council Resolutions; the need to co-operate in the delivery of humanitarian aid; the obligation to co-operate wholeheartedly in international monitoring, peacekeeping and arms control operations; and the need for an international guarantee to ensure full implementation of agreements reached within the framework of the International Conference.

The full Conference would be resumed by the Permanent Co-Chairmen on the recommendation of their permanently engaged representatives. These were to be the Co-Chairmen of the Steering group which would run the International Conference in Geneva. The Steering Group would be under the Co-Chairmanship of the EC and UN Special Envoys (Owen and Vance), and would comprise the Troika of the EC, the Troika of the CSCE, the five permanent members of the UN Security Council, one representative from the Organisation of the Islamic Conference, two representatives from the neighbouring states of the Former Yugoslavia, as well as the outgoing chairman of the defunct EC Conference, Lord Carrington, and the chairmen of the six working groups created at London. These were on: Bosnia and Hercegovina, Humanitarian Issues, Ethnic and National Communities and Minorities, Succession Issues, Economic Issues, and Confidence, Security-building and Verification Measures.

Work on this last set of issues looked set to take on an immediate significance as the 'Specific Decisions' and 'Statement on Bosnia' papers both contained agreement for action on specific arms control measures with reference to Bosnian Serb heavy weapons. One of the key successes claimed for the London Conference, particularly by the UK Foreign and Commonwealth Office which was particularly involved, was an accord that the Serbian camp would notify the UN of all heavy weapons and their positions within 96 hours, and place the weapons under UN supervision within seven days. The Bosnian Serb leader Radovan Karadžić agreed to this in a special agreement with Douglas Hogg, the UK deputy foreign minster. Although this was a re-hash of the agreement achieved by Carrington's EC team which had exacerbated the friction between the EC and the UN — one of Boutros-Ghali's chief complaints was that the UN was not equipped to implement the agreement - there was still no mechanism for implementation; the deal struck by the UK had once more been made without involving either Boutros-Ghali, or his special envoy, Vance. In some ways, this did not matter because the agreement did not specify when the 96-hour and seven-day periods were due to begin. Even when the UN did begin to supervise Serbian heavy weaponry around Sarajevo, it could do no more than watch artillery pieces being fired on the town. Quickly it appeared that the agreement bore all the hallmarks of international ineffectiveness.

However, that early agreement was taken, particularly by the Conference organisers as a cause for optimism and an example of what the concerted international pressure at the Conference could achieve. Had implementation of that agreement been secured, as well as the introduction of monitors on the Serbian-Bosnian border, as Milan Panić had said his country (the Federal Republic of Yugoslavia) would permit, then the history of the Yugoslav War of Dissolution, and in particular its Bosnian phase might have been irrevocably changed for the better, as one senior American admitted:

History might have taken a different course if, the day after the London Conference, we had started instisting that all the terms of the London Conference agreement were upheld. There was a serious debate and there was serious concern. We felt, even then, that the willingness to use force to enforce the terms of the London Confernce was probably essential, that that was the only thing that the Serbs would really respect.[16]

However, in spite of the activity at ICFY, the follow-through was weak — as it was in all other areas of international activity. The momentum of the London diplomatic success was not maintained. In part this was because there was much sighing in relief that the Conference had been successful, followed by sitting back on perhaps too-flimsy laurels; it was also due to the desire to give some time to the efforts of Milan Panić. However, his defeat in the Serbian presidential elections at the end of 1992, in which Slobodan Milošević was re-elected, was the precursor to a vote of no-confidence in the Yugoslav parliament which the Prime Minister lost. However, the international community invested its hopes in what turned out to be the twin chimeras of the London Conference: that the presence of Panić made a difference and that strong words, urgent diplomacy and concerted international pressure, without a will to enforce compliance, might just be enough. As the Bosnian Serbs, initially worried, saw through the scarecrow military presence of the humanitarian escort agency announced at the end of the London Conference to carry out Security Council Resolution 770 (but not deployed until three months later),

---

16 David Gompert, Senior Director for Europe and Eurasia, National Security Council Staff with the Bush Administration in the US, in 'Diplomacy and Deceit', Channel 4 TV, 2 August 1993: *Bloody Bosnia*, Media Transcription Services, MTS M2578.WPS, p.9.

international diplomacy became exposed.[17] In these circumstances the International Conference on Former Yugoslavia began its work in Geneva, confident that everything would be settled by Christmas.[18]

Geneva and the Vance-Owen Plan

The International Conference on Former Yugoslavia (ICFY) formally became the successor to the European Community Conference on Yugoslavia and convened for the first time on 3 September at the UN headquarters in Geneva, the Palais des Nations (the seat of the inter-war League of Nations). Sponsored by the EC and the UN,[19] ICFY was provided with a small secetariat, run by an execuritive director, in addition to which the each of Co-Chairmen was to have his own modest personal staff. For Vance this meant a senior US diplomat and an aide secured from his own law firm in New York. Owen's staff originally comprised a senior British diplomat, formerly Ambassador in Belgrade,

17 This force was originally announced within the framework of the Council of Minsters of the WEU (Western European Union, *Communiqué*, Extraordinary Council of Ministers, London, 28 August 1992). These troops were eventually deployed, after considerable delay, as an extension of UNPROFOR in Bosnia. See Chapter 6.

18 At a joint press conference of the Co-Chairmen with John Major, held at the end of the London Conference, Boutros Boutros Ghali explained that 'the internatonal confernce will remain in being until a final settlement of the Yugoslav problem. In other words the two chairmen can decide to have a meeting of the international conference in the next two or three months....' 'Transcript of Press Conference Given by the Prime Minister Mr. John Major, Mr. Cyrus Vance, Mr. Boutros Boutros-Ghali and Mr. Douglas Hurd at the London Conference on Thursday, 27 August 1992', ECMG for COI Radio Technical Services, Transcript A — PM — PC — London Conference, 27 August 1992. It was not impossible to imagine that, had the momentum of the London Conference been maintained and appropriate measures been taken to enforce compliance with the 'Specific Decisions' of the Conference, the greater part of a settlement could have been achieved in this period.

19 The Conference — the first formal collaboration between the UN and a regional arrangement — was to be funded in the ratio 45-55 respectively by the EC and the UN. However, once the contributions of EC members through the UN were taken into account, the proportions came close to being inverted, with the Twelve, in reality, paying over half the ICFY budget. (Graham Messervy-Whiting, *Peace Conference: the Politico-Military Interface*, London Defence Study No.21, Brassey's for the Centre for Defence Studies, London, 1994, note 21, p.39.)

and a private secretary supplied by the UK Foreign Office (Owen was later to ask for and be given a military adviser[20]).

The Conference was in permanent session, with most of the time spent in Working Groups which would prepare work for Plenary Sessions. The work of the special groups was, however, limited in most ways, with the spotlight constantly falling on the questions of Bosnia. This indicated the weakness in the conception of ICFY. It was structured sensibly to handle negotiations on the future of the post-Yugoslav states and their relationships, but this was more appropriate for peacetime discussion than for encompassing the politics behind war, let alone stemming the course of 'ethnic cleansing'.

The general inadequacy of the ICFY framework was demonstrated with reference to discussion of military affairs. There could be signs of scope for movement on steps towards de-militarisation in Bosnia and Hercegovina following the agreement of all parties to the political document on constitutional principles proposed by Vance and Owen and the agreement in principle to the military document. Yet, further discussion in the military working group on Confidence, Security-building and Verification measures (CSBMs), as well as implementation on the ground, was not forthcoming. Implementation was dependent on two factors: the need to gain agreement on the borders of the autonomous regions into which the country would be divided and the good faith of those making the agreements.

The question of good faith was at the heart of all the agreements. The record indicated that all parties were capable of making agreements in bad faith and that the Serbian camp seemed incapable of making them in good faith. The problem in Bosnia and Herecegovina was going to be how to avoid repeating the situation in Croatia where neither demilitarisation nor population return had been accomplished. The documents agreed at the beginning of 1993 provided for the need to establish compliance mechanisms, but it was clear that these would be

20 This was Brigadier Graham Messervy-Whiting who, on finishing his tour in Geneva, spent three months as a Research Associate at the Centre for Defence Studies at King's College London where not only was the author able to benefit from his front-line knowledge, but he also wrote a valuable study of working in ICFY, as much for its worth as an authoritative document in its own right as for its analysis of the Conference at work and the Vance-Owen Plan. (Graham Messervy-Whiting, *Peace Conference*.)

achieved only with great difficulty. Yet without a way of ensuring compliance, there was little prospect that agreements would work.

In general the 'Specific Decisions by the London Conference' adopted on 27 August were violated openly and on a large scale. Again the Serbian camp was responsible for the overwhelming majority of transgressions. Those decisions included an effective and durable cessation of hostilities, an early lifting of the sieges of towns, international supervision of heavy weapons, ensuring central control of all regular and irregular forces, withholding assistance to self-proclaimed governments and elements internal to neighbouring states, progressive reduction of weapons in the region under international supervision, and a ban on military flights over Bosnia and Hercegovina. At the beginning of 1993 none of those specific decisions had been implemented.

The inability of ICFY to make progress on substantive matters, apart from in the Bosnia Working Group which absorbed most of the Conference's time, eventually led to a restructuring of the Conference in which a number of working groups were placed in suspended animation on 1 July 1993. ICFY's organisational structure did not go beyond the Working Groups established by the London Conference, meaning that there was no formal division of labour or real management — even though several officials with experience made efforts to improve this situation as they joined the staff. In reality, however, the inner workings of ICFY were chaotic, according to Lord Owen's military adviser, and the main reason it 'worked as well as it did was the generally high quality of the people who made up what was, in comparison with the size of its task, a very small team'.[21] This was an almost inevitable fact of life, given the ochlocracy governing Bosnia and which dragged the ICFY agenda with it.

The main focus of international diplomacy and most of ICFY's attention were both, inevitably, on the war in Bosnia. While the terrors of Bosnia were continuing, officials at ICFY in Geneva were working on a plan which might have been appropriate to the accommodation of any genuine fears in the Serb communities in Bosnia and Hercegovina. The earlier idea of 'cantonisation' was rejected in favour of new principles for the constitutional settlement of the war in Bosnia-Hercegovina. The EC effort had been based on the adoption of an idea

21 Messervy-Whiting, *Peace Conference*, p.32.

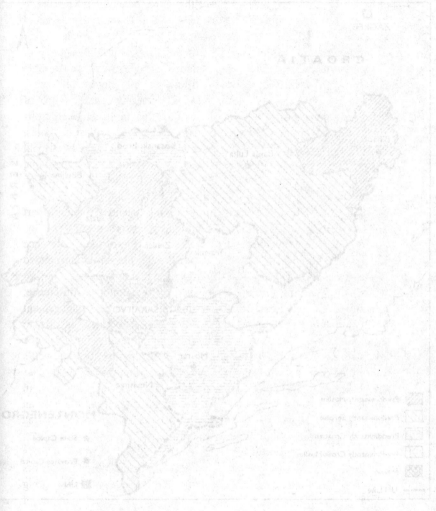

ZAGREB

CROATIA

Bihać

Banja Luka

Bosanski Brod

Bijeljina

SERBIA

Tuzla

Travnik

Zenica

SARAJEVO

Mostar

Nevisinje

MONTENEGRO

Predominantly Muslim
Predominantly Serbian
Predominantly Croatian
Predominantly Croat/Muslim
Miixed
UN Line

★ State Capital
● Province Capital
■ UN

N

2. The Vance-Owen plan

— ethnic territories or 'cantons' — which had been propounded by the Serbian side during 1991. Understood by the EC negotiators as a means to propitiate the Serbs and avoid war, it had served in reality as a charter for 'ethnic cleansing': ethnically designated cantons created the basis for ethnically pure territories. The constitutional plan, devised by the Bosnia Working Group in Geneva headed by the Finnish diplomat Martti Ahtisaari (elected President of Finland in 1994), was a major improvement on the 'cantonisation' proposals at the EC Conference in that it did not take ethnicity as a starting point, although it was a factor taken into account.

What was to evolve into the Vance-Owen Plan was initially prepared in the Bosnia Working Group and presented to the plenary Steering Group meeting in Geneva on 27 October 1992 under the label 'Options for BiH'.[22] At this stage the document envisaged a set of 7-10 regions, most of which would have ethnic majorities but which were to be constitutionally designed as multi-cultural.[23] Rather than being divided into three ethnically founded 'cantons', the country would be 'regionalised' in a larger number of units.[24] Critically, from the point of view of both the Bosnian leadership and the international community, the document specified that a single Bosnian state with a central government (albeit in a weak form) would be retained.

Discussions continued throughout the autumn in the Working Group and with the leaders of the warring parties in Bosnia. The enhanced plan was presented as the Vance-Owen Plan in January and comprised three parts — one military, one political and the third a map.[25] The core of the Vance-Owen Plan was to create a de-centralised state of ten provinces, although the most insurmountable questions would concern the map (see Map 2).

22 The 'Options for BiH' document was presented to the UN Security Council in a Report by the Secretary General on 11 November 1992 ('Report of the Secretary General on the International Conference of the Former Yugoslavia', UN Doc. S/24795, 11 November 1992.UN Doc. S/24795).

23 See 'Report of the Secretary General on the International Conference of the Former Yugoslavia' UN Doc. S/24795, 11 November 1992. Most people closely involved accepted, at least unofficially, that there would be some areas in the country to which ejected populations would never return and in which the multi-cultural provisions would have little meaning in reality, at least in the near future.

24 Leonard J. Cohen, *Broken Bonds: The Disintegration of Yugoslavia*, Westview Press, Boulder CO, 1993, p.243.

25 UN Doc. S/25221, 2 February 1992.

The first of four plenary meetings during January 1993 was held on the 2nd and brought together in the same room for the first time the political leaders and military chiefs from all three sides. Following the opening session, it was decided by the Co-Chairmen that tactically it was advisable that the question of the provisional map be effectively put aside for another occasion by being attached in an annex. They proposed that the Plan should be discussed in two groups. One would look at constitutional issues and the other military matters. Ahtisaari, head of the Bosnian Working Group, would take charge of the former and the UNPROFOR commander, Lieutenant-General Satish Nambiar, an Indian, of the latter.[26]

Nambiar's role in charge of the negotiations made sense both practically and in terms of tactics. Over the latter, it avoided the problems which had faced Carrington the previous July when Boutros-Ghali had refused to let the UN take on responsibilities for an agreement it had not made. Practically, the inclusion of UNPROFOR, especially the Bosnia (BH) Command, in the negotiations made sense because it was they who would have to implement an agreement and they who best knew the conditions on the ground. Therefore, when the first outline military implementation plan was drawn up on 13 January,[27] this was done by the Chief of Staff BH Command, at that time Brigadier Roddy Cordy Simpson, and his staff.

There was considerable optimism at the Palais des Nations in Geneva during January as early progress was made at the 10-12 and 23 January plenums, as well as in discussions in different parts of former Yugoslavia in between sessions of the Steeering Group. The Co-Chairmen felt confident enough to put before the Steering Group on 30 January a somewhat optimistically titled 'Agreement for Peace in BiH'. This came in two parts: the military agreement and the constitutional document with the provisional map as an annex. The task of the Co-Chairmen was to obtain six signatures from the three communal leaders

26 Nambiar and his commander in Bosnia, General Philippe Morillon, had both attended the Steering Group meeting in mid-December in the run-up to the January phase. However, while Nambiar took on the task of mediation at ICFY, Morillon returned to Sarajevo where he spent most of this period preoccupied with the acutely embarrassing murder by a Bosnian Serb of Bosnian Deputy Prime Minister Hakija Turajlić while travelling in a French UNPROFOR armoured vehicle on 8 January (Morillon, *Croire et Oser. Chronique de Sarajevo*, Grasset, Paris, 1993, pp.141ff.)
27 UN Doc. S/25050, 13 January 1992.

in Bosnia — one on each paper (although this was quickly to become nine when the map came to be treated separately from the constitutional document).

The Bosnian Croat leader Mate Boban, displaying even more ambiguity than during the Cutilheiro talks the previous year, signed the whole package almost straight away for the Croats. The Bosnian Croats (and Croatia behind them) had nothing to lose whatever happened to the Plan — in their own eyes, they would gain if the Plan were accepted and they could not lose if it were not. Therefore, in a sense it was no surprise, therefore, that the Croats accepted the Vance-Owen Plan.

A greater surprise was the early progress on the military document. This document included provision, where possible with a timetable, for the separation of forces, for control and monitoring of heavy weapons by UNPROFOR, and for the demilitarisation of Sarajevo. After brief hesitation, Karadžić signed the military agreement (presumably because his military commander, General Ratko Mladić, had calculated that implementation would depend on agreement on the other parts of the package and could in any event be frustrated). There had been a modified Bosnian Army and HVO (Croatian Defence Council) agreement already signed at the beginning of the month, but now, whereas Boban had signed the slightly amended agreement, the Bosnian President said that he had reservations about the arrangements for heavy weapons.

Both the Bosnian President Alija Izetbegović and Karadžić could not accept the map and therefore refused to sign the constitutional paper. The response of the Co-Chairmen was to de-couple the constitutional provisions from the map. This meant that all three contingents would have agreed on the political future of the country as an amalgam of ten provinces. Each of these would have considerable autonomy, with provision both for the return of those displaced during the war and for the protection of the rights of minorities. The provinces would form part of a federal-type structure in which central government in Sarajevo would be confined to the external affairs of the state and areas of economic policy. It was envisaged that ultimately the country would become demilitarised, when it could be assumed security matters would become the preserve of Provincial police forces.

PROVINCE	CAPITAL	GOVERNOR	VICE-GOVERNOR	IPG*	
1	Bihać	Muslim	Serb	Muslims	7
				Serbs	2
				Croats	1
2	Banja Luka	Serb	Muslim	Serbs	7
				Muslim	2
				Croats	1
3	Bosanski Brod	Croat	Serb	Croats	5
				Serbs	3
				Muslims	2
4	Bijeljina	Serb	Muslim	Serbs	5
				Muslims	4
				Croats	1
5	Tuzla	Muslim	Serb	Muslims	5
				Serbs	3
				Croats	2
6	Nevesinje	Serb	Muslim	Serbs	7
				Muslim	2
				Croats	1
7	Sarajevo	Special status	Special status	Muslims	3
				Serbs	3
				Croats	3
8	Mostar	Croat	Muslim	Croats	6
				Muslims	3
				Serbs	1
9	Zenica	Muslim	Croat	Muslims	6
				Croats	2
				Serbs	2
10	Travnik	Croat	Muslim	Muslims	5
				Croats	4
				Serbs	1

* Interim Provision Government

This arrangement had the potential to create a variety of Provincial irredentisms, as Leonard Cohen accurately observed.[28] To help protect against this, at least for an interim period, there would be direct involvement by international bodies in running the country — roles were envisaged in the constitutional court, in electoral and human rights protection agencies and in the formation of police and any residual defence forces for representatives from ICFY, the EC, the UN, the CSCE and possibly other international bodies.[29] Government within the country as a whole would involve all three ethno-national groups, as it would in the Provinces.

The arrangements for the Provinces were of critical importance. While Province 7 (Sarajevo) was to have special status as the capital designated to have equal representation from each of the communities, the others would have political structures proportionately based one ethnic distribution in the 1991 census, held before the break-up of Yugoslavia, the outbreak of war and, crucially, 'ethnic cleansing'. In each Province the majority community would nominate the Provincial Governor, the second largest group would designate the Vice-Governor and the ten-person government would be composedin proportion with the ethnic composition of the Province according to the 1991 census (see table on page 238). Province 2, for example, according to the census, would have comprised 65 per cent Serbs, 19 per cent Muslims and 9 per cent Croats. This would have translated into a Serb-nominated Governor, a Muslim-nominated Vice-Governor and the remainder of a Provincial Government made up of 7 Serbs, 2 Muslims and 1 Croat.

The importance of these provisional governmental arrangements should be emphasied. For the international community, as well as for the Bosnian government, the insistence on proportionality in the Provincial political structures represented a principled, if belated, step back from the curse of ethnic 'cantons'.[30] Of course, it was not hard to snipe at this provision, given that, by the time the plan was on the

---

28 Leonard J. Cohen, *Broken Bonds*, p.246. This point is amplified in Marie-Janine Calic, *Der Krieg in Bosnien-Hercegovina; Uraschen, Verlaufsformen, und Lösungsmöglichkeiten*, SWP-S 386, Stiftung Wissentschaft und Politik, Ebenhausen, 1993, pp.57-8.

29 It should be noted that many well-informed and respected observers regarded the prospects of fully implementing the Vance-Owen Plan as being marginal. See, for example, C.J. Dick, *Prospects for Conflict Termination in Former Yugosalvia*, Occasional Brief 20, Soviet Studies Research Centre, RMA Sandhurst, May 1993.

30 Marie-Janine Calic, *Der Krieg in Bosnien-Hercegovina*, pp.48-52.

negotiating table, 'ethnic cleansing' had been under way for almost a year in Bosnia. For some this obviously meant that the merits of the Vance-Owen Plan were wiped out.[31] It was hard realistically to be convinced that implementation of the provisions for the return of refugees 'cleansed' would be achieved in certain areas, notably Province 2 around Banja Luka. However, the Plan had two real virtues: recapturing some of the democratic and moral ground lost (albeit inadvertently) in the 'cantonisation' scheme discussed at the EC Conference a year before; and imposing at least superficially both recognition of the 1991 census and adherence to the principle of a multi-ethnic community on the ethnic purifiers.[32]

In addition to the obligation of a formal rejection of 'ethnic cleansing' which Vance-Owen placed on the Serbs, it also placed a major obstacle in the way of their ambitions to create contiguous ethnically purified territories. The division of Bosnia into the ten largely self-governing Provinces identified on the Geneva map would have broken any prospect of unified Serbian lands: even if there were to be no mass return of refugees to north-western Bosnia, implying *de facto* Serbian control of Province 2 in spite of the formal governmental structures, Province 3 would break any connection with Serbia proper (see Map 2). Agreement to arrange a UN 'throughway' (an UNPROFOR-controlled road) to cross Province 3 dealt again with any genuine Serb fears — if there were any — that Serbs in western Bosnia would be cut off from other Serbs in eastern Bosnia and Serbia and would not be able to receive supplies.[33]

31 See Noel Malcom, *Bosnia*, p.248.

32 The Bosnian Serbs would have been obliged in the short term to have at least token Muslims and Croats in the governmental structures of areas in which there had been 'ethnic cleansing'. In the longer term the formal, if disingenuous, acceptance of the principles at stake might come to undermine ethnically authoritarian power structures, rather as assent to the humanitarian documents of the CSCE ultimately came to undermine the communist regimes in Central and Eastern Europe and, to a lesser extent, in the Soviet Union.

33 This was, of course, at odds with the realities of life for Serbs and others in north-western Bosnia before the demise of Yugoslavia. Serbs from Banja Luka and its region, for example, gravitated towards Zagreb rather than Belgrade for university education, and the local economy was more closely integrated with that of Croatia.

While elaborating a constitutional arrangement and a map which would deal with the ostensible concerns of the Serbs,[34] on account of which they claimed to have gone to war to 'defend' themselves, the Vance-Owen Plan would have denied them their two cardinal war aims: ethnic purity and, yet more important, contiguous territories. This was, as Lord Owen admitted, nothing more than the best that could be achieved in poor circumstances.[35] It could not be claimed as a perfect rejection of the Serbian policy, but it was better than allowing it to succeed in its essential aspects.

In general this was missed by the many critics who insisted on seeing it as a continuation of the 'cantonisation' project and as nothing more than an immoral acceptance of 'ethnic cleansing' and the attempt to establish new borders through the use of force. This was at the heart of the sharp American criticism of the Plan which was eventually to kill it. Of course, they were right to point out, as the negotiators understood only too well, that the Plan's virtues were also the very reasons why it would be hard to get the Bosnian Serbs to agree to the plan, especially the Provincial map.

Thus the early rapid advances made by the team in Geneva, while giving them confidence, were in the easier domains — however great the surprise that so much had come so quickly. With six out of nine signatures in place, Owen and Vance had to set about trying to close their deal by overcoming the starkest problems: in the final analysis, wars are fought for territorial control — even if other matters of politics are at stake, they will only be decided through a hold on land. The hardest questions were bound to be on the map. The Geneva negotiators had the unenviable task, therefore, of persuading the Bosnian President and the leader of the Bosnian Serbs to sign on the appropriate dotted lines.

The game of 'hunt the signature' was to take three months and was to be accompanied by an effort to secure international backing for the Plan. This should have been a sideshow, but came to be the main event as the strong opposition to Vance-Owen coming from the incoming

---

34 This was explained by Lord Owen to the UK Parliament's Foreign Affairs Committee. Foreign Affairs Committee, *The Expanding Role of the United Nations and its Implications for UK Policy*, Minutes of Evidence, HMSO, London, p.105.

35 Lord Owen, 'Yugoslavia', the 1993 Churchill Lecture delivered on 25 November 1993 at the Guildhall in London.

Administration of President Bill Clinton in the US, in some ways, became more of a challenge to the prospects for the Plan than the reactions of either Izetbegović or Karadžić — indeed, Washington's clear lack of support for it could only encourage them, for different reasons, to think that they would have better options than to sign the agreement.

This was clearly the opinion of Lord Owen who believed that the Bosnian leadership was convinced that the American distaste for Vance-Owen would be followed by military assistance. He said there was a belief in the government of Bosnia-Hercegovina, the Muslim delegation effectively, in his terms, that all they had to do was go on appealing to President Clinton — and that the US cavalry would run in and help them, save them, and intervene. While it was clear that, beyond support for use of air power and lifting the arms embargo, particularly during the presidential election campaign, there was absolutely no American taste for military engagement in Bosnia. However, the prospect that US rhetoric on air power and the arms embargo might gain substance, added to American unwillingness effectively to support the Vance-Owen Plan, did nothing to persuade Izetbegović that he should sign the Plan.

It was certainly understandable that the Bosnian President would want to reject a plan which was far from perfect from his point of view. Nor was it wholly incomprehensible that those directing national security in the new Adminstration in Washington would not want to back something which was less than ideal — those involved at ICFY, the EC and the UN felt the same.[36] However, given the realities of the Bosnian war and the difficulties in the international community over doing more than was already being done, the American position seems to have been diplomatically immature. It was ironic that, with the exception of taking the lead on recognition of Bosnia and the imposition of sanctions on Belgrade, the US had been in the back seat of international diplomacy under the Bush Administration, yet now that it was taking a prominent and strong position under Clinton, it was working against the grain of international efforts to end the war in Bosnia.

With the initiative being lost in Geneva, ICFY decided to take the Vance-Owen Plan to New York where, it was hoped, backing could be obtained through a Security Council Resolution. However, although four

36 See Noel Malcolm, *A Short History*, p.251.

out of the Permanent Five (P5) Members of the Security Council were already set to back the Plan through a Security Council Resolution, the US flatly refused.[37] Where ICFY had hoped that Vance would be able to establish a useful link with Clinton's Secetary of State Warren Christopher (who had been Vance's deputy at the State Department under the Carter Administration in the late 1970s), this did not materialise and Vance, who had already signalled his intention to resign at an appropriate moment, gradually began to withdraw from the scene, finally to be replaced by the former Norwegian Foreign Minister Thorvald Stoltenberg on 1 May. Lord Owen was increasingly taking the lead. In an effort to get the merits of the Vance-Owen Plan across in the US, where he perceived no willingness even to find out what the Plan really was, he made a number of television appearances in the hope that understandings would change and that there would be pressure for the Administration to back it. However, these performances only antagonised the Administration further — even if Secretary of State Warren Christopher was forced to adjust US policy (see below).[38]

ICFY's problems with the US could to some extent be attributed to inevitable discontinuity as policy and personnel changed with the incoming Administration and the merely practical problems which the changing of the guard could present. However, the real problem was US opposition to the Plan. The Clinton team held rigidly to their conviction that the Plan was unacceptable because they judged it to be unfair to the Muslims, even though its starting point was the 1991 census and proposals by the Bosnian government at the time of the London Conference]. Moreover, there was reason to suppose that the top levels in the Administration were not even familiar with the contents of the Plan and were reluctant to be told,[39] even though those working in US governmental departments were more than receptive.

---

37 Messervy-Whiting, *Peace Conference*, p.17.
38 'Diplomacy and Deceit', Channel 4 TV, 2 August 1993, Media Transcription Service, *Bloody Bosnia*, MTS/M2578.WPS, p.11.
39 See Messervy-Whiting, *Peace Conference*, p.17. Messervy-Whiting points out that in spite of repeated offers to brief the incoming Clinton team on the Vance-Owen Plan and the work of ICFY, these were not taken up and that when eventually the ICFY team met Christopher, it emerged that he had not even known that the plan had three parts, including a military document which had already been signed by all three parties in Bosnia.

On 10 February, in an attempt to calm relations with its allies and Russia, Secretary of State Christopher issued a statement of the six principles guiding US policy on Bosnia: a special envoy would be appointed to the peace negotiations;[40] any settlement would be negotiated, not imposed; sanctions would be tightened and pressure increased on Serbia, and the threat to intervene militarily if Belgrade initiated a conflict in Kosovo, made originally by President George Bush on Christmas Day 1992, was reaffirmed; steps to reduce suffering and bloodshed as the conflict continued; preparedness, even with the use of armed force if necessary, to help implement and enforce a negotiated agreement; and broad consultation with friends and allies in the search for peace.[41] This statement offered backhanded support for Vance-Owen, and in his introduction of the principles Christopher praised the tireless efforts of the two envoys to ICFY. The US offered to assist militarily in implementing any agreement they might accomplish. Most of all, the US was not mentioning its preferred approach — the much proclaimed 'lift and strike' recipe, which would see a temporary use of air power and the lifting of the UN arms embargo in favour of the Bosnian government.

On the other hand, Christopher's emphasis in the principles on a 'negotiated' settlement and his assertion that the world could not 'allow a new member to be dismembered by force', while not actually contrary to the Geneva Plan, implicitly weighed against it.[42] Christopher's principles were a coded rebuff both for Owen's canvassing support for Vance-Owen in the UN Security Council and for the Plan itself, which was (wrongly) understood by Washington as a cryptic concession of Bosnia's borders to the Serbs.[43] In effect the US was sticking with its

40 The Special Envoy was Reginald Bartholomew, US Ambassador to NATO — his association with NATO being intended to add weight to US policy. Two days later Russian Deputy Foreign Minster Vitaly Churkin was appoined as Special Representative for his government. There was a crucial difference of experience, however: whereas Russia had been a strong supporter of the international diplomatic effort in Geneva and Churkin had been close to the process there, neither the US nor its Special Envoy had been near to it.
41 *USIS Wireless File*, 11 February 1993.
42 Quoted in Fiona M. Watson, 'Peace Proposals in Bosnia-Herzegovina', House of Commons Library Research Paper No. 93/35, 23 March 1993, p.12.
43 The US had other objections to Vance-Owen, of which the primary one was its non-viability in terms of military implementation. (See *ibid.*, pp.11-17.)

policy but pretending, for want of a better option, to lend its support to the work of ICFY.

The fall-out from the February disagreements was to leave US-European — especially US-UK relations — in their worst condition since the Suez crisis of the 1950s. As both sides made efforts to repair the damage, the US agreed, albeit a little reluctantly, to use its influence with Izetbegović to persuade him to sign the remaining parts of the Plan. This did not reflect a sudden fondness for Vance-Owen, but unwillingness to ease relations with the Europeans and acceptance of the ICFY strategy to get the Serbs isolated.

The negotiators' strategy following the harvest of signatures at the end of January was to engage Izetbegović first, with a view to leaving Karadžić alone in opposition to Vance-Owen, thereby enabling all international pressure, including possible threats of coercive violence, to be brought to bear on the Serbian camp. On 3 March the Bosnian President signed the agreement on military forces in New York. This came as a result of the moderated American position, as well as additional written assurances on the control of heavy weapons from Nambiar on the eve of his departure as UNPROFOR commander. Finally Izetbegović was persuaded by talks with the Americans in Washington to sign up on 25 March for the provisional map, following adjustments with regard to Sarajevo, again in New York.[44]

As a result, President Clinton could announce that the 'full-court press' of international diplomacy was to bear down on the Serbian side to assent to the Vance-Owen Plan.[45] Even so, on 30 March the US still refused to support a British-drafted endorsement of Vance-Owen in the Security Council.[46] The self-proclaimed Bosnian Serb Assembly, while declaring support for the peace process, rejected the map on 2 April. The weight of international opinion urged the Serbs to sign the plan. On 17 April the UN Security Council (Resolution 820) called on the Serbs to sign Vance-Owen and threatened that if they did not a new set of sanctions would come into effect after a 9 day-delay. This would tighten the international economic stranglehold on Belgrade and on its proxies.

---

44 See Cohen, *Broken Bonds*, note 71, pp.261-3.
45 Quoted in Cohen *ibid.* note 71, p.263.
46 Fiona M. Watson and Richard Ware, 'The Bosnian Conflict — a turning point?', House of Commons Library Research Paper No.93/56, 28 April 1993, p.1.

Owen went to Belgrade as part of a regional tour between 21 and 26
April, and urged President Milošević and President Dobrica Ćosić (then
president of the 'Federal Republic of Yugoslavia') to use their positions
to get the Bosnian Serbs to sign the Plan. The Bosnian Serbs met again
on April 25-6, but rather than either rejecting or accepting Vance-Owen,
decided to put the Plan to a referendum. This was done, presumably, in
the hope both of adding a veneer of legitimacy to the political
leadership's repudiation of the map and of delaying the imposition of
sanctions. The former carried little weight with international diplomats,
and the latter did not work: tighter sanctions came into force at 5 am on
27 April,[47] supplemented by a further Security Council Resolution
(821) on 28 April recommending Yugoslavia's expulsion from the UN's
Economic and Social Committee (ECOSOC), where representatives
from Belgrade had continued formally to participate in the seat of the
old Socialist Federative Republic of Yugoslavia. Yugoslavia's exclusion
from ECOSOC was confirmed the following day by the UN General
Assembly.

With the US publicly and strongly advocating the use of air power
against Serb targets both in Bosnia and in Serbia itself if the Bosnian
Serbs did not sign the Plan, although there were no actual threats made,
an emergency meeting was convened in Athens at the beginning of
May. There Presidents Milošević and Ćosić, along with its Greek Prime
Minister Mitsotakis attempt to cajole Karadžić and his colleagues into
accepting. On 2 May, after Owen had convinced the Serbs that air
strikes would begin the next day, Karadžić, through the conduit of
pressure from Milošević and Mitsotakis, eventually signed the final part
of the Vance-Owen Plan. However, any sense of euphoria was quickly
dampened by doubt as the Bosnian Serb leader made it clear that his
signature was subject to ratification by his assembly in Pale. Milošević,
however, expressed his confidence that Pale would ratify the agreement
— that gave reason for some optimism.

The apparently credible threat of air strikes (which had no basis in
reality), channelled through pressure from Belgrade and Athens, had

47 The new sanctions hit Serbia and Montenegro hard. They effectively closed the borders
of the Federal Republic of Yugoslavia, stopping not only trade with it, but also transit of
goods across the country which had been allowed until that time and had provided one
way for the sanctions to be broken. In addition, all financial assets were frozen, with
loopholes in the first round of sanctions, such as assets being transferred to individuals,
being closed.

forced Karadžić to place his name on the Vance-Owen Plan. However, amendments to the arrangements on the map and for implementation discussed towards the end of April had given the Bosnian Serb leader enough scope to argue that his signature had been possible because of the changes to the Plan. These had focused on the strategic corridor of vital importance to the Serbs in northern Bosnia. Recognising that General Mladić's primary strategic aim was to widen and strengthen the Brčko corridor, and unwilling to accept a Bosnian Serb swathe of territory through Province 3 on the map, ICFY contrived to create a 'super throughway'. This would comprise the original 'blue route' throughway plus a 5 kilometre demilitarised zone on either side of it.[48] In addition, the ICFY negotiators brought more public attention to the 'super throughway' concept with a press briefing in Belgrade where it was likened to the Berlin Corridor during the Cold War (most of the journalists understood the idea of the blue route as a new development rather than an amplification of an existing element in Vance-Owen). The assistance of Russia and Greece was invoked to help 'sell the idea' to the Serbs.[49]

However, the amendments were not enough to persuade the Pale politicians to endorse Vance-Owen. Milošević, Ćosić, Mitsotakis and the Montenegrin President Momir Bulatović all travelled to Pale to address the Bosnian Serb Assembly. There was a general belief that the collective authority of these four, not to mention Milošević's considerable hold on the Bosnian Serbs, would lead to acceptance of Vance-Owen. Despite a shared long-term programme, Milošević was insistent that, at least tactically, the Plan had to be ratified. However, he came away shaken, genuinely furious and, it was said, humiliated.[50] Instead, the Pale Assembly again insisted on a referendum throughout the 'Bosnian Serb Republic', and this was held on 15-16 May. The outcome, somewhat predictably, was reported by the Bosnian Serbs to be a 96 per cent rejection of the map. The international community immediately disregarded the result of the referendum: it had been hastily arranged under conditions of war, leaving big question marks

---

48 These features were published at the Athens talks, May 1-2 1993, as "Explanations and amplifications on various aspects of the peace plan."
49 Messervy-Whiting, *Peace Conference*, p.7.
50 'Diplomacy and Deceit', Channel 4 TV, 2 August 1993, Media Transcription Service, *Bloody Bosnia*, MTS/M2578.WPS, p.13.

about its reliability and leading to a failure to recognise the result internationally. However, there was no doubting the meaning of the whole farrago: Bosnian Serb agreement was not forthcoming.[51] By this time the diplomatic and coercive momentum of Athens had been lost.

Washington, 'Safe Areas' and the Death of the Vance-Owen Plan

The shortcomings of the principal governments leading the international community's response when it came to carrying through the momentum of the Athens meeting was critical. The failure to succeed with the Vance-Owen Plan only encouraged issues to become blurred by growing clashes between nominal allies, the Muslims and the Croats, in central Bosnia. There the message of international diffidence and division was understood as 'everyone for himself'. Hesitation and uncertainty condemned Bosnia to a new round of ferocious inter-communal fighting which, as well allowing the Serbs off the hook on which they had been placed, acted as a catalyst in the Croat-Muslim conflict. International debility also meant that the prospect of finding a place for the London Principles in an eventual settlement were negligible and that in effect these were being abandoned. International inadequacy was confirmed in Washington on 22 May when a hasty agreement between the US and the foreign ministers of the main troop-contributing countries in Bosnia, plus Russia, announced a 'Joint Action Programme' emphasising 'safe areas' in Bosnia. In reality, this was a project of inaction, unsafe areas and future headaches. It was also an American device for killing the Vance-Owen Plan.

After the Pale rejection, there was still at least one way forward, but with the Washington Declaration the international community failed to take it. That way would have been to agree to deploy new forces in Bosnia to begin what the Russian Foreign Minister Andrei Kozyrev, in a joint statement with Lord Owen, called 'progressive implemenatation' of the Vance-Owen Plan.[52] This could have meant the use of armed

---

51 One of the main opposition leaders in Serbia, Vuk Drašković, suggested that the international community, not recognising the legitimacy of the Bosnian Serb Assembly, should take Karadžić's signature in Athens as legal and enforce the Vance-Owen Plan. (See Milan Andrejevich, 'Serbia's Bosnian Dilemma', *RFE/RL Research Report*, Vol.2, No.23, 1993, p.16.)
52 *Daily Telegraph*, 17 May 1993.

forces to begin implementation of the Plan in areas under the control of Croatian and Bosnian forces, as was discussed and agreed with Bosnian and Croatian leaders on 18 May 1993.[53]

'Progressive implementation', according to Kozyrev, implied a gradual approach to quelling the Bosnian turmoil. 'We can put out the fire in former Yugoslavia step by step,' he argued, concluding that the international community 'did not have to wait until the last Bosnian fighter endorses the plan'.[54] A move of this kind would have required the international community, through the UN, to provide an implementation force. NATO had been laying plans, in conjunction with the UN, to deploy a 50-75,000-strong implementation force if the Vance-Owen Plan were to be accepted. Planning was carried out on the basis that the US had made a public commitment to contribute up to 25,000 personnel to an implementation force, should the various Bosnian parties accept the plan. However, planning was dogged by uncertainty as it was not clear either in exactly what circumstances the US would supply the troops promised, or who else would provide whatever additional forces would be needed in the event of an agreement. There were plans, but these were all conditional on governments making appropriate offers to the UN. No country was prepared to make a categoric commitment until the circumstances of agreement and potential deployment had become clear. In short, no one was willing to take a risk. These doubts automatically undermined any thought of a partial implementation.

Partial implementation, however, as discussed by Owen and Kozyrev, would have made a great deal of sense in terms of bringing the war to a halt. At the time when the plan was being contemplated by the Bosnian Serbs, the Bosnian government-cum-Muslim forces and the Croats in Bosnia were still ostensibly on the same side diplomatically, although on the ground their relations were rapidly deteriorating.[55] As

---

53 'Heads of Agreement' were drafted in a meeting at Medjugorje on 18 May. (Messervy-Whiting, *Peace Conference*, note 13, p.38.)

54 *Daily Telegraph*, 17 May 1993.

55 From October 1992 onwards there had been local clashes between HVO and Bosnian army units in central Bosnia, as well as a growing number of incidents of 'ethnic cleansing' by the Croats. For the most part the impact of these was kept to a minimum. Incidents began to become more prominent during April, following a Croat ultimatum to Bosnian army units to vacate certain areas which the HVO asserted were designated as theirs under the Vance-Owen Plan. By the end of April, the HVO was clearly

Kozyrev and Owen called for 'progressive implementation', the Muslim-Croat relationship hung in the balance. International action would have helped avert the coming war, both by building on the peace in the large areas in Bosnia which at that stage were not yet ravaged by war, as well as creating the sense in Croatian minds in particularly, that the international community was prepared to do something in which it was worth their having a stake.

There should be no doubt that a programme geared to progressive implementation would have made sense. For one thing, given the relative shortage of manpower from which the UN would have suffered had implementation begun, building on more propitious circumstances in certain areas would have allowed concentration of forces — which in itself would have added to the credibility of any implementation force. Given the reluctance of the major governments involved in Bosnia to engage in a war with the Bosnian Serbs, it was obvious that implementation could begin in areas under Croat or Bosnian government control. Thus, at a minimum, implementation could have begun in Provinces 8 and and 10, before quickly being extended to Province 9 and possibly Province 5.

A partial implementation of this kind would have damped down the flames of war in a substantial way and satisfied growing demands for the creation of 'safety zones' in Bosnia along the lines of the 'safe havens' created for the Kurds in northern Iraq in the wake of the Gulf War.[56] This, in response to events in Bosnia during the spring, especially at Srebrenica (see Chapter 6), had led to the designation of six 'safe areas' in Bosnia.[57] However, partial implementaion might well have left the Serbs in a dominant position and able to consolidate

implementing plans to remove Muslim forces from territories they deemed to be Croat and the Croat 'cleansing' of Mostar on 9 May added seriously to the momentum towards war beteen Croats and Muslims in Bosnia, which would break into full hostilities by the end of May. In the following months, the most intense battles in Bosnia were fought between the Bosnian army and the HVO in central Bosnia, with an increasing frequency of Muslim atrocities against Croats. See James Gow, 'One Year of War in Bosnia and Herzegovina', *RFE/RL Research Report*, Vol.2, No.23, 4 June 1994, pp.10-11.

56 See Lawrence Freedman and David Boren, 'Iraq' in Nigel Rodley ed., *To Loose the Bands of Wickedness: International Intervention in Defence of Human Rights*, Brassey's for the David Davies Memorial Institute, London, 1992.

57 Under Resolution 819 (16 April 1993), Srebrenica was designated a UN 'safe area'. Five other towns were added to this under Resolution 824 (6 May 1993) — Bihać, Tuzla, Sarajevo, Žepa and Goražde.

their control of territory already under occupation, as well as leaving them able to fight on in other regions. Those probabilities meant that a partial implementation of this kind would have been morally unacceptable to certain Western governments, most notably the United States. However, there would have been two further dimensions to partial implementation.

The first of these was that any partial implementation, by being progressive, would not have represented a final resolution of Bosnian questions, but it would have offered the possibility of restraining the fighting in the country and saving lives. A scheme of this kind would have left all other questions open: just as Germany, or Cyprus, had remained for many years with a *de facto* partition but with retention of the *de jure* integrity of the state, the same could have been done for Bosnia. It was not impossible to imagine that, with the will to maintain pressure over the longer term, the fate of Bosnian Serb territories, especially if divided in two (as described below), could have been similar to that of the German Democratic Republic.

The second additional aspect of partial implementation concerned the strategic impact of carrying it out. Even if the effort to implement had been restricted to the provinces identified above, Bosnian army and HVO forces in alliance would have been free to mobilise their limited resources against the Bosnian Serb army (VRS) in other areas — assuming that the VRS had not taken the major UN presence as a sign of serious intent and a reason to make an agreement. However, a more ambitious approach to partial implementation would have gone beyond the initial calming of non-Serb areas to a strategic implementation in Province 3.

This would have been to strike at the strategic centre of gravity of the Serbian campaign in the region which included key stretches of the all-important Posavina Corridor in northern Bosnia — the Serbs most vital territorial interest.[58] VRS forces would have been divided between those in western Bosnia and those in eastern Bosnia, and the vital link between Serbia proper and Serb-controlled eastern Bosnia and, beyond the corridor, western Bosnia, with the Serbian stronghold around Banja Luka and the Serb-occupied Krajina region in Croatia would have

58 See James Gow, 'One Year of War in Bosnia and Herzegovina', *RFE/RL Research Report*, Vol.2, No.23, 4 June 1994, p.12.

been cut. Implementation in Province 3, had it been carried out, would have broken the back of the Serbian military campaign.

With other parts of Bosnia becalmed and requiring relatively small forces to patrol them, the bulk of the implementation force could have been concentrated in Province 3. This would have required basing in Croatia and the use of the US contingent, supplemented by other high-quality troops prepared to engage in combat in order to take control of parts of the Province from the VRS. The overwhelming force which the implementers would have been able to concentrate in the Province would have enabled it to deal relatively easily on flat terrain with any Serb resistance to implementation.[59]

Any possibility of this happening depended on the presence of US troops, but an emergency meeting in Washington four days later resulted in a virtual abdication. With Kozyrev and Owen supporting progressive implementation, the prospect of a UN Security Council resolution to authorise a move in this direction seemed a likely next step, with Russia calling for a ministerial meeting of the Security Council to discuss implementation of the Vance-Owen Plan.[60] However, Washington said that it would not attend and began discussions with Moscow,[61] and then with other key capitals on a new common strategy.[62] The foreign ministers of the main Western troop-

59 Assuming the implemetation force to be 75,000, by the time the mission focused on Province 3 the situation in the 'easier' provinces would have needed to be brought to a level where they could be assumed to demand no more than 5-10,000, leaving 60-70,000 soldiers to pack the critical Province. In reality it might only have required a relatively small number of US troops in this Province to end the war, had Washington been prepared to deploy them. Karadžić confirmed that the Bosnia Serb judgement had been that if 5,000 NATO troops were deployed in Province 3, then their cause would effectively have been lost. (*The Death of Yugoslavia*, Programme 5, Brian Lapping Associates/BBC, 1995.] At the same time, the presence of the implementation force would have acted as a restraint on Croat and Muslim forces, creating conditions for Croatian and Bosnian Government co-operation, much as was to happen in 1995.

60 David Owen, *Balkan Odyssey*, Victor Gollancz, London, 1995, p.168.

61 According to one report, Koyrev had presented Christopher with "a proposal to carry out the Vance-Owen plan in stages," but the US Adminstration, against putting its own troops on the ground, argued a need for "reasonable borders". *International Herald Tribune*, 22-23 May 1993.

62 Owen discovered in Foreign Office telegramme mistakenly passed to him on 21 May that, for the sake of Transatlantic harmony, the UK and France were preparing to reach an accommodation with the US which would in practical terms kill of Vance-Owen. (Owen, *ibid.*)

contributing countries (France, Spain and the UK), in addition to Kozyrev, flew to the US where, instead of the Security Council meeting Russia in New York that Russia had wanted, the foreign ministers were deflected to Washington.

There, a meeting of foreign ministers was held, at which the notion of progressive implementation could have been discussed. However, the US appears to have discussed the issue bi-laterally with the Russian Federation in such a way that it placed Kozyrev in a position where (incorrectly) he appeared to drop support for implementing Vance-Owen.[63] This US stroke of diplomacy, juduciously leaked in the press, created a *fait accompli* to present to the other countries coming to Washington. After the meeting on 22 May, Kozyrev, along with the foreign minsters of the United Kingdom, France and Spain, left the meeting with their US counterpart, and together issued a 'Joint Action Declaration' which included emphasis on the military protection of six 'safe areas' designated by UN Security Council Resolutions 819 and 824.[64] In effect, this meant the end of the Vance-Owen Plan, which the joint statement re-labelled 'Process' rather than Plan.

A 'Union of Republics of Bosnia and Hercegovina'?

With the Vance-Owen Plan discarded, the initiative in what was to continue as the 'Vance-Owen process'[65] rested with those implicated in the war. Owen, with Stoltenberg, continued efforts on the basis of a joint Serb-Croat proposal for a tri-partite ethnic division of the country within its borders, while implicitly creating *de facto* Greater Serbia and

63 The language of a US **[briefing]** apparently rejecting the concept of a partial, evolutionary implementation indicates this. On 20 May, as Kozyrev travelled to Washington, the *New York Times* published a story claiming that the US and the Russian Federation were preparing to do a deal which would mean accepting Serb gains for the time being. That was an inaccurate interpretation of what Kozyrev had been proposing — something to which the US, in any case taking the high ground, would not agree. 'Diplomacy and Deceit', Channel 4 TV, 2 August 1993, *Bloody Bosnia*, Media Transcription Services, MTS M2578.WPS, p.14.

64 France, in particular, had been pushing for the creation of safety zones in Bosnia for some time.

65 The 'Vance-Owen process' was an American invention to replace the eponymous Plan which was being laid to rest at the Washington meeting on 22 May — an ironic innovation, given that Stoltenberg had replaced Vance as UN Envoy at the beginning of May.

Greater Croatia. This phenomenon would be known incongruously as the 'Union of Republics of Bosnia and Hercegovina'.[66] Its worth for the international mediators lay in the fig-leaf preservation of a single Bosnia, internally partioned into a confederation of ethnically defined mini-states.

The 'Union of Republics' plan was devised at a meeting in Geneva on 15-16 June between President Milošević of Serbia and President Tudjman of Croatia and was further elaborated at a meeting between Karadžić and Boban, the Bosnian Serb and Bosnian Croat leaders, in Montenegro on 20 June.[67] This was essentially a return to the principles of cantonisation. The collective Bosnian Presidency, headed by President Izetbegović, found this proposal unacceptable although, so as not to give the impression of complete intransigence, it gave indications that it would be prepared to continue discussions. It also called for a reconvening of the London Conference to restate the principles on which the ICFY was based since the proposed tri-partite division was regarded as being in conflict with them.

In Geneva, at this point, the original structure and principles set down by the London Conference, while retained formally, were in practice mothballed at a Steering Group meeting on 1 July 1993. Instead, the *de facto* structure became working groups on Croatia, Bosnia-Hercegovina, the Federal Republic of Yugoslavia and Macedonia. This last group represented a complete departure from the London framework, where Macedonia was not treated separately and was barely mentioned. The formation of a group on Macedonia was a reflection of the continuing trouble with Greece over the country's name and the deteriorating security situation which had led to the preventive deployment of UN peacekeepers in the country (see Chapter 5).

At ICFY efforts continued to make progress, with the mediators meeting all the parties in the hope of keeping options for peace alive. In this phase the Co-Chairmen, who had throughout being trying to optimise the position of the Muslims, were now more than ever effectively 'trying to ride shotgun for Bosnian Muslim vital interests' while the Bosnian President refused to engage fully in the Geneva

---

66 The joint Serb-Croat proposals were first fully presented in Geneva on 28 June 1993 and published in the Secretary-General's Report, UN Doc. S/26066.
67 Patrick Moore, 'Endgame in Bosnia and Herzegovina', *RFE/RL Research Report*, Vol.2, No.32, 13 August 1993, p.17.

process.[68] In particular, this meant persuading the Serbs and Croats that the 25 per cent of Bosnian territory they were proposing for the Muslim Republic in the Union would not be enough, to satisfy either the Bosnian government or the international community.

Gradually Izetbegović became more involved in discussions as the potential for an agreement on a 'Union of Republics' grew. By 20 August, the 'Union' plan had developed considerably and incorporated the following: a constitutional agreement, with provision for human rights courts; agreed arrangements for making the 'Union' work, such as an access authority; a draft ageement guaranteeing the Muslim Republic access to the Adriatic; and an agreement on military aspects of implementing a peaceful settlement, signed by all the military chiefs on 11 August at Sarajevo airport.[69] There was also what was in reality an agreement to disagree for the time being — that is, to undertake a comprehensive review of all the outstanding territorial issues. These were numerous and obvious, and brought the other points of agreement into doubt-inducing relief.[70]

The negotiators came near to closing an overall deal on the 'Union' plan on 20 September at negotiations on board the British warship HMS *Invincible*. All parties agreed to the constitutional package and territorial arrangements on the table. The *Invincible Acquis* would have given the predominantly Muslim Republic 30 per cent of the country, with access to the port at Brčko on the River Sava in the north, a navigable port for container ships on the River Neretva which would be linked to the Adriatic through guaranteed access via the port of Ploče in Croatia, which would be held on a 99-year lease from Croatia.[71] In addition,

68 Of course, the protection of Muslim interests was a relative concern. From the point of view of ICFY, this meant arguing for more for the Muslims in any settlement, whereas for the Muslims and the Bosnian Government which they dominated the most urgent interest was military action, either through external intervention or through a lifting of the arms embargo.

69 See Messervy-Whiting, *Peace Conference*, note 15, p.38.

70 These included the Brčko corridor and the Posavina area, eastern Bosnia, the Bihać pocket, eastern Hercegovina, central Bosnia and Sarajevo. (*Ibid.*)

71 Lord Owen, 'Yugoslavia: the Lessons for the European Union', 1994 Winston Churchill Memorial Lecture, Fondation Pescatore, Luxembourg, 11 March 1994. The label *acquis* was applied to what was an agreement of principles on which a firm agreement could be made. The term is commonly used for such agreements by diplomats.

Sarajevo and Mostar would come under external adminstration — the UN would run the former and the EU the latter.

The prospects for agreement on the ironic 'Union' seemed good. This was especially so following agreement between Izetbegović and Momčilo Krajišnik, leader of the Bosnian Serb Assembly, that after an agreed delimitation of land between their two Republics the Muslim Republic would not stand in the way of the Serbian Republic if it held a referendum on secession and wished to leave the Union.[72] In making this agreement, Izetbegović appeared to have accepted the inevitability of ethnically-based republics and the break-up of Bosnia implicit in such an arrangement.[73] However, while the Bosnian Serb and Bosnian Croat Assemblies agreed the *Invincible Acquis* on the proposed 'Union', the Bosnian Parliament in Sarajevo rejected it.[74]

Although another opportunity for agreement had gone, the *Invincible Acquis* remained the firm basis for continuing talks. Lord Owen, as EU Envoy to ICFY, requested the EU Foreign Affairs Council to back an expanded version of the 'Union' concept, in which agreement in Bosnia would be part of an overall regional settlement. This was framed by the

---

72 *Ibid.*

73 Izetbegović's agreement with Krajišnik should not be taken completely at face value. The provisions for possible secession of the republics in the draft agreements foresaw any one of them leaving only with the consent of the other two. Izetbegović's gesture appeared to give a clear exit from the 'Union' to the Bosnian Serb Republic because the Bosnian Croat Republic, itself seeking to leave the 'Union' and unite with Croatia, would not stand in the way of the Serbs. However, the wily Izetbegović could theoretically could create a stalemate by refusing to agree to secession by the Bosnian Croat Republic, on the assumption that the Bosnian Croats would veto an exit by the Bosnian Serbs if they themselves were to be blocked from leaving the 'Union'. In addition, there were clearly signs that, whereas the Hercegovina element leading the Bosnian Croats favoured union with Croatia, there was strong commitment to Bosnia in other Bosnian Croat areas, leading the mediators to believe that there was enough support among the Bosnian Croats to make a closer union with the Muslims thinkable.

74 For the Bosnian political leadership there were two major points of opposition to the prospective 'Union'. First, although rationally access to the modern port at Ploče made sense, there were strong arguments that Bosnian access to the sea should be at Neum, a small town on the tiny part of Bosnia and Hercegovina which is on the coast, even though the waters there would not be navigable to large vessels. The second matter for Bosnian opposition was the proportion of territory the Muslim Republic would receive — 30 per cent was judged to be too little.

French and German Foreign Ministers, Alain Juppé and Klaus Kinkel and became known as the 'EU Action Plan'.[75]

The 'Action Plan' was essentially a way of appearing to offer something different and of interest in the Yugoslav region as a whole, but it looked as though it were window-dressing for a package to entice Bosnian agreement to the 'Union' scheme through an improved share of the land: in spite of raising the prospect of an easing of the sanctions on Belgrade, the key element in the 'Action Plan' was a commitment that the Muslim-majority Republic should have at least one-third of Bosnia. As a result, long negotiations ensued, notably between the Bosnian Serbs and Bosnian Croats, until a new map was proposed. This would give the predominantly Muslim Republic 33.56 per cent of the country and the Bosnian Croat Republic 17.5 per cent.[76] However, on 22-23 December at a meeting in Brussels between the three Bosnian parties and the foreign ministers of the Twelve, Izetbegović rejected the 33 per cent share of Bosnia, at the same time as Karadžić walked out, declaring that he would no longer agree to UN adminstration of Sarajevo.[77] The prospects of a settlement were no nearer.

In this context the international community, divided as ever, was beginning to show its frustration with the problems of Bosnia. Far from the Statement of Principles at the London Conference, international mediators and the governments which delegated them were struggling to obtain agreement to the latest and, in terms of integrity, the most inglorious proposal for settlement in Bosnia. The international community remained divided and confused, with the US lending, at most, half-hearted backing to European initiatives but mostly avoiding giving them backing at all unless the Bosnian government had done so first.

The combined diplomatic efforts of ICFY, the EU and the UN and varous governments were stalled on the details of a map to go along with either the Vance-Owen Plan or *Invincible Acquis*. This appeared to confirm to some that what would really make a difference were

---

75 Lord Owen, 'Yugoslavia: the Lessons for the European Union'.
76 Lord Owen, 'Yugoslavia: the Lessons for the European Union'.
77 Discussions on the UN Administration of Sarajevo began again with the Bosnian Serbs in the new year, as Karadžić's deputies Krajišnik and Deputy President Nikola Koljević met Owen in Paris on 3 January 1994.

'developments on the ground'.[78] However, there was an important sense in which it was the situation in the world outside former Yugoslavia which determined that situation. The failure of the international community, having given a mandate to ICFY, to back the Plan which emerged was crucial. It was the absence of an external commitment, notably by the US, to be prepared even partly to implement the Vance-Owen Plan which made the demise of that Plan the central moment in the international handling of the Yugoslav War of Dissolution. The leaders of international diplomacy established a framework in which ICFY had to square the circle of ending the war, securing key international principles and interests yet without the option to call on the use of armed forces. They had promised to implement any agreement, but reluctance to take responsibility and opposition to the Plan meant that implementation forces were not forthcoming. Once that became clear, the Bosnian Serbs, in particular, and the Bosnian Croats — and probably the Bosnian government as well — decided that there was no need to adhere to agreements.

Instead, the priority was clearly to ensure physical control of as much territory as possible through the use of armed force — within the new context of ethnic statelets within an ironic 'Union'. The 'Union', embraced the abandonment of key international principles: resisting ethnic purification and denying territorial contiguity achieved through force as parts of any settlement. Not even the acceptance of the 'Union' proposal on HMS *Invincible*, could meet with sufficient international commitment to make the parties take their own plans seriously when there was an opportunity to make a settlement on that basis in September 1993. As international disarray grew and Bosnia flared as a triangular war, and physical control of territory remained the stumbling-block barring a settlement, Lord Owen and some of the leading contributors both to international diplomatic efforts and to the troubled legions of UNPROFOR began to question the value of keeping the UN force in Bosnia. They suggested, like the French parliamentarian Pierre Lelouche (an advisor of President Chirac), that 'Western democracies' were 'being ridiculed'.[79]

The Vance-Owen Plan had been killed by international disagreement. This had outwardly concerned the merit of the plan, although in reality

78 Patrick Moore, 'Endgame in Bosnia', p.17
79 Quoted in *The Independent*, 27 January 1994.

the plan seems to have been sunk out of American reluctance to implement it. Along with the demise of Vance-Owen, a vital opportunity to embrace the Russian Federation in a common crisis management approach was lost. The general lack of cohesion in international approaches and the incoherence of US initiatives was critical. Not even after crucial principles about resisting ethnic purification and opposing the forcible capture of territory had bee dropped, there was still insufficient international political will to make the Bosnian parties implement their own agreements. This raised questions about the value of persevering with an international presence. If there were to be any future for international involvement, it would require common purpose, cohesion and, above all else, an American commitment.

10

THE PEACE PLANS:
DAYTON — ACCORD FROM CONTACT

Discord in international diplomacy had characterised the early initiatives to handle the Yugoslav war, had bedeviled discussion on military operations, had divided the major players in the international diplomacy over the war and had been responsible for the failure of the Vance-Owen Plan. Conversely, if international action were to be successful, it would require coherence, common purpose and commitment. As will be shown below, by the time the Dayton Accords were signed in November 1995 these characteristics were present — albeit largely because the Americans, whose position on Vance-Owen had been critical, became seriously engaged and were acknowledged as leading international diplomacy the second half of 1995. As will be argued, American commitment to the international effort was the most significant factor which changed between the period in which the Vance-Owen Plan was the focus of attention in 1993 and the agreement at Dayton. The evolution of greater cohesion in international approaches to the Yugoslav war began with the formation of the Contact Group, comprising representatives from the US, Russia, France, Germany and the UK, and its formulation of a plan.

Emperors With No Clothes: the Contact Group Plan

Conclusive confirmation of international debility and disrepute, as well as the underlying lack of cohesion, was provided by the experience of the Contact Group during 1994 and 1995. The Contact Group represented the first point in the international involvement in the Yugoslav conflict where the major players, despite their divergent perspectives and preferences, attempted to act decisively with an agreed political objective and as one. Formed in April 1994 to give cohesion to the various international initiatives which had been taking place, sometimes at cross-purposes, the Contact Group simultaneously had two membership sets. Officially it comprised representatives of the US and Russian envoys, who had been providing the main pulse of international diplomacy in the early part of 1994, as well as three technically from ICFY.[1] The latter three would notionally represent the EU, the UN and ICFY itself. In reality, behind this official facade, as was all too readily spotted by observers and status-conscious outsiders such as Italy, the three representatives were being nominated by Germany, France and the UK. While the latter two were essential because of their involvement on the ground and their position as permanent members of the UN Security Council, Germany was considered to be important because of its major position in the EU, alongside France and the UK, and its potential influence over Croatia, in particular.

The emergence of a military and political stalemate at the beginning of 1994 provided the opportunity for the international community to establish a single, coherent international policy on the Bosnian war. A plan was devised to capitalise on the gridlock of war (there had been little movement on the ground for several months) and the sense of unity and purpose in the international community. At its most basic, this envisaged an internally divided, confederal Bosnia, with Muslims and Croats taking 51 per cent of the territory between them (the Muslims 34 per cent and the Croats 17 per cent), while the Serbs, having given up 20 per cent of the territory they had dominated since the early stages of the war in Bosnia, would hold on to the remaining 49 per cent.

The limitations of the parties were straightforward. The Bosnian Serb army had plenty of weapons but lacked manpower; the Bosnian army-Croatian Defence Council, once again beginning to co-operate, following the ending of the Muslim Croat conflict, had the manpower available but not the weaponry. Without a much greater tank and heavy gun capability, as well as lacking command and control experience, expertise and communications technical capability at the strategic level, the Bosnian army had difficulty taking advantage of its manpower superiority. It could not launch attacks on enough fronts simultaneously to put real pressure on the Serbs. The Serbs, although short of numbers,

---

1 See David Owen, *Balkan Odyssey*, Victor Gollancz, London, 1995, p.276.

had a strong logistical capability and could always move enough troops around to block Bosnian offensives if necessary. Even with such arms the Bosnian army faced an uphill task to expand the 33 per cent of territory controlled by the Federation to the 51 per cent proposed by the Contact Group.

The underlying basis for the Contact Group plan was twofold: the *Invincible acquis* of September 1993, in which agreement in principle had been established on the creation of a Union of Republics; and the Bosnian Federation, established in February 1994 under the aegis of the US, between the Muslims and Croats in Bosnia. The initial steps in this direction were taken by the US Ambassador to Zagreb Peter Galbraith and Special Envoy Charles Redman.[2] Their work was directed towards ending the Croat-Muslim Conflict which had broken out in 1993. Before the Muslim-Croat conflict an alliance between the HVO (Croatian Defence Council) in Bosnia and the Bosnian army had at least made life difficult for the Bosnian Serb army (VRS) in vital areas, such as the northern corridor at Brčko linking Serbia with Serb-held areas in western Bosnia and in Croatia. Although the HVO had initiated the war with the Bosnian government forces, it was dealt a series of defeats in central Bosnia during the 1993-4 winter in spite of reinforcements from Croatia. The Croatian leadership therefore finished the winter militarily and diplomatically constrained — and keenly seeking an end to a losing war. Croatia was not strong enough to fight on two fronts, i.e. in Croatia against the Krajina Serbs and in Bosnia against the Muslims and, in some places, the Serbs.

In this context the initiatives of Charles Redman, prepared by Ambassador Galbraith, became attractive to the Croatians. For them it was a way to turn military defeat into success and to place Croatia in American diplomatic 'good books', from which there would be some kind of reward. A hallmark of Croatian ambivalence has been the apparent desire to be taken seriously by the West. The Redman initiative worked, therefore, because the Muslims trusted the US and the Croats were keen to be taken seriously by its officials.

---

2 According to many close to events, Galbraith was able to build on and, ultimately take credit for, much hard work performed by others, especially the German diplomat Michael Steiner (later to be a Contact Group representative), as well as two ambassadors at ICFY, Geert Ahrens, another German, and Kai Eide, a Norwegian.

CROATIA

N

Bihać

Banja Luka

Tuzla

Jajce

Srebrenica

SARAJEVO

Žepa

Goražde

Mostar

Serbian territories

Croatian - Muslim
Federation territories

Sarajevo - UN
administration

line of confrontation

0   100

kilometres

FEDERAL REPUBLIC
OF
YUGOSLAVIA

3. The Contact Group plan

3. The Contact Group plan

Its success not only freed forces which had been in combat with each other to combine, in theory, against the VRS, but it also made the smuggling of weapons to the Bosnian army far easier, given that consignments did not have to be brought through quite such hostile lines — thus the Bosnian government clearly saw the merit of the Redman plan. In addition, the advice to the two groups from Redman's military adviser, General John Galvin (former Supreme Allied Commander in NATO), on the establishment of joint forces meant that weapons could in theory be smuggled to a combined force which would be able to mount significant actions.

However, the nature of the Federation agreement meant that its success would depend on continued US input: unless the Americans bound it together, it would not be successful in providing a political and military counterbalance to the Bosnian Serbs, and if it were not successful, the arrangement would fall apart in renewed Croat-Muslim fighting. Thus while the Federation showed signs of working in certain areas such as Zenica and Orašje, in others such as Mostar it was to remain frail. This was in spite of considerable effort by the EU, which took transitional responsibility for the administration of Mostar. At the same time military co-operation was limited. However, it did occur in the autumn of 1994, when the HVO, with HV and Bosnian Army assistance successfully captured strategically vital high ground at Kupres. This was clearly because Croatia had an interest in securing an objective which, when seized, would increase the military pressure on Knin, the capital of the self-declared Republic of Serbian Krajina in Croatia. The Federation — as an achievement, albeit mainly on paper — supplemented the *Invincible acquis* as the basis for a settlement.

While the political and constitutional elements of a settlement could be agreed in principle, the map on which it would be based could not. The Contact Group proposal was framed to create an internal partition on the political and constitutional lines already agreed in principle by all the parties. To this was added a map which would be based on an internal partition, with 51 per cent going to the Muslim-Croat Federation and 49 per cent to the self-styled Republika Srpska. (See Map 3.) This was presented on a take-it-or-leave-it basis: only 'yes' or 'no' answers would be acceptable. If not, the international community would relinquish its efforts, leaving different Bosnian armies to fight another bout of war, that was likely to be more intense than the previous ones, probably having withdrawn UNPROFOR and lifted the arms embargo.

This was not quite what happened. The Bosnian Serbs rejected the plan. However, the response of President Milošević of Serbia — to cut off links with the Bosnian Serbs was not foreseen. This meant that the planned Contact Group strategy of applying further coercive pressure to Belgrade, before ultimately moving to exempt the Bosnian government from the UN arms embargo on former Yugoslavia was not appropriate. The Milošević decision, however, made a significant difference to the military balance in Bosnia. The Bosnian Serbs had relied heavily on support from Belgrade both for military assistance and logistical back-up and supplies — especially for finance. Without these the ability of the Bosnian Serbs to wage war was diminished: now, not only were they short of manpower but they would find it increasingly difficult to move men around to ward off Bosnian army attacks.

At the same time, having made a take-it-or-leave-it proposal which was rejected, the Contact Group neither left the matter nor carried out any of the actions threatened as consequences of repudiation. Despite the cohesive initiative with which the Contact Group began its work in April, already by July international resolve had again been found wanting, as Serbian leaders began to provoke differences among the countries contributing to the group. The US favoured tough measures against the Bosnian Serbs, the Russians urged the easing of sanctions against Belgrade, and the Europeans found their way through the middle ground. Lord Owen, the EU negotiator was increasingly recommending to his EU masters that there should be a policy of 'leave, lift and strike', if the Bosnian Serbs continued to reject the Contact Group Plan.[3] This, it was thought, might gain Russian acquiescence, providing there was no action against Serbia and Montenegro. However, it was the US which proved most reluctant to adopt such a policy. While it still favoured 'lift and strike', the priority was, it seemed, to keep British and French troops in place.[4]

Instead of the promised decisive, robust and coherent response to the Bosnian Serb non-acceptance, there followed a period of seventeen months in which various representatives of the Contact Group sought ways to move forward and a curious initiative from the Bosnian Serbs

---

3 Owen, *Balkan Odyssey* p.290ff.
4 This was made clear to the author by officials in Washington.

saw a fleeting appearance by former US President Jimmy Carter, seen by Pale as a potential mediator.[5] It was suggested that, although the Contact Group had made a take-it-or-leave-it offer, this did not mean that the Bosnian government and the Bosnian Serbs could not negotiate changes to the plan among themselves. These were always likely to be negotiated as much on the battlefield, however, and not in the chambers of international diplomacy unless there was a concerted attempt at international diplomacy backed by the will to apply force.

A Sense of Purpose and Lacking Will: Wisdom in the End?

International diplomacy towards the Yugoslav War of Dissolution had been stripped of all credibility. With diplomatic initiatives ground to a halt, the already limited possibilities of using coercive and defensive air power apparently largely neutralised by Serbian tactics and UNPROFOR subject to ever greater humiliation, the international community entered the final phase of its involvement. At the end of May 1995, something changed. The UK and France, with a small Dutch contribution, formed a Rapid Reaction Force (RRF) to deploy to Bosnia in support of UNPROFOR, following the robust use of airpower.[6] However long it took, whatever the outcome, the decision at the end of May 1995 to strengthen UNPROFOR by providing a combat-capable reaction force represented the final gasp. If it were to fail, it would be hard for the international community to avoid admitting failure and moving to a complete withdrawal from the Bosnian fray. Even if this deployment proved successful, it would only highlight the earlier failures of political will. Either UNPROFOR would be more effective or it would be effectively finished.

With the deployment of combat-capable troops London and Paris, while covering themselves for the first stage of a withdrawal,[7] were

---

5 Patrick Moore, 'January in Bosnia: Bizarre Diplomacy', *Transition*, Vol.1 No.3, 15 March 1995.

6 Authorisation for this force came on 16 June 1995, under UN Security Council Resolution 998.

7 The unwelcome prospect of possible withdrawal was presumably on the agenda by the middle of 1995 when the EU Council held its summit meeting at Cannes on 27 June, outlining a programme for the RRF. This opened the two way channel — either more forceful positive action, or an exit. Both options were reinforced two days later when US President Clinton signed an authorisation for American naval and air assistance to the UK;

more importantly creating one final opportunity to display resolve and operate robustly. The UN operation in Bosnia would be able to operate far more effectively within the given mandates. The key to this was the UK's decision to provide the critical mass for a theatre reserve force to support UNPROFOR. This decision to dispatch the 5,500 strong 24 Airmobile Brigade was soon supplemented by the French 1st Rapid Reaction Corps with 4,000 personnel, and a company of Dutch Marines augmented with a mortar detection unit, totalling 180 men. These troops were all combat-capable and designed for mobility and raiding, and they were cohesive military units, unlike the pot-pourri of battalions characteristic of traditional UN operations.

The new forces, in spite of difficulties in gaining authorisation and funding for the force in the UN Security Council, increased chances of UNPROFOR's being effective and generally added some credibility to international initiatives. The difficulties in gaining Security Council authorisation involved the US Administration, under pressure from Congress, demonstrating its reluctance to have the additional troops financed by the normal UN assessment mechanism, which would have meant the US paying 31 per cent of the estimated $350 million costs for the an initial six-month period; finally, at the end of June, President Clinton allocated $15 million — the maximum he could without Congressional approval, with the promise of a similar amount later.[8] The troops nonetheless gave a crucial element of credibility to any international diplomatic initiatives to coerce the warring parties in Bosnia — above all the Bosnian Serbs — into upholding agreements already made, or even into making new agreements. That in turn might increase the pressure on the Bosnian Serb leadership, both from the international community and from the ever more confident Bosnian army as it captured territory, and, critically from the Serbian President Milošević, if he could be obliged to maintain leverage on the Bosnian Serb leadership to make concessions in pursuit of both an early end to hostilities and survival. The tempo had been increased, and if it could be sustained, it would result either in success or in the final failure of international diplomacy, precipitating withdrawal.

The linchpin of the new initiative was London. The decision to boost UNPROFOR followed two days of air strikes against ammunition

however, this agreement would be more important in the event of a pull-out.
8 The *Daily Telegraph*, 30 June 1995.

The linchpin of the new initiative was London. The decision to boost UNPROFOR followed two days of air strikes against ammunition dumps at the Bosnian Serb headquarters at Pale and the seizure of 400 UN hostages by the Bosnian Serbs. The immediate response of many was to interpret the UK government's decision as a panic-stricken response to an ill-judged move precipitated by US pressure for air strikes — as much as it was a response to UNPROFOR's demand that the Bosnian Serbs should comply with agreements they had previously made, but since been breaking on heavy weapons. A more reflective and rational approach to these events suggested an alternative reading.

As seen in Chapter 6, Bosnian Serb commander General Ratko Mladić had found an extremely successful counter-coercive (and counter-compliance) tactic with which to neutralise the limited coercive and enforcement uses of air power by the international community: seizing hostages. Hostage-taking in response to air strikes could easily be foreseen, and therefore had to be factored into any decision to use air strikes. Lieutenant-General Rupert Smith, since January the British commander of the UN force in Bosnia, would not have been so irresponsible as to jeopardise the security of so many of his troops had he not known that troops taken hostage would not be killed. His calling for air strikes in full knowledge that hostages would be taken, having established with certainty that the Bosnian Serbs would not take further steps, suggested that General Smith was sure that he could count on strong backing from London when hostages were taken. London's announcement of reinforcements in turn meant that the critical mass for the theatre reserve force was already in place, although there was some improvisation. The extra troops were provided on a painting-by-numbers basis: these were the forces ear-marked throughout for any emergency withdrawal. They were, therefore, deployed without too specific a sense of what they were to do. It would not take long for Smith to integrate them in his thinking, however. This meant that others — particularly the French, who had been pushing for a move of some kind and who carried the greatest part of the military and diplomatic effort in Bosnia — would also join a rapid reaction force.

It was always likely that General Smith, an individual of great character, intuition and intellect would seek ways to make the force more effective. With this understanding of the General, the initial interpretation of the air strikes at the end of May and subsequent events was off the mark. Discussion was dominated by the notion that the US had precipitated air strikes and that this caused an all too predictable and avoidable mess. The reality was actually rather different. General Smith had precipated them in order to create a mess which would result in a better position once it had been cleared up. The outcome was clear: UNPROFOR was placed in a position to be more effective and to cover a re-configuration of forces which would enhance its capability and its capacity to use coercive measures, including the threat and execution of air strikes, without being more vulnerable than it was capable of inflicting damage. General Smith and the international community were making provision to demonstrate that they were able to counter and neutralise the Bosnian Serbs' primary counter-coercive instrument.

Not only was the counter-coercive instrument of the Bosnian Serbs neutralised, but the Pale leadership for the first time began making significant miscalculations and backing themselves into a corner from which there were few ways out. They could kill some hostages — always a possibility, though almost certainly never a real option: this would clearly have resulted only in Western attempts to rescue the hostages, which, would also have brought NATO into combat with the Bosnian Serbs and doing them irretrievable harm in the process. The second option was to hold on to the hostages. However, as most terrorists discover taking and holding hostages has little value: the longer they are held, the more the hostage-takers become hostage to their hostages and therefore weaker. Eventually, it could be assumed, holding on to hostages for too long would only precipitate a situation in which rescue missions, backed by the reaction force and NATO, would put the Bosnian Serbs in a combat position in which their forces would be overwhelmed. This was, therefore, not a realistic option. The third option was to get rid of the hostages as quickly as possible: this way, the more distant prospect of combat could be avoided and the concessions would be fewer.

The Bosnian army, increasingly if slowly, had for some time been gaining ground from an overstretched Bosnian Serb force, although it continued to be weak in mounting operations at the operational level. The Bosnian army moved in mid-June to relieve the strangulation of Sarajevo, forcing the Bosnian Serbs to fight in fifteen places. Although the net effect of this was to leave the situation largely unchanged on the ground, it signalled the growing capability of the Bosnian army to mount operations of some complexity and left it better placed for future operations. The Sarajevo campaign was a sign of the way in which the tide of the Bosnian war had turned — a turn which could not be wholly divorced from the presence over three years of UNPROFOR. With the Bosnian Serbs overstretched and being drawn away from numerous siege positions, the Pale leadership found itself not only diplomatically and militarily in a weak position but also under pressure from Belgrade.

President Milošević was flirting with the Contact Group over a deal on Belgrade recognising Bosnia — the first step being taken with Montenegro's announcement on 3 June that it recognised Bosnia within its international frontiers. Milošević also clearly decided to try to take control of the Serbian armed forces in Croatia and Bosnia. The former came through the appointment of General Mile Mrkšić (previously deputy chief of staff of the *Vojska Jugoslavije* — Milošević's Belgrade military) as commander of the Krajina Serb army; the latter could be the product of a meeting lasting several hours between Milošević and General Mladić on 21 April.

It seemed that the Serbian President was putting himself in a position to end the war in Bosnia at the earliest possible stage, in order to have the sanctions regime against Belgrade lifted — an essential part of Belgrade's economic and diplomatic strategy since January 1994 was the removal of sanctions by the summer of 1995. This also suggested that the Bosnian Serb leader Radovan Karadžić, having avoided the grasp of Milošević during 1994 and becoming a Frankenstein's monster with a life of its own, was at risk of being reclaimed and possibly removed by his master, perhaps before the summer was over.

As a result of the developments on the Bosnian battlefields and within the various Serbian political-military leaderships, London's decision to back General Smith and lead the international reinforcement of UNPROFOR in Bosnia added considerable weight to international diplomatic initiatives. The prospects for international diplomacy and, if necessary, limited coercion to secure compliance with existing agreements or indeed make new ones were probably better than they had been since the Vance-Owen Plan. Now that the initiative had been taken which created the circumstances for positive developments, it was important that the mistakes of the past should be avoided. On several occasions, as seen throughout this volume, having achieved apparent success, international coercive initiatives lacked resolution as either political will or credibility was found wanting, pressure was removed, and there followed a modified return to a situation in which the Bosnian Serbs held most of the initiative. There was now a last opportunity, albeit late in the day, to salvage some respect for the international role and, after three years of war in Bosnia and so much diplomatic discord, to resolve the coercive cadence.

The UK government's decisions in support of General Smith demonstrated clear political purpose and made greater credibility and effectiveness possible. Now there would be less time, either for sighs of relief that a critical moment had passed or for relaxation. The opportunity was there to extract concessions from the Bosnian Serbs and to bring an end to the conflict. This required concentration, pressure and the credible coercive potential that was becoming available — with London more than ever responsible for what happened. So often pusillanimous realists, Prime Minister John Major, Foreign Secretary Douglas Hurd and Defence Secretary Malcolm Rifkind (who was soon to replace Hurd at the Foreign Office) appeared surprisingly to have added a little courage to their realism. The cowardly British lion, having found its courage, was in a position to rehabilitate the pride of international diplomacy.

With the international community more united than at any time in the Yugoslav War of Dissolution and with UNPROFOR moving into a position where it could operate robustly, there were three broad ways in which the involvement in Bosnia could conclude. Each would affirm that lack of political will among members of the international community had been the critical factor in diplomatic failure. One outcome was business as usual: having seized the initiative, riven either by disparate policies or by a lack of will, UNPROFOR would become quiescent. It would do as much as it could when it could, but would not ensure that humanitarian assistance was always delivered, or that 'safe areas' were protected, or that it could be used in efforts to bring the war to an end. This was the UN preference. The Secretary-General's Report to the Security-Council on 30 May 1995, tried to remove enforcement measures from UNPROFOR's mandate — in almost direct response to Franco-British initiatives.[9] Over time, it seemed that

9 In the Secretary-General's Report (UN Doc. S/1994/444) there was an attempt to suggest that the use of 'all necessary measures' to assist in the delivery of humanitarian assistance was not part of UNPROFOR's mandate. This, it was said, was because Security Council Resolution 770 (13 August 1992), in the mandatory framework of

business-as-usual was unlikely to be sustained — key governments, such as France and the UK, would instead confirm international failure by looking to withdraw from Bosnia.

The second possible outcome was that the initiative taken would be sustained and pressure would be applied against the Bosnian Serbs, including a limited move towards combat to defend the force or to secure compliance — but that this would result in failure and, in face of likely turmoil and combat, withdrawal of the force. Such a withdrawal, following a last determined initiative, could be marked down as an honourable failure. Nonetheless, it would be a failure — moreover, one resulting from the lack of will to act firmly and forcefully earlier, as well as to sustain the new undertaking to the end.

Finally, it was possible that a firm and consistent policy would result in success — as had been signalled on so many occasions. If attempted, it would probably succeed, but it would require commitment, cohesion and preparedness to use force not previously in evidence. Even such success, as the expression of a belated will to use force if necessary, would emphasise the lack of will which had produced four years of failure. By demonstrating what could be achieved with cohesion and the political will to use force, the international community, while redeeming itself a little, would only highlight what could have been achieved earlier — and how many years of war could have been avoided, had there been the will to use force at earlier stages.

This range of possible outcomes was confirmed in July 1995 when the Bosnian Serb army overcame the Srebrenica 'safe area', expelling

Chapter VII of the UN Charter, had not been addressed to UNPROFOR but to member states 'acting nationally' or through 'regional arrangements', whereas Resolution 776 (14 September 1992) authorising the enlargement of UNPROFOR neither made reference to the 'use of all necessary measures', nor was it under Chapter VII. The reality was that operative paragraph 2 of Resolution 776 had explicitly stated that the enlargement of UNPROFOR was to implement paragraph 2 of Resolution 770 — including the use of 'all necessary measures'. There was a similar UN attempt at a sleight of hand involving Resolution 836 (4 June 1993) on the protection of UN-declared 'safe areas' in Bosnia, as reference to paragraph 9 was omitted, including the mandate, acting in self-defence, 'to take the necessary measures, including the use of force, in reply to bombardments against the safe areas'. In the Secretary-General's report, there was no mention of a mandate to reply using enforcement measures, but only one to deter (derived from paragraph 5) without the threat of force being used in reply to attacks on the safe areas. Paragraph 9 of Resolution 836, incidentally, made explicit reference to Resolution 770 as part of the mandate for UNPROFOR.

completed five days later.[11] The Bosnian Serb attack was relatively easily accomplished. Although there was some resistance from the small Dutch UN force, the bulk of the Bosnian government troops in the area had already withdrawn at least twenty four hours before the attack came, including the commander of the local forces, General Naser Orić. It seemed that Orić, who was alleged to bear responsibility for atrocities against civilian Serbs in eastern Bosnia around Bratunac at the end of 1992, had prior knowledge of the imminent assault. Indeed, it was believed that arrangements might have been made both locally and at leadership levels concerning the fate of Srebrenica.[12]

Whatever the truth concerning the fall of Srebrenica, the starkness of the Bosnian Serb takeover was terrible. As Mladić's troops advanced, several thousand Muslims fled in two ways. Around 15,000, mostly men, left through the woods from Šušnjari towards the town of Tuzla. This column of flight was interrupted near the village of Buljim and attacked by the VRS. Around one third of the group escaped to Tuzla, the remainder were trapped on VRS controlled territory.

A second group of men, women and children looked to the immediate security of the Dutch UN compound at Potočari, where they remained from 11 until 13 July, and after which they were transported on around sixty buses General Mladić had waiting with Bosnian Serb military drivers to remove them to Bosnian Government controlled territory. As the VRS burned and looted Muslim houses, Mladić personally assured the Muslims that they would not be harmed, but would be safely transported out of Srebrenica. However, as the Muslims boarded the buses on 13 July, VRS personnel separated the men from the women and children. The latter were escorted out of Bosnian Serb controlled territory, while the men were taken to various other locations in the area. Although some of the Muslim men were told they would be exchanged Bosnian Serbs being held by government forces in Tuzla, the

---

11 The following is based on the Indictment confirmed by the International Criminal Tribunal for the Former Yugoslavia on 14 November 1995. This indictment was made against Karadžić and Mladić in connection with the Srebrenica events and alleged, *inter alia*, genocide.

12 According to officials in The Hague, units of the Bosnian Army appeared to have been given instructions from Sarajevo to prepare for withdrawal a few weeks before the attack came, indicating readiness to concede the town. Similarly, the Bosnian Serbs were rumoured to have made efforts both to infiltrate Srebrenica to intimidate the locals and to come to an arrangement with Orić.

majority were taken to Bratunac and then Karakaj where they were killed at two sites between noon and midnight on 14 July. By 23 July, one way or another, the Muslim population of the Srebrenica area had been "virtually eliminated," in circumstances of "unimaginable savagery." Srebrenica was a scene "from hell, written on the darkest pages of human history."[13]

The massacre at Karakaj was perhaps the most callous act in a litany of atrocities during the war in Bosnia. It was also, perhaps, the hubristic work of Bosnian Serb military and political leaders who had come to believe that they would never face an international response that would seriously damage them, just at the point where the tide had changed. It was perhaps also the action of men who had misjudged the degree to which Serbia's President Milošević would be able firmly to control them. Both these miscalculations would place the Bosnian Serb leaders in Milošević's grasp: the first as they would need him to negotiate a way out of NATO bombing; the second as they would need him to protect them from international (or other) justice for crimes so brazenly committed.

In the meantime, no doubt filled with overconfidence, the Bosnian Serbs swiftly moved on to the Žepa and Bihać 'safe areas', having been deterred (temporarily, at least) over Goražde, by the British presence which had been critical in stalling the Bosnian Serb assault at the end of May and a growing international realisation that a stand would have to be made somewhere, probably there.[14] Increasing international commitment was emerging in July to use air power in a substantial way to assist the force in Goražde. Moreover, the relative strength of local Bosnian government forces also had to be taken into account. As the international community absorbed the horror of Srebrenica and prepared to make some kind of a stand at Goražde, the inevitable collapse of the Žepa 'safe area' came on 25 July. Although on defensible high ground, Žepa had always been too small and too cut off for their to be a credible effort to save it. There was certainly little that the small Ukrainian UN presence could be expected to achieve. This placed

---

13 Judge Fouad Riad, 'The Prosecutor v. Radovan Karadžić, Ratko Mladić. Review of the Indictment', International Criminal Tribunal for the Former Yugoslavia, IT-95-18-I, 16 November 1995.
14 1st Battalion Royal Welch Fusiliers, *White Dragon. The Royal Welch Fusiliers in Bosnia*, Royal Welch Fusiliers, Wrexham, 1995, pp.49-50.

critical pressure on the future of the UN operation in Bosnia, as the heroic failure of 470 Dutch troops in Srebrenica and the impotence of 79 Ukrainians in Žepa left it threadbare.

These dismal events occurred as part of a series of developments which threatened to make UNPROFOR's position untenable within little more than a month unless it were to take on a more forceful aspect. The first of these was legislation in the US Senate, sponsored by the Republican majority leader Robert Dole, to force a unilateral US lifting of the arms embargo in favour of the Bosnian government. Even though this could only be the beginning of the Congressional process and there remained the possibility that the Dole 'Bosnia Self-Defence Bill' might receive less than the two-thirds majority needed to resist a presidential veto, impact on UNPROFOR's standing could not be avoided.

Secondly, there was the prospect that further Bosnian Serb humiliations would make the UN mission untenable in troop-contributing capitals. This was compounded by the growing prospect that UNPROFOR's position in Bosnia would become impossible as the signs grew that the Bosnian government would withdraw its co-operation and consent — in a pincer movement with the US Senate and in a mood of complete despair with the UN's inability to prevent the fall of 'safe areas' such as Srebrenica and Žepa and, worse, to be powerless in the face of atrocities.

All of this was against the backdrop of the need to make a decision in August if the NATO plan to evacuate UNPROFOR, involving 60,000 military personnel — 25,000 of whom were due to be provided by the US — were to bring about a withdrawal before winter arrived. The plan — 40104, codenamed Determined Effort — assumed a five- month period of withdrawal, fraught with difficulties and combat situations. It was the prospect of combat that governed the size of the force, almost three times larger than UNPROFOR itself. However, fed up as the UK and France were, they had little inclination to endure the humiliation of withdrawal, however much in practice they were coming to regard it as inevitable. Most of all, the Clinton Administration in Washington, previously determined to keep its ground forces out of Bosnia but having committed itself to the NATO plan which would involve US troops in combat roles, had a strong desire to see UNPROFOR remain but becoming more robust.

For all involved, it was clear that there was no longer a choice which involved UNPROFOR remaining in Bosnia in its existing mode. The real options were war to withdraw or war to withstand. This realisation finally forced France, long impatient to use force, and the UK to work with a US proposal to provide massive air protection to the remaining 'safe areas', most notably Goražde, at the same time as the European Reaction Force (RRF) began to deploy to Mount Igman in order to open up a secure access route into Sarajevo.

However, these commitments were initially toned down as the key countries concerned with the future of the UN operation in Bosnia met in London on 21 July 1995. At that meeting the Russian Federation blocked the issuing of a clear ultimatum, and for a few days it appeared to many sceptics that the apparent Western will and cohesion emerging in the run-up to the meeting would be neutralised by Russian reservations. However, within days elements of the RRF were deployed to secure the Igman route, while a senior officer from each of the three key Western countries was present in Belgrade to deliver a joint ultimatum on the use of massive air power, specifically in response to any attack on Goražde and generally to protect the other 'safe areas'.

Having faced the question of war to stay or war to go, France, the UK and the US then had to address a further question: Western will or international cohesion. The London conference of contributing countries had achieved minimal consensus, revealing division and equivocation among the Western allies but crucially with the Russians. Having opted for Western will, the West now had to give a visible demonstration of that will at an early opportunity to ensure the credibility of the threats made. The pressures which had forced the issue of staying and fighting or going and fighting remained, as did the August deadline. Time was running out for action. After three years of hesitation, bluff and vacillation, there would be no further opportunities if there were to be stalling now.

Following the London conference of concerned countries in July 1995, the questions of cohesion and will had effectively become alternatives: it was either international cohesion that included the Russians, or the will of the West. The West, having opted for its will, then had to demonstrate intent quickly. If not, there would be a messy withdrawal involving NATO. If there were success with the new forceful measures utilising the Reaction Force on the ground and the threat of massive air power, it would be little and it would be late, but better late than never. Ironically, this would only indicate that which might have been achieved sooner, for want of political will. The essential locus of that political will was in Washington.

The Road to Dayton and Accord

In 1995 there were major changes on the battlefield in Bosnia, following three years of stalemate. The United States lay behind much of the change. First, it had begun to give military assistance to Croatia. This led to a significant strengthening of Croatia's military capability which was turned against the Serbs, first in Croatia, then in western Bosnia — the latter giving support to Bosnian Government forces in forcing the Bosnian Serbs from large tracts of land during August.

Secondly, the US had realised that there was a growing likelihood, following a hostage crisis at the end of May and the reconfiguration of the UN force in Bosnia that key countries like the United Kingdom and France might withdraw in November. This was supplemented with signals from London and Paris that withdrawal was contemplated (in particular, newly elected President Jacques Chirac had publicly indicated that French troops would not remain in Bosnia for another winter without a more positive role). A withdrawal would confront Washington with two unacceptable alternatives: honouring a commitment to deploy troops to help an evacuation of UNPROFOR in Bosnia, or facing the humiliation of not keeping its word. Instead, it began a series of strong diplomatic initiatives.

These included intensive shuttle diplomacy between the various former Yugoslav capitals, as well as the preparation and consolidation of common approaches within the international community. This was especially true within NATO, where views coalesced around a commitment to extensive use of air power. After a mortar attack on the Sarajevo market place on 28 August, NATO began a sustained bombing campaign to force the Bosnian Serbs to withdraw heavy weaponry from around Sarajevo, as well as in other areas of Bosnia. In effect, if not intention, this complemented the joint Croatian-Bosnian military action already under way.[15] As a result of the shift in the military balance, the way was paved for diplomatic talks on reaching a settlement —

15 See, for example, Patrick Moore, 'An End Game in Croatia and Bosnia?', *Transition*, Vol.1 No.20, 3 November 1995.

leading to the Dayton agreement in November, signed in Paris on 14 December. This ended four and a half years of war in the former Yugoslavia and led NATO to its first ever ground operation as it organised a 60,000 strong implementation force — IFOR — to secure the military parts of the Dayton Accords.

The turning point on the road to Dayton was the decision to deploy the RRF following the air strikes against Pale at the end of May. This created circumstances in which threats to use force became credible — even if they were not believed by the Bosnian Serb command which seems hubristically to have come to believe it would never face a serious use of force. It also created a situation in which British and French withdrawal became feasible. With the fall of Srebrenica and Žepa, by default, helping the process of force reconfiguration begun after the events at the end of May, UNPROFOR had greatly reduced its vulnerability. The US, confronted by a situation in which the use of air power was more possible, yet in which a withdrawal might occur, was catalysed. Already, in May, the US had begun to lead international efforts as Contact Group member and Special Envoy Robert Frasure entered into direct discussions with Milošević on achieving peace. Frasure's approach was realistic, but was also, in fact, a marked shift from previous US policy onto ground which the Europeans had already been treading.[16] The essence of the deal Frasure was seeking to make was that sanctions against Belgrade would be lifted in return for Serbia and Montenegro's recognising Bosnia. Although an agreement was reached on 18 May, it lasted no more than a few days as Milošević realised that the Americans intended that sanctions would only be suspended — meaning that they could be reapplied at any moment, whereas he had expected a full lifting which would then have required reimposition of sanctions to need a new resolution which the Russians would veto. Montenegrin recognition of Bosnia on 3 June was no doubt a sign of good faith engineered by Milošević.

Frasure continued unstintingly with a shuttle-diplomacy mission between various regional and international capitals. He was generally regarded as making good progress. He had certainly eclipsed the EU-UN efforts of ICFY, where Owen had resigned at the end of May to be replaced as EU mediator by former Swedish Prime Minster Carl Bildt on 9 June. Although Bildt and Stoltenberg continued to be significantly

---

16 See Owen, *Balkan Odyssey*, p.324.

involved, this was in a lower register and somewhat in the background. The American diplomatic dynamic was broken on 19 August when Frasure, along with two members of his negotiating team and a French soldier died in a road accident in Bosnia. However, fortunately, circumstance was to prevent this being the setback it might have become. Within ten days, the Frasure mission had been taken over by his State Department superior, Assistant Secretary for State Richard Holbrooke. From late August onwards, it was Holbrooke who led the American (and therefore international) diplomatic drive. His work was significantly assisted by the use of NATO air power.

On 28 August a Bosnian Serb mortar killed over 30 people in Sarajevo. This was the cue for NATO to begin a campaign of aerial bombardment against the Bosnian Serbs. This had the effect of providing air support for combined Croatian and Bosnian military offensives in Bosnia - which were themselves, at least in part, a result of American assistance in training. Croatia had weathered some international criticism following the failure of UN-brokered talks between Zagreb and the Knin authorities at the beginning of August. On 4 August, Croatia launched its 'Operation Storm', a two day campaign in which all parts of Croatia which were still under Serb control were captured, with the exception of eastern Slavonia. In the wake of this, Croatian forces pressed on into Bosnia and undertook co-ordinated action against the Bosnian Serbs, resulting in a series of gains throughout the autumn. By November 1995, the situation on the ground was radically different from that which it had been at the beginning of the year in both Croatia and Bosnia: Croatian Serb control of territory had been reduced from 23 per cent to less than 5 per cent; Bosnian Serb controlled land had been reduced from around 70 per cent to under 50 per cent. Most significantly of all, the use of NATO air power and, around Sarajevo, the RRF artillery, had put the Bosnian Serbs on the receiving end of overwhelming firepower for the first time.

The physical and psychological impact of the NATO and RRF engagements against the Bosnian Serbs meant that Milošević, still seeking to make deals with the Americans, was suddenly in stronger position to do so. Karadžić, that Frankenstein's monster, had now been returned to his master on a plate. The Bosnian Serb leadership, losing territory, had little choice other than to accept that Milošević would represent them in negotiations, short of facing further armed action from either the international community or their foes in Bosnia. This was to be of absolute significance as the combined elements of US diplomacy, international action and Milošević side-lining the Bosnian Serbs made proximity talks at the Wright-Patterson Air Base, Dayton, Ohio, possible. The focus of international involvement had shifted from the UN to NATO in military terms and from the UN to the US regarding diplomacy.[17]

The Dayton Proximity Talks: Approximating Peace

The Dayton proximity talks began on 1 November 1995 and were to last for three weeks.[18] At the end of that period, following three weeks of incarceration, albeit in relative luxury, on a US airbase, the leaders of Bosnia, Serbia and Croatia initialled an accord on ending the war in Bosnia, under the gaze of American diplomats.[19] The talks were to finish nervously with absolute deadlines being extended amid fears that a settlement would not be reached. However, the conditions which had created the possibility of Dayton were also the conditions which made it impossible to walk away without an agreement. Although there were worries that, in the final analysis, the process adopted for Dayton might not work and the issues under discussion might prove too great, as will be shown, an accord was agreed out of necessity.

There were four key conditions which paved the way to Dayton. Two of these concerned the US. The first had been the tireless diplomatic mission carried forward by Holbrooke after Frasure's death. This had given the US a concerted and focused approach to the Yugoslav war for the first time. That initiative had come in face of the growing prospect that the Clinton Administration would be caught between the rock of Capitol Hill moving to force the arms embargo issue and the hard place of the growing prospect that the Europeans at the heart of the UN military operation in Bosnia would pull out.

17 UN Special Envoy Yasushi Akashi left his post on 10 October 1995 to be replaced by Kofi Annan, responsible for peacekeeping at UN Headquarters in New York. Annan's was a temporary appointment, while his role appeared primarily to be the facilitation of a handover from the UN to NATO in Bosnia.
18 The following section is largely based on discussions with British and other officials.
19 Although the EU and Russian partners in the Contact Group were present, they were largely marginalised. Their role was to be one of lending superficial collective authority to what was an American affair.

The second, related, factor was that Holbrooke and Frasure had shifted the US attitude to Milošević's Serbia. This reflected a move towards the European position since the second half of 1993 when the EU Action Plan had been put forward, based on a trade-off in which sanctions against Serbia and Montenegro would be eased in return for co-operation in ending the war and recognition of the Sarajevo government by Belgrade. With Holbrooke in charge of the US diplomatic initiative and the threefold limitation imposed on US policy,[20] There was a more pragmatic and creative US approach than had been the case in the past. The key to this was the adoption of a policy based on getting Belgrade to recognise Bosnia within its borders, as a precondition for peace, in exchange for the suspension of sanctions. Thus rather than the outright opposition to Serbia and the Serbian President which there had been in 1993 at the time of the Vance-Owen Plan, Washington now saw him as an essential partner for peace.

US policy contributed to what was easily the most significant condition for the Dayton process. This was the delicate military-political balance which had emerged on the ground by the autumn on 1995. The Bosnian Serbs had lost the strategic initiative and had been losing territory. Without renewed backing from Milošević, there would be no further Bosnian Serb interest in further fighting. Substantially renewed support from Milošević was unlikely because his main concern was to obtain a settlement and the removal of sanctions. The Bosnian Government was in a stronger position militarily than it had been at any stage in the war. But, it continued to be short of sufficient quantities of heavy weapons and, therefore, to be dependent on support from Croatia and from the Americans — without their help, even if the Sarajevo leadership wanted to continue the fighting, it would be unable to do so. Croatian support, which had been essential for the military successes of the summer and autumn, was not going to be forthcoming for two reasons: Zagreb wanted to keep the Bosnian Government in a relatively weak position; and Croatia wanted to keep on the right side of Washington. The US, with a major political and diplomatic stake now placed on achieving a settlement, had indicated to Zagreb that further

---

20 The threefold constraint on US policy involved the Administration's aversion to placing its troops on the ground in Bosnia, its relationships with its Allies and the Russian Federation and the grave difficulties associated with the apparently simple alternative of supplying the Bosnian Army with the weapons it required.

operations were not desirable and would not receive the quiet approval given to the military action during 1995. Thus, there was little room for manoeuvre and little reason for anyone to continue fighting. At Dayton, all involved were constrained by the prospective cost of a return to armed hostilities.

The military-political balance reinforced the final factor in creating the conditions for successful negotiations. This concerned the delegations taking part in the talks themselves. The events of the summer had put Milošević in a strong position: he was to negotiate on behalf of the Bosnian Serbs. Although a Bosnian Serb contingent was included in the Milošević delegation, it did not include either Karadžić and Mladić. Moreover, the senior Bosnian Serb figures present were excluded from much of the negotiation.[21] Tudjman also came to Dayton in a relatively strong position. Following the outcome of 'Operation Storm' and the removal of the majority of the Serb population in Croatia, there were few sensitive outstanding issues for Zagreb. Croatia's interest lay in keeping on the right side of the US and in sustaining an influential position in Bosnia. Both Tudjman and Milošević were working from positions which were undivided because these were their own. The Bosnian Government delegation, in contrast, was in a weaker position. It reflected at least two internal divisions. The first was between the Croats and Muslims who represented the Federation — any official Bosnian position had to represent a compromise between their distinct perspectives. The second internal division was within the Muslim leadership of the Bosnian Government delegation. Earlier in the year, a dispute over the Islamic content of Bosnian Government policy and links with ideologically Islamic countries had led Bosnian Prime Minster Haris Silajdžić (who argued for the Muslim-Croat Federation, for good links with Croatia and with the US, as well for placing emphasis on the multi-cultural aspects of Bosnian policy, to tender his resignation). Although the resignation was withdrawn, the disagreements, particularly with Foreign Minster Mohammed Šaćirbey, continued through to Dayton. These political

21 The Bosnian Serb contingent was led by former speaker of the Bosnian Serb Assembly and recently designated President of Republika Srpska Momčilo Krajišnik (who had formally replaced Karadžić) and included the apparently more moderate Deputy President, Nikola Koljević.

divisions did nothing to compensate for the military limitations of the Sarajevo government's position.

If the conditions for Dayton indicated that there would be a high price for failure, success still depended on the process working and the issues being resolved. The process, to begin with, was important in itself. The concept of proximity talks meant that all the concerned parties would be in one place at the same time, but would not have to meet each other in set piece confrontations in which formal positions were reiterated and no progress was made. Instead, there was a series of bi-lateral meetings, bringing together the delegations for close discussions.

The programme for these meetings was set by the US hosts of the talks, arranging which issues would be discussed by whom at what time — although as the three weeks developed discussions between the main parties to the talks were to occur on their own initiative. The US framework was based on Holbrooke continuing the shuttle diplomacy which had made Dayton possible over the previous months, except he would race between rooms and buildings at Dayton, rather than fly between capitals and headquarters. As well as a series of intensive bi-lateral meetings and meetings with American representatives, pace was an important part of the process. The first days at Dayton seem to have involved some degree of relaxation and confidence building. This slow beginning was to give way to great pressure and extreme pressure in the later stages to ensure that agreement was made and, eventually, the setting of an absolute deadline. Finally, in contrast with the media diplomacy which had characterised much of the international diplomatic work towards a settlement in the past, the chief virtue of the Dayton airbase location, was that media access was strongly controlled (although some delegations managed to give background briefings). This meant that the confidential nature of the discussions would not risk serious disruption, or immediate re-interpretation in public at press conferences. That would make it easier to reach agreement, in itself.

Aside from the fact of arranging talks, the most important part of the Dayton process was to build the elements which would create the context for an agreement. In particular, this meant dealing with the questions requiring resolution with regard to Croatia and consolidating the Bosnian Federation. These were building blocks for achieving a settlement in Bosnia. Both were parts of the process, but were linked to important issues to be dealt with in any settlement over Bosnia.

4. The Dayton Accords

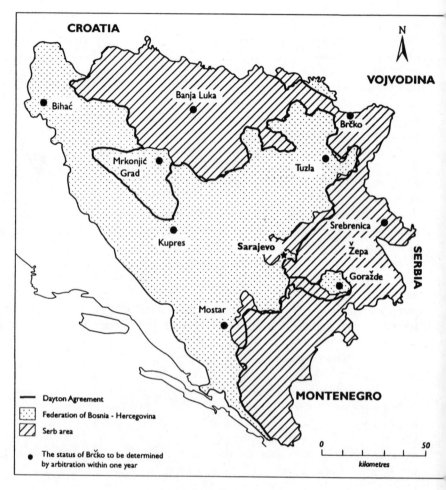

CROATIA

VOJVODINA

Bihać

Banja Luka

Brčko

Mrkonjić
Grad

Tuzla

Kupres

Srebrenica

Sarajevo

Žepa

SERBIA

Goražde

Mostar

Dayton Agreement

Federation of Bosnia - Hercegovina

Serb area

The status of Brčko to be determined
by arbitration within one year

MONTENEGRO

0   50

kilometres

4. The Dayton Accords

There were four principle questions concerning Croatia. The most important of these for Belgrade was the Prevlaka Peninsula (see Chapter 9). Coveted by the JNA and its successor the Yugoslav Army, Milošević and members of his team approached the Croatian delegation constantly at Dayton with a view to arranging a deal on the peninsula. Milošević was reported to have suggested land swaps. These involved territory for the Bosnian Croats behind the Dalmatian coast which would provide greater security for Dubrovnik, in return for Prevlaka which had been traditionally a military possession and which dominated access to the Bay of Kotor and the only naval bases available to the Belgrade military following the Yugoslav dissolution. The Serbian President was able to convey the impression that an arrangement had been discussed and, in principle, made. However, the Croatian delegation afterwards made clear that it was always prepared to talk, but that any possible transfer of territory was out of the question as it would never gain the approval of either the Zagreb parliament, or a Croatian referendum, both of which would be necessary. Prevlaka was, therefore, unresolved — although the fact that Croatia talked about it eased the way to agreement on other questions and enabled Milošević to imply that Prevlaka would be transferred to Montenegro and so to the federation with Serbia. That made it easier to make concessions on other matters.

One of the most significant concessions was over eastern Slavonia, the one area of Croatia which remained under Serbian control at the time of the talks. It was an economically important area in which the Belgrade military had come to have an key interest. Milosević was able to strike an agreement with Tudjman on returning this region to Croatian control (in which the prospect of reacquiring the seemingly more important Prevlaka territory was an important compensation for the Belgrade military). The agreement rested on a transitional authority, under the UN. Whereas Serbia wanted this to be for two years, Croatia argued that it should be for only one. In the end, it was agreed that the transition would be for one year which could be extended to two, if necessary.

In addition to the chimera concerning Prevlaka, Milošević appeared to use the question of the Posavina corridor across northern Bosnia as an element in the bargaining over eastern Slavonia. In return for agreement on restoring full Croatian control within Croatia, Zagreb agreed to the ceding of territory by the Bosnian Croats in the Posavina corridor — a decision which led to the announcement of the resignation of the Bosnian Croat leader and Prime Minster of the Federation, Krešimir Zubak (although this was retracted later). Although there was agreement, the issue of the corridor was not completely resolved and would not be, even at the end of the Dayton process, where it was the last issue being discussed. That was nine days after the first serious news to emerge from Dayton confirmed the agreements resolving eastern Slavonia.

The Posavina problem and Zubak's resignation were sensitive matters when it came to strengthening the Bosnian Federation. Many Bosnian Croats, like Zubak, were unhappy at the cession of territory in the Posavina corridor which had been majority Croat areas. Equally. Zubak as a well-regarded moderate on the Croat side, was important for the credibility of the Federation. Without figures such as him and his Muslim counterpart Silajdžić, the fragile federation was a hopeless venture. There were even more important divisions which threatened to weaken the Federation.

The Muslims and Croats in the Federation had little common policy. In particular, the Muslims insisted on the disestablishment of the Croatian para-state Herceg-Bosna and the reunification of the town on Mostar which was divided. The Bosnian Croats wanted to create a strong Federation which they would dominate (and which would be a *de facto* 'Great Croatia', whereas Sarajevo wanted to make the central institutions as strong as possible. Differences of emphasis on this question ran within the Muslim element in the leadership, with Silajdžić unable to resist Izetbegović's tendency to support a decentralised Bosnia and a stronger Federation.

The relationship of the entities, as they were coming to be called, with each other and with central authorities was one of the vital issues for the success of the Bosnian state. With this is mind, the EU, as the prospective lead agency for a programme of reconstruction and rehabilitation, emphasised the importance of central institutions. As the EU's only significant contribution to the Dayton process, this was critical, both practically for channelling assistance and politically for encouraging co-operation in forging a united Bosnian state.

Bosnia's reality was that power was highly decentralised. Real power already lay away from the centre in most respects. Within the Federation, the real issue was whether decentralised power lay with the Federation authorities, or with the Croat and Muslim controlled territories within it. The formal decision to disband Herceg-Bosna did little to persuade anyone that all would be well with the Federation, or that it would be strong. However, to counterbalance the Bosnian Serb entity, especially for the purposes of negotiation, it was necessary to make the Federation as strong as possible. The strength of the Federation depended in large part on the US which had taken responsibility for putting it together in the first place. For its part, the US seemed to believe that the majority of thorny political matters could not be solved in the negotiations and would have to be dealt with following elections which would renew political opinion throughout Bosnia. In the meantime, easily the most vital question in Washington's eyes was to get a settlement

In the final analysis, all the issues under discussion were subordinate to territorial questions — as the Posavina corridor indicated. In addition to this, key points of negotiation concerned the capital Sarajevo, Goražde and the Drina valley and north-western Bosnia. The principle for sharing our the land was adapted from the Contact Group proposal and envisaged 51 per cent of territory going to the Federation and the other 49 to the Bosnian Serbs. The Bosnian Government did not achieve territory on the Drina, or on the Sava, which would have fatally impaired the Serbian entity. Nor did manage to persuade anybody that the territorial disposition proposed in the Contact Group map should be adhered at Dayton — something which would have meant the return of Srebrenica, Žepa Višegrad and a number of other places to Government control. The Bosnian authorities did, however, secure agreement on the control of the whole of Sarajevo, as well as the establishment of a corridor to Goražde. The Goražde corridor created problems as Milošević, who wanted it to be narrower than was proposed, was convinced by US computer mapping technology that it could not be narrower.

Milošević's agreement on Goražde created a problem. When the US military computers added up all the territory, it emerged that rather than the proposed 49 per cent, Bosnian Serb land amounted to no more than 45 per cent. As a result, the Federation agreed to transfer Mrkonjić Grad in western Bosnia. This had been a Serb majority town, but had been captured in the summer of 1995 by Croatian forces. The Croatian forces, by giving it up were also implicitly weakening the position of the Muslims as the town lay on the major road connecting Sarajevo and central Bosnia with the Bihać area. This was not enough, anyway. The

Serbian President had continued to seek more land at Brčko, the key point in the Posavina corridor. The Bosnian Government, came under pressure from Holbrooke and others to make concessions.

Instead, it took the talks into a final phase of brinkmanship by demanding, among other things, control of the town of Brčko, in proposals to revise a map which was otherwise believed to have been settled. The talks had already gone into a final phase of brinkmanship, with the Americans turning up the pressure to obtain an agreement, by imposing a deadline of midnight on 18-19 November for agreement to be reached — a deadline which was then moved to 10 a.m. on 20 November. As both deadlines passed, everybody, in spite of having no interest in returning to war, began preparing to leave, with pressure falling on the Bosnian Government to come to terms. Faced with the prospect of losing American sympathy, Croatian support and being charged with responsibility for the collapse of the talks, the Bosnian Government delegation withdrew its counter-proposal map and agreed to an arbitration mechanism over the width and delineation of the corridor at Brčko. Although the Brčko question was left open, agreement to subject it to binding arbitration meant that the full range of agreements that had been made on all other matters could become the Dayton Accords.

The Dayton Accords

The Dayton Accords were initialled on 21 November and signed as a full peace agreement in Paris on 14 December. The relatively brief ten point accord was supplemented with eleven annexes (twelve in practice, as the first annex on military matters was in fact two separate documents), as well as one hundred and two maps. Although international attention at the end of 1995 seemed only to treat the military aspects of the agreement and the imminent deployment of a new NATO force to implement the agreement, the military part of Dayton was the most straightforward. The bulk of the Dayton Accords, around five sixths of the documentation, concerned civilian aspects of the settlement. It was in the civilian aspects of implementation that the real test of the Dayton process would come. Civilian implementation would define the peace and would delineate Bosnia's future.

Only one sixth of the Dayton-Paris peace concerned the ability to wage war. Annexes 1A and 1B concerned military matters. Annex 1A established the arrangements and timetable for the separation of forces and the deployment of IFOR, the NATO-organised military peace implementation force which would be responsible for ensuring the military parts of the Dayton agreement. In spite of initial attention given to NATO's IFOR and the possible problems it would face, in reality this was the easiest part of making the settlement work. Although incidents in which IFOR was presented with a challenge could be expected, for the most part IFOR could anticipate a relatively unproblematic mission.

This was for two reasons: the character of the deployment itself and the interests of the warring parties in Bosnia. First, the IFOR was to deploy with a simple and clear mission. More than 60,000 troops, three quarters from NATO countries, had a simple and single mandate: to enforce the line of separation. In practice, this was a primary mandate. There were also secondary mandates to assist in the creation of conditions for other agents to carry out there part of any implementation plan. But, the secondary mandates were to be very much secondary. If the tasks involved could be accomplished as a by-product of carrying out the primary mission, it would be. If, however, it required any diversion of attention or troops from the military mission, or the use of additional forces, it would not happen.

IFOR was little more than a very large, quasi-peacekeeping force with the task of reminding the armies on either side of the zone of separation that they had decided to cease combat. IFOR was to enforce a demilitarised zone of separation four kilometres wide. It was also mandated to patrol either side of the line of separation in which the opposing armed forces would still have military capability, albeit withdrawn to barracks by set dates. IFOR's rules of engagement were robust, permitting prompt and comprehensive military action to suppress any breach of the ceasefire. However, it was likely that this would only be used in the event of local infractions of the ceasefire. Were there to be an overall breakdown of the ceasefire along the length of the separation zone (over 1,000 kilometres), then IFOR would probably move to withdraw quickly. Neither NATO, nor the contributing countries were likely to stay to uphold a ceasefire that military-political leaders in Bosnia did not wish to preserve. However, there was every chance that, whatever local problems the IFOR might face in several sensitive areas (such as the front line near Prijedor, the Posavina

Corridor, access to Goražde and Sarajevo), it was in no one's interest
to return to armed hostilities.

The second annex regarding military matters addressed issues of
regional stabilisation. This envisaged confidence and security building
measures, as well as talks on arms control which would work on the
principle of a 5:2:2 ratio of forces for Serbia and Montenegro, for
Bosnia and for Croatia, respectively (although the Bosnian Serbs would
be entitled to one third of the Bosnian share).[22] However, given the
military-political conditions which had brought the war to an end and
which left none of the parties with a viable option for returning to
armed hostilities in the near or medium term future, military
implementation was going to be relatively straight forward, although it
would not mean either the disestablishment of the rival armed forces in
Bosnia or their unification. The longer term fate of those armed forces
and the peace made in Dayton and Paris would rest with the civilian
parts of the agreement and civilian implementation. Only if there was
adequate implementation would there be a prosperous and viable state
and the elimination of conditions for a return to armed hostilities in the
years ahead.

The Dayton Accords defined a single state, to be called Bosnia and
Hercegovina (dropping the previous designation 'Republic of'), albeit
a state that would be in the anomalous of being effectively partitioned
with more than one army for the foreseeable future. That state would
carry forward the political independence, territorial integrity and
sovereignty of the previous state.[23] That state was defined as being the
state of three constituent peoples and others, and comprised two entities,
The Federation of Bosnia-Hercegovina and the Republika Srpska.[24]
Each of the entities was given authorities other than those specified as
belonging to the Institutions of Bosnia and Hercegovina. The central

22 'General Framework Agreement for Peace in Bosnia and Hercegovina' (hereafter
'Framework'), Annex 1-B ('Agreement on Regional Stabilisation'), Article IV.3. This ratio
would come into force in the absence of an agreed arms control regime negotiated within
180 days of the agreement being signed. If this mechanism were needed, the agreement
stipulated that the baseline would be the weapons holdings of Serbia and Montenegro (the
Federal Republic of Yugoslavia). Belgrade would limited to 75 per cent of this figure in
designated categories, while Croatia and Bosnia would be restricted to 30 per cent of that
figure.
23 'Framework', Annex 4, ('Constitution of Bosnia and Hercegovina'), Article I.1.
24 'Framework', Annex 4, Preamble and Article I.3.

institutions were given responsibility for foreign policy and various aspects of economic policy, as well as for inter-entity communications and criminal law enforcement.[25] Crucially, although the entities would be able to establish 'special parallel relationships with neighbouring states', these would have to be 'consistent with the sovereignty and territorial integrity of Bosnia and Hercegovina'.[26] The entities would not be entitled to conduct a separate foreign policy, although with the consent of the Parliamentary Assembly, they could be allowed to enter into specific agreements with states or international bodies.[27] Thus there was some scope for the Federation to have links with Croatia and for Republika Srpska to have links with Serbia and Montenegro, but there was no provision for either supervening the independent international legal personality of Bosnia and Hercegovina.

The degree to which the formality of a single state reflected in the agreements and the constitutional provision inhibiting independent international activity would result in a strong and united state was dependent on the way the political institutions of Bosnia and Hercegovina worked. As indicated already, there was to be a Parliamentary Assembly which would be responsible for approving the external activity of the entities, as well as for regulating citizenship matters, approving budgets and preparing and promoting legislation. The Parliamentary Assembly was one of the key areas in which the fate of the new Bosnia would be defined. It contained both the mechanisms to prevent radical legislation against the self-defined interest of any group, as well as the possibility for creating irreconcilable differences which might tend to resolution in extra-parliamentary ways.

The Parliamentary Assembly was designated with two chambers, the House of Peoples and the House of Representatives.[28] The former was given fifteen members, five from each constituent people, that is ten from the Federation and five from the Bosnian Serb entity. The Muslim and Croat delegates would come from the House of Peoples of the Federation, and the Serbs would be nominated by the Republika Srpska Assembly. For it to be quorate, the House needed nine delegates in total and at least three from each community to be present. In the House of

25 'Framework', Annex 4, Article III.1.
26 'Framework', Annex 4, Article III.2(a).
27 'Framework', Annex 4, Article III.2(d).
28 'Framework', Annex 4, Article IV.

Representatives, which would have forty two members directly elected within the entities — two thirds from the Federation and the remainder from the Republika Srpska. The key to the future of Bosnia lay less in these structures themselves, however, than in the procedures attached to them.

A majority vote of those present in both chambers was set as the basic requirement for taking decisions in the Parliamentary Assembly. However, the Constitution provided an effective veto to any national group. The constituent peoples had the prerogative of declaring any prospective decision of the Parliamentary Assembly to be 'destructive of a vital interest'.[29] In the event of this mechanism's being invoked, the proposal would then require 'a majority of the Bosniac, of the Croat, and of the Serb Delegates present and voting' in the House of Peoples.[30] With this mechanism, decisions could only be made on the basis of a broad consensus and not against the declared vital interest of any national community.[31]

The exercise of the 'vital interest' mechanism could be challenged if a majority of one of the other communities' delegates raised an objection. In this event, the Chair of the House of Peoples would promptly convene a three-delegate Joint Commission (one from each community). If this commission failed to find a solution within five days, the matter would be referred to the Constitutional Court which would where its procedural propriety would be reviewed.[32] The Constitutional Court, in theory, therefore, might have an extremely important and delicate role. (See below.) Its decision would determine whether the use of the 'vital interest' mechanism, or its rejection was properly used and therefore would define the outcome of a particular decision.

This constitutional mechanism could be seen as a litmus paper for the progress being made in the political reconstruction of Bosnia. Infrequent use would indicate a broad degree of consensus. Frequent and accepted use of the mechanism would indicate a politically stagnant and stalemated country in which decisions could not be easily made, but in

29 'Framework', Annex 4, Article IV.3(e).

30 The term Bosniac was used to refer to the Slav Muslim population in Bosnia.

31 The assumption was inherent in this mechanism that the representatives in the House of Peoples would be the best placed to define the vital interests of the Muslims, Serbs and Croats in Bosnia.

32 'Framework', Annex 4, Article IV.3(f).

which the failure to be able to take decisions was thought to require the use of alternative means to assure effectiveness. Finally, constant recourse to the mechanism, accompanied by frequent challenge would signal a lack of faith in these political institutions and lead in the direction taken by the Socialist Federative Republic of Yugoslavia — stagnation and constitutional-political deadlock. At a minimum, however, it meant that there was no formal or legal mechanism for making significant changes to the form, structure or composition of the country without broad consensus. This mechanism for inaction, was also, however, a recipe for potential constant deliberate frustration of the Parliamentary Assembly's work.

The 'vital interest' mechanism was also present in provisions for the Presidency. This three-person body was stipulated to require one Muslim and one Croat, both to directly elected from the territory of the Federation and one Serb, directly elected from the Serbian entity, one of whom would chair the Presidency. Again, the procedures were designed to prevent radical steps being taken against the interest of one community. Although the Presidency was charged with endeavouring to adopt its decisions consensually, a majority decision was possible. However, a limitation was placed on a two-to-one decision. Provision was made for a three day period following a decision in which one the Presidency members could declare a decision taken to be "destructive of vital interest'.[33] Following the invocation of this mechanism, the decision would be referred to either the Republika Srpska Assembly, or either the Muslim or Croatian delegates in the House of Peoples in the Federation. A confirmation of the challenge by a vote of two thirds of the relevant group within ten days would render the decision null and void.

Taken together, the mechanisms for effective veto in the Parliamentary Assembly meant that the Bosnian Constitution foresaw little that could be done without broad agreement. Moreover, it also confirmed the importance of the entities and the authority of ethnic politics. The Presidency would be directly elected from the entities, on the basis of ethnicity. The 'vital interest' mechanism in the Presidency would be validated by the relevant group in the entity assemblies. In the Parliamentary Assembly, the 'vital interest' mechanism would in the control of Delegates of particular ethnic background from the entity

---

33 'Framework', Annex 4, Article V.2(d).

assemblies. Thus, the degree to which Bosnia would have a positive and co-operative future depended on the degree to which the ethnically defined politicians in the entity assemblies were prepared to see value in taking that option.

The final central political institution established by Dayton was a government, the Council of Ministers. The Council, appointed by the Presidency and approved by parliament was also subject to ethnic and territorial conditionality. No more than two thirds of all ministers should come from the Federation and deputy ministers should not be of the same constituent people as the minster. Thus, the Constitution agreed at Dayton enforced a further ethnic mechanism on the a central institution, while paving the way for potential difficulties in which either there would be friction between ministers and deputies from different entities or constituent peoples within the government, or there would be unfilled ministerial posts because of a refusal by one party or another to co-operate with the others. To a lesser extent than the 'vital interest' mechanism, this was nonetheless another device for creating inertia and impeding strong central government (in the absence of consensus).

The longer term prospects for the Dayton-Paris deal, therefore lay in the way in which the formal provisions of the documents would be put into practice and the degree to which future mechanisms adopted by the Parliamentary Assembly would help or hinder co-operative relations between the entities, between the entities and the central institutions, and between the constituent peoples. Much of this would, in turn depend on the outcome of elections scheduled to take place between six and nine months after the signing of the peace agreement. The elections, provided for in Annex 3 to the agreement, were vital to renew Bosnia politically. They would be the critical instrument for ensuring that those indicted by the International Criminal Tribunal (ICTY) for the Former Yugoslavia established in The Hague could not hold political or official positions. Elections would also provide some degree of validation for the new arrangements.

Successful elections were also to be a measure of the extent to which other parts of the settlement were being implemented. In particular, elections would demonstrate the degree to which aspects of the Accords, such as inter-entity co-operation, freedom of movement and the right of displaced people to return to the places of origin. The situation of displaced persons was an especially sensitive matter. Citizens, according to the agreement, were expected to vote in the municipality where they had been registered in 1991, prior to the war, unless they had specifically requested otherwise.[34] In one significant respect, therefore, the Dayton Accords, while in many other ways firmly cementing an ethno-political partition within Bosnia, held out the prospect of resisting the reality of ethnic cleansing for those determined and brave enough to try to turn back the tide of the previous four years.

It was certain that, after years of war and deepening animosity, there was no real prospect that the complex arrangements for Bosnia's future could be implemented by the former warring parties without an external helping hand. For this reason the agreements made significant provision for international involvement in implementation of the peace settlement. Overall co-ordination of civilian implementation was given to a High Representative under the authority of the UN Security Council.[35] This job was to be given to Carl Bildt who had been acting as EU mediator. The High Representative had responsibility for co-ordinating all aspects of the civilian implementation, as well as co-ordinating his activities with those of the IFOR Commander and maintaining contact with the UN, the Contact Group and other important international actors.

Within Bosnia, there was a serious international civilian involvement. This was the case, for example, with regard to appointments in key posts during the transition by international bodies of persons neither citizens of Bosnia, nor of its neighbouring states. These included: the Human Rights Ombudsman,[36] appointed by the OSCE for the first five years of implementation; the first Governor of the Central Bank,[37] appointed by the International Monetary Fund for a six year term; and the membership of the Constitutional Court,[38] where three out of nine representatives were to be designated by the President of the European Court of Human Rights. These appointments held great saliency. For an initial period financial control would be outside day to day Bosnian politics and the critical issues that would face the Constitutional Court in the event of the 'vital interest' mechanisms being invoked would not be entirely subject to inter-communal difference.

34 'Framework', Annex 3 ('Agreement on Elections'), Article IV.1.
35 'Framework', Annex 10 ('Agreement on Civilian Implementation of the Peace Agreement'), Article I.2.
36 'Framework', Annex 6 ('Agreement on Human Rights'), Article IV.2.
37 'Framework', Annex 4, Article VII.2
38 'Framework', Annex 4, Article VI.1(b).

The need for a strong international presence in civilian implementation was manifest in other ways. There was a broad role for international bodies in monitoring and overseeing the fulfilment of human rights agreements, including an invitation to all such bodies to monitor the situation with 'unrestricted' access and co-operation.[39] It was also evident in the role assigned to the OSCE over the preparations for and conducting of elections. The OSCE was charged with supervising this, as well as of establishing a Provisional Election Commission to manage the various tasks of running polls in the several elected political institutions which comprised Bosnia and its entities.[40]

Complementing these international roles, there was provision for an International Police Task Force (IPTF), potentially one of the most vital elements in facilitating the conditions for elections and in returning Bosnia to some kind of order. This was especially true in light of IFOR's particularly narrow military focused mission and the twin demands for freedom of movement within and between the entities and for co-operation with ICTY. Although the IPTF had an apparently weak mandate to assist and advise, and to monitor and observe,[41] in the absence of IFOR's taking this kind of role much would rest on the interpretation of the mandate and the nature of its implementation. The intention of the IPTF mandate was to encourage the Bosnian police and the entity police forces to take the primary role in law enforcement and inspection. However, advice could be advice on who a known war crimes suspect is, where they are and how they might be apprehended; facilitating might mean helping the local police to investigate and even arrest persons indicted by ICTY, particularly given that the various local police forces and authorities were obliged to allow IPTF personnel to have access to anything requested in accordance with its duties.[42] The essential point was that the interpretation of its mandate by the IPTF Commissioner, the High Representative and others was flexible enough to permit strong interpretation, while managing not to appear excessively intimidating so as to be unacceptable as an agreement.

---

39 'Framework', Annex 6, Article XIII.
40 'Framework', Annex 3, Article II.2 and 3.
41 'Framework', Annex 11 ('Agreement on International Police Task Force'), Article III.1.
42 'Framework', Annex 11, Article IV.

The key lay in the reserve potential the IPTF had should co-operation not emerge. This meant that if the IPTF met any obstruction or 'refusal to comply with an IPTF request' (which might, hypothetically, be a request to apprehend and indicted war criminal),[43] then IPTF Commissioner was obliged to notify the High Representative and the IFOR Commander of the failure, and may then request the High Representative to 'take appropriate steps' which might include 'further responses' following consultations with other relevant parties.[44] Finally, the IPTF was charged with special responsibilities with regard to violations of human rights, where relevant information was to be passed to the Human Rights Commission established under Annex 6 of the 'Framework Agreement', ICTY or 'other appropriate organisations'.[45] The 'Parties' to the agreement are then compelled to co-operate with the designated organisations.[46] The degree to which the agreement bound the local police and local authorities to co-operate with the IPTF meant that the scope of its activity would only be constrained by its own interpretation of its mandate. The need for freedom of movement, law and order and, most of all, an element of justice for peace to be built suggested that the IPTF would have to interpret its mission flexibly and potently.[47]

Justice was a vital element in making peace and peace building was the main issue. The real test for the international community, as well as for the various Bosnians themselves, was rebuilding Bosnia in such a way as to make it whole and functioning. This required vast resources — Bildt mentioned the sum of five billion US dollars, a figure which was agreed and promised at the conference of donor countries organised by London on 8-9 December. The resources would have to be made available. The World Bank and the IMF could be expected to play significant roles. Most of all, the EU, as probably the only source of finance on the scale required and as designated lead agency, would have to take the bulk of the responsibility — virtually bringing the diplomatic handling of the war full turn. While US diplomatic leadership would

---

43 'Framework', Annex 11, Article V.1.
44 'Framework', Annex 11, Article V.2.
45 'Framework', Annex 11, Article VI.1.
46 'Framework', Annex 11, Article VI.2.
47 The initial signs, however, were that the IPTF would struggle to gain its full complement or receive sufficient backing to act with authority.

continue to be vital in making the settlement work, the responsibility for post-war reconstruction fell to the EU.

Implementing the Bosnian peace would be as much of a major test for the international community and for the EU in particular as managing crisis and war had been. Peace offered the chance to compensate for earlier inadequacies. However, the experience of the EU-run PHARE and TACIS Programmes (as well perhaps as the experience of EU peace-building in Mostar) did not suggest an inspiring record. In the absence of international success, however, Bosnia would remain a divided country with more than one armed force and vulnerable to renewed armed hostilities in the years ahead.

Peace building meant an understanding of reconstruction which was wider than one of simply restoring physical infrastructure. It included the fostering of economic and political co-operation, suitable treatment of the displaced and refugees (whose future was vital to the longer term success of the settlement) and an educational policy that favoured understanding of the past and notions of reconciliation.[48] Alongside this, as representatives of ICTY made clear,[49] a vital task is to ensure that, even if only a few of former Yugoslavia's multitude of war criminals eventually would face trial, the process of making the truth known was of psychological, as well as social and political value. This was central to any process of rehabilitation and reconciliation.

US diplomacy played a vital role in bringing the Bosnian part of the Yugoslav War of Dissolution to an end and creating conditions for settlement of the war. With Washington fully engaged and facing a set of unpalatable alternatives, it was able to force a policy which was broadly accepted by other significant players in the international management of the Yugoslav war. This meant that international policy more than at any previous stage during the conflict was characterised by a degree of agreement, even if in the background there were always

---

48 For a valuable preliminary study of the aspects of peace-building in the Bosnian context, see Vesna Bojičić, Mary Kaldor, Ivan Vejvoda, 'Post-War Reconstruction in the Balkans. A background report prepared for the European Commission', *Working Papers in Contemporary European Studies*, Sussex European Institute, University of Sussex, Brighton, 1995.

49 For example, Senior Trial Attorney at ICTY Minna Schrag, speaking at King's College London, 18 October 1995.

difference of emphasis. As the conditions for settlement emerged, for the first time there was a concerted international effort to secure peace. By the time the Dayton proximity talks began, Washington was leading the way with everybody else playing very minor supporting roles.

With a settlement reached which inevitably included a strong international presence, the focus moved to how to make the peace work. For there was as much work in implementing peace as there had been in managing conflict. However, as the peace implementation process began at the end of 1995, it was not clear that the basic recipe for success was understood. Although most of the ingredients had been identified, with the military aspects of the agreed peace set to be fully implemented, it was not certain that civilian implementation would be as successful. This is because there was no evidence of an understanding that the same fundamental characteristics which had been essential for successful international management of the Yugoslav war, were equally vital to building its peace. A failure to unify the country would mean its continuing to be a state in which there was more than one armed force. The war had finished, but there could be no certainty that it would not return after some years if peace were not successfully implemented. Dayton had worked where Geneva had not, but questions remained.

11

CONCLUSION:
TRIUMPH OF THE LACK OF WILL

The Dayton Accords, which brought the Yugoslav War of Dissolution to a close, although at an immediate level a success, the peace agreement signed in Paris also served to confirm the essential failure of international diplomacy over the break-up of Yugoslavia. International efforts had failed to hold together the old federation. This was understandable as it was an almost impossible aim. More notably, the international community had failed peacefully to manage the dissolution. Instead, ever greater attention and resources were devoted to attempts to resolve the dispute and to halt the fighting.

The initial well-meaning but hurried and ill-planned venture of the then EC troika led seemingly ineluctably to the expansion of the EC role, to the inclusion of the OSCE, the WEU and the UN in various ways, and eventually to the incorporation of NATO and the US. With each inevitable increase in international involvement, the international stake rose. This escalation of involvement is reflected in the structure of the present volume: from the early diplomatic initiatives of the EC, the CSCE and the UN in the first section, to the increasing military engagement dealt with in the second and the growing salience for relations between the major states involved in international diplomacy and strains in the relationships between them; finally, there were the major efforts to provide a concerted diplomatic focus and the focus which fell on the peace plans put forwards as a test of international honour. The Yugoslav war moved from being an important question for Euroepan stability and security and a test of the then CSCE's brand new Conflict Prevention Centre, to being a test of the future of EU Common Foreign and Security Policy; from that it moved to being a test of UN diplomacy and UN peacekeeping; from that, it became a test of European, Transatlantic and East-West relations and post-Cold War co-operative security; and finally, it became a test of NATO credibility and with that of international and particularly American credibility. Despite the commitments that went with these tests, for four years international diplomacy struggled to end the war.

When the triumph of Dayton emerged, it embraced failure itself and it underlined the failure of the previous years. Dayton, although a success in terms of ending the fighting, was a failure because although it maintained the territorial integrity of Bosnia which was the cardinal aim of the international community, it effectively abandoned the other two which had been present three years before, as will be shown below. In addition to establishing this failure, Dayton highlighted the record of international failure in three ways. First, it demonstrated that it was possible for international action to be instrumental in ending the conflict. Secondly, the conditions for obtaining a settlement at Dayton confirmed the fundamental characteristics of failure during the previous four years, as will be identified below. Finally, by confirming the funamentals of earlier failure, Dayton also led to the conclusion that the Bosnian conflict and the Yugoslav war as a whole could have been drawn to a close two and a half years earlier at the time of the Vance-Owen Plan.

As will be argued through this concluding chapter, apart from securing an end to the war, the international community got less from the agreements negotiated at Dayton than it would have from implementation of the Vance-Owen Plan. However, the conditions for implementing both plans were the same: Dayton worked where Vance-Owen failed because there was a willingness to use force and, crucially, because the US was behind the plan, rather than opposing it. This will be shown through comparison of Vance-Owen and Dayton. That analysis rests on drawing out the elements which characterised the failures of international diplomacy prior to Dayton.

A Peace-making Assessment: the Fundamentals of Failure

There were four fundamental features of international failure in handling the Yugoslav war: bad timing, inappropriate measures, incoherence, and lack of political resolve.[1] Of these the most important was political nervousness about the use of force to back policies and ensure respect. The dissipation of the Contact Group during 1994 and subsequent moves towards a potentially more robust use of force demonstrated the indispensable need for both cohesion and political will.

Bad timing was always a problem. International efforts suffered from the start because by the time the EC arrived to mediate between Belgrade and Ljubljana after the declarations of independence — and later tried to broker an agreement based on the confederal positions previously advocated by the republics which had declared independence but rejected by Belgrade — it was already too late: once force was used against Slovenia and Croatia, there was no real prospect of their being able to accept re-integration into a Yugoslav state. This involvement came late in the day considering that for several months, if not three years, there had been clear signals that a situation was developing which required attention.

The international community generally reacted to events rather than anticipating them. Consequently, action which could have made a great difference three or six months earlier came late and usually with too little commitment. The clearest example of this was the fate of Bosnia. Although there had been unmistakable signs that the republic was teetering on the verge of war for over a year. In August and September 1991 the Yugoslav army had completed the deployment of tanks at major communications points throughout the country, had all but abandoned barracks in the major towns in non-Serbian populated areas, and had dug in heavy artillery on high ground around the towns.[2] When, in March 1992, this arsenal began the last and worst phase of the attempt to destroy Bosnia, the international response was meagre: there was an internationally co-ordinated move to grant recognition of independence to the country.

---

1 Much of the analysis in this chapter is drawn, adapted and expanded from James Gow, 'Nervous Bunnies: the International Community and the Yugoslav War of Dissolution — the Politics of Military Intervention in a Time of Change', in Lawrence Freedman, ed., *Military Intervention in European Conflicts*, Blackwell for the *Political Quarterly*, Oxford, 1994.

2 It is important here to recall that international recognition did not cause war in Bosnia, although the Serbian camp used this as a pretext and it fuelled their campaign (see Chapters 1, 2 and 3).

That there was a threat of widespread violence had been made clear by Radovan Karadžić, the local Serbian leader. That the EC, as well as other parts of the international community, were aware of the threat was also clear from the fact that from February 1992 onwards the EC Conference and other international efforts were geared towards avoiding war in Bosnia. The EC effort was essentially based on the adoption of an idea — ethnic territories or 'cantons' — propounded by the Serbian camp.[3] Understood by the EC negotiators as a means to propitiate the Serbs and avoid war, it was in reality a charter for 'ethnic cleansing': ethnically designated cantons created the basis for ethnically pure territories.

Some months later, in the wake of the terror which swept the country in the spring and summer, the EC-UN backed ICFY in Geneva came up with a plan which might have been appropriate to the accommodation of any genuine fears in the Serb communities in Bosnia. The constitutional plan, devised by a working group under the Finnish diplomat Martti Ahtisaari, was much better in that it did not take ethnicity as a starting point, although it was a factor taken into account. The end-product was a set of regions which had ethnic majorities but were constitutionally designed to be multi-cultural.[4] However, by the time the Ahtisaari plan was called the Vance-Owen plan and placed on the negotiating table, 'ethnic cleansing' had been realised.

A further example of inappropriate measures was the decision to declare 'safe areas' in Bosnia and make a commitment to implementing them. Two, Srebrenica and Žepa, were never going to be viable, while two more, Goražde and Bihać, were on crucial strategic axes in the war and therefore always unlikely to be left alone as 'safe areas' by the Bosnian Serbs — in so far as they were left alone, they would be zones in which elements of the Bosnian army could prepare for action. Sarajevo and Tuzla, for reasons of size and either international presence or degree of control by Bosnian government forces, would remain the focal points of fighting, but were unlikely ever to become completely vulnerable to military operations.

What was certain in any case was that without secure logistics lines and a large UN presence the isolated enclaves in eastern Bosnia would

3 See Milan Andrejevich, 'The Future of Bosnia and Hercegovina: A Sovereign Republic or Cantonisation?', *RFE/RL Report on Eastern Europe*, 5 July 1991.
4 See Chapter 5.

be indefensible. They would therefore be no more than symbolically 'safe' at the same time as they were hostages to fortune. This placed the UN on a hook for a variety of reasons. First, the Security Council had made a commitment to protecting these areas; secondly, UNPROFOR was unable genuinely to deter attacks purely by a presence in the 'safe areas'; thirdly, deterrence relied on the threat of using close air support to defend the troops, or possibly air strikes, in response to bombardment of the areas; and fourthly, the threat of using air power was neutralised by the vulnerability of the troops on the ground in those areas, deployed in small pockets and cut off from the main force. In such a situation there would always be calls to take action, as per the declarations of the Security Council and then inevitable and bitter criticism when the amalgam of UN, NATO and other international instruments failed effectively to implement the ill-thought out 'safe area' concept.

The 'safe area' concept was drafted almost on the back of an envelope at the time of the Washington Declaration of 22 May 1993 as a face-saving device for foreign ministers seeking to overcome the divisions within their ranks presenting a positive front. This was a deformed manifestation of the importance of cohesion in the international response to the war. Indeed, the inappropriateness of steps taken and the way in which the international response lagged behind events can be explained largely in terms of the nature and composition of the various bodies involved. All were intergovernmental organisations, all requiring discussion and agreement between member states, and some requiring consensus before decisions could be taken. Therefore, over a controversial question such as the collapse of Yugoslavia there was much disagreement between the individual governments which made up the international agencies. This made quick responses to situations which required them impossible.

Differences of opinion were most notable on the questions of recognition, the deployment of military personnel and the use of armed force. Even where there was some kind of agreement on what was to be done, there were different perspectives on implementation. Once it had been decided that the European countries would offer troops to support the UN's humanitarian effort in Bosnia, there were differences of emphasis between the French who wished to use the WEU to plan the operations and the British who favoured NATO for the role. Later, on the question of enforcement of a UN air exclusion zone over Bosnia, the US wished to have the right to strike targets on the ground and in

Serbia itself, whereas the French preferred to limit operations to Bosnia and, if possible, to aerial targets. This was a reflection of the general tension between the aerial bullishness of the US and the greater caution of those carrying out the humanitarian mission with troops on the ground.

The crucial problem concerned compliance and the use of force. The pattern of international activity indicated that, although there were numerous efforts to mediate, progress towards either ceasefire or political agreement only emerged after some form of coercion had been applied, usually against the Serbian camp.[5] However, the logic of this pattern was not readily extended to the use of armed force.

Even after almost a year of war, the Vance-Owen Plan, in spite of considerable complexity, had a role to play in moving towards an end to hostilities in Bosnia. The plan, it will be recalled, involved the creation of ten provinces in a single Bosnian state, in each of which there would be a multi-ethnic government and, in nine of the ten, a governor nominated by one of the three constituent ethnic groups (the capital, Sarajevo, would have had a separate status). Both in January and in May, agreement on all elements of the Vance-Owen Plan appeared close, and on each occasion an apparently growing threat of US-led air strikes helped to induce Serbian co-operation. However that co-operation proved short-lived when it became clear that the organisation of a force to implement the plan was still subject to debate and that some crucial countries, notably the US, were reluctant to become involved if not actually opposed, both if this required their own ground troops and if it appeared morally unacceptable in their terms.

The reluctance of relevant governments to commit armed forces in the Balkans, for good and bad reasons, had the effect of giving a green light to those who would go the limits of what they could do without being brought to account. As one senior UN official engaged in the handling of the Yugoslav break-up observed: 'Force is the ultimate arbiter and any diplomatic policy that does not rely on carrots and sticks will not really get you very far. Without a club in the closet, without a

---

5 See James Gow, 'The use of coercion in the Yugoslav crisis', *The World Today*, Vol.48, No.11, November 1992.

credible threat of force, policy becomes bluff, bluster.'[6] From the outset, categoric declarations that there would be no use of force stripped diplomatic efforts of one of their key instruments: the threat of force in circumstances where other means proved inadequate or unpersuasive.

Using Force: the Political Equation

There were many aspects to the international debate on using force. The issues used in argument included history, ethics, interest, the basis for armed action (both political and legal), the nature of the conflict and the resources required, available or in use.[7] From the point of view of those in Western capitals facing the question of an armed intervention, the matter was not clear-cut. While it was evident that Belgrade had been responsible for the initiation of large-scale organised campaigns of violence in Bosnia (something recognised in the UN Security Council Chapter VII resolutions, especially on sanctions against Serbia), the aggression was not a classic cross-border adventure involving a well-established member of the UN — as with Iraq and Kuwait. It was, rather, a hybrid war. The continuing presence in Bosnia after independence of the JNA, loyal to Belgrade, meant that although there were significant incursions across the River Drina between Serbia and Bosnia, there were also 80,000 troops already based in Bosnia. Their presence there was a consequence of Bosnia's predicament as a state emerging to independence from the Yugoslav federation.

The transitional nature of the situation in Bosnia confused some of the questions relating to the basis of intervention. So too did the fact that it was only in part a war of external aggression. The fact that the bulk of the JNA and later its successor, the army of the Serbian Republic (in Bosnia), comprised Serbs from Bosnia gave the war a strong element of internal conflict. Civil wars have been conventionally (to some extent, prudentially) judged to be matters internal to the state and therefore subject to the general proscription of interference in domestic affairs — although in reality there is often external backing

---

6 Herbert Okun, UN Special Adviser and Deputy-Head of Civilian Affairs UNPROFOR, Interview, 'Diplomacy and Deceit' Channel 4 TV, 2 August 1993, Media Transcription Service, *Bloody Bosnia*, MTS/M2578.WPS, p.4.
7 For more extensive discussion of some of these see Gow, 'Nervous Bunnies'.

for different sides in civil wars. Even though there was a critical question over the inviolability of the state's borders, the internal dimension was a counterweight to the need to take similar action, particularly where there was little appetite for doing so.

However, for all the factors of practicability and principle which complicated the question of military intervention in Bosnia, the crucial matter was the politics of intervention. Experts and officials generally recognised the complexities of the situation in Bosnia and the region, but there was also a general awareness that only the use of force, or perhaps the threat of it, would decisively affect events on the ground. While much was made of comments by military figures about their fears of sending troops to Bosnia, those fears were generally not so much to do with the strictly military factors involved as concerns over the relationship of the use of force to political objectives.

For example, Field-Marshal Sir Richard Vincent, chair of the Military Staff Committee at NATO, was widely reported when he took the rather unusual step of publicly voicing worries that, without a proper political dynamic, military intervention in Bosnia could parallel the Charge of the Light Brigade. Less noticed was that his point concerned not the use of force but its linkage to a political objective. Even less noticed was his reported private assessment that intervention was possible and necessary at different levels.[8]

That opinion could be heard in private discussion from many, if not all, corners of officialdom, both civilian and military. The assessment was that politicians were the major constraint on policy. In a different way this was conceded by Douglas Hurd: 'The only thing which could have guaranteed peace with justice would have been an expeditionary force, creating if you like a new Northern Ireland, being there for how many years? And no government, no government has at any time proposed that.'[9] More strikingly, the understanding expressed by the then NATO Secretary-General Manfred Wörner was that the reason there had been no military intervention was that the politicians making

8 See, for example, Andrew Marr,'Politicians let NATO down over Bosnia', *The Independent*, 11 September 1993.
9 Douglas Hurd, interview, 'Diplomacy and Deceit', Channel 4 TV, 2 August 1993, Media Transcription Service, *Bloody Bosnia*, MTS/M2578.WPS, p.4.

up those governments lacked 'political will'.[10] Various plans had been made and policies recommended of a more interventionist nature, but various ministers had not had the stomach for them. If there was an overall policy failure, its central feature was the absence of armed force as a bottom line. The reason for that absence was a lack of the 'political will' to act forcefully in a transitional situation that appeared to be both laced with risk and not absolutely indispensable.

The fact that from an early stage of the Yugoslav break-up, politicians in almost every significant country had decided that the situation was practically and politically uncertain, unclear, complex, danger-ridden and potentially costly meant that armed intervention was always unlikely. Where the only clear common perspective was that the problem was too difficult to be dealt with using the kind of armed force which might be made available, it was more or less ruled out. It was that mixture of no intelligible political aim and political queasiness which most prompted the fears of senior military personnel.

The political worries of Western politicians concerned popular opinion and the need to win votes at the next election. The prospect that the mission might go wrong, given the complexity of the problem and its apparently intractable nature, made these political leaders reluctant to contemplate intervention seriously enough. The fear that it could be another Northern Ireland, Dien Bien Phu or broader Vietnam weighed heavily on the minds of politicians wanting to avoid similar problems, particularly critical in this respect was the shadow of Vietnam hanging over US political and military leaders. Because of the key US role in NATO as well as the size of its armed forces, no sizeable military intervention with ground forces was conceivable without US involvement.[11] Had the US been prepared to commit its ground troops, then there would have been little prospect that the UK, for all the worries shared by the Foreign and Defence Secretaries, would not have been involved alongside. Likewise, whatever French rhetoric might suggest, France was committed in practice to international operations in

10 Manfred Wörner, Secretary-General, NATO, 'NATO's Role in a Changing Europe', IISS Adelphi Paper no.284, Brassey's for the IISS, London, 1994, p.98.
11 Of course, much of this discussion was based on the notion of large-scale intervention. One alternative for the future use of armed forces such as those of the UK and France would be a modernised return to the practices of their imperial past — small, high-quality forces designed for raids directed at the centre of gravity of opposing forces, something which could have been relevant had there been a decision to use force in Bosnia.

a way which made it hard to imagine Paris not associating itself, with special considerations, with any intervention there might have been in Bosnia.

The US was therefore the linchpin of any concerted international military operation. Both the Bush and the Clinton Administrations were hamstrung by domestic considerations: the need to deal with the country's own economic difficulties; the lack of confidence that there would be public opinion support for an intervention, especially if it went wrong; the absence of a perceived interest significant enough to warrant overcoming Vietnam sensitivity and making a commitment of forces anyway; and the absence, also of a political campaign to explain such a commitment to public opinion.

In the final analysis, the critical factor in the failure of Western countries to intervene was the refusal of the US to put ground troops into the ring. It was only when Washington was forced to accept that admitting the possibility, if not inevitability, of placing troops on Bosnian soil that international diplomacy could begin to address all the fundamentals of failure. The same attributes of international diplomacy were appropriate for Vance-Owen and Dayton. The conditions for success of both were the same. Dayton was concluded where Vance-Owen was condemned because there had been crucial changes in those conditions.

Comparing Peace Plans: Vance-Owen and Dayton

Vance-Owen and Dayton represent the two major international attempts to achieve a settlement in Bosnia and to bring the Yugoslav War of Dissolution to an end. The purpose of the following section is to offer analysis of why one worked where the other did not. That analysis will incorporate assessment of the plans themselves, as welll as the aims of, and the situation and resources of, the four main groups involved: the Serbs, the Bosnian Government, the Croats and the International Community.[12] As indicated, the most important difference between the two plans was the US position. Although there were several differences in the plans and in the conditions in which they were under discussion, this was the critical one.

12 The terms 'the Serbs' and 'the Croats' have been explicitly adopted here to include Serbia and the Serbs outside Serbia, and Croatia and the Bosnian Croats.

The need of any peace plan was to represent the desires of the international community, while trying to present arrangements for an accommodation between the Bosnian belligerents. Any plan, therefore, had to be understood in the context of the aims of all concerned. At the heart of this was the essence of the war: the clash of state projects between the Serbs, seeking to establish new borders through force and other Yugoslav republics, notably Croatia and Bosnia seeking to uphold the integrity of the existing borders.

There were changes in the aims of those involved between the pre-Vance-Owen and the Dayton periods. In the early stages of the conflict, Serb aims were threefold: to establish the borders of a new entity (whether a mini-Yugoslavia, a Great Serbia, or a Union of Serbian States); to establish territorial contiguity of Serb areas; and to make those areas ethnically pure. By the time of the Dayton talks, it was clear that there were divisions among the Serbs. The Bosnian Serbs still sought new borders, meaning either or both of the following: independence or union with Serbia. Serbia, however, appeared to have abandoned this project, temporarily at least. The common Serb aim continued to be contiguous and ethnically pure territories.

The Bosnian Government, in contrast, was interested at the beginning of the war in Bosnian state integrity; in promoting a multicultural society; in protecting the position of the Muslims in the country; and in gaining international support. As the conflict evolved, although emphasis on maintaining a multicultural society continued to be declared, the Bosnian Government's unstated aim was increasingly concerned with the Muslim position. Although the overall aim continued to be the maintenance of Bosnia as a state, as far as a divided leadership had a core aim, it was to maximise the weak position of the Muslims, in terms of territory, political influence and military capability.

The Croats were always in a more ambiguous situation. Like the Bosnian Government, their aim was to preserve the territorial integrity of Croatia; however, in similar vein to the Serbs, there was also an inclination to seek new borders by seizing parts of Bosnia; the ambiguity in these contrasting aims was highlighted by the desire to keep on the right side of the international community. By the time of the Dayton talks, Croat aims, while retaining ambiguity, had become a little more coherent. The importance of Croatia's territorial integrity had been established as a priority and much done in connection with that aim. The trade-off for relinquishing any ambitions over establishing new borders was the aim (largely being accomplished) of having substantial influence in Bosnia. Finally, to complete the Croats' being able to have almost all their cake and eat most of it, the Croats had established good international ties, particularly with the US.

Finally, the aims of the international community at the time of Vance-Owen fell into two categories. With regard to the situation in Bosnia, there were three aims: to uphold the principle of state integrity and to resist attempts to change borders through force; to resist ethnic purification; and to deny the Serbs contiguous territories. There were two further aims with regard to the international community itself: to maintain common positions; and to avoid making commitments judged to be too great, including using force. Vance-Owen was designed to accomplish the three aims on Bosnia and to square a circle by satisfying the international community's self-focused aims.

Although all three aims in the first category no doubt remained as aspirations, after the demise of Vance-Owen — certainly by the time of Dayton — international aims ceased seriously to include opposing territorial contiguity and (*de facto*) ethnic cleansing. Furthermore, even the desire to maintain a unified Bosnian state was apparently weaker in the Bosnian peace settlement agreed at Dayton. Where Vance-Owen envisaged demilitarisation of Bosnia, Dayton accepted that the state would have at least two armed forces for the foreseeable future. This was surely more realistic as an approach and the issue was one to be dealt with in the talks on regional stability agreed at Dayton. But, it also lent continuing encouragement to ideas of permanently dividing the country. On the international side, where the aim of a common front over Vance-Owen was strained by American criticism, the aim was constitently present in the Dayton process. Most critically, the aim of avoiding a use of force had given way to the aim of using the force, or its potential, constructively.

These changes at the level of aims reflect changes regarding situation and resources. The Serbs, in 1993, had a superabundance of weaponry, but a relative manpower shortage. They controlled up to seventy per cent of Bosnia, as well as twenty two per cent of Croatia, as a result of their initial superiority. This gave the Serbs in both countries a strong psychological advantage. However, their position was dependent on support from Belgrade. As the Bosnian Serb leadership attempted to pursue a separate line, backing from Belgrade, while never completely cut off, was greatly reduced with serious impact on capability, morale and the renewal of some resources.

However, for the Serbs, apart from their own intra-Serbian problems, the most critical change in situation concerned the amount and the effectiveness of force used against them. The Bosnian Serbs were able to defy Milošević and the international community over the Vance-Owen plan because there was no use of force available to encourage them. As the Vance-Owen Plan, anyway, ran counter to their aims they had no desire to accept it. Under duress, the plan was signed, but, as was seen in Chapter 9, it could eventually be rejected because there was no prospect of its being enforced. By contrast, by the time of Dayton, both the Croatian and Bosnian Serbs had faced a substantial use of force by their enemies in the war, as well as by the international community which was also now prepared to provided a strong ground force under NATO command to implement the deal. In this situation, psychological and physically diminished, and without backing from Belgrade for resistance, the Bosnian Serbs were forced to accept terms and to allow Milošević to negotiate for them.

The situation and resources of the Bosnian Government had also changed. The Bosnian Army had always had enormous manpower potential, but had been short of weapons throughout. Although enough weapons had been smuggled to increase the number of troops, these had mostly been man-portable. So the Bosnian Government forces had developed a large infantry force, but lacked weapons of heavy calibre with which to damage the Serbs seriously. This situation was compounded by the fact that there was relatively little territory actually under Government control and what territory there was had to be defended often on all sides and was cut off from easy access to arms supplies.

In a militarily weak position, the Bosnian Government's need for international support was essential. To some extent, therefore, its actions were always geared towards an international audience, if not constrained by the need to sustain international sympathy. Although probably unhappy about any plan which envisaged some division of Bosnia, the Sarajevo government because of its weak position was likely to accept so as to keep on the right side of international opinion. Aside from international opinion, the Bosnian Government was in a difficult position psychologically. It had lost control of most of the country in the course of the war, particularly in the early stages and represented the decimated and displaced Muslim community. This put the Government in the position of being a victim and apparent loser. The sense that any agreement might be regarded as an admission of defeat encouraged the Bosnian Government to fight on, even were this to prove futile, for the sake of dignity.

By the time of Dayton, the Bosnian Government's situation had been modified. It had been able to place a large part of its manpower reserve under arms and had been carrying out operations jointly with Croatian forces. As a result, the Bosnian Serbs had been forced off substantial tracts of land and Bosnian pride a little repaired. Even more significantly, the combined use of force by NATO planes in the air and the artillery of the Rapid Reaction Force supporting UNPROFOR on the ground dealt the Bosnian Serbs a substantial blow, both physically and psychologically. In doing this, it provided a boost to the Bosnian Government and made it far easier psychologically to make terms. It was also encouraged to do this by the reality that although Sarajevo might have preferred to continue the war in order to press the Bosnian Serbs further, its dependence on both Croatian and international, especially American, support meant that it was in no position politically or militarily to do so when Zagreb and Washington had decided it was time to call a halt. (Indeed, to have tried to continue alone might only have opened the way for the Croats to turn on the Muslims again.) The Bosnian Government was constrained from going further, but had achieved enough to find honour in a settlement.

The Croats, consistent with their ambiguous aims, were in an equivocal situation. Croatia had begun the war, like the Bosnian Government in a significantly weaker position than the Serbs. However, it had been able to acquire weapons, including heavy weapons and aircraft via its maritime and continental, non-Yugoslav borders. As a result, by the second half of 1995, they had a better ratio of men to arms than either the Serbs, excluding Belgrade, or the Bosnian Government. Whereas the former had weapons and the latter manpower, Croatia had men and weapons (albeit fewer men than the Bosnian Army and fewer weapons than the Serbs). Zagreb was able to use this capability, with Washington's muffled approval, to restore control over most of Croatia. It was then able to press its position with the US and with the Bosnian Government by giving assistance to the Bosnian Government in western Bosnia. Thus, in spite of some international criticism of Croatian Army behaviour in the campaign in Croatia,

Zargeb had been ab'e to offer itself as a strategic pivot for the Americans. Psycholog'cally, the Croats were confident: of their usefulness to the Americans; of their victory within Croatia's borders; and of their influence in Bosnia, whatever happened.

The biggest changes between spring 1993 and autumn 1995 were in the international sphere. At the time of Vance-Owen, the military presence in Bosnia was not designed for a major use of force and, deployed in small packages on long communications lines, was vulnerable. However, among the more significant contributors to UNPROFOR, there was preparedness to take on the role of implementing Vance-Owen under a NATO command. Secondly, Washington was dead-set against using American troops, either as part of an operation while the conflict continued, or to implement an agreement. By the end of 1995, in terms of manpower and military capability, there were two significant differences. First, the insertion of the Rapid Reaction Force in the summer of 1995 along with the force reconfiguration which began as a result of the hostage taking crisis at the end of May meant that there was a less vulnerable force on the ground with a greater capaility for using force. Secondly, the US had accepted that it would have to place its forces on the ground in the event of a settlement. That made a settlement both more likely and more credible.

These movements on the military side reflected significant political-diplomatic shifts. The Vance-Owen Plan was conceived to achieve international interests without making too many internaitonal sacrifices. In the end, although it had some degree of political backing from most parts of the international community, it was clear that there was an absence of coherent approval for the plan, with the US leading the way with an attitude which was to make implementation of the plan impossible and so allow the Bosnian Serbs the luxury of being able to reject it. The lack of cohesion marked by the US perspective was reinforced by a lack of political commitment to making the plan work. Where the US opposed the plan, none of the European governments were sufficiently committed to it to carry it forward — and the Russians who did try were therefore easily rebuffed by Washington (with important consequences for Russian attitudes in the future). Circumstances were radically different for Dayton. The whole international community, including the major players in the Contact Group, were behind the American initiative. This reflected the strong political commitment of all involved, particularly the, US. This also signalled the willingness to commit troops to a settlement inplementation regime — that is, to back diplomacy with force, if necessary.

The Vance-Owen and Dayton plans were significantly different. Vance-Owen offered more in terms of the original aims of the international community. It maintained a single Bosnian state, through its system of provincial governments it maintained the principle of multi-ethnicity through the provision of ethnic proportionality in government, and through the placing of Province 3, it denied the Serbs any sense of territorial contiguity (see Chapter 9). Beyond providing a mechanism to secure internaitonal aims, the requirement for demilitarisation, although making implementation more difficult, also enhanced the chances of reconstituting a unified Bosnia. In these senses, it was a better plan than that which was achieved at Dayton.

It is ironic that the Clinton Adminstration effectively destroyed Vance-Owen through allegations that it rewarded aggression and condoned ethnic cleansing. The Dayton Accords accepted the principle of an ethnically defined Serbian territory which would run contiguously from eastern Bosnian across the north and onto the north-western part of the country. The principles of resisting ethnic cleansing and Serbian territorial contiguity had been conceded. Although Vance-Owen had been condemned by Washington for such concessions, it had made significant formal efforts to avoid them. Having refused to attempt implementation of Vance-Owen on these grounds in 1993, the US was prepared to oversee and contribute significantly to a deal which was worse, regarding the principles at stake.

Dayton did, however, secure the absolute minimun for the international community: agreement on the territorial integriry of Bosnia and its continuing indpendent poiltical and legal international personality. This secured the principle of resisting attempts to change borders through force. However, the future of that partitioned Bosnian state would be fragile for some time to come and its future almost entirely dependent on international, especially US, commitment. One major shadow was the continuing presence of more than one armed force — another significant and unfavourable contrast with the demilitarisation envisioned by Vance-Owen, in terms of principle.

There were two ways in which Dayton compared more favourably with Vance-Owen. First, it was easier to implent. The numerous boundaries of the Vance-Owen provincial map were replaced with one single (albeit long and winding) border between two entitites. This certainly won more favour in US military thinking than Vance-Owen had. It is hard to see this as an overwhelming compensation for the abandoning of the princples involved when Vance-Owen, for all its complexity and imperfections, could have been the framework for an implemented settlement.

The most significant way in which Dayton exceeded Vance-Owen, of course, was its success. It was agreed and implementation was begun almost immediately. This, in itself, was a substantial and welcome achievement. All credit was due to the American diplomatic team which had engineered this outcome. Peace at the cost of some princple was, by this stage, both inevitable and preferable to continuing war which ethnic lines of division would become more pronounced and bitterness deeper. However, it was also hard to avoid the conclusion that similarly strong US support for implementation of Vance-Owen in 1993 would have ended the war two and a half years sooner, and on better terms.

There were important differences in the prevalent conditions for Vance-Owen and Dayton. By the time of Dayton, the situation on the ground provided a situation in which no party had sufficient interest or prospect in prolonging the fighting and therefore had some interest in a settlement. This was true in terms of territorial control, strategic position and psychological attitude. However, without these changes, a settlement could have been agreed in 1993, in spite of the reluctance of the belligerents.

The changes which made a real difference were at the international level. On the ground in Bosnia, the salient changes flowed from the appointment of General Smith as UNPROFOR Commander and the force reconfiguration and reinforcement which occurred in 1995. However, these shifts were only indications of what might have been possible in 1993 had there been strong moves towards implementing the Vance-Owen Plan. In the final analysis, the critical differences between 1993 and 1995 lay in the degree of diplomatic cohesion behind the initiatives and the preparedness to use force. Central to both of these was the US position. With the US at the heart of diplomacy, those it had criticised gave their backing and entrusted it to accomplish the task. In doing so, they were more confident in the possibility of using force and moving towards implementation of a settlement because the US had placed a major stake on the outcome and committed a good deal of political capital to achieving it. It was unfortunate that this US commitment had not been present in 1993 to forestall a further two and a half years of war. It was to be hoped that the US commitment would be sustained into the peace to prevent a return to war in the years ahead and to enable Washington to achieve due credit.

The State of International Diplomacy

International efforts, first to prevent the break-up of Yugoslavia and then to end the War of Dissolution, resulted in the emergence of five states from the six republics which had formed the Socialist Federative Republic of Yugoslavia (with the possible separation of Montenegro and Serbia in the years to come not wholly out of the question[13]) and a war in Bosnia which, after three years of efforts and the contribution of vast resources by the international community, continued into the summer of 1995. Thus there could be little argument that international diplomacy had failed in its major objectives. Although the diplomatic resistance to changes in the borders of either Bosnia or Croatia through a use of force was firm — representing the only cardinal concern of the international community in the outcome of the Yugoslav War of Dissolution — neither of those states would escape conflict and the legacy of war. Neither could expect to have large parts of their pre-war Serb populations integrated into the life of the state, in the short term at least, and for both the prospect seemed to be internal partition. However, both were likely to see an eventual re-integration of federated Serbian elements through circumstances as communications and economic needs required co-operation. In spite of this prognosis, there was no avoiding the conclusion that, even if the Serbian project to carve new borders from Croatia and Bosnia could be denied, the essence of multi-cultural societies had been destroyed.

The impact of war and dissolution, as well as international attempts at crisis management, had resulted in a set of troubled independent states, although Slovenia could look to a reasonably healthy future as part of Central and Eastern Europe and ever-improving relations with the EU and, possibly, NATO, provided that hiccups in relations with

---

13 See James Gow, 'Serbia and Montenegro: Small 'FRY', Big Trouble', *RFE/RL Research Report*, Vol.3 No.1, 7 January 1994, pp.130-32.

Italy could be overcome, as seemed likely.[14] For the other states future prosperity depended on two developments. The first was assistance and trade from those countries and bodies which had been involved in the international management of the conflict. In particular, this would mean the EU, albeit not in isolation, playing a major role in the rehabilitation and reconstruction of economic, social and political life. Without this there could be no prospect of longer-term security and stability in the region.

The second need, symbiotically interwoven with the first, was for good neighbourhood relations. This meant not only the establishment of economic and other links between different parts of the territory of the former Yugoslavia, but also between the post-Yugoslav states and the neighbouring countries — Italy, Austria, Hungary, Romania, Bulgaria, Greece, Turkey and Albania. This entailed the elaboration of trading links and possibly political co-operation. It certainly required the negotiation of a regional arms control regime to bring the armed forces of the Yugoslav states into line with the ceilings imposed on their neighbours by the 1990 Conventional Forces in Europe Treaty (CFE). This had limited the weapons holdings of NATO and Warsaw Pact countries in particular categories, but had not included Yugoslavia. Bulgaria, Romania and Hungary in particular had more than ample reason to see Belgrade's military capability limited by an international treaty, negotiated within the OSCE Forum on Security Co-operation and possibly annexed to the CFE Treaty. Otherwise, already suffering various repercussions from the Yugoslav war such as the impact of implementing sanctions, these countries could feel vulnerable to future instability — or bellicosity — emanating from a regime in Belgrade with a violent record (even if that regime had revealed its war weariness and its capacity to absorb mistakes and move on). However unlikely, this was not a possibility which Belgrade's neighbours, such as Hungary and Bulgaria, were going to dismiss lightly.

Above all, this situation arose from the fact that President Milošević, having set a series of violent conflicts in train, would remain in power. With no obvious prospect of his being able to take a peaceful and early retirement, it seemed that the outlook would be either a future with Milošević ruling from Belgrade until his demise, or his regime collapsing in violence. In the mean time, there was the ironic possibility

14 See Anton Bebler, 'Slovenia and Europe', *The World Today*, Vol.51 No.5, May 1995.

that he might be awarded the Nobel Peace Prize for his role in bringing
the war in Bosnia to a conclusion. Although this was not a major
possibility, his relationship with the various emissaries of international
diplomacy and their sponsors was increasingly positive — with plaudits
for his statesman-like behaviour coming from all sides. At the
minimum, all this reinforced the sense that having led most of his
Yugoslav counterparts and most of the international community, for
most of the time, on a string Milošević would — metaphorically, at
least — have got away with murder.

In small, somewhat perverse ways Milošević along with the other
Yugoslavs, had helped those engaging in diplomacy on behalf of the
international community to understand their own limitations and needs.
The attempts to handle the Yugoslav war internationally catalysed
certain processes in the evolution of European security and international
relations at the end of the twentieth century and demonstrated a number
of things. Among these was the difficulty for the UN to operate in a
complex, strategically dynamic conflict with a force broadly constructed
to operate in a consensual environment, but spiced with elements of an
enforcement mission. This difficulty was compounded by divisions
between the major states in the Security Council and the need to work
with other bodies such as the EU and NATO. While many doubted the
value of the experiments which UNPROFOR and other UN-backed
activity in the former Yugoslavia represented, and although there were
clearly great problems associated with them, there was also scope for
learning lessons and, rather than ruling out such operations due to
simplistic and lazy analysis, making them less vulnerable and more
creative in the future.

Otherwise, for the UN the former Yugoslavia offered confused
signals. The great expectations created by the Gulf conflict of 1990-1
were suitably diminished by the entanglement in Bosnia. Yet
involvement also created new expectations and larger burdens on the
UN system. New modes of operation, requiring massive manpower
commitments, placed great strain on the UN's organisational and
financial capacities. Thus, with the UN increasingly debt-ridden and
unpopular in the US, its major financial contributor, there would be
further strains, limiting the its capacity to act in a world whereever
more would be expected of it, in spite of the disappointments not only
in former Yugoslavia but also in Somalia and Rwanda. Financial
worries, along with criticisms from certain quarters of the Security

Council about indifference in Bosnia, could only add to pressures for reform of the UN and particularly the Security Council.

Otherwise, history would judge the UN's role in the former Yugoslavia harshly. It seemed likely to be kinder to UNPROFOR than its contemporary critics, which at the very least was likely to be judged as an operation which, albeit a great cost, did some good. Beyond this there was the possibility that even though it had not perhaps been intended that way, UNPROFOR could emerge in retrospect as the international force which, without going to war, did enough to contain the conflict in Bosnia until the Bosnian government forces were in a position to counter Serbian aggression.

The other major historical test of the UN's record in the former Yugoslavia would be the performance of the International Criminal Tribunal on War Crimes in Former Yugoslavia (ICTY). Established as an *ad hoc* court, under Chapter VII of the UN Charter, ICTY was based on existing international humanitarian law and the laws of international armed conflict, including the Geneva Conventions and Protocols, and the Genocide Convention. It represented perhaps the most ambitious of the precedent-setting initiatives arising from the international involvement in the dissolving Yugoslavia.

The Tribunal, established in The Hague, was under great pressure with severely limited resources to deliver results, preferably spectacular ones, within a year of the Chief Prosecutor, a South African, Judge Richard Goldstone, and the first senior trial lawyers (i.e. the prosecutors) and investigators beginning work in the summer of 1994. Partly there was pressure because many, including those in governments, assumed that ICTY had been in operation since Security Council Resolution 827 (25 May 1993) decided to create it or since, Security Council Resolution 857 (20 August 1993) announced a list of candidates to be the judges. By mid-1995 almost one year after the first real work had begun at ICTY, there had been five indictments, but in only one case was the person charged in the Tribunal's custody. At the minimum, the spectre of ICTY (and its counterpart established to deal with war crimes in Rwanda again with Goldstone as Chief Prosecutor), cast the shadow of international humanitarian law over conflicts in the future. More optimistically, the test over time of the Tribunal and again of international political will must be to bring an element of international justice to Bosnian in the future.

For NATO former Yugoslavia represented an opportunity to put itself in the forefront of European security initiatives. By forging links with the UN through various support roles in connection with former Yugoslavia, it moved into areas which saw its first use of force. However, the expectations of NATO's potential were primarily based on the US contribution — yet the evidence of the international handling of the Yugoslavia War of Dissolution was that the transatlantic links on which West Europeans had relied for fifty years were not likely to be as strong in the future as in the past. Thus, while NATO retained political and military utility — as the most integrated and technologically-advanced collection of military assets in history — it would be subject to further diplomatic strains and organisational evolution. In this context European developments were significant.

The development of Common Foreign and Security Policy (CFSP), one of the great hopes of European Union integration, proved to be more difficult than its supporters had hoped. The hopes raised by the end of the Cold War met a rather dismal crisis surrounding the dissolution of the Yugoslav federation. Nonetheless. for all the justifiably grey clouds surrounding the first major attempt at CFSP and the bleak failure of attempts to end the war in former Yugoslavia, small, potentially important silver linings could be identified.

Seen initially as the test-bed for CFSP, involvement in the Yugoslav crisis proved an immense challenge to those seeking to forge a common European policy, whether for reasons of interest or belief. That the involvement was a general failure and did considerable damage to the idea of CFSP, at least in the short term, was undeniable. However, this was not to say that the involvement was without merit. Moreover, for all the muddle created by the EC (later EU) and international experience in former Yugoslavia, that involvement appears to have been the catalyst for the evolution of a European defence capability to underpin an eventual maturation of CFSP which would otherwise have taken years of argument.

CFSP was damaged by the arguments between Germany and many of the other members in the autumn of 1991, and both Germany and the Union as a whole spent the following years recovering. In addition to this, there were problems in CFSP involving Greece and Macedonia. This kind of argument undermined the credibility of any body claiming to be a major force, with a security policy and interests to pursue, yet unable to resolve a question over what a small state in a fragile situation should be called. Even though, with American influence, Greece and Macedonia were able to sign an interim agreement at the UN on 13 September 1995 which went a long way in resolving their differences and in establishing openings for co-operation, the name issue was left for some unspecified future date.

However, the European Union developed, in terms of its CFSP, in the relationship with the UN — as the UN developed regional arrangements with the EU, NATO and others. This was seen to be the creation of ICFY. For the EU, developing its CFSP and taking on a new role, this was a significant development providing the prototype for possible future co-operation between regional and global bodies. At the minimum, it had to be acknowledged that in spite of the failures in former Yugoslavia, the degree of co-operation between the various countries in the EU, as well as between the EU and other organisations, represented a historic point of achievement: the competition and use of clients which in the past had spread war to the rest of Europe had been averted.

From the outset EU policy was constrained in several ways by the absence of a military capability. It ruled out any kind of intervention, irrespective of whether there was any political commitment for one. In addition, the arguments with the US over the best approach to handling Bosnia demonstrated a partial US withdrawal and a change in the Atlantic Alliance. There was now a situation in which the Europeans were being forced to look for ways to handle things themselves in the future.

The lessons learned from the Yugoslav failure included the realisation that, whatever else might limit CFSP, the absence of a military capability to underpin policy was critical. Furthermore, the seasoning of transatlantic relations which accompanied this forced an understanding that the US could no longer be relied on to be there — and might well not be reliable when it was. It was thus imperative for the Europeans to develop their own military potential while continuing to work with the Americans. Without the awful experience of Yugoslavia this might not have been realised clearly for many years — until there was a more directly pressing crisis, by which time it would be too late.

Here there was a clear shift in favour of the idea of a European pillar within NATO. The WEU would be developed as the defence arm of the EU and the focus for European collective decision-making, with planning and operational capability. Moreover, the NATO Combined

Joint Task Forces scheme,[15] through which force packages could be created both within NATO and with collaborators in the Alliance's Partnership for Peace programme launched in January 1994, would facilitate the development of a European capability, with a variety of bilateral and multi-lateral formations already emerging in 1995 such as the Anglo-French Rapid Reaction Force. It would still be tied to NATO and rely on NATO assets, but it would not have to rely on the Americans.

To a notable extent the development of a European capability, albeit backed up by NATO, became a reality with the decision of the UK, France and the Netherlands in May 1995 to create a rapid reaction force to support UNPROFOR. That decision also confirmed that for all the interweaving of international bodies and the friction which could sometimes emerge, those bodies were all underpinned by their member states. It was the understanding, capability, cohesion and will of those states which shaped the engagement of each of the international organisations. Indeed it was the key states, through both their joint action and their differences, which moulded international involvement in the Yugoslav War of Dissolution.

The EU, collectively and as individual Member States, set the tone of international intervention in the conflict, as well as determining the growing international stake in its successful resolution. The initial European intervention demonstrated excessive ambition, the absence of a common understanding and the frailty of a common policy. Whereas France and the UK were guided by misplaced analysis of the conflict until it was too late — by that time they had already committed themselves to a policy difficult to reverse, Germany which possibly showed greater, if incomplete, understanding of the conflict, was clumsy in translating this into policy arguments.

The problem for Germany, the UK (especially), France and other European countries was that understanding of the conflict was essentially irrelevant since they were all guided in approaching the challenge of the Yugoslav War by an overwhelming commitment to what they would not do. With France there were occasional considerations of a more forceful approach, but these were always

15 See G.C. de Nooy, *Towards a Military Core Group in Europe?*, Clingendael Paper, Clingendael — The Netherlands Institute for International Relations, The Hague, March 1995.

limited and restricted by the UK and others. For the UK, even where there was a grudging acknowledgment that force could be necessary to sustain the position of UNPROFOR or of international efforts more broadly, this was always dogged by lingering caution. More than any other country, the UK set the tone of international involvement in the Yugoslav War of Dissolution.

However, in spite of the UK's central role, international disarray owed most to the position of the US. Whereas Moscow balanced internal pressures with the desire to co-operate internationally with the West until it judged that it would have to assert itself more, the US ebbed and flowed, acutely so under the Administration of President Clinton. From the outset, the US position was critical. The Bush Administration's decision to remain in the background in the early stages allowed the hubristic Europeans to set in train the chain of misconceptions, fallacies and failures permeated international diplomacy towards the Yugoslav War. However, as Bush gave way to Clinton, US policy moved from virtual inaction to limited activism, against the grain of existing international approaches, resulting in a dislocation of international diplomacy and the dissipation of pressure on Washington for serious commitment in line with its partners and allies on the international scene.

The Clinton Adminstration arrived late on the scene and although its analysis of the conflict may have been morally correct, its lack of any commitment to serious action was iniquitous. For all the misreading of the crisis and mistaken, shambling, contradictory and attenuated policy manoeuvres by other states, particularly in the West, and the demeanour of some UN officials, it was the Clinton Adminstration and most of all its destruction of the Vance-Owen Plan, which was responsible for the dereliction of international diplomacy. The inexperienced domestic reform President, in fact, had matured into a masterful foreign policy President after three years: he was the successful 'President Peacemaker' — not only in Bosnia, but in the Middle East and elsewhere. Clinton's team was to recover much of its position, to make important concessions of principle and to be responsible for the eventual settlement in Bosnia for which it was due enormous credit. But there was still no escaping the whispers of conscience that the war could have been stopped two and a half years earlier, meaning more lives saved and a more principled peace.

The Triumph of the Lack of Will

There were important ways in which the activity of the institutions concerned with European security made a positive difference in the course of the Yugoslav crisis. Moreover, ill-equipped and inappropriate institutions predicated on the Cold War division between East and West were clearly pitched against a multiplex problem. In difficult circumstances, with limited means, some of the bodies involved achieved more than was generally credited to them by critics. However they were not adequate to the challenge.

Overall, international action was ineffective or only of limited effect, for four reasons: timing was wrong, there was inconsistency, there was a lack of co-ordination and agreement and, finally, there was an ever-present weakness over the linked issues of ensuring compliance and the use of force. Ultimately it was a lack of will to back initiatives with the possible use of force which allowed the Serbian leadership, even if its new borders project were denied, effectively to destroy Bosnia and to cripple Croatia, before abandoning the Croatian Serbs to ethnic displacement, and to survive. That lack of will also severely impaired the credibility of collective approaches to regional crises and conflicts. A consequence was bound to be a greater propensity to use force — by those seeking either to change the political-territorial order or to preserve it. Perhaps the most critical aspect of the international failure to end the war in Bosnia was the implication for situations in the former Soviet Union, particularly for the Russian Federation. This was true of Russia's relationships both within the former Union and with the West.

The handling of the Yugoslav crisis, following on from the Gulf Conflict, offered the chance for the West to confirm a partnership with Moscow which would have accorded the Russian Federation status and strengthened the positions of the reformers and 'Westernisers', who would thus have had something to show for their positive and friendly relations with the West. Instead, critically, over the Vance-Owen plan (as was argued in Chapter 9) the chance to lock Moscow into a collective crisis management framework was lost. Russia's initiatives were, in effect, dismissed and its willingness to back Western initiatives was taken for granted or ignored, and both resulted in a Russian retreat from open co-operation. The loss of this historic chance to cement post-Cold War co-operation — one of the most important aspects of international failure — was a function of the lack of political will in

Western capitals either to deal with the war in Bosnia or to seal the relationship with Russia.

It was evident from the point of the Vance-Owen Plan's demise at the latest, that international efforts had failed. Although Dayton was undoubtedly successful in bringing the war to an end, it only cast a more revealing light on the overall failure. The 'triumph' which emerged in the Bosnian settlement exemplified what could have been achieved earlier, for want of the political will which drove the Dayton diplomacy. The absence of political will at earlier stages meant four things. First, although Bosnia's borders might remain, this was a somewhat hollow achievement as the principles of rejecting ethnic purity and the seizure of land through force had, in effect, been abandoned. In practice, ethnic purification, by mass murder and deportation, had been accepted. This 'triumph' of an ethno-national will was facilitated by the lack of will in the international community adequately to block it.

Secondly, it was made clear to Slobodan Milošević that he could play the role of peacemaker and be taken seriously by Western diplomats and survive in power, having set the war in train. Thirdly, the strength and credibility of international and particularly Western power — at a peak after the Gulf conflict — were diluted by irresolution. And finally the post-Cold War opportunity to build a genuine partnership between the West and Moscow was wasted, encouraging the Russian Federation to turn towards its own resources to solve its own problems. If the West had not lacked the will to act collectively on Bosnia, the later Russian actions in Chechnia and its role in Georgia, Tajikistan and in Armenia and Azerbaijan might have been handled differently. Although, in the short term Russia might not have been completely lost, the longer-term trend was for considerably cooler and more complex East-West relations. If not a new Cold War, then a Cold Peace seemed assured.

With the partial withdrawal of the United States from its commitment to European security, the cooling of Western relations with Moscow placed a greater emphasis on the Europeans to be able conduct their own collective security engagements — in line with the evolution which had been catalysed by the involvement in former Yugoslavia. The first clear manifestation of this was the decision of France and the UK (backed by the Netherlands), building on the historically unparalleled co-operation established between them already forged by the experience in Bosnia, to commit around 10,000 troops to the strengthening of

UNPROFOR at the end of May 1995. This stepped up the pace of international engagement in handling the war in Bosnia and set the stage for the final phase of international diplomacy. The success of that force, in the context of strong US diplomacy, while desirable, ironically only underlined the scale of general failure. It only confirmed the way in which the lack of political will, especially in Western capitals, was the mainspring of international deficiency.

Like losing gamblers, the masters of international involvement in the Yugoslav crisis constantly hoped that they would strike lucky. Having laid one losing bet after another on half-measures, diplomacy and non-violent pressures which did not achieve their prime objective of resolving the conflict, the major powers and the principal bodies responsible for European security played double-or-quits. International diplomacy, with the US at its heart, finally came good and Dayton was signed, but only in the ironic shadow of past failure and present surrender of principle.

It was Bosnia's fate and, indeed, the former Yugoslavia's, that it presented a problem for the whole of Europe and in particular for those integrating in the West, in the EU, but that it was not enough of a problem to warrant full attention when it was required. The conflict was too close to be ignored — something had to be done. However, Bosnia was not so close or so immediate that there was an overriding need to decide to take the kind of action necessary to resolve the situation — the use or threat of armed force.

In this sense both the US and the various Europeans, even though they sometimes had radically different ideas about the situation in former Yugoslavia, knew and understood most of the detail. However, they still failed, individually and collectively, to gain a sharp focus on events in Bosnia and establish a perspective on its political future. Without such a perspective none of them could clearly analyse the situation seriously address the question of military intervention. Probably there was no desire to do so. This was why the best opportunity to stop the war was missed with the demise of the Vance-Owen Plan.

Full or partial implementation of Vance-Owen was one of five obvious points at which a different international response might have made a crucial difference. The first was the approach to the prospect of Yugoslav dissolution. Had there been more openness to states' becoming independent, given the ineluctable break up of the old federation prior to declarations of independence and armed conflict, an overall solution could have been shaped and war avoided (but not violent unrest). Had the EC Conference which began in September been organised to help the Yugoslav republics talk to each other, in the framework of a possible right to independence prior to declarations and fighting when there was great uncertainty, its chances of success would have been good.

The second point at which policy might have been different was the EC decision to dispatch the troika to mediate in the Yugoslav conflict at the end of June 1991. This was a decision taken without clear planning and co-ordination. It was taken hurriedly because the EC leaders were meeting for the Luxembourg summit. It was right for the EC to be concerned over a major question of European and international security. It was correct that it took an active interest in the situation on the territories of the disintegrating Yugoslav federation following the onset of armed hostilities, even if it had not done so sufficiently earlier. The EC Council should, however, have paused to work through the implications of a seemingly innocuous step, as well as to establish a more comprehensive policy framework. While recognising the pressures and constraints which work on those engaged in international diplomacy, there can be no sense in which it was acceptable to initiate a major security policy venture without due attention having been paid and options worked through.

The third moment in which another international policy could have made a significant difference concerned recognition. Once the independence of those states seeking it was accepted, there should have been the possibility of a full commitment to establishing the independence of those states either through the establishment of transitional arrangements, including a strong international military peace operation, or by taking steps, including the lifting of the arms embargo against the Yugoslav territories, which would have offered them the possibility of facing up to their own problems and being wholly responsible for them.

The fourth point at which a different approach could have been beneficial was the decision to deploy an international force to Bosnia. There may be many 'what ifs...?' in connection with this. One crucial mistake was the decision to allow the UNHCR's programme to determine international policy and the deployment of these troops. This happened in the absence of a clear policy objective for an international community nonetheless conscious that there was a major security policy question at stake which required a response using armed forces. It would have been better for those states involved to have conceived of their deployment in clear, rather than vague, security policy terms and to have established a coherent operation from the outset.

Of all these, once the war had started, implementation of Vance-Owen represented the best and most coherent opportunity to have taken international diplomacy and the war in a different direction. Although the later 'Union of Republics' and Contact Group plans also represented chances for the international community to seize an opportunity to press for a settlement, Vance-Owen was significant because it held out the prospect of an objective around which international opinion could have formed strongly. With commitment to implementing the plan, as with the later but ethically lesser Dayton Accords, there was the chance to stop the war. The Vance-Owen plan was, in the end, lost in the interplay of weak and contradictory international interests.

Throughout, the main interests in the dissolution of Yugoslavia for those in the US, the EU Member States and Moscow were the repercussions of the war on their mutual relations, on the various international bodies through which they exercised aspects of their foreign and security policy — in the future and stability of which they all had serious if sometimes conflicting interests — and on the norms of international order, particularly the principle that border changes must not be allowed through the use of force. These were the concerns of the major and minor players in the international arena. The needs and interests of the parties to the Yugoslav War of Dissolution were of no more than indirect interest, other than at the level of resisting attempts to alter international borders by force, or, when the credibility and strength of particular international agencies were at stake. Where the various Yugoslavs were concerned in different ways with blood and borders, the agents and instruments of international diplomacy were preoccupied with order and organisations. For the Serbian side, as well as the objects of its military and terror campaigns (who were not beyond repeating Serb practices), the war was about territory and victory. In some periods, this was true for Croatia, as well. For the international community it was about containment of both the conflict and the diplomatic damage caused by it, and about simply, bringing the war to an end.

Containment was seen as an alternative to direct intervention. However, much of the international involvement in the former Yugoslavia was close to intervention, not necessarily purely military and never outright: the deployment of UNPROFOR in Bosnia was something accepted by the parties under pressure against their will rather than welcomed by them. This was expecially true of the Serbs, to whom it was only welcome in so far as it was a deployment of armed forces which did not threaten to stop their campaign through combat. Nonetheless, the presence of armed international troops was an impediment which they would rather have avoided. It was also a presence which stemmed the flow of the war and, in practice, bought time for Croatia and Bosnia, even though this may not have been the intention of deciding to deploy them. Finally, it provided the framework for the eventual use of force, in conjunction with NATO, which brought the conflict to its culmination.

Bosnia was, in the end, not only the borders of the state. Nor was it only the borders of the entities agreed at Dayton and which were thought by some to be possible successors to the Bosnian state. Bosnia also represented the historic boundary between east and west, Islam and Christianity. Most of all, it represented the limits of European integration, of humanitarian concern and of political interest. It was the contemporary border between what was close enough not to be ignored, but not so close that it had to be dealt with fully. Nor was it important enough that it had to be clearly understood and something done about it. However, the longer the conflict lasted and the deeper international involvement became, the higher the international stake in the outcome became. WIth that the importance of Bosnia rose. In these circumstances there was an ever greater premium on cohesion and resolve in the international community. Finally, there was more or less a coherent international position once the US took a strong lead. That US lead was only engendered by fear of the alternatives, as the prospect of a military withdrawal by the major European contributors, requiring US assistance, became more likely.

When the war was brought to an end, that only affirmed earlier failure and the reality that the war could have been stopped well before it was. Success required willingness to use force and accept certain risks. However, although Bosnian bridges were burned, those of the Western capitals were not. Those capitals, either alone or jointly, had not been not prepared to mount a full-scale armed intervention, despite frequent calls for strong action to uphold aspects of international order and collective credibility, to stop the shocking brutality and suffering in Bosnia, and to save either people or bridges. By the time they were and the agreements made at Dayton were put into effect, this was a success cast in the dismal colours of four years of failure. It would only become a meaningful 'triumph' if the international focus, force, cohesion and commitment which had been the conditions for settlement were maintained. Those same elements which had been essential to success and failure in conflict and crisis management were the detrminants of success and failure in peace. The US, in particular, had come through, but would have to realise the stake it had placed in the settlement and sustain its military and diplomatic involvement. The EU would have to ensure the resources for reconstruction. With the fighting over, the international community had the opportunity to redeem its failure by building peace. Real success would mean a durable peace. That required absolute international commitment to justice and reconciliation through the work of the International Tribunal; and to reconstruction and rehabilitation by rebuilding Bosnia's famous bridges physically and with them the social and political bridges between its peoples.

INDEX